W9-CTH-610

DATE DUE

			PRINTED IN U.S.A.

FOR REFERENCE

Do Not Take From This Room

Authors & Artists for Young Adults

ISSN 1040-5682

Authors & Artists for Young Adults

VOLUME 18

Thomas McMahon
Editor

GALE

DETROIT • NEW YORK • TORONTO • LONDON

SEP   '96

Riverside Community College
Library
4800 Magnolia Avenue
Riverside, California 92506

REF

PN1009.A1 A88
Garrett, Agnes.
Authors & artists for young
adults.

Thomas McMahon, *Editor*

...elly Andrews, Joanna Brod, Sheryl Ciccarelli, Alan Hedblad,
Kevin S. Hile, Motoko Huthwaite, Gerard J. Senick, Diane Telgen, Kathleen Witman,
Contributing Editors

Diane Andreassi, Janet L. Hile, Kevin Hillstrom, Laurie Collier Hillstrom, David P.
Johnson, J. Sydney Jones, Nancy Rampson, Megan Ratner, Susan Reicha, Pamela L.
Shelton, Kenneth R. Shepherd, Tracy J. Sukraw, Laura M. Zaidman,
Sketch Contributors

Victoria B. Cariappa, *Research Manager*
Cheryl L. Warnock, *Project Coordinator*
Tamara C. Nott and Michele P. Pica, *Research Associates*
Alicia Noel Biggers, Julia C. Daniel, and Michelle Lee, *Research Assistants*

Marlene S. Hurst, *Permissions Manager*
Margaret A. Chamberlain, Maria Franklin, and Kimberly F. Smilay,
Picture Permissions Specialists
Diane Cooper, *Permissions Associate*

Mary Beth Trimper, *Production Director*
Deborah Milliken, *Production Assistant*

Randy Bassett, *Image Database Supervisor*
Sherrell Hobbs, *Macintosh Artist*
Robert Duncan and Mikal Ansari, *Imaging Specialists*
Pamela A. Hayes, *Photography Coordinator*

While every effort has been made to ensure the reliability of the information presented in this publication, Gale Research Inc. does not guarantee the accuracy of the data contained herein. Gale accepts no payment for listing; and inclusion in the publication of any organization, agency, institution, publication, service, or individual does not imply endorsement of the editors or publisher. Errors brought to the attention of the publisher and verified to the satisfaction of the publisher will be corrected in future editions.

The paper used in this publication meets the minimum requirements of
American National Standard for Information Sciences—Permanence Paper
for Printed Library Materials, ANSI Z39.48-1984.

This publication is a creative work fully protected by all applicable copyright laws, as well as by misappropriation, trade secret, unfair competition, and other applicable laws. The authors and editors of this work have added value to the underlying factual material herein through one or more of the following: unique and original selection, coordination, expression, arrangement, and classification of the information.

All rights to this publication will be vigorously defended.

Copyright (c) 1996 by Gale Research
835 Penobscot Building
Detroit, MI 48226-4094

All rights reserved including the right of reproduction in whole or in part in any form.

Library of Congress Catalog Card Number 89-641100
ISBN 0-8103-9942-3
ISSN 1040-5682

10 9 8 7 6 5 4 3 2 1

Printed in the United States of America

Authors and Artists for Young Adults

NATIONAL ADVISORY BOARD

A five-member board consisting of teachers, librarians, and other experts on young adult literature was consulted to help determine the contents of *Authors and Artists for Young Adults*. The members of the board for this volume include:

Patricia Campbell
General Editor, Twayne's Young Adult Author Series, and author of column "The Sand in the Oyster" for *Horn Book Magazine*

Cathi Dunn MacRae
Librarian, young adult advisory board director at the Boulder Public Library in Colorado, book review editor for *Voice of Youth Advocates*, and author of *Presenting Young Adult Fantasy Literature*

Tom Reynolds
Adult/Young Adult Librarian for the Sno-Isle Regional Library System in Edmonds, Washington

Pam Spencer
Coordinator of library services for the Fairfax County Public Schools in Virginia and author of *What Do Young Adults Read Next?*

Nancy Vogel
Professor of English at Fort Hays State University in Kansas and author of *Robert Frost, Teacher*

Authors and Artists for Young Adults
TEEN BOARD ADVISORS

A number of teen reading boards were consulted to help determine series' content. The teen board advisors for this volume include:

Barbara L. Blosveren
Head of Young Adult Services and advisor for the Youth Review Board at the Stratford Library in Connecticut

Dana Burton
Youth Services librarian and advisor for the Bloomington Teen Council at the Monroe County Public Library in Indiana

Barbara Hoffman
Advisor to the Teen Advisory Board and Young Adult librarian at the Patchogue-Medford library in New York

Cathi Dunn MacRae
Librarian, young adult advisory board director at the Boulder Public Library in Colorado, book review editor for *Voice of Youth Advocates,* and author of *Presenting Young Adult Fantasy Literature*

Diane Tuccillo
Member of the Young Adult Advisory Council and Young Adult Services Supervisory librarian at the Mesa Public Library in Arizona

Renee J. Vaillancourt
Young Adult librarian at the Carmel Clay Public Library in Indiana

Cheryl Karp Ward
Advisor to the Teen Advisory Board and Library/Media Specialist at Windsor Locks Middle School in Connecticut

Authors and Artists for Young Adults

TEEN BOARD

The staff of *Authors and Artists for Young Adults* wishes to thank the following young adult readers for their teen board participation:

Michael Arawy
Rebecca Athan
Andrew Bagley
Catharine Banasiak
Melissa Barnaby
Allison Barrett
Devin Barry
Amy Becker
Melanie Beene
Dara Bonetti
Jesse Bonware
Jessica Buchser
Emily Burleson
Dylan Burns
Annie Burton
Rachel Campominos
Abby Conover
Christy Cook
Teresa Copeland
Jordan Copes
Heather Lee Cordeira
Lin Costello
Kate Cottrell
John Crower
Jennifer Dennis
Joanne M. Dimenno
Alison Dougherty
Josh Dukelow
Joe Eckert
Ellis Farmer
Kylin Follenweider
Alda Fox
Michelle Gagnon
Sarah Gangstad
Mary Genest
Eric Gilbert
Kate Gunther

Grant Hamilton
Alice Harnisch
Mark Haseltine
Allen Heinecke
Erin Hooley
Laura Huber
Maeghan Hurley
Kristin Hursh
Kristina Ivanisin
Tom Ivers
Adam James
Amanda Joy
Austin Joy
Ian Kelly
Alysia Kulas
Sarah Kulik
Dana-Jean LaHaie
Rolland LaHaie
Sarah Lairy
Aaron Landini
Sarah Lawhead
Erin Lewis
Nisha Low-Nam
Jamie Luna
Chenda Ly
Lauren Makowski
Jaimie Mantie
Kimberly Marie Rutkauski
Jen Mathiason
Megan McDonald
Niamh McGuigan
Allison C. Mikkalo
Jocelyn Miller
Glynn Miller II
Neal Mody
Shannon Murphy
Jason Nealy

Pablo Nevares
Brittany Pagella
Carlene Palmer
Krista Paradiso
Daniel Pereira
Eric Peters
Brian Petersen
Leah M. Pickren
Anne Pizzi
Mike Quilligan
Jessi Quizar
Christina Rampelli
Matthew R. Reese
Eric Rice
Benjamin Rockey
Meghan E. Rozarie
Tony Ruggiero
Peter Ryan
Erica Sebeok
Amee Shelley
Elizabeth Shouse
Kersten Stevens
Erin Stick
Mark Strauss
Avery Thatcher
Adam Tierney
Dan Uznanski
Melissa Vosburg
Rebecca Weide
Jonathan Weinberg
Lynn Weisee
Joe Wenzel
Kenyon Whitehead
Alisson Wood
Brandon C. Wood
Ally Wright
Josh Yorke

Contents

Introduction

Authors and Artists for Young Adults is a reference series designed to serve the needs of middle school, junior high, and high school students interested in creative artists. Originally inspired by the need to bridge the gap between Gale's *Something about the Author,* created for children, and *Contemporary Authors,* intended for older students and adults, *Authors and Artists for Young Adults* has been expanded to cover not only an international scope of authors, but also a wide variety of other artists.

Although the emphasis of the series remains on the writer for young adults, we recognize that these readers have diverse interests covering a wide range of reading levels. The series therefore contains not only those creative artists who are of high interest to young adults, including cartoonists, photographers, music composers, bestselling authors of adult novels, media directors, producers, and performers, but also literary and artistic figures studied in academic curricula, such as influential novelists, playwrights, poets, and painters. The goal of *Authors and Artists for Young Adults* is to present this great diversity of creative artists in a format that is entertaining, informative, and understandable to the young adult reader.

Entry Format

Each volume of *Authors and Artists for Young Adults* will furnish in-depth coverage of twenty to twenty-five authors and artists. The typical entry consists of:

—A detailed biographical section that includes date of birth, marriage, children, education, and addresses.

—A comprehensive bibliography or filmography including publishers, producers, and years.

—Adaptations into other media forms.

—Works in progress.

—A distinctive essay featuring comments on an artist's life, career, artistic intentions, world views, and controversies.

—References for further reading.

—Extensive illustrations, photographs, movie stills, cartoons, book covers, and other relevant visual material.

A cumulative index to featured authors and artists appears in each volume.

Compilation Methods

The editors of *Authors and Artists for Young Adults* make every effort to secure information directly from the authors and artists through personal correspondence and interviews. Sketches on living authors and artists are sent to the biographee for review prior to publication. Any sketches not personally reviewed by biographees or their representatives are marked with an asterisk (*).

Highlights of Forthcoming Volumes

Among the authors and artists planned for future volumes are:

Jane Austen	Anne Fine	Jim Murphy
Marion Dane Bauer	Neil Gaiman	Kit Pearson
T. Ernesto Bethancourt	Terry Gilliam	K. M. Peyton
Jorges Luis Borges	Ernest Hemingway	Terry Pratchett
Kenneth Branagh	Brian Jacques	Faith Ringgold
Gwendolyn Brooks	Welwyn Wilton Katz	Mary Shelley
Joseph Bruchac III	R. R. Knudson	Randy Shilts
Lois McMaster Bujold	Kathryn Lasky	Jan Slepian
Robert Cormier	Myron Levoy	Robert Swindells
Clive Cussler	Maya Lin	Theodore Taylor
Philip K. Dick	Chris Lynch	Frances Temple
John Donovan	William Mayne	Mark Twain

Contact the Editor

We encourage our readers to examine the entire *AAYA* series. Please write and tell us if we can make AAYA even more helpful to you. Give your comments and suggestions to the editor:

BY MAIL: The Editor, *Authors and Artists for Young Adults*, Gale Research, 835 Penobscot Building, 645 Griswold St., Detroit, MI 48226-4094.

BY TELEPHONE: (800) 347-GALE

BY FAX: (313) 961-6599

BY E-MAIL: CYA@Gale.com@Galesmtp

Authors
& Artists
for Young
Adults

Isabel Allende

■ Personal

Surname is pronounced "Ah-*yen*-day"; born August 2, 1942, in Lima, Peru; daughter of Tomás (a Chilean diplomat) and Francisca (Llona Barros) Allende; married Miguel Frías (an engineer), September 8, 1962 (divorced, 1987); married William Gordon (a lawyer), July 17, 1988; children: (first marriage) Paula (deceased), Nicolas; Scott (stepson). *Education:* Graduated from a private high school in Santiago, Chile, 1959.

■ Addresses

Home—15 Nightingale Lane, San Rafael, CA 94901. *Agent*—Carmen Balcells, Diagonal 580, Barcelona 21, Spain.

■ Career

United Nations Food and Agricultural Organization, Santiago, Chile, secretary, 1959-65; *Paula* (magazine), Santiago, journalist, editor, and columnist, 1967-74; *Mampato* (magazine), Santiago, journalist, 1969-74; Canal 13/Canal 7 (television station), television interviewer, 1970-75; worked on movie newsreels, 1973-75; Colegio Marroco, Caracas, Venezuela, administrator, 1979-82; writer. Guest teacher at Montclair State College, New Jersey, 1985, and University of Virginia, 1988; Gildersleeve Lecturer, Barnard College, 1988; teacher of creative writing, University of California, Berkeley, 1989.

■ Awards, Honors

Eva Luna was named one of *Library Journal*'s Best Books of 1988.

■ Writings

NOVELS

La casa de los espíritus, Plaza y Janes (Barcelona), 1982, translation by Magda Bogin published as *The House of the Spirits*, Knopf (New York City), 1985.

De amor y de sombra, Plaza y Janes, 1984, translation by Margaret Sayers Peden published as *Of Love and Shadows*, Knopf, 1987.

Eva Luna, Plaza y Janes, 1987, translation by Peden published under same title, Knopf, 1988.

Cuentos de Eva Luna, Editoral Sudamericana (Buenos Aires), 1990, translation by Peden published as *The Stories of Eva Luna*, Atheneum (New York City), 1991.

Plan infinito, Editorial Sudamericana, 1991, translation by Peden published as *The Infinite Plan*, HarperCollins (New York City), 1993.

OTHER

Civilice a su troglodita: Los impertinentes de Isabel Allende (humor), Lord Cochran (Santiago), 1974.
La gorda de porcelana (juvenile; title means "The Fat Porcelain Lady"), Alfaguara (Madrid), 1984.
Paula (memoir), HarperCollins, 1995, translation by Peden published under same title, 1995.

Also author of several plays and stories for children. Author of weekly newspaper column for *El Nacional* (Caracas), 1976-83. Contributor to books, including *Paths of Resistance,* edited by William Zinsser, Houghton, 1989. Contributor to periodicals, including *Discurso Literario* and *Revista Iberoamericana.*

■ **Adaptations**

The House of the Spirits and *Of Love and Shadows* were adapted as motion pictures and released in 1994.

■ **Sidelights**

Chilean novelist Isabel Allende has been critically acclaimed for her unique prose style. In addition to her use of a technique called "magic realism," Allende's works are noted for their underlying feminism and her sensitive depiction of both Latin and American culture. Now making her home in California—Allende has lived in the United States since 1988—she brings her vivid Latina storytelling skills to each of her works, creating memorable characters and vivid settings. Writing her first novel only after spending several years hard at work as a journalist in her native Chile, Allende has been forced by circumstance to deal with several personal tragedies. While difficult emotionally, such events have, perhaps, helped inspire within her a writer's muse that has propelled Allende to prominence as the first internationally acclaimed Latin American woman writer. Her books—which the multilingual Allende continues to compose in Spanish—have been consistently popular with both English- and Spanish-speaking readers, and she continues to top bestseller lists around the world.

Allende was born August 2, 1942, in Lima, Peru, the daughter of Chilean diplomat Tomás Allende and his wife, Francisca Llona Baros Allende. When Allende was only two years old, her parents divorced; she and her mother went to live with her maternal grandparents, Isabela and Augustin Llona, in Santiago, Chile. Allende's grandmother was, like the young girl's own mother, a wonderful teller of tales as well as a devout spiritualist; both women would prove to be a strong influence on the budding writer. Allende remained at the home of her doting grandparents until her mother married a man who—like her former husband—was a member of the diplomatic service. Allende's new stepfather brought his new wife and stepdaughter with him on his travels around the world, giving her the opportunity to live in a variety of locations, including Bolivia and the Middle East, as well as in several major European cities.

Allende's first novel, the multi-generational tale of the Truebas, a Chilean family, blends the supernatural with the real.

In 1957, when the political upheaval in Lebanon—where her stepfather was currently posted—intensified, Allende was sent back to Chile to finish her high school education. After graduating two years later at the age of sixteen, she found her first job as a secretary for the United Nations' Food and Agricultural Organization, staying there until 1965. In 1962 Allende married Miguel Frías, with whom she would have two children prior to the couple's separation in 1978. Meanwhile, her job at the United Nations brought her into contact with many members of the press; she became interested in writing and began to plan her own career as a journalist.

In 1967 Allende took a job with *Paula*, a radical feminist women's magazine that had a national circulation. While at *Paula* she worked as a reporter, editor, and as an advice columnist whose "Impertinences" made interesting reading for many Chilean women. Allende supplemented her work at *Paula* with editorship of the popular children's magazine *Mampato*, beginning in 1969. She also appeared on Chilean television's Canal 13/Canal 7, where she interviewed numerous guests on a weekly program, and worked behind the scenes. Unfortunately, her career as a successful journalist was not meant to be; it would soon come to an abrupt end under tragic circumstances.

Military Coup Changes Writer's Life

The September 11, 1973, assassination of President Salvador Allende as part of a military coup against Chile's socialist government hit twenty-nine-year-old Allende harder than it did many of her fellow Chileans: the progressive, Marxist president had been her uncle. "I think I have divided my life [into] before that day and after that day," Allende told Amanda Smith of *Publishers Weekly*, recalling the twenty-four hours of bloodshed that were sparked by the four-man military junta—or council—led by General Augusto Pinochet Ugarte in his successful bid to take control of the country. "In that moment, I realized that everything was possible—that violence was a dimension that was always around you."

After eighteen months of political repression and violence, during which she helped others find food and shelter and sometimes escape military persecution—Allende helped transport several people to safety in her own automobile—Allende

and the other members of her family were warned by the Mexican Embassy that it was no longer safe for them to remain in Chile. Given asylum by the democratic government of Venezuela, she and several other members of her family fled to Caracas in 1975. "At the beginning it was very hard because I had no status of political refugee," she told the *Atlanta Constitution*'s Betty Parham and Gerrie Ferris, recalling her first days in Venezuela: "I was just an illegal immigrant, a person who had arrived with a tourist visa and stayed. So it took me a while to get papers. I didn't have friends. I didn't have money." To make things even more difficult, despite her considerable experience as a journalist, Allende found it impossible to find a job that would allow her to remain in her field. Resolutely, she put thoughts of writing aside and worked as a teacher for several years.

It was a telephone call from her aged grandfather—who, having remained in Chile and reaching almost a hundred years of age, had decided that it was time to die—that prompted Allende to begin writing again. "My grandfather thought people died only when you forgot them," she later told Harriet Shapiro in *People Weekly*. "I wanted to prove to him that I had forgotten nothing, that his spirit was going to live with us forever." In 1981 she took paper and pencil and began to write the old man a letter recounting her memories. "I think I knew from the beginning that it was not a letter," Allende revealed to Jean W. Ross in an interview for *Contemporary Authors*. "What I didn't know was if I was just writing my memories, writing to salvage fragments of the past that I thought were becoming very blurred by time and distance. I wanted to get back all I had lost. But I didn't tell anybody, not even myself, that it was a book. I would just sit down and write. When my children asked what I was doing, I would say 'Writing,' and they wouldn't ask further."

A Weave of Fantasy and Politics

Those memories of family and home ultimately became Allende's first novel, 1982's *La casa de los espíritus* (*The House of the Spirits*). Organized as the diary of Clara, a woman Allende based on her beloved grandmother, the novel follows three generations of the Trueba family through both domestic and political upheavals. *The House of the Spir-*

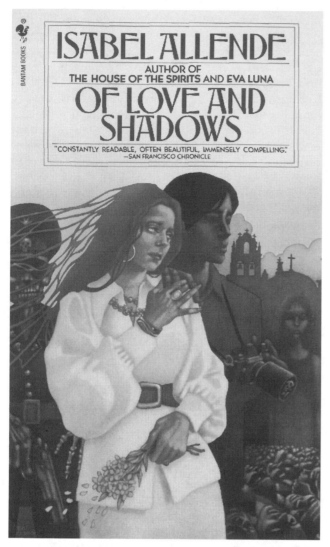

Originally published in 1984, this work follows a journalist and a photographer who investigate a political murder committed in a repressive Latin American nation.

its "is a novel of peace and reconciliation, in spite of the fact that it tells of bloody, tragic events," asserted Alexander Coleman in the *New York Times Book Review*. Allende's use of fantasy, deep sensitivity, and an ambitious structure caused some critics to compare the work to noted author Gabriel García Márquez's dreamlike *One Hundred Years of Solitude*. Allende responded to the comparison in her interview with Ross: "I think that not only in Latin America but everywhere in the world there are things that are invisible that we systematically deny: emotions, passions, dreams, superstitions, myths, legends. They are everywhere all the time, and they effect our lives. . . . [In] the Third World we are willing to accept those

realities. . . . We know there is a dimension of uncertainty in which we move constantly, and that is what in literature has been translated as magic realism."

The House of the Spirits includes, in addition to its mystical element, political approaches similar to other Latin American works of literature, particularly those of Peruvian novelist Mario Vargas Llosa. In explanation, Allende noted the status of the writer in a continent rife with political instability, where, as she stated during a lecture presented in 1988 and later included in *Paths of Resistance: The Art and Craft of the Political Novel*, "a book is almost a luxury," where a novel would cost the average laborer almost four weeks wages—if he could even read it. "Some writers are considered witch doctors, or prophets, as if they were illuminated by a sort of natural wisdom. . . . Jorge Amado has to spend part of the year away from Brazil in order to write, because people crowd into his house seeking advice. Mario Vargas Llosa directs the opposition to [president] Alan Garcia's government in Peru. García Márquez is a frequent middleman for Central American presidents. . . . These writers have interpreted their reality and told it to the world, . . . put into words the hidden thoughts of their people, which of course include social and political problems, because it is impossible to write in a crystal bubble, disregarding the conditions of their continent."

In many ways uncharacteristic of Latin American fiction, *The House of the Spirits*—which Allende dedicated to "my mother, my grandmother, and all the other extraordinary women of this story"—also contains "an original feminist argument that suggests women's monopoly on powers that oppose the violent 'paternalism' from which countries like Chile continue to suffer," Bruce Allen noted in the *Chicago Tribune*. Family patriarch Esteban Trueba is a strict conservative who exploits his employees and lets his rigid beliefs distance him from both his wife and his children—even in the face of catastrophic events. Allende sees herself as one of the women in Latin America who are "breaking the rule of silence and raising a strong voice" to question this rule of patriarchy—the domination of the culture by men. "In all my books there's a character who is silent," she told Ross, explaining that "in a way, maybe it is because I feel that, in my continent, women have been condemned to silence, and speaking up, having a voice, is a very subversive thing for a woman."

Of Love and Survival

The twin themes of politics and giving voice to the concerns of women appear throughout Allende's later works, threaded in and out of a variety of story lines. At the start of her 1984 novel, *De amor y de sombra* (*Of Love and Shadows*), two babies with identical names are switched shortly after birth; one of them grows to womanhood only to become the focus of a woman journalist's investigation. After the reporter and her photographer\companion expose the political murder of the girl, they find themselves on the run and are forced to flee the country. "Love and struggle a la 'Casablanca'—it's all there," described Gene H. Bell-Villada in the *New York Times Book Review*, commenting on the novel's exciting surface plot. "Ms. Allende skillfully evokes both the terrors of daily life under military rule and the subtler form of resistance in the hidden corners and 'shadows' of her title." Although political plottings comprise a large part of the story, *Of Love and Shadows* can also be read as a love story about two people witnessing a battle between the forces of good and evil, tossed together by the tide of history-altering circumstance.

The illegitimate, orphaned protagonist in Allende's third novel works as a scriptwriter and, recalling *The House of the Spirits*, a storyteller. In 1987's *Eva Luna*—released in English in 1988—Eva becomes romantically involved with an Austrian-born film maker who is haunted by memories of his Nazi father. In the novel's sequel, *Cuentos de Eva Luna* (*The Stories of Eva Luna*), published in 1991, Eva spins her colorful tales to her boyfriend in an effort to help separate him from the pressure of his job and the memories and guilt that continue to haunt him. While centering several of her stories on the political upheavals common to Latin America, in *The Stories of Eva Luna* Allende ultimately depicts strong women who are capable of survival, even in the midst of violence and turmoil.

Although many of the novel's themes reflect Allende's previous work, writing *Eva Luna* and its sequel marked a change for the novelist. "It was probably the first time I acknowledged to myself that I was writing a novel," Allende admitted to Ross, "so I planned it and I knew what I was

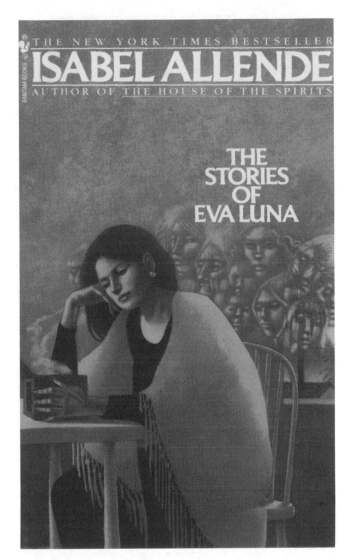

A woman enchants her lover by spinning colorful tales in this 1990 sequel to *Eva Luna*.

going to say exactly. I wanted to write a novel on several levels, that could be read as a story, as *A Thousand and One Nights*, as a picaresque novel [describing the adventures of a roguish main character], but also as a story about writing, about storytelling, about being a woman."

Survival again provides the focus of Allende's fifth novel, 1991's *El plan infinito* (*The Infinite Plan*), translated into English in 1993. Taking place in California, this novel covers a forty-year span in the lives of its three main characters: Gregory Reeves, Carmen Moralez, and Gregory's sister, Judy. When Reeves, the son of a footloose traveling preacher, falls ill during a stop on the touring circuit, his father decides to put down roots, settling his family in the barrio of East Los An-

If you enjoy the works of Isabel Allende, you may also want to check out the following books and films:

Jorge Amado, *Doña Flor and Her Two Husbands*, 1966.

Lois Duncan, *Who Killed My Daughter?*, 1992.

Laura Esquivel 1989 work *Like Water for Chocolate*, which was made into a film in 1993.

Carlos Fuentes, *Old Gringo*, 1985.

Gabriel García Márquez, *One Hundred Years of Solitude*, 1967.

Mario Vargas Llosa, *Aunt Julia and the Scriptwriter*, 1977.

geles. For the Reeves children, their new Hispanic neighborhood welcomes them almost like a family. During the novel, Reeves, Judy, and Moralez—an energetic Latina with a lust for life—travel in and out of the lives of others: neighbors, lovers, friends, and family. Each of the characters' personal weaknesses and strengths, their ability to cope with the ever changing forces of birth, life and death, their moments of anger and the problems that result, and the passion of their love, intertwine throughout the work.

The Loss of a Child

The author's own encounter with tragedy is the subject of 1995's *Paula*. Written while at the bedside of her twenty-eight-year-old daughter Paula, who, fatally afflicted with a hereditary metabolic disorder called porphyria, lay comatose in a Madrid hospital, Allende's book is an intimate, almost painful, collage of memories. The personal—beloved family members like her mother, brother, and grandparents, and recollections of her first husband and their relationship—and the political—the progressive reforms that led up to the death of her uncle in 1973, her strong feminist beliefs, and her personal challenge in gaining a voice in a patriarchal culture—are layered within Allende's account of the days leading up to her daughter's death.

In later years, Allende has been able to return to her native Chile. "All my roots are there," she told

Ross. "I have felt a foreigner everywhere in the world since I left my country." No longer living in Latin America on a full-time basis, she now makes her home in San Francisco, where she lives with her second husband, lawyer William Gordon. In addition to writing, the issue of women's rights—both in Chile and elsewhere—are a major concern to this politically attuned former journalist, who was only allowed to revisit her homeland in 1988. "For women in the United States, the issues are equality through political and economic power," she told Stephen Foehr in the *Chicago Tribune*. "For Latin American women, the issues are still food and shelter for their children." Allende views her chosen profession from a feminist perspective as well: "Women think in terms of process," she explained to Foehr in *Hispanic*. "For them the journey is more important than the place you get to. I think men are motivated by their goals. . . . Thinking in terms of process makes good mothers. Being a mother is an eternal process. My children taught me that. I have tried to apply that to all aspects of my life."

The sense of optimism and the willingness to move forward in the face of adversity that has characterized Allende's life has found another home in her novels. As Jason Wilson wrote of her work in *Contemporary World Writers*: "Behind all Allende's writing lies a sheer joy in storytelling, like a latter-day Scheherazade, a fascination with women, politics, the poor, and destiny, and interest in all kinds of lives related to the best gossip, and an exuberant sensuousness that is in part her style, and in part her outlook on life. She believes in happy endings despite the atrocious history of Latin America and deserves her immense popularity."

■ Works Cited

Allen, Bruce, review of *The House of the Spirits*, *Chicago Tribune*, May 19, 1985.

Allende, Isabel, "Writing As an Act of Hope" (transcript of lecture), *Paths of Resistance: The Art and Craft of the Political Novel*, edited by William Zinsser, Houghton, 1989, pp. 39-63.

Bell-Villada, Gene H., review of *Of Love and Shadows*, *New York Times Book Review*, July 12, 1987.

Coleman, Alexander, review of *The House of the Spirits*, *New York Times Book Review*, May 12, 1985.

Foehr, Stephen, "Of Exile and Love," *Hispanic*, October, 1990, pp. 12-14.

Foehr, Stephen, "For Isabel Allende, the Struggle for Freedom Continues from Afar," *Chicago Tribune*, November 17, 1991, p. 3.

Parham, Betty, and Gerrie Ferris, interview with Allende in *Atlanta Constitution*, May 29, 1993, p. A2.

Ross, Jean W., interview with Allende in *Contemporary Authors*, Volume 130, Gale, 1989, pp. 7-9.

Shapiro, Harriet, "Isabel Allende, Salvador's Niece, Builds a House of the Spirits from the Ashes of Exile," *People Weekly*, June 10, 1985, p. 145.

Smith, Amanda, interview in *Publishers Weekly*, May 17, 1985.

Wilson, Jason, "Isabel Allende," *Contemporary World Writers*, St. James Press, 1993, pp. 17-18.

■ For More Information See

BOOKS

Coddou, Marcelio, editor, *Los libros tienen sus propios espiritus: Estudios sobre Isabel Allende*, Universidad Veracruzana, 1986.

Contemporary Literary Criticism, Volume 39, Gale, 1986.

Erro-Peralta, Mora, "Isabel Allende," in *Dictionary of Literary Biography*, Volume 145: *Modern Latin-American Fiction Writers, Second Series*, Gale, 1994, pp. 33-41.

Hart, Patricia, *Narrative Magic in the Fiction of Isabel Allende*, Fairleigh Dickinson University Press, 1989.

Rojas, Sonia Riquelme, and Edna Aguirre Rehbein, editors, *Critical Approaches to Isabel Allende's Novels*, P. Lang, 1991.

PERIODICALS

Boston Globe, April 23, 1993, p. 14.

Christian Science Monitor, June 7, 1985; May 27, 1987; June 10, 1993, p. 14.

Globe & Mail (Toronto), June 24, 1985; June 27, 1987.

Los Angeles Times, February 10, 1988.

Los Angeles Times Book Review, June 16, 1985; May 31, 1987; June 6, 1993, p. 13; April 30, 1995, pp. 3, 8.

New Statesman & Society, July 5, 1985; July 2, 1993, pp. 38-39.

Newsweek, May 13, 1985.

New York Review of Books, July 18, 1985.

New York Times, May 2, 1985; May 20, 1987; February 4, 1988.

New York Times Book Review, October 23, 1988; May 2, 1993, p. 13; May 21, 1995, p. 11.

People Weekly, June 1, 1987; May 2, 1994; June 5, 1995.

Publishers Weekly, March 1, 1985.

Time, May 20, 1985.

Times (London), July 4, 1985; July 9, 1987; March 22, 1989; March 23, 1989.

Times Literary Supplement, July 5, 1985; July 10, 1987; April 7-13, 1989.

Tribune Books (Chicago), October 9, 1988.

Village Voice, June 7, 1985.

Voice Literary Supplement, December, 1988.

Washington Post Book World, May 12, 1985; May 24, 1987; October 9, 1988; May 23, 1993, p. 6.

World Literature Today, spring, 1993, pp. 335-36.*

—Sketch by Pamela L. Shelton

William H. Armstrong

■ Personal

Born September 14, 1914; son of Howard Gratton (a farmer) and Ida (Morris) Armstrong; married Martha Stone Street Williams, August 24, 1943 (died November, 1953); children: Christopher, David, Mary. *Education:* Augusta Military Academy, diploma, 1932; Hampden-Sydney College, A.B. (cum laude), 1936; graduate study at University of Virginia. *Politics:* Independent. *Religion:* Christian. *Hobbies and other interests:* Carpentry, sheep farming.

■ Addresses

Home—Kimadee Hill, Kent, CT 06757.

■ Career

Virginia Episcopal School, history teacher, 1939-44; Kent School, Kent, CT, history master, 1945-96; writer. Also farmer and real estate agent. *Member:* Phi Beta Kappa, Omicron Delta Kappa.

■ Awards, Honors

National School Bell Award of National Association of School Administrators, 1963, for distinguished service in the interpretation of education; Lewis Carroll Book Shelf Award, 1970; John Newbery Medal, American Library Association, 1970, Mark Twain Award, Missouri Association of School Librarians, 1972, and Nene Award, Hawaii Association of School Librarians and Hawaii Library Association, all for *Sounder;* Academy Award nomination, 1972, for the media adaptation of *Sounder;* Jewish-Christian Brotherhood Award, 1972; Sue Hefley Award, 1976; D.Litt., Hampden-Sydney College, 1986.

■ Writings

YOUNG ADULT FICTION

Sounder, illustrated by James Barkley, Harper, 1969, Gollancz, 1971.
Sour Land, illustrated by David B. Armstrong, Harper, 1971.
The MacLeod Place, illustrated by Eros Keith, Coward, 1972.
The Mills of God, illustrated by Armstrong, Doubleday, 1973.
JoAnna's Miracle, Broadman, 1978.
The Tale of Tawny and Dingo, illustrated by Charles Mikolaycak, Harper, 1979.

YOUNG ADULT NONFICTION

Tools of Thinking: A Self-Help Workbook for Students in Grades 5-9, Barron's, 1968, published as *Word Power in 5 Easy Lessons: A Simplified Approach to Excellence in Grammar, Punctuation, Sentence Structure, Spelling and Penmanship*, 1969.

Barefoot in the Grass: The Story of Grandma Moses, Doubleday, 1970.

(Adaptor with Hana Doskocilova) *Animal Tales*, translated from Czechoslovakian by Eve Merriam, illustrated by Mirko Hanak, Doubleday, 1970.

Hadassah: Esther the Orphan Queen, illustrated by Barbara Byfield, Doubleday, 1972.

My Animals, illustrated by Hanak, Doubleday, 1973.

The Education of Abraham Lincoln, illustrated by William Plummer, Coward, 1974.

ADULT PUBLICATIONS

Study Is Hard Work, Harper, 1956, new edition, Godine.

Through Troubled Waters, Harper, 1957.

(With Joseph W. Swain) *Peoples of the Ancient World*, Harper, 1959.

87 Ways to Help Your Child in School, Barron's, 1961.

Study Tapes, Barron's, 1975.

Study Tips: How to Improve Your Study Habits and Improve Your Grades, Barron's, 1976, revised edition published as *Study Tactics*, 1983.

OTHER

Armstrong's manuscripts are housed in the Kerlan Collection, University of Minnesota.

■ Adaptations

Sounder was adapted into a film released by 20th-Century Fox, 1972.

■ Sidelights

"But there was no price that could be put on Sounder's voice. It came out of the great chest cavity and broad jaws as though it had bounced off the walls of a cave. It mellowed into half-echo before it touched the air. . . . Each bark bounced from slope to slope in the foothills like a rubber ball. But it was not an ordinary bark. It filled up the night and made music as though the branches of all the trees were being pulled across silver strings. . . . [A]ll over the countryside, neighbors, leaning against slanting porch posts or standing in open cabin doorways and listening, knew that it was Sounder."

Sounder, the mixed-breed hound for whom William Armstrong's prize-winning novel is named, is known for his unique voice, a voice shaped and made distinct by the particular kind of body that produces it and through the resonance given it by the natural features of a certain geography. And so it also is with Armstrong, whose storytelling voice has been shaped and made distinct by particular life experiences distilled by memory, and a deep knowledge of how history—both ancient and recent—marks individuals and events.

At various times a history teacher, author, father, sheep farmer, house builder, and nature lover, Armstrong has written more than fifteen books. Over half of these are for young adults, including six works of fiction as well as biographies of historical and biblical figures and materials to help people learn study techniques. As varied as his body of work is, major themes remain constant throughout: the nobility of hard work, the rewards of education, the importance of religious faith, and a respect for nature and its sometimes beautiful, sometimes harsh lessons. When asked if his books reflect his life, Armstrong told an interviewer for the *Hartford Courant*, "I guess they do quite a bit. I'm a loner and some of the characters in my books begin to appreciate the quiet harvest of aloneness, the quiet symphony of creation and earth, the quiet music of the earth—and its deep agony."

Great Lessons Learned from "Small World"

Armstrong was born in 1914 on his parents' hardscrabble farm near the village of Collierstown (near Lexington) in Rockbridge County, Virginia. It was here that he grew up with his two older sisters under the influence of parents who believed in the value of hard work and education. His religious mother read the Bible to them every day. The demanding work required by a farming life during economic hard times and the close-knit village community of friends and neighbors also seem to have made lasting impressions on Armstrong, and these make their way into his writing. "Growing up in that little world many great lessons awaited me, not least of which were love of earth and respect of nature," Armstrong wrote in an essay for the *Something about the Author Autobiography Series (SAAS)*. Characters who are knowledgeable about plants and animals and therefore seem near to and at peace with the mysteries of nature—of life and death—are central to Armstrong's stories, as are detailed observations about the natural world. Other portraits from real life are visible in his work as well— mothers who both teach and entertain their children by telling Bible stories; fathers who stoically make sacrifices in order to provide for their families' needs; exceptional teachers whose influence make a real difference in the lives of students.

For a man who would end up spending nearly his whole life in school—first as student, then as teacher—it is interesting to note that Armstrong's early school days were not happy ones. He described himself in *SAAS* as an easy target for other students because of his small size, glasses, chronic asthma, and a speech problem that caused him to talk with a stutter for a time. But things changed for him in the sixth grade when a memorable teacher singled him out in front of the class for having the neatest paper. "Now, suddenly, I knew where I could win. I could have the most nearly perfect written work—whether spelling, multiplication table, or sentence. . . . That day began a Depression-born country boy's determined journey toward 'the gates of excellence,'" Armstrong continued in *SAAS*.

Books were scarce when Armstrong was a schoolboy, and in *SAAS* he wrote that when he visits elementary schools today he tries to convey to young people "the great thrill of owning my first book—other than regular schoolbooks." It was Lord Charnwood's 468-page *Life of Abraham Lincoln*, purchased for $1.65, money Armstrong had earned digging sassafras sprouts from the pasture for five cents an hour. (Armstrong would go on to one day write his own book about Abraham Lincoln, *The Education of Abraham Lincoln*, in 1974, which a reviewer for the *Wall Street Journal*, quoted in *SAAS*, described as "unbounded by categories—a book of simplicity, beauty, and wisdom for all readers.")

In this 1969 novel, a faithful coon dog is shot while trying to protect his master, a poor black sharecropper who is arrested after stealing some food for his hungry family.

Armstrong began his secondary schooling in 1928 at Augusta Military Academy, where two key assignments set him on the path toward his future vocations: first, a theme paper about the origin of geometry gave him an introduction to ancient history—a subject he would take up later in both his teaching and writing—and, second, a short story for composition class about a wheelchair-bound boy who helplessly watches as his cat destroys a nest of baby birds. It was so good—and so distinct from the other boys' stories of sports and summer activities—that he was accused of copying it from another source. Armstrong worked hard at odd jobs to meet the expenses of staying in school and graduated in 1932. Rather than continue with military schooling, he instead decided to attend Hampden-Sydney College in Prince Edward County, Virginia, where he studied Greek, wrote for the school newspaper, served as editor of the school literary magazine and saw his first plays on stage. He graduated cum laude in 1936.

A Teacher First

Though he had considered becoming a journalist, the influence of his own teachers held sway, and Armstrong decided to become a teacher himself. He taught at an Episcopal school in Lynchburg, Virginia, and did graduate study at the University of Virginia before taking, in 1944, a teaching position at Kent School in Kent, Connecticut, where he spent the rest of his teaching career. Explaining in *SAAS* how he was able to devote almost a lifetime to the same job in the same place, he wrote, "I learned that teaching is more than the subject and the textbook; it's hopefully directing some young wanderer in a direction that will add quality, and, in rare cases, love of learning, to a life." His love of village life may well have something to do with it also. "I get away and visit other places just so I can appreciate Kent a little more, just enough to be anxious to get back," he related in his interview for the *Hartford Courant.*

As his teaching career progressed, so did Armstrong's family life; he married Martha Stone Street Williams in 1943 and they had three children, Christopher, David, and Mary. He still lives in the pine house overlooking the Housatonic River that he built for his family and at which he also raised Corriedale sheep. The year 1953 brought a tragic turn in his life; his wife died suddenly and he was left with three small children—aged 8, 6, and 4—to raise and a household to run. "You know, when you have tangles to comb out of your daughter's hair and vitamins rolling off the table you stop thinking," Armstrong pointed out in his *Hartford Courant* interview, explaining how he began his disciplined schedule of getting up in the early morning hours to do his writing. "Early in the morning is my time to write—from 4:00 A.M. to 7:00 A.M.," he explained in *SAAS.* "There is something very satisfactory about having one big job done before breakfast— like back on the farm with the milking before breakfast."

Armstrong has said that he thinks of himself as a teacher rather than a writer, and in fact it was his success as an educator that led to his first

published work. In 1950, the Kent School headmaster proposed that Armstrong write a book about how to study. Titled *Study Is Hard Work* and published in 1956, it deals with such topics as listening skills, practice methods, and motivation. It was followed in 1957 with *Through Troubled Waters,* a lyrical account of how Armstrong and his children together made their way through the loss of their wife and mother, Martha. But it is *Sounder,* published in 1969 and the recipient of several awards, including the American Library Association's prestigious John Newbery Medal in 1970, for which young readers in schools across the country have come to know him.

A Childhood Story Remembered

In the book's author's note, Armstrong explains that *Sounder* is based on a story from his childhood, told to him by the gray-haired black teacher from the nearby rural school for black children. The teacher did farm work for Armstrong's father after school and in the summers, tutoring the Armstrong children at the kitchen table in the evenings. After their lessons, the teacher would tell stories from Aesop, the Old Testament, Homer, and history. But on one occasion, Armstrong recalls, the teacher told the story of Sounder, a coon dog. "It is the black man's story, not mine. . . . It was history—*his* history," Armstrong wrote in the author's note, concluding that though the world has greatly changed since that time, "the story remains."

Sounder, which was made into a movie in 1972 by Twentieth-Century Fox, takes place in the early part of this century in the rural South. It is the story of a black sharecropping family—which Armstrong does not name—struggling to get by with little opportunity and scarce resources, other than their dignity, determination, and family bonds. Sounder is their coon dog, beloved as a family pet but also important to their livelihood, since the money the father earns by hunting coons and selling their hides ensures that the family will have food to eat during winter.

When *Sounder* opens, it is a particularly bleak winter and the hunting has not been profitable. So one night, the desperate father steals a ham. He is brutally apprehended by the white authorities and hauled away like an animal. Sounder, trying to protect his master, is shot down in the road and crawls away to die. The oldest son, who channels his fear and grief for his father into similar feelings for the missing Sounder, does his best to help his mother manage the farm. He also journeys far and wide in his free time, looking for his missing father, who was sentenced to a hard labor camp in an unknown location. On one search, he meets an old black teacher, who takes him in during the winter so that he can attend school. Sounder does reappear, permanently maimed from the shooting and without his beautiful voice, and spends the rest of his life waiting for his master to return. When the father does come home—after many years—crippled from an explosion in the prison quarry, it is to live out the short remainder of his life in the presence of his loved ones.

Like other young adult books of this type—*Old Yeller* or *Where the Red Fern Grows*, for example—

HARPER TROPHY By the Newbery Medal-Winning Author of SOUNDER $3.95 US $5.25 CDN

SOUR LAND
William H. Armstrong

Racial hatred leads to violence when a black man tutors three white children in a southern farming community in this 1971 work.

Sounder is not essentially about a dog that dies, but rather, is about the boy who is left behind and the life lessons about love, sacrifice, and relationships that carry him into manhood. Mary Lystad, writing in *Twentieth-Century Young Adult Writers*, noted that "*Sounder* is one of the few books of mid-century focused on black adolescents in the South." And, indeed, racial injustice and the painful transitions of growing up are among the primary themes that Armstrong takes up in *Sounder*.

"There is an epic quality in the deeply moving, long-ago story of cruelty, loneliness, and silent suffering. The power of the writing lies in its combination of subtlety and strength," wrote Ethel L. Heins in *Horn Book*. Similarly, Zena Sutherland observed in the *Bulletin of the Center for Children's Books* that *Sounder* is "written with quiet strength and taut with tragedy. . . . Grim and honest, the book has a moving, elegiac quality that is reminiscent of the stark inevitability of Greek tragedy." As these reviewers and others have noted, *Sounder* stands out because Armstrong does not shy away from making plain the violence and tragedy that marks his characters' lives. As June Meyer Jordan, writing in the *New York Times Book Review*, pointed out: "There are no lies. But I am not sure children should read this book." In it, she continued, "We engage a history frozen around loving people who never scream, who never cry: they search, they continue any way they can, and they wait. It seems that *Sounder* is worth reading—by young and not so young adults."

This history, which includes a variety of racial issues, was also the cause of some critical debate. "What the white author of *Sounder* has done to the black characters is to diminish their role as instruments in effecting change," Rae Alexander concluded in *The Black American in Books for Children: Readings in Racism*. Dorothy M. Broderick, in *Image of the Black in Children's Fiction*, wrote, "We do not need any more books like William Armstrong's *Sounder*, where a black child who watches his father destroyed by racism overcomes the horrors of childhood to attain the lofty position of being allowed to sit in the white man's kitchen and help the white man's children become intellectually stimulated." But John Rowe Townsend, in his *Written for Children: An Outline of English Language Children's Literature*, gave his support to *Sounder*, saying that some of the criticism against Armstrong's novel was "misguided." "A charge of lack of authenticity is hard to evaluate; it depends on what you mean by authenticity. To me it has always seemed that truth in a novel is truth to the enduring, underlying realities of human nature; and that these enduring realities are recognizable whatever the context. . . . *Sounder*, though by no means a masterpiece, is a brief, bleak book that tells an elemental story of hardship, suffering, endurance; tells it memorably and well."

Nameless and Universal

A question that critics and young readers alike have asked many times about *Sounder* is why the author chose not to name his characters. Armstrong explained in *SAAS* that because of the ambiguities inherent in the Bible stories he heard as a boy, he was able, by using his imagination, to become a part of those stories. This, he says, is the basis for his "wholesale omissions" in *Sounder*. "If the boy's age was not given the reader could become a part of the story: 'The boy must be about my age.' . . . And no names for the family. With names they would have represented one family; without names they became universal—representing all people who suffer privation and injustice, but through love, self-respect, devotion, and desire for improvement, make it in the world."

Armstrong's second novel, *Sour Land*, published in 1971, is a sequel, of sorts, to *Sounder*, featuring the boy from that book as its main character. He is now an old man with a name: Moses Waters. Moses arrives in a southern farming community to teach in the black school and fulfill his dream of owning his own place. With deep knowledge of books and the natural world and a master at whatever he puts his hand to, he is befriended by the town's storekeeper and moral force, Enoch Morris, and the Stone family—a recently widowed farmer and his three young children, David, eight; Jonathan, a year-and-a-half younger; and Mary, five. Moses works on the Stone farm after school and during the summer and tutors the Stone children in the evenings, becoming a well-loved part of the family. The Stones' openness, however, is the exception in a time and place where ignorance and racism are otherwise the rule. Many villagers disapprove of the white family's association with the black man, and after a series of threatening events, Moses is mysteriously murdered for

speaking out about the murder of a young black girl.

Reviews for *Sour Land* were mixed. Strong points cited by critics include its attempts to indict prejudice and violence and its "beautiful descriptions of nature, seasonal change, and the peculiar peace and understanding possible to a man who works with the soil," described Diane G. Stavn in *School Library Journal*. She ultimately found, though, that such a picture didn't make up for "passionless

---

If you enjoy the works of William H. Armstrong, you may also want to check out the following books and films:

Ouida Sebestyen, *Words by Heart*, 1979.
Mildred D. Taylor, *Roll of Thunder, Hear My Cry*, 1976.
Alice Walker, *Meridian*, 1976.
Old Yeller, Disney, 1957.
To Kill a Mockingbird, MCA/Universal, 1962.

---

characters and a lack of drama that is incredible given the potentially stirring situations" of the book's plot. Others found Moses Waters too noble and too perfect to be interesting or convincing. "A sincerely idealistic and elegiac presentation of one of America's tragic dilemmas," concluded Paul Heins in *Horn Book*.

Clearly, elements of *Sour Land* are drawn from Armstrong's own life. "Perhaps it is because I was treated so miserably at school that I remember only older people, my parents' contemporaries, as friends. They are the models for the adult characters in my books, the good and the bad," he related in *SAAS*. Armstrong himself, as a boy and as a man, figures into the story too: the terrible incident of young David's pony getting trampled to a pulp by the other horses really happened to Armstrong as a boy; Armstrong gives David the same grief-stricken stammer that resulted from the experience. And anyone who has read Armstrong's *Through Troubled Waters* will recognize in the Stone family the grown Armstrong and his children grieving for their dead wife and mother.

Armstrong's other works of fiction include *The MacLeod Place*, published in 1972, which is an "ecological fable" (as described by Maggie Scarf in the *New York Times Book Review*) about a boy whose grandparents' Virginia mountain farm is threatened by the government's plans to build a highway through it; *The Mills of God*, published in 1973, which is a story about a boy named Aaron and his dog set in Appalachia during the Depression; *JoAnna's Miracle* (1978), and *The Tale of Tawny and Dingo* (1979), a picture book about the friendship between a sheepdog and a lamb. Among Armstrong's nonfiction titles for young adults are several biographies of historical figures: *Barefoot in the Grass: The Story of Grandma Moses* (1970), *Hadassah: Esther the Orphan Queen* (1972), and *The Education of Abraham Lincoln* (1974).

Living History, Living Memory

Having grown up in a region of the country that Armstrong has described as "living history"—riding through the Shenandoah Valley where Robert E. Lee rode after the Civil War, worshipping in the church where Stonewall Jackson taught Sunday school, hearing stories connecting family members with famous figures—it's not surprising, then, that his stories are the weaving together of personal life experience and the larger legacy of history. "I write with a pencil on a lined tablet," explained Armstrong of his method in *SAAS*, adding that he was afraid the use of a typewriter or word processor would get in the way of the slow process of translating feeling into story. "For most of my books begin with an idea that I take inside and keep there for a long time before I write a single word. It gets into my blood and is filtered through my heart until it is a part of me."

Armstrong's reflection, in *Something about the Author*, about a late-night walk and the creative process that brought forth *Sounder* could well speak to the origin of his own authorial voice: " . . . what good is a sprig of memory except to twirl between the fingers of the mind as one walks? Who looks a second time at the dead twig that has been snapped from a branch while walking, peeled of its dead bark, glanced briefly at its velvety smooth nakedness, then cast away in a bed of fallen leaves? . . . So the sprig of memory is rolled between the fingers of the mind, first smooth, then sharpened until its point becomes a

splinter. And on the night walk along the Housatonic it pricks and pricks; agonizing, destroying the rhythm of leaves dancing, wrinkling the golden carpet that a Hunter's Moon has laid upon October fields. I must use this memory."

■ Works Cited

Alexander, Rae, "What is a Racist Book?," *The Black American in Books for Children: Readings in Racism*, Scarecrow, 1972.

Armstrong, William H., in an interview for the *Hartford Courant*, November 25, 1973.

Armstrong, comments in *Something about the Author*, Volume 4, Gale, 1973.

Armstrong, essay for *Something about the Author Autobiography Series*, Volume 7, Gale, 1989.

Armstrong, *Sounder*, illustrated by James Barkley, Harper, 1969, Gollancz, 1971.

Broderick, Dorothy M., *Image of the Black in Children's Fiction*, Bowker, 1973.

Heins, Ethel L., review of *Sounder*, Horn Book, December, 1969.

Heins, Paul, review of *Sour Land*, Horn Book, June, 1971.

Jordan, June Meyer, review of *Sounder*, New York Times Book Review, October 26, 1969.

Lystad, Mary, essay on William H. Armstrong for *Twentieth-Century Young Adult Writers*, St. James Press, 1994.

Scarf, Maggie, review of *The MacLeod Place*, New York Times Book Review, November 5, 1972.

Stavn, Diane G., review of *Sour Land*, School Library Journal, March, 1971.

Sutherland, Zena, review of *Sounder*, Bulletin of the Center for Children's Books, February, 1971.

Townsend, John Rowe, *Written for Children: An Outline of English Language Children's Literature*, Lippincott, 1974.

■ For More Information See

BOOKS

Hopkins, Lee Bennett, *More Books by More People*, Citation, 1974.

—Sketch by Tracy J. Sukraw

W. H. Auden

Personal

Full name, Wystan Hugh Auden; born February 21, 1907, in York, England; immigrated to the United States, 1939, became a citizen, 1946; died in his sleep September 28, 1973 (officially recorded as September 29) in Kirchstetten, near Vienna, Austria; son of George Augustus (a doctor) and Constance Rosalie (a nurse; maiden name, Bicknell) Auden; married Erika Mann (a writer and daughter of German author Thomas Mann), June 15, 1935, so she could acquire a passport out of Nazi Germany (divorced); companion of Chester Kallman, 1939-73. *Education:* Christ Church College, Oxford, B.A., 1928.

Career

Poet, essayist, dramatist, librettist, critic, editor, anthologist, scriptwriter, and translator. Larchfield Academy, Helensburgh, Scotland, teacher, 1930-32; Downs School, Colwall, England, teacher, 1932-35; cofounder, Group Theatre, 1932; film writer, General Post Office film unit, 1935; St. Mark's School, Southborough, MA, teacher, 1939-40; faculty member, American Writers League School, 1939; New School for Social Research, New York City, teacher, 1940-41, 1946-47, and 1948; faculty member at Olivet College and University of Michigan, 1941-42, Swarthmore College and Bryn Mawr College, 1943-45, Bennington College, 1946, Barnard College, 1947, University of Virginia, 1949, and Mount Holyoke College, 1950; Smith College, Northampton, MA, W. A. Neilson Research Professor, 1953; Oxford University, Oxford, England, professor of poetry, 1956-61. Cofounder and editor (with Lionel Trilling and Jacques Barzun), Reader's Subscription Book Club, 1951-59, and of Mid-Century Book Society, 1959-63. *Wartime service:* Broadcaster, ambulance driver, and stretcher-bearer for Loyalists during Spanish Civil War, 1937; research chief of Morale Division, U.S. Strategic Bombing Survey in Germany, 1945. *Member:* American Academy of Arts and Letters.

Awards, Honors

King's Gold Medal for Poetry, 1937; Guggenheim fellowships, 1942, 1945; Award of Merit Medal, American Academy of Arts and Letters, 1945; Pulitzer Prize in Poetry, 1948, for *The Age of Anxiety;* Bollingen Prize in Poetry, 1954; National Book Award, 1956, for *The Shield of Achilles;* Feltrinelli Prize (Rome), 1957; Alexander Droutzkoy Memorial Award, 1959; shared Guiness Poetry Award (Ireland) with Robert Lowell and Edith Sitwell, 1959; honored on Chicago Poetry Day, 1960; Honorary Student (Fellow), Christ Church College, Oxford University, 1962-73; Austrian State Prize for

European Literature, 1966; National Medal for Literature of the National Book Committee, 1967, for lifetime contributions to literature; Gold Medal of the National Institute of Arts and Letters, 1968. Recipient of honorary doctorates from Swarthmore College, 1965, Oxford University, 1971, and University of London, 1972.

■ Writings

POETRY

Poems, S.H.S. [Stephen Spender], 1928.

Poems, Faber, 1930, 2nd edition, 1933, Random House, 1934, revised edition with foreword by Spender, Elliston Poetry Foundation of the University of Cincinnati, 1965.

The Orators: An English Study, Faber, 1932, revised edition with new foreword, Random House, 1967.

Look, Stranger!, Faber, 1936, published as *On This Island,* Random House, 1937.

(With Louis MacNeice) *Letters from Iceland,* Random House, 1937, revised edition, 1969.

Spain, Faber, 1937.

Selected Poems, Faber, 1938.

(With Christopher Isherwood) *On the Frontier,* Faber, 1938.

(With Isherwood) *Journey to a War,* Faber, 1939, revised edition, 1973.

Another Time, Random House, 1940.

Some Poems, Faber, 1940.

Three Songs for St. Cecilia's Day, privately printed, 1941.

The Double Man, Random House, 1941, published as *New Year Letter,* Faber, 1941.

For the Time Being, Random House, 1944.

The Collected Poetry of W. H. Auden, Random House, 1945.

Collected Shorter Poems, 1930-1944, Faber, 1950, Random House, 1951.

Nones, Random House, 1951.

The Shield of Achilles, Random House, 1955.

The Old Man's Road, Voyages Press, 1956.

W. H. Auden: A Selection by the Author, Penguin, 1958, published as *Selected Poetry of W. H. Auden,* Modern Library, 1959.

Homage to Clio, Random House, 1960.

W. Auden, A Selection, notes and essay by Richard Hoggart, Hutchinson, 1961.

The Common Life, translated from original German by Dieter Leisegang, Blaeschke, 1964.

The Cave of the Making, translated from original German by Leisegang, Blaeschke, 1965.

Half-Way (limited edition), Lowell-Adams, 1965.

About the House, Random House, 1965.

The Platonic Blow, [New York], 1965, published with *My Epitaph,* Orchises Press, 1985.

Collected Shorter Poems, 1927-1957, Faber, 1966, Random House, 1967.

Portraits, Apiary Press, 1966.

Marginalia, Ibex Press, 1966.

A Selection by the Author, Faber, 1967.

Selected Poems, Faber, 1968, revised edition, Random House, 1979.

Two Songs, Phoenix Book Shop, 1968.

Collected Longer Poems, Faber, 1968, Random House, 1969.

Secondary Worlds, Faber, 1969.

City without Walls, and Many Other Poems, Random House, 1969.

Academic Graffiti, Faber, 1971, Random House, 1972.

(With Leif Sjoeberg) *Selected Poems,* Pantheon, 1972.

Epistle to a Godson, and Other Poems, Random House, 1972.

Poems and Lithographs, edited by John Russell, British Museum, 1974.

Poems, lithographs by Henry Moore, edited by Vera Lindsay, Petersburg Press, 1974.

Thank You, Fog: Last Poems, Faber, 1974.

Collected Poems, edited by Edward Mendelson, Faber, 1976.

Sue, Sycamore Press, 1977.

The English Auden: Poems, Essays, and Dramatic Writings, edited by Mendelson, Faber, 1977, Random House, 1978.

Selected Poems, edited by Mendelson, Vintage, 1979.

Juvenilia: Poems, 1922-1928, edited by Katherine Bucknell, Princeton University Press, 1994.

Tell Me the Truth about Love: Ten Poems, Random House, 1994.

The Language of Learning and the Language of Love: Uncollected Writings, New Interpretations, edited by Mendelson Bucknell and Nicholas Jenkins, Clarendon Press, 1994.

As I Walked out One Evening: Songs, Ballads, Lullabies, Limericks, and Other Light Verse, selected by Mendelson, Vintage Books, 1995.

CRITICISM AND ESSAYS

(With T. C. Worsley) *Education, Today, and Tomorrow,* Hogarth, 1939.

The Enchafed Flood: The Romantic Iconography of the Sea, Random House, 1950.

Making, Knowing, and Judging, Clarendon Press, 1956.

The Dyer's Hand and Other Essays, Random House, 1962, published as *Selected Essays*, Faber, 1964.

Louis MacNiece (memorial address), Faber, 1963.

Secondary Worlds (T. S. Eliot Memorial Lectures at University of Kent, 1967), Faber, 1968, Random House, 1969.

A Certain World: A Commonplace Book, Random House, 1970.

Forewords and Afterwords, edited by Mendelson, Random House, 1973.

PLAYS

(With Isherwood) *The Ascent of F6: A Tragedy in Two Acts* (produced in London, 1931, produced in New York City, 1939), Faber, 1936, Random House, 1937, 2nd edition, 1956.

The Dance of Death (produced in London, 1934, and New York, 1935; produced in Poughkeepsie, NY, as *come out into the Sun*, 1935), Faber, 1933, 2nd edition, 1935.

(With Isherwood) *The Dog beneath the Skin; or, Where is Francis?* (produced in London, 1936, revised version produced in New York City, 1947), Faber, 1935.

(Adaptor with Edward Crankshaw) Ernst Toller, *No More Peace! A Thoughtful Comeday* (produced in London, 1936, and New York, 1937), Farrar & Rinehart, 1937.

On the Frontier: A Melodrama in Three Acts (produced in London, 1939), Random House, 1938.

The Age of Anxiety: A Baroque Eclogue (verse play; produced Off-Broadway, 1954), Random House, 1947.

(With Isherwood) *Two Great Plays* (contains *The Dog beneath the Skin* and *The Ascent of F6*), Random House, 1959.

Plays and Other Dramatic Writings: W. H. Auden and Christopher Isherwood, 1928-1938, edited by Mendelson, Princeton University Press, 1988.

Also author of documentary screenplays in verse, including *Night Mail*, 1936, *Coal Face*, 1936, and *The Londoners*, 1938; author of radio plays, including *Hadrian's Wall*, 1937, *The Dark Valley*, 1940, and *The Rocking-Horse Winner* (adapted from a D. H. Lawrence story).

LIBRETTOS AND LYRICS

Our Hunting Fathers, music by Benjamin Britten, Boosey & Hawkes, 1936.

Fish in the Unruffled Lakes, music by Britten, Boosey & Hawkes, 1937.

On This Island, music by Britten, Boosey & Hawkes, 1937.

Two Ballads, Boosey & Hawkes, 1937.

Now through the Night's Caressing Grip, music by Britten, Boosey & Hawkes, 1938.

Ballad of Heroes, music by Britten, Boosey & Hawkes, 1939.

Paul Bunyan (performed in New York, 1941), music by Britten, Faber, 1976.

Hymn to St. Cecilia for S.S.A.T.B., music by Britten, Boosey & Hawkes, 1942.

For the Time Being: A Christmas Oratorio (first performed at Carnegie Hall, New York City, 1959), music by Marvin David Levy, [New York], 1944.

The Duchess of Malfi (adapted from the play by John Webster), music by Benjamin Britten, produced in New York, 1946.

(With Chester Kallman) *The Rake's Progress: Opera in Three Acts* (produced in Venice, 1951, New York, 1953, and London, 1962), music by Igor Stravinsky, Boosey & Hawkes, 1951.

(Adaptor with Kallman) *The Magic Flute: An Opera in Two Acts* (telecast, 1956), music by Wolfgang Amadeus Mozart, Random House, 1956.

(With Noah Greenberg) *The Play of Daniel: A Thirteenth Century Musical Drama*, Oxford University Press, 1959.

Five Poems (performed in New York, 1959), music by Lennox Berkeley, J. & W. Chester, 1960.

The Seven Deadly Sins of the Lower Middle Class (adapted from the work by Bertholt Brecht), music by Kurt Weill, produced in New York, 1959, Edinburgh and London, 1961, published in *Tulane Drama Review*, 1961.

(With others) *Time Cycle, for Soprano and Orchestra*, performed at Carnegie Hall, 1960.

(With Kallman) *Elegy for Young Lovers: Opera in Three Acts* (produced in Stuttgart and Sussex, 1961), music by Hans Werner Henze, Schott, 1961.

(Adaptor with Kallman) Lorenzo Da Ponte, *Don Giovanni*, music by Mozart, Schirmer, 1961.

Elegy for J.F.K., music by Stravinsky, Boosey & Hawkes, 1964.

(Adaptor with Kallman) *Arcifanfano, King of Fools*, performed in New York, 1965.

The Twelve: Anthem for the Feast Day of Any Apostle, music by William Walton, Oxford University Press, 1966.

(With Kallman) *The Bassarids: Opera Seria with Intermezzo in One Act* (adapted from *The Bacchae* by Euripides; produced in Salzburg, Austria,

1966, and Santa Fe, NM, 1966), music by Henze, Schott, 1966.

(With Kallman) *Love's Labour's Lost* (adapted from the play by William Shakespeare; produced in Edinburgh, 1971), music by Nicholas Nabokov, Boat & Bock, 1972.

Also author, with Kallman, of *Delia; or, A Masque of Night*, published in *Botteghe Obscure*, 1953.

RECORDINGS

Reading His Own Poems, Harvard Vocarium, 1941.
Reading from His Works, Caedmon, 1954.
Auden, Argo, 1960.
Selected Poems, Spoken Arts, 1968.

EDITOR

(With Charles Plumb) *Oxford Poetry, 1926*, Basil Blackwell, 1926.
(With C. Day Lewis) *Oxford Poetry, 1927*, Appleton, 1927.
(With John Garrett) *The Poet's Tongue*, G. Bell, 1935.
(With Arthur Elton) *Mechanics*, Longmans, Green, 1936.
(With Horman Holmes Pearson) *Poets of the English Language*, 5 volumes, Viking, 1950.
(With Marianne Moore and Karl Shapiro) *Riverside Poetry 1953: Poems by Students in Colleges and Universities in New York City*, Association Press, 1953.
(With Kallman and Greenberg) *An Elizabethan Song Book: Lute Songs, Madrigals, and Rounds*, Doubleday, 1956, published as *An Anthology of elizabethan Lute Songs, Madrigals, and Rounds*, Norton, 1970.
Van Gogh: A Self Portrait (selected letters), New York Graphic Society, 1961.
Joseph Jacobs, *The Pied Piper, and Other Fairy Tales*, Macmillan, 1963.
(With Louis Kronenberger) *The Viking Book of Aphorisms*, Viking, 1963, published as *The Faber Book of Aphorisms*, Faber, 1964.
Walter de la Mare, *A Choice of de la Mare's Verse*, Faber, 1963.
Selected Poems of Louis MacNeice, Faber, 1964.
(With John Lawlor) *To Nevill Cognill from Friends*, Faber, 1966.
Selected Poetry and Prose of George Gordon, Lord Byron, New American Library, 1966.
MacNeice, *Persons from Porlock, and Other Plays for Radio*, BBC Productions, 1969.

G. K. Chesterton: A Selection from His Non-Fictional Prose, Faber, 1970.
George Herbert, Penguin, 1973.

Also coeditor of "The Looking Glass Library" series of children's books.

EDITOR AND AUTHOR OF INTRODUCTION

Oxford Book of Light Verse, Oxford University Press, 1938.
A Selection of the Poems of Alfred Lord Tennyson, Doubleday, 1944, published as *Tennyson: An Introduction and a Selection*, Phoenix House, 1946.
Henry James, *American Scene*, Scribner, 1946.
John Betjeman, *Slick but Not Streamlined*, Doubleday, 1947.
The Portable Greek Reader, Viking, 1948.
Edgar Allan Poe, *Selected Prose and Poetry*, Rinehart, 1950, revised edition, 1957.
The Living Thoughts of Kierkegaard, McKay, 1952, published as *Kierkegaard*, Cassell, 1955.
Selected Writings of Sydney Smith, Farrar, Straus, 1956.
The Criterion Book of Modern American Verse, Criterion, 1956, published as *The Faber Book of Modern American Verse*, Faber, 1956.
Nineteenth Century British Minor Poets, Delacorte, 1966, published as *Nineteenth Century Minor Poets*, Faber, 1967.
Selected Songs of Thomas Campion, Godine, 1973.

Also editor and author of introduction for the "Yale Series of Younger Poets," 1947-59, which published poets such as Adrienne Rich, W. S. Merwin, John Ashbery, and James Wright.

OTHER

The Complete Works of W. H. Auden, Princeton University Press, Volumes I and II: *Libretti and Other Dramatic Writings, 1939-1973*, edited by Mendelson, 1989, Volumes III-VI: *Essays and Reviews*, 1988, Volumes VII-VIII: *Complete Poetry*, 1988.
The Map of All My Youth: Early Works, Friends, and Influences, edited by Bucknell and Jenkins, Oxford University Press, 1991.
The Prolific and the Devourer (aphorisms), Ecco Press, 1993.

Author of introductions and afterwords to numerous books. Contributor of poems and essays to numerous books and periodicals. Auden also translated (often with others) several poems, operas, plays, and essays by Brecht, Goethe, and others.

The Berg Collection of the New York Public Library holds the most important collection of Auden's papers, and the Humanities Research Center at the University of Texas, Austin, houses an extensive collection of manuscripts, prompt books of his plays, and other materials.

■ Sidelights

"America may break one completely, but the best of which one is capable is more likely to be drawn out of one here than anywhere else," W. H. Auden wrote a friend soon after immigrating to the United States, Richard Johnson related in *Concise Dictionary of British Literary Biography.* Despite seeing America as a "terrifying place," Auden decided the only worthwhile goal was "to attempt the more difficult" and "to live deliberately without roots." He had uprooted himself from both the British literary scene and his family and underwent a self-imposed alienation, as Johnson concluded; in his writing and in his life, Auden assumed the exile's role.

Auden died in 1973 in Austria, far from his adopted country, but no less an American. In a special Auden issue of *Shenandoah,* Robert Lowell agreed with fellow poet John Crowe Ransom's remark that America "had made an even exchange, when we lost [T. S.] Eliot to England, and later gained Auden. Both poets have been kind to the lands of their exile, and brought gifts the natives could never have conceived of." Labeled an Anglo-American, Auden established an international reputation transcending national boundaries; as John Hollander asserted in the *Atlantic,* Auden spoke "not for national affairs or victories, but on events and crises in the world of the moral imagination."

Indeed, Auden enjoyed wide acclaim as a poet, essayist, playwright, critic, editor, translator, scriptwriter, and librettist. His prestigious literary awards included the 1948 Pulitzer Prize in Poetry and the 1956 National Book Award. Some critics found a decline in his artistic achievement over the five decades of his literary career. In the *Concise Dictionary of British Literary Biography,* Johnson related that "'the decline of Auden' became a criti-

cal commonplace during the last thirty or even forty years of Auden's life" until Monroe K. Spears's *The Poetry of W. H. Auden: The Disenchanted Island* (1963) countered this "decline theory" by showing Auden to be a "serious, intelligent, growing poet."

Spears argued in a *Contemporary Poets* essay that Auden indisputably inherited the title of "greatest living poet" when T. S. Eliot died in 1965, and deserved it on the basis of his "generous abundance" and "dazzling display of metrical virtuosity." During his lifetime and since his death in 1973, many critics have acknowledged his preeminent reputation as a twentieth-century poet, noting that Auden focused on moral issues and strong political, social, and psychological concerns; the body of his work represents a quest for an orderly ideology in an increasingly complicated and perplexing world.

A Precocious Childhood

The industrialized northern England of Auden's youth shaped his world view; in his poetry it manifested itself as an allegorical landscape filled with machinery, abandoned mines, and technological references. Auden also paid close attention to social landscape and human behavior. Born in York, he grew up in the industrial city of Birmingham. Critics often mention Auden's vast knowledge and impressive talents in many areas of expertise and comment on how his parents undoubtedly influenced Auden with their extensive literary, scientific, scholarly, social, and cultural interests. His father, a prominent doctor, was knowledgeable in both science and the mythology and folklore of his Icelandic ancestry; his mother, a nurse, was an accomplished musician and devout Anglican. Despite being raised in a pious home, as Auden told Daniel Halpern in a 1971 *Antaeus* interview, when he was sixteen he decided "all this was nonsense," and he did not return to the church until he was thirty-two.

Educated at preparatory schools in Surrey and Norfolk, England, Auden had established certain academic and personality traits early in his childhood. When Halpern asked Auden about the accuracy of childhood friend Christopher Isherwood's description of him—"a sturdy, podgy little boy, precociously clever, untidy, lazy, and with the masters, inclined to be insolent"—Auden, who had

This manuscript, a page from "O love, the interest itself in thoughtless Heaven,"
is taken from Auden's 1932 poetry notebook.

known Isherwood since he was eight and Isherwood was ten, admitted he did like to shock his elders. For instance, when the headmaster's wife asked him how he liked the first day of school, he replied that he "liked coming to school to see the various types of boys." Said Auden to interviewer Halpern, "That shut her up." Not only did Auden agree with Isherwood about the truth of his childhood interests—"thick scientific books on geology and metals and machines"—but also he admitted to being "quite sophisticated in the ways of sex at a rather early age" since he had access to his father's many medical books. Psychology was another area of Auden's precocious knowledge, as he told Halpern; he was always teasing people by asking questions such as, "Do you know why you did that?"

Having earned a scholarship in science to Oxford University, Auden switched to an English major because of his fascination with modernist poets such as T. S. Eliot, who influenced his early work. Other early influences on Auden's work included Thomas Hardy, Gerard Manley Hopkins, Edward Thomas, and Robert Frost. Discussing his development as a young poet with Halpern, Auden admitted that his early poetry was "quite clearly imitative" of Hardy; in fact, "anyone who read it would say at once, oh yes, you've been reading Hardy." He added that it took time for his own voice to emerge after this teenage period of apprenticeship and that he was twenty when he wrote the first poem he kept. As for imitating the writers he read, Auden remarked to Halpern that it was a natural stage in the development of the young poet, although he hoped that "later on people [wouldn't] know what I've been reading."

The "Curious" Auden Generation

At Oxford University and in the ten years following graduation, Auden served as the center of a group of writers—often referred to as the "Oxford Group" or the "Auden Generation"—that included Christopher Isherwood, Stephen Spender, Cecil Day Lewis, and Louis MacNeice. Years later, Auden was quoted as saying: "How odd it is to recall that at one time there stalked through the pages of literary journalism a curious chimaera named *Daylewisaudenmacneicespender*." Isherwood was quoted by Frederick Buell in his *W. H. Auden as a Social Poet* as he described how this close circle of friends spoke in codified language: "Our conversation would have been hardly intelligible

to anyone who had happened to overhear it; it was a rigamarole of private slang, deliberate misquotations, bad puns, bits of parody, and preparatory school smut." This terse style of private communication can be seen in Auden's writing of this period; according to Robert Bloom's *PMLA* essay, "the omission of articles, demonstrative adjectives, subjects, conjunctions, relative pronouns, auxiliary verbs—form a language of extremity and urgency. Like telegraphese . . . it has time and patience only for the most important words."

Because Auden's voice seemed to define this Oxford group of young writers, critics often called them the Auden Generation. Their social, economic, and political concerns reflected communist and anti-fascist doctrine. However, Auden told interviewer Halpern that he objected to the "annoying" label "group," saying it was an invention of journalists reviewing the work of these poets. "We all happened to be more or less the same generation, we happened to be personal friends; now, naturally people of more or less the same age, living in the same world, are going to have certain things in common, but what they have in common is the least interesting; what is interesting is the way in which they differ."

Among the commonalities Auden shared with Isherwood (who had spent "two academically inglorious years at Cambridge") were their Saint Edmund's prep school years, their literary aims and talents, and their homosexuality; consequently, they "became lovers and allies" in the 1930s, stated Michael J. Sidnell in a 1982 *Dictionary of Literary Biography* article. Because Isherwood was a novelist and Auden a poet, they could collaborate in the theater in an uncompetitive way, the critic added. Auden's differences did set him apart, however, and sometimes the multiple differences within his own canon can be confusing. As Spears pointed out in *Contemporary Poets*, Auden felt the duty of interpreting his times, diagnosing society's ills and dealing with the intellectual and moral dilemmas concerning the public; on the other hand, Auden felt the need "to express the deeply personal world of the dream and the unconscious." Using his gifts to express these two concerns—the outer and the inner world—has made Auden's poetry "sometimes bewildering in its variety," Spears believed.

Another aspect of Auden's multiple voices is the difference in his temperament and imagination

Auden (left) meets with John F. Kennedy, John O'Hara, and Herbert Kubly at the 1956 National Book Awards ceremony.

throughout his many works. Spears compared Auden to a scientist in his poetic attitude—exhibiting "a certain tough-mindedness, a detachment, sometimes a remoteness"; then again, Auden balanced this distancing attitude with a more "Dickensian quality of his imagination, vividly concrete and specific, and [with] the compassion, tolerance, and sympathy for 'ordinary' people and things." By collecting his poems, revising them, and presenting them chronologically in two volumes (for shorter and longer poems), Auden ordered his world of poetry for easier access to the multiplicity of his work. Similarly, to order the Auden canon from a critical perspective, Spears divided Auden's career into four stages.

The first period begins in 1927 with the early poems as an Oxford student and goes through 1932 with *The Orators.* His first published work, *Poems,* appeared in 1928—approximately forty-five

copies hand-printed by Spender. Johnson commented in a 1983 *Dictionary of Literary Biography* article that perhaps "no other poet since Keats has shown such precocious brilliance" as was demonstrated by this collection. In 1928 Auden graduated from Oxford (with an undistinguished degree of third-class honors) and lived in Berlin for a year and a half. Why did he choose Germany? Auden once attributed his attraction to Germany to prep-school days during World War I: "If I took an extra slice of bread and margarine, some master was sure to say: 'I see, Auden; You want the Huns to win,' thus establishing in my mind an association between Germany and forbidden pleasures." To this he added, in the interview with Halpern, that when his parents said he could have a year abroad after college, he decided that since Paris had attracted the previous intellectual generation, he was not going to France; instead, to be in Berlin in the last days of the Weimar Republic was much more exciting. Auden took full advantage of this excitement and freedom. Johnson remarked that the music of political cabaret songs provided Auden with inspiration for his later songs. Although briefly engaged to a woman during this time, Auden confirmed his homosexuality by having affairs with young German men.

In late 1929 Auden returned to England to teach at two schools; by Johnson's account, he was "an enthusiastic, eccentric, inventive, and popular schoolmaster." Auden used these early years of his teaching career to quickly establish himself as an important poet by age twenty-five. His first major work, a verse play titled *Paid on Both Sides: A Charade*, written while still at Oxford, impressed T. S. Eliot so much he published it in his magazine *Criterion* in 1930. Johnson saw Eliot's *The Waste Land* as the play's most important influence, given its "irony, humor, fragmentary structure, and 'unpoetic' verse"; the drama also reflects Auden's extensive reading of early Germanic literature (particularly Anglo-Saxon poetry) and Icelandic sagas (which Auden had known since childhood). Johnson suggested that Auden's "charade" connects the two worlds of bloody Icelandic sagas and school officer-training corps.

Also in 1930, Auden's second volume titled *Poems* appeared in commercial publication. This volume "must be one of the most unexpected books ever to have made its author's reputation," Peter Porter asserted in *Encounter*, noting that in these early works "the tone is completely new. And like Byron's tone, which enabled him to wake one morning and find himself famous, Auden's won instant recognition." Early on, Auden conveyed his psychological and political concerns through concrete images and colloquial language. His next work, *The Orators: An English Study*, used modernist and surrealist techniques to describe and deride fascism and the stagnation of British life and institutions; however, because of private allusions, jokes, and references to friends it can be difficult to understand much of the work. Asked by Halpern nearly forty years later what he thought of these early poems, Auden replied that "they're all right," adding that he got "tired of warhorses that appear in all the anthologies."

"The Age of Anxiety"

The second period, 1933 to 1938, marks Auden as the "hero of the Left," as Spears stated in *Con-*

temporary Poets. The most important events and works of this time include his marriage to Erika Mann (daughter of German writer Thomas Mann) to provide her with British nationality and a passport that allowed her to leave Nazi Germany; the publication of *Look, Stranger!* (American title, *On This Island*); the plays written with Christopher Isherwood; the trip taken to Iceland with Louis MacNeice, described in the later *Letters from Iceland*; his experiences in Spain during the Civil War, resulting in the later works *Spain* and *Journey to a War*; and his trip to China with Isherwood.

Auden's style of verse from the mid-1930s shows a gradual evolution of form. For instance, his 1936 poetry collection *Look, Stranger!* reflects quite disciplined patterns. A dedicatory inscription in this work to Erika Mann supports Auden's belief that the form and truth of poetry can make sense of the world's disorder and lies. Johnson, writing in *Dictionary of Literary Biography*, thinks these brief four lines of dedication summarize the poet's shifting concerns:

Since the external disorder, and extravagant lies,
The baroque frontiers, the surrealist police;
What can truth treasure, or heart bless,
But a narrow strictness?

Form and order remained important criteria for Auden in the decades that followed. The writer told Halpern in 1971 that he disapproved of contemporary poets' neglect of form: "I look on poetry as a sort of rite or game of a fairly solemn kind, but it's fun to do." In fact, he preferred to call poets "Makers," a direct translation of the Greek word for "poets." Comparing poem-making to carpentry, Auden gave Halpern this illustration: "You make a verbal object, and this should be the first thing you think about. You like a table to stand up and not fall down. It's intended to last." He took delight in having fun with poetry, especially "the playful things involved in complicated forms" such as a scholarly Scandinavian metrical pattern. Auden admitted to Halpern that his test of the merit of critics—those who judged his writing—was whether or not they knew and enjoyed the same complexities of language.

Because of Auden's intensely formal style, the author avoided Romantic idealism and modernism; his style was seemingly intended to offset the chaos of contemporary society. Decades later

Auden would call himself "a passionate formalist" who believed that "you can't play a game without rules." While a few poets, like D. H. Lawrence, succeed in writing in free verse, Auden wrote in *The Dyer's Hand*, his 1962 collection of critical essays: "The poet who writes free verse is like Robinson Crusoe on his desert island. He must do all his cooking, laundry, darning and washing himself. . . . More often the result is squalor, dirty sheets on the unmade bed and empty bottle on the unswept floor!"

Because critics judged Auden as the best of his generation of poets, his pronouncements were taken seriously. When Jeremy Robson evaluated Auden's longer poems in *Encounter*, he called him "the most accomplished and versatile" poet of his time, one who dominated "the generation of the 1930s with a power and range that few could approach." By the middle of this decade, Auden's poetry began to demonstrate an "anti-Romantic impersonality" as well as tendency towards the use of light verse, "a sharp, impersonal instrument" to attack self-deception, observed John G. Blair in *The Poetic Art of W. H. Auden*. Because Auden had such an "impressive facility in speaking through any sort of dramatic persona," Blair warned, one cannot be sure the speaker of an Auden poem is actually Auden himself. Equally impressive demonstrations of mastery were his many forms of writing and his passionate expression of beliefs. Auden remained influential and impressive despite "see-sawing beliefs" and "his worst lines," argues Robson. The critic predicted that Auden's eventual reputation will rest on "the magnificent early lyrics—far away from the world of Spain and Fascism against which he cried out so forcefully in much-quoted poems he no longer favours." Clearly, by the time the poet moved to America, he had moved away from interests that dominated his work in the 1930s.

Coming to America, Returning to Faith

Auden's third period, spanning the years 1939 to 1947, begins with his move to the United States with Isherwood. Outstanding works he produced during this time include *Another Time*, a collection including songs and topical poems; *The Double Man* (published in England as *New Year Letter*), which depicted the spiritual and intellectual changes leading to his return to the Anglican church in 1940; *Collected Poetry; For the Time Be-*

ing, a Christmas oratorio; *The Sea and the Mirror: A Commentary on Shakespeare's The Tempest*; and finally, *The Age of Anxiety*, which won the Pulitzer Prize in 1948.

Spears suggested that these last three works defined the religious, aesthetic, and social-psychological beliefs that remained at the heart of all Auden's work after 1940. These longer poems, stated Robson, also exemplify what Spender called Auden's "odd impersonality" and typify the "colder, more distant, more cerebral" Auden—a marked change from earlier attitudes of ideal conceptions of love or brotherhood. The theme of the isolation of the individual recurs in Auden's poetry, although he denied to interviewer Halpern in 1971 that he himself was isolated, because he had very good friends. On the other hand, he admitted that he liked mostly to be alone (a condition different from isolation) and that "aloneness" is the real condition of humanity.

A more scientific attitude toward the individual's role in history is dominant in this period. Writing about Auden in her book *Ancient Myth in Modern Poetry*, Lillian Feder argued that the poem "September 1, 1939" reflects Auden's delusion with love, the mythical entity Eros, stating that "the poet's hope is fragmented by his experience of the limitations of Eros, the sole productive element in history, which too often operates in both individual and social life as a narcissistic and deceptive influence." *The Double Man* also typified Auden's poetry of the early forties in that it depicts Eros as an ineffective, even "destructive social and political force"; to quote one of Auden's poems from this collection, "Love's vigour shrinks to less and less." Ever since the 1940s, Auden's poetry affirmed the religious perspective of "the Incarnation as a climactic historical event," concluded Feder.

Especially important is the addition of Christianity to his world view after his return from Spain. Whereas at fifteen he had lost interest in the devout religion of his parents and had grown disenchanted with the secular belief systems of D. H. Lawrence and Karl Marx in the 1930s, he underwent a religious conversion at the end of this decade, observed Johnson in *Dictionary of Literary Biography*. One major influence in effecting this change was Charles Williams, editor at Oxford University Press and "sometime theologian"; Auden wrote that the effect of Williams's "presence of personal sanctity" transformed him, even though they never discussed anything beyond literary business. Johnson's essay also suggests that Auden's conversion to Christianity may have been motivated by the shock of finding himself the "prey of demonic powers" in his personal life. When asked by interviewer Halpern about his reaffirmation of Christianity, Auden agreed his overall philosophy is based on a religious view of life. He told this interviewer, "Everything I've written since 1940 has been theologically orthodox. . . . It doesn't mean that I talk directly about religious subjects, necessarily, but the value is implied."

The last period of Auden's work, beginning in 1948, includes not only all the work until his death in 1973, but also the several posthumous publications of his work edited by others. Some of the principal volumes from this time are the *Collected Shorter Poems, The Shield of Achilles, Homage to Clio, About the House,* and *City without Walls.* Spears used no further demarcations to describe the poet's career because Auden's poetry reflected no major change in his social, political, or religious philosophy after these books.

Even with Auden's undisputed reign as greatest living poet in the early 1970s, not all critics accepted his brilliance without challenge. Writing in 1970, Gerald Burns confessed in *Southwest Review,* "I could never hang onto Auden poems—that high-pressure 'Watch me be impossibly cultivated' and 'let me ENTERTAIN you'. . . . I'm too young to be awed by his reputation." But despite this admission of being bored with Auden's "impossibly self-conscious poems," Burns admitted that 1970's *City without Walls* "knocked me down— pages of wonderful, effortless verse. It's as if he gave up all hope of writing for effect—or no longer needs to write for fame."

Auden's homosexuality offers still another angle of vision in understanding his life and art. Having known he was homosexual since adolescence and having actively embraced that lifestyle as an adult, Auden fell in love with Chester Kallman, a student at Brooklyn College, soon after arriving in New York in 1939. Although still legally married to Erika Mann (through an arranged formality), Auden considered himself married to Kallman; consequently, Auden was devastated to discover early in their relationship that Kallman had an affair with another man, Johnson related in *Gay*

and Lesbian Literature. This profound betrayal triggered Auden's return to the Anglican religion of his youth, Johnson asserted. Also playing an integral role were the "demonic forces" (that is, Hitler and Nazism) being unleashed in Europe. Both situations confirmed Auden's keen awareness of the world's evil forces, both psychological and historical. Formal religion, then, offered Auden a means of coping with these private and public dilemmas.

Despite the betrayal and lack of commitment, Kallman remained a lifelong partner; he died soon after Auden's death in 1973. Johnson concluded that both "had independent sexual lives, with Auden continuing to feel a particular emotional dedication to Kallman." In their successful professional collaboration, they wrote librettos for numerous works, including Igor Stravinsky's *The Rake's Progress,* Wolfgang Amadeus Mozart's *The Magic Flute* and *Don Giovanni,* and Bertholt Brecht's *The Seven Deadly Sins of the Lower Middle Class.*

While Auden never denied his homosexuality, he did not write about it directly. As Johnson asserted in *Gay and Lesbian Literature,* "When homosexuality or Auden's love for a particular man is behind a given poem, either the gender is disguised or it is revealed indirectly—or the poem is left unpublished." For example, when Auden lived in Germany from 1928 to 1929, he wrote six poems addressed to young men whom the speaker has paid for sex; however, these sexually explicit poems written in German were left unpublished until the posthumous *"The Map of All My Youth"* (1991). Also published after his death was the 1965 poem, "Glad," in which the speaker addresses a Viennese prostitute and presents various reasons for being happy about their friendly, contractual relationship; Johnson suggested that "beneath the knowing tone is a sadness," such as that found in the early German poems.

In addition to these posthumous publications of explicit sexuality, Auden mentioned homosexuality in his writing at times during his lifetime. He occasionally slipped homosexual slang into his poetry; more frequently, stated Johnson in *Gay and Lesbian Literature,* Auden would rely on riddles and ambiguity in approaching sexuality; thus, his playful tone serves to mask the personal relationships behind the poems and thereby distance the poet from the persona. During his lifetime

Auden's one published piece of erotica, "The Platonic Blow," only used his own name in unauthorized editions, according to Johnson. Other love poems that Auden published in his lifetime tended to portray the characters as androgynous: neither lover's sex is revealed. In fact, noted Johnson, Auden followed the advice given in his poem "'The Truest Poetry is the Most Feigning'" (the title is taken from Shakespeare's *As You Like It*), in which the persona suggests "Re-sex the pronouns" as a way to disguise the poet's true intentions in writing love poetry.

Because Auden avoided explicit sexuality in his work, much of the critical writing on Auden does the same. Auden himself had urged that people read his work without reference to his personal life, and he directed his literary executors to ask that all letters from him be destroyed upon his death. As Johnson pointed out, separating the literary work from biographical information "ac-

Auden's memorial stone was unveiled in Poets' Corner, Westminster Abbey, in October 1974.

corded with the generally accepted assumptions" of literary criticism of Auden's day.

However, in the decades following Auden's death, scholars such as Richard Johnson have analyzed how the poet's homosexuality both affected and is reflected in his work; for instance, critics have found the theme of sexual infidelity in *For the Time Being: A Christmas Oratorio,* and have noted how guardedness, disguise, and androgyny tend to be the rule in Auden's love poetry. Adding a sharpened sensitivity to Auden's sexuality in studying his works, particularly his puzzling poetry, argued Johnson, can offer a fuller understanding of Auden's homosexuality "not only as an abstract quality and not only as a set of biographical facts but also in terms of a particular moment in history." Auden's having to protect himself from public censure and personal danger resulted "in his sensitivity to certain aspects of love, in some of the games, riddles, indirections, 're-sexing' of pronouns, deflections, omissions, and rearrangements of his work," Johnson concluded in *Gay and Lesbian Literature.*

Auden did write explicitly about the political and social evils he saw in the world. When interviewed in 1971, however, Auden said he doubted whether political poetry had any significant impact upon society, for poetry can't change the course of history. Somewhat of an embarrassment almost forty years later, he confessed to Halpern, was his political writing. He said he would not take back the statements he made because what he said was quite true, but what he found embarrassing was that he was the only person who really benefitted because they gave him a certain literary reputation. "But nothing I wrote prevented one Jew from being gassed or spared the war by five seconds," he observed.

On the other hand, as Halpern related in his interview, Auden felt the only effective ways to combat political and social evil were political action and "absolutely straight journalistic reportage for the facts." Auden admitted that without a free press, a writer risks liberty—even life—and sometimes can have a political effect because people cannot get the information anywhere else. In the free world, however, writers "must not imagine that we can affect anything by this." Auden went further: "The political and social history of Europe would be what it has been if Goethe, Dante, Shakespeare, Michelangelo, Mozart, Beethoven and whom you like, had never lived. We'd have missed an awful lot of pleasure, but the political and social history would have been more or less the same."

Reinventing through Revision

Auden defied labeling as he continued to reinvent himself. He admitted to Halpern that as he matured, he looked at life a little differently and thus wrote differently; consequently, his interpretation of the world depended on certain beliefs held at

---

If you enjoy the works of W. H. Auden, you may also want to check out the following books and films:

C. Day Lewis, *Overtures to Death and Other Poems*, 1938.

T. S. Eliot, *The Waste Land*, 1922.

Thomas Hardy, *The Complete Poems*, 1976.

Christopher Isherwood, *Lions and Shadows* (autobiographical), 1938.

Stephen Spender, *Collected Poems, 1928–1985*, 1985.

Four Weddings and a Funeral (includes recitation of Auden's "Funeral Blues"), Gramercy Pictures, 1994.

---

the time. This he considered "a lucky gift," not a weakness. The writer called himself "a Liberal Humanist" and even boasted to Halpern, who inquired if he had ever heard himself described with the labels "Spiritual Physician" and "Lunatic Clergyman," that "I believe I really invented them myself. I don't think I'm particularly lunatic, though."

Just how "liberal" was Auden in his attitudes about current events? Besides discussing his work with interviewer Daniel Halpern, Auden expressed his views on several contemporary issues of interest to young adults of his time. With the war in Vietnam still raging, Auden remarked that he felt writers could say what they liked about the war without fear of censorship, but they must not imagine they could affect the course of history. What about the generation gap? The age of a grandparent, Auden thought he got along more easily with young people than their own parents' generation could. What did he think of the drug

scene? "I deplore it," Auden said. He experimented with LSD once under medical supervision but experienced nothing except "some slight schizoid associations." "All drugs, even the harmless ones like pot, deprive people of a real wish to communicate. They talk, but they talk nonsense." Auden disapproved of young people's using pot because it produces a harmful "ego inflation." Nevertheless, he favored legalizing pot because it might prevent youth from associating with dealers and others who are on harder drugs. As far as his taste in contemporary writers, Auden told Halpern that he did not subscribe to any current literary magazines (instead he took periodicals such as *Scientific American* and *Natural History*) and that he read poetry of the past.

Auden also reworked his own poetry of the past, and as he revised this earlier work, he reshaped his critical reputation. The most controversial changes followed his reaffirmation of the Christian faith in the late 1930s. "When Auden edited, retitled, omitted, and scrambled the order of his poems for his *Collected Poetry* of 1945, some critics saw an attempt at revising his radicalism out of, and his rediscovered Christianity into, his early work," as Johnson observed in *Gay and Lesbian Literature;* furthermore, many considered his return to the church to be "an apostasy, considering the radical and irreverent Marxist, Freudian, and Darwinian echoes" of his earlier poetry. Auden himself criticized his previous work; for instance, Frank Kermode, writing in the *Yale Review,* mentioned that in the Foreword to the 1966 *Collected Poems,* Auden apologizes for the "dishonest, the bad-mannered and the boring" poems. His most famous rejection is the line "We must love one another or die" from "September 1, 1939," which he omitted from later anthologies. When Halpern mentioned this much-anthologized piece, Auden replied that he shouldn't have written this "unauthentic" poem because "the rhetoric is too high-flown. It's not in my handwriting and it's a forgery." He admitted that he very much dislikes poetry that is written because "it sounds poetically effective" rather than because the poet "believes it to be true."

Another reason for reinventing himself as poet was that Auden changed with the times—just as the English language changes to reflect changing times. As he said to interviewer Halpern in 1971, "I think it's frightfully important to be one's age. There are certain things you should write at a certain period; when you've learned how to do that, then you've got to do something else." Besides letting go of subjects he found no longer interesting, Auden understood that words change their meaning over time; he gave Halpern this ironic example: "You can't write about fairies any more in a poem; you have to call them elves."

"Famed Stranger and Exalted Outcast"

Whether delighting in double entendres that resulted from changes in the English language or how doubleness affected many aspects of life, Auden astutely scrutinized his world in both literature and life. Critics mention his being an exile or an outsider (whether it be his British background, his homosexuality, or his elite intellectualism); perhaps they are conscious of his double vision, a position that allowed him a unique distancing. In *Gay and Lesbian Literature* Johnson discussed Auden's complexity by relating an anecdote about the 1941 publication, *The Double Man* (which was published as *New Year Letter* in England the same year). The critic noted that the title of this long poem, which was inspired by homosexuality but vividly expresses heterosexuality, comes from Montaigne: "We are, I know not how, double in ourselves, so that what we believe we disbelieve, and cannot rid ourselves of what we condemn." Auden inscribed Kallman's copy of *The Double Man* "To Chester who knows both halves." Johnson surmised that the poem treats different kinds of doubleness—"the private and public spheres of life, war and peace, faith and doubt, body and soul, Eros and Agape (i.e, physical and spiritual love), and so on." In a similar manner, Auden remained very aware of doubleness in various aspects of life.

Doubleness and multiplicity characterize Auden's extensive canon. In her book *Auden*, Barbara Everett enumerated the poet's formidable facility with many voices: "In his verse, Auden can argue, reflect, joke, gossip, sing, analyse, lecture, hector, and simply talk; he can sound, at will, like a psychologist on a political platform, like a theologian at a party, or like a geologist in love." His brilliance, exemplified by these extraordinarily diverse persona, impressed his readers over the decades.

Auden's claim to fame includes his labeling the 1930s as "the age of anxiety" to describe how his generation attempted to survive moral, social, and political dilemmas. With new generations of readers came reevaluations of the opinion that Auden's later work reflects a decline or collapse in artistic merit. As Clive James offered in this appreciative assessment in *Commentary*: "Famed stranger and exalted outcast, Auden served a society larger than the one in which he hid. In his later work we see not so much the ebbing of desire as its transference to the created world, until plains and hills begin explaining the men who live on them. Auden's unrecriminating generosity towards a world which had served him ill was a moral triumph. [Those] who try to understand it too quickly ought not to be trusted with grown-up books."

■ Works Cited

Auden, W. H., *Look, Stranger!*, Faber, 1936, published as *On This Island*, Random House, 1937.

Auden, W. H., *The Double Man*, Random House, 1941, published as *New Year Letter*, Faber, 1941.

Auden, W. H., *The Dyer's Hand*, Random House, 1962.

Blair, John G., *The Poetic Art of W. H. Auden*, Princeton University Press, 1965, 210 p.

Bloom, Robert, "The Humanization of Auden's Early Style," *PMLA*, May, 1968, pp. 443-54.

Buell, Frederick, *W. H. Auden as a Social Poet*, Cornell University Press, 1973.

Burns, Gerald, review of *City without Walls*, *Southwest Review*, spring, 1970, 213-14.

Everett, Barbara, *Auden*, Oliver & Boyd, 1964.

Feder, Lillian, "W. H. Auden: Unconscious Forces of History," in *Ancient Myth in Modern Poetry*, Princeton University Press, 1971, pp. 317-343.

Halpern, Daniel, interview with W. H. Auden, *Antaeus*, spring, 1972, pp. 135-149.

Hollander, John, "Auden at Sixty," *Atlantic*, July, 1967, pp. 84-87.

James, Clive, "Auden's Achievement," *Commentary*, December, 1973, pp. 53-58.

Johnson, Richard, "W. H. Auden," *Dictionary of Literary Biography*, Volume 20: *British Poets, 1914-1945*, edited by Donald E. Stanford, Gale, 1983, pp. 19-51.

Johnson, Richard, "W. H. Auden," *Concise Dictionary of British Literary Biography*, Volume 6: *Modern Writers, 1914-1945*, Gale, 1991, pp. 3-35.

Johnson, Richard, "W. H. Auden," *Gay and Lesbian Literature*, edited by Sharon Malinowski, St. James Press, 1993, pp. 16-22.

Kermode, Frank, "Another Auden," *Yale Review,* summer, 1978, pp. 609-614.

Lowell, Robert, in *Shenandoah,* winter, 1967.

Porter, Peter, "Auden's Cornucopia: The 1930s Texts," *Encounter,* February, 1978, pp. 64-70.

Robson, Jeremy, "Auden's Longer Poems," *Encounter,* January, 1970, pp. 73-74.

Sidnell, Michael J., "W. H. Auden," *Dictionary of Literary Biography,* Volume 10: *Modern British Dramatists, 1900-1945, Part 1: A-L,* edited by Stanley Weintraub, Gale, 1982, pp. 12-24.

Spears, M. K., "W. H. Auden," *Contemporary Poets,* 2nd edition, edited by James Vinson, St. Martin's Press, 1975, pp. 41-49.

■ **For More Information See**

BOOKS

Ansen, Alan, *The Table Talk of W. H. Auden,* Ontario Review Press, 1990.

Bahlke, George W., editor, *Critical Essays on W. H. Auden,* G. K. Hall, 1991.

Bloom, Harold, editor, *W. H. Auden,* Chelsea House, 1986.

Boly, John R., *Reading Auden: The Returns of Caliban,* Cornell University Press, 1991.

Carpenter, Humphrey, *W. H. Auden: A Biography,* Houghton, 1981.

Contemporary Literary Criticism, Gale, Volume 4, 1975, pp. 33-35, Volume 14, 1980, pp. 26-34.

Davenport-Hines, Richard, *Auden,* Pantheon, 1996.

Farnan, Dorothy J., *Auden in Love,* New American Library, 1984.

Hecht, Anthony, *The Hidden Law: The Poetry of W. H. Auden,* Harvard University Press, 1993.

Johnson, Wendell Stacy, *W. H. Auden,* Continuum, 1990.

Miller, Charles H., *Auden: An American Friendship,* Scribner, 1983.

Osborne, Charles, *W. H. Auden: The Life of a Poet,* Harcourt, 1979.

Poetry Criticism, Volume 1, Gale, 1991, pp. 1-41.

Rowse, A. L., *The Poet Auden: A Personal Memoir,* Weidenfeld & Nicolson, 1988.

Spears, Monroe K., *The Poetry of W. H. Auden: The Disenchanted Island,* Oxford University Press, 1963.

PERIODICALS

New Republic, September 26, 1934, pp. 189-190.

New York Times, June 25, 1970, p. 43.

New York Times Book Review, September 24, 1972, pp. 4, 30; December 2, 1973, p. 75; July 18, 1975, pp. 5, 20.

Paris Review, spring, 1974, pp. 32-69.

Poetry, June, 1939, pp. 148-156.

Publishers Weekly, April 13, 1970, p. 81; July 31, 1972, p. 63; January 15, 1973, p. 62.

Sewanee Review, July-September, 1951, pp. 392-425; fall, 1974, pp. 672-681.

Shenandoah (special Auden issue), winter, 1967.

Southern Review, autumn, 1941, pp. 326-49.

Times Literary Supplement, March 17, 1966, p. 224; June 11, 1971, p. 664; January 12, 1973, pp. 25-26; October 12, 1973, p. 1212; November 11, 1977, p. 1310.

■ **Obituaries**

Partisan Review, 1973, pp. 546-548.

Sewanee Review, fall, 1974, pp. 672-681.*

—*Sketch by Laura M. Zaidman*

Terry Brooks

■ Awards, Honors

Best Young Adult Books selection, American Library Association, and Best Books for Young Adults selection, *School Library Journal*, both 1982, both for *The Elfstones of Shannara;* Best Books for Young Adults selection, *School Library Journal* 1986, for *Magic Kingdom for Sale—Sold.*

■ Personal

Full name Terrence Dean Brooks; born January 8, 1944, in Sterling, IL; son of Dean O. (a printer) and Marjorie Iantha (a housewife; maiden name, Gleason) Brooks; married Barbara Ann O'Banion (an office manager), April 23, 1972; married Judine Elaine Alba (a bookseller), December 11, 1987; children: (first marriage) Amanda Leigh, Alexander Stephen. *Education:* Hamilton College, B.A., 1966; Washington & Lee University, LL.B., 1969.

■ Addresses

Home—Seattle, WA. *Agent*—c/o Ballantine/Del Rey, 201 E. 50th Street, New York, NY 10022.

■ Career

Lawyer and writer. Besse, Frye, Arnold, Brooks & Miller, Attorneys at Law, Sterling, IL, partner, 1969-86. Writer, 1977—. *Member:* American Bar Association, Illinois State Bar Association, Author's Guild.

■ Writings

"SHANNARA" TRILOGY

The Sword of Shannara, illustrated by the Brothers Hildebrandt, Random House, 1977.
The Elfstones of Shannara, illustrated by Darrell K. Sweet, Del Rey, 1982.
The Wishsong of Shannara, illustrated by Sweet, Del Rey, 1985.

"HERITAGE OF SHANNARA" TETRALOGY,

The Scions of Shannara, Del Rey, 1990.
The Druid of Shannara, Del Rey, 1991.
The Elf Queen of Shannara, Del Rey, 1992.
The Talismans of Shannara, Del Rey, 1993.

"MAGIC KINGDOM OF LANDOVER" SERIES,

Magic Kingdom for Sale—Sold, Del Rey, 1986.
The Black Unicorn, Del Rey, 1987.

Wizard at Large, Del Rey, 1988.
The Tangle Box, Del Rey, 1994.
Witches' Brew, Del Rey, 1995.

OTHER

Hook (based on screenplay by Jim V. Hart and Malia Scotch Marmo), Arrow, 1991.
First King of Shannara (prequel to *The Sword of Shannara*), Del Rey, 1996.

■ Adaptations

The Sword of Shannara was adapted for cassette, Caedmon, 1986; *The Scions of Shannara* was adapted for cassette, read by Theodore Bikel, and published as *The Heritage of Shannara,* Dove Audio, 1991; the CD-Rom game *Shannara,* based on Brooks's "Shannara" novels, was produced by Legend in 1996.

■ Sidelights

How would you like a high-paying job writing stories about elves, gnomes, trolls, and dwarfs? Although Terry Brooks worked as an attorney for seventeen years before he was able to work full-time on his famous Shannara fantasy series, he now receives million dollar advances for his novels about gnomes and dwarfs and fairies. As for fame—all of Brooks' novels have made the *New York Times Best-Sellers* list, and three of them have held the second spot on the list; it may be just a matter of time before someone decides to make a motion picture out of one of his action-packed novels. Two of Brooks' books have also been selected by the American Library Association and *School Library Journal* as best books for young adults.

Of course, Brooks is not a successful writer just because he writes books about gnomes and trolls. According to critics and fans alike, he is the only writer who has come close to filling the shoes of J. R. R. Tolkien, author of *The Lord of The Rings.* While the influence of Tolkien in Brooks' first novels may have been a factor in their popularity, critics acknowledge that Brooks' books about Shannara, the alternative, fictional world he has created, have developed in his own style; his reliance upon humor in the Magic Kingdom of Landover novels is authentic Brooks.

Critics have also noted Brooks' talent for telling tales. He once explained that he is committed to quality story-telling: "I believe that telling a good story is a fantasy writer's first obligation to his readers." Brooks also communicates important messages about faith and courage, and develops concerns about environmental crisis in the novels. As Brooks himself asserted in *People,* he is "not just writing about elves and dwarfs." His books touch "themes that affect our lives."

Terry Brooks was born and raised in a midwestern steelmaking town surrounded by farmland. He spent a great deal of time alone with his imagination and books. He enjoyed the Hardy Boys

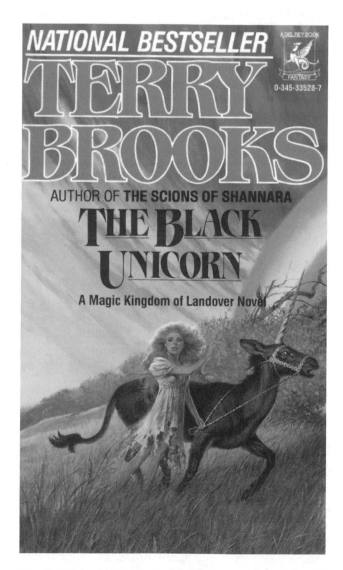

Ben Holiday falls prey to a treacherous wizard named Meeks, who owns a powerful magic medallion, in this 1987 novel.

mysteries, *The Black Stallion*, and the works of science fiction writers like Robert A. Heinlein and Ray Bradbury. He once commented, "The European adventure story writers probably influenced me the most." Brooks began to write his own stories when he was just ten years old, and managed to get his first piece published in the eighth grade after winning a short story contest. Brooks continued to write in earnest in high school, and he completed a science-fiction novel. Although, as Brooks once confided, this novel is "now too awful to contemplate," he sent it to a children's book editor. Due to a fortunate contact, he received a review from this editor which encouraged him to pursue his dream of becoming a writer.

The First "Shannara" Trilogy

Although he was intent on furthering his career as a writer, Brooks was determined not to starve as he developed his talent. After completing college, he began law school and a new novel. He continued to write and rewrite this novel as he accepted a job at a law firm in his hometown. Finally, seven years after he first began writing it, Brooks sent the manuscript to Ballantine Books. According to Marilyn Achiron and Nick Gallo in *People,* after he "plucked" Brooks' manuscript "from the slush pile" and read it, editor Lester del Rey deemed it the best science fiction since J. R. R. Tolkien and published it in 1977. In a short time, Brooks was not only a published author—he was a best-selling author.

The Sword of Shannara presents readers with a fantasy world where magic dominates science and people live in the midst of Trolls, Dwarfs, Elves, and other mutants. The novel also introduces a magical druid, Allanon, who is determined to abolish evil from the land. The mysterious Allanon cleverly enlists the help of various members of the Ohmsford family, descendants of Shannara's royal house, to assist him. In return, Allanon leads these youths in the development of their extraordinary, if little understood, talents. In *The Sword of Shannara*, Allanon sends a son of the Ohmsford family on a hunt for a magic charm. According to Frank Herbert, the author of *Dune*, writing in the *New York Times Book Review*, Brooks seemed to discover the importance of telling "a rousing story" in *The Sword of Shannara*'s later chapters. Herbert also reported that, while Brooks presented

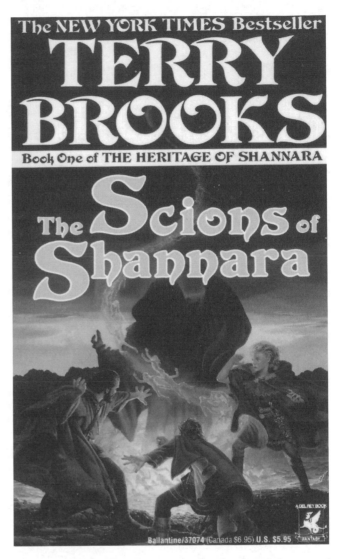

This 1990 work, the first in the "Heritage of Shannara" tetralogy, follows the efforts of Par and Coll Ohmsford to prevent the evil Shadowen from destroying their territory, the Four Lands.

a number of details in the novel, he managed to integrate them into the plot in a meaningful manner.

The second book of the "Shannara" trilogy, *The Elfstones of Shannara*, follows the efforts of Wil Ohmsford and Amberle to save a magical tree, the Ellcrys, from death; without the tree, their land will be ravaged by demons. It is Wil's job to protect Amberle, the only person who can perform the ritual which can save the tree. Brin Ohmsford, a young woman, is the main protagonist in *The Wishsong of Shannara*; tested as the men in the series are, she meets challenges with strength and courage.

In this 1991 sequel to *The Scions of Shannara,* four unlikely partners set out in search of the black Elfstone, which rests in the hands of the Stone King.

The "Heritage of Shannara" Tetralogy

The Scions of Shannara, which begins the "Heritage of Shannara" tetralogy, jumps ahead three hundred years after the Druid Allanon's death. Many changes have occurred since then: the Federation has consolidated its control of the Four Lands, suppressed the Gnomes, enslaved the Dwarfs, and allowed the Trolls to roam freely. Druids and Elves have disappeared, and the use of magic is prohibited. Given the wishes of Allanon's ghost, it is up to the descendants of Shannara's Elfin line, especially Par Ohmsford and his wishsong, to liberate the land and end the threats of the terrible Shadowen.

As many reviewers noted, readers who have not read the first "Shannara" trilogy will not have trouble understanding this book. According to Gene LaFaille in *Wilson Library Bulletin, The Scions of Shannara* "totally" captivates "the reader in its magic." "It's not Tolkien," wrote David Hiltbrand in *People,* "but it's about the best we've got." "[T]eens will be clamoring for the sequel" to this "fantasy epic," concluded Barbara A. Lynn in *School Library Journal.*

The Druid of Shannara follows Walker Boh as he attempts to find the Black Elfstone in Paranor. At the same time, Quickening, the daughter of the King of the Silver River, is also on a quest for the lost magic Elfstone. As Barbara A. Lynn of

---

If you enjoy the works of Terry Brooks, you may also want to check out the following books and films:

Piers Anthony, *A Spell for Chameleon,* 1977, and other "Magic of Xanth" books.
David Eddings, *The Diamond Throne,* 1989, first book of the "Elenium" trilogy.
Nancy Springer, *Madbond,* 1987, first book of the "Sea King" trilogy.
J. R. R. Tolkien, *The Lord of the Rings,* 1954– 55.
The Dark Crystal, Universal, 1982.
Dragonslayer, Disney, 1981.

School Library Journal remarked, "fans will not be disappointed" with this second book in the "Heritage of Shannara" series.

The Elf Queen of Shannara continues the story of the quests of the Elfin descendants. Par and Coll Ohmsford have set out to find the Sword of Shannara, and Walker Boh seeks the Druids of Paranor. Wren Ohmsford strikes out on her own to find the lost Elves and return them to the lands of Men, and *The Elf Queen of Shannara* is her story. With her mentor Garth, Wren encounters the Elves in Arborlon. She discovers that she is descended from the Elves and is challenged to use the Shannara Elfstones to complete the task set out for her by Druid Allanon's ghost. In the opinion of Jackie Cassada of *Library Journal,* Wren is both "self-sufficient" and "tough"— the author's "most successful character to date." According to a critic for *Publishers Weekly,* this novel is "[f]inely tuned and occasionally elegiac;" Brooks' "world becomes more complex, ambiguous and credible with each volume."

The Talismans of Shannara is the final novel in the "Heritage of Shannara" series. Par Ohmsford, Walker Boh, and Wren have fulfilled their individual quests, but they must confront a further challenge to save their people from the Shadowen. Although Par still possesses the magic wishsong, he finds it difficult to control, and he hesitates to use the Sword of Shannara which he has recovered. His brother, Coll, pursues him and Damson Rhee. After he is trapped by the Shadowen, Walker Boh must escape from Paranor. Wren and

Wren and Garth must travel through demon-infested lands to find the vanished race of Elves and convince them to return to their homelands in this 1992 novel.

the Dwarfs must confront the evil Federation. Roland Green of *Booklist* commented that *The Talismans of Shannara* "drags in spots and reaches compelling power in others." Jackie Cassada of *Library Journal* asserted that Brooks "orchestrates an exciting" conclusion to the series.

The "Magic Kingdom of Landover" Series

Brooks' "Landover" series, which he introduced with *Magic Kingdom for Sale—Sold* in 1986, is also popular with fantasy readers. While Roland Green, a critic for *Booklist*, suggests that the magic kingdom of Landover is a "somewhat more original creation" than Shannara, Jackie Cassada of *Library Journal* asserts that the series "displays the author's genuine flair for humorous fantasy."

Like Brooks, the King of Landover, Ben Holiday, is an ex-lawyer. After Ben allows two exiles to return to the Kingdom in *The Tangle Box*, he finds they have treacherously released the terrible Gorse from his prison—the Tangle Box. The fairies who trapped the Gorse, an evil sorcerer, in the box are in danger. Before Ben can help them, however, the Gorse traps him in the box, along with a witch and a dragon. Meanwhile, Ben's non-human wife, Queen Willow, is preparing for the birth of their child, and Horris Kew, one of the exiles, wreaks havoc in the kingdom. While a critic for *Publishers Weekly* found *The Tangle Box* to be "slower and less charming" than *Magic Kingdom for Sale—Sold!* and *Wizard at Large*, the critic asserted that the novel "is still likely to please readers already hooked."

In 1986, as Brooks traveled on a book tour, he met Judine Alba. They married in 1987, and Brooks purchased a lavender-colored home overlooking the Puget Sound in Seattle. Although, as Marilyn Achiron and Nick Gallo wrote in *People*, Brooks' wife Judine suffered through a bout of breast cancer soon after they met, the cancer has disappeared, and Brooks "is thrilled with his life." With Judine, he walks through Seattle and enjoys the markets, restaurants, ballet, and symphony. Brooks also likes to spend time traveling. He owns three acres of Oregon coastal forest and a home in Hawaii. His children, who live in Pittsburgh with their mother, visit him frequently.

Brooks is not content to rest on his laurels. "I am a writer who is compelled to write; I am not complete without my work. The writing of the book is the best part of the process," he once explained. In addition, as he told Achiron and Gallo in *People*, Brooks wants "to be No. 1" on the *New York Times Best-Seller* list. Readers should not expect Brooks to abandon his style for such a goal. He once explained that he believes in writing for himself: "that is, if I write something that I would enjoy reading, it will find an audience."

■ Works Cited

Achiron, Marilyn and Nick Gallo, "Laying Down the Law," *People*, May 10, 1993, pp. 53-54.

Cassada, Jackie, review of *The Elf Queen of Shannara*, *Library Journal*, February 15, 1992, p. 200.

Cassada, Jackie, review of *The Talismans of Shannara*, *Library Journal*, February 15, 1993, p. 196.

Cassada, Jackie, review of *The Tangle Box*, *Library Journal*, April 15, 1994, p. 117.

Review of *The Elf Queen of Shannara*, *Publishers Weekly*, December 20, 1991, p. 68.

Green, Roland, review of *The Talismans of Shannara*, *Booklist*, January 1, 1993, p. 770.

Green, Roland, review of *The Tangle Box*, *Booklist*, March 15, 1994, p. 1302.

Herbert, Frank, review of *The Sword of Shannara*, *New York Times Book Review*, April 10, 1977.

Hiltbrand, David, review of *The Scions of Shannara*, *People Weekly*, April 23, 1990, p. 30.

La Faille, Gene, review of *The Scions of Shannara*, *Wilson Library Bulletin*, January, 1991, p. 115.

Lynn, Barbara A., review of *The Scions of Shannara*, *School Library Journal*, September, 1990, p. 226.

Lynn, Barbara A., review of *The Druid of Shannara*, *School Library Journal*, July, 1991, p. 96.

Review of *The Talismans of Shannara*, *Publishers Weekly*, March 29, 1993, p. 39.

Review of *The Tangle Box*, *Publishers Weekly*, April 4, 1994, p. 62.

■ For More Information See

PERIODICALS

Library Journal, February 15, 1990, p. 215; March 15, 1996.

Publishers Weekly, January 4, 1991, p. 62.*

—Sketch by David P. Johnson

Octavia E. Butler

Award, Nebula Award, Science Fiction Writers of America, Locus Award, *Locus* magazine, and Best Novelette Award, *Science Fiction Chronicle Reader*, all 1985, all for novelette "Bloodchild"; Nebula Award nominations, 1987, for novelette "The Evening and the Morning and the Night," and 1994, for novel *Parable of the Sower*; MacArthur Foundation fellowship, 1995.

■ Personal

Born June 22, 1947, in Pasadena, CA; daughter of Laurice and Octavia Margaret (a maid; maiden name, Guy) Butler. *Education:* Pasadena City College, A.A., 1968; attended California State University at Los Angeles, 1969.

■ Addresses

Home—P.O. Box 61293, Pasadena, CA 91114. *Agent*—Merrilee Heifetz, Writers House, 21 West 26th St., New York, NY 10010.

■ Career

Freelance writer, 1970—. Has worked variously in factories, warehouses, and offices, and as a dish washer, inventory taker, and telephone solicitor. *Member:* Science Fiction Writers of America.

■ Awards, Honors

YWCA Achievement Award for the Creative Arts, 1980; Hugo Award, World Science Fiction Convention, 1984, for short story "Speech Sounds"; Hugo

■ Writings

"PATTERNIST" SERIES; SCIENCE FICTION

Patternmaster, Doubleday, 1976.
Mind of My Mind, Doubleday, 1977.
Survivor, Doubleday, 1978.
Wild Seed, Doubleday, 1980.
Clay's Ark, St. Martin's, 1984.

"XENOGENESIS" SCIENCE FICTION TRILOGY

Dawn: Xenogenesis, Warner Books, 1987.
Adulthood Rites, Warner Books, 1988.
Imago, Warner Books, 1989.

OTHER

Kindred, Doubleday, 1979, 2nd edition, Beacon Press, 1988.
The Evening and the Morning and the Night (novelette), Pulphouse, 1991.
Parable of the Sower, Warner Books, 1993.

Bloodchild: Novellas and Stories, Four Walls Eight
   Windows, 1995.

Contributor to anthologies, including *Clarion,* 1970,
and *Chrysalis 4,* 1979. Contributor to periodicals,
including *American Visions, Essence, Future Life, Isaac
Asimov's Science Fiction Magazine, Omni, Transmis-
sion,* and *Writers of the Future.*

■ **Sidelights**

A winner of the coveted Nebula and Hugo
awards, Octavia E. Butler is one of the leading
science fiction authors writing today. Butler's talent was already evident by the time she had finished her first three novels, *Patternmaster, Mind of
My Mind,* and *Survivor. Extrapolation* contributor
Frances Smith Foster argued in a 1982 article that
"there should exist no doubt that in [Butler's]
contribution [to science fiction] this writer has already given us 'something really first rate,'" while
John Pfeiffer asserted in *St. James Guide to Science
Fiction Writers* that several of Butler's stories and
novels "are among the most important science fiction works written in the late twentieth century."

Butler stands out among science fiction writers for
another reason: she is one of the few black writers of science fiction, and is among the first black
women to venture into the genre. By 1994, as
Thomas Wiloch noted in the *Bloomsbury Review,*
Butler enjoyed "a solid reputation among both
science fiction aficionados and feminists for her
novels featuring strong African American women
characters." Yet while Butler's identity as a black
woman enriches her work and often generates it,
she told Lisa See in a *Publishers Weekly* interview
that the fact that her leading female characters are
black "is not the most important thing on my
mind. I'm just [as] interested in telling a story,
hopefully a good one. . . . I write about the things
that interest me."

Butler has loved science fiction since she was a
child. Her father died when she was a baby, and
she was raised by her mother, grandmother, and
other relatives with strict Baptist discipline in
Pasadena, California. Butler felt alienated from
children her own age; she preferred the company
of adults and books. "My mother read me bed-
time stories until I was six years old," the author
related in *Essence.* "It was a sneak attack on her
part. As soon as I really got to like the stories,

she said, 'Here's the book. Now you read.'"
Butler's mother, who had been limited to only
three years of school before she began working,
"believed passionately in books and education. She
wanted me to have what she had been denied."
Her mother would bring home all the discarded
books she could collect while working in other
people's homes, and Butler read as many as she
was able. It was not long before she outgrew
children's books, and she attempted to read books
from the adult section at the public library. As
the library didn't allow children in the adult section, Butler moved to the magazine section of the
supermarket and discovered science fiction.

An uncomfortably shy child, Butler used added
writing as means of escape. "I believed I was ugly
and stupid, clumsy, and socially hopeless," she
revealed in *Essence.* "I also thought that everyone
would notice these faults if I drew attention to
myself." Unfortunately, the adolescent Butler grew
to the stately height of six foot, making her an
easy target for ridicule. "I hid out in a big pink
notebook—one that would hold a whole ream of
paper. I made myself a universe in it. There I
could be a magic horse, a Martian, a telepath. . . .
There I could be anywhere but here, any time but
now, with any people but these." By the time she
was twelve, she was writing her own science fiction stories, and at thirteen she started pecking
them out on a portable typewriter her mother had
purchased for her and submitting them to magazines.

At Pasadena City College, where she won a short
story contest, Butler majored variously in English,
history, business, and anthropology. When she left
school, she took occasional extension classes at
UCLA and attended classes given by the Writers
Guild of America West Open Door program. However, it was not until she participated in the
Clarion Science Fiction Writers' Workshop, where
she learned a great deal about her craft from other
science fiction writers, that she sold two stories.
Meanwhile, Butler supported her writing career by
working as a dish washer, inventory taker, and
telephone solicitor. "My size and strength were
advantages in factories and warehouses," she recalled in *Essence.* "And no one expected me to
smile and pretend I was having a good time," as
they did when she did clerical work.

Finally, in 1975, Butler began to concentrate full-
time on her writing and made swift progress;

Patternmaster, based on the first stories she had written as a child, was published by Doubleday in 1976, and two more novels soon followed, *Mind of My Mind* and *Survivor*. In these first books of the "Patternist" series Butler examined sexual roles much as other women writers had but also, according to Foster, demonstrated that she "is not just another woman science fiction writer. Her major characters are black women, and through her characters and the structure of her imagined social order, Butler consciously explores the impact of race and sex upon future society." The novels of the Patternist series each deal with the descendants of Doro, a Nubian who has survived for over four thousand years by taking over healthy bodies—of all races, sexes, and ages, but preferably black male ones like his original Nubian body—and relinquishing them before they fail. By carefully selecting his mates and regulating his offspring, Doro has created a line of mentally and physically superior descendants who have the potential to be linked telepathically.

The 1980 novel *Wild Seed*, set on Earth during the years 1690 to 1840, sets up the story of Doro and the Patternists. Blending historical fact with science fiction, it describes Doro's more distant past and the lives of Africans from the time before Europeans began to sell them as slaves to just before the Civil War in the United States. When the long-lived Doro encounters Anyanwu, a 300-year-old Onitsha priestess whose considerable mental and physical powers include skill in healing, he immediately recognizes her as a mate who can enrich the gene pool of his descendants. She, in turn, is attracted to him as a potential lifelong companion, but at the same time his violent methods of extending his life and ensuring his power over his children repel her. Writing in the *Washington Post Book World*, Elizabeth A. Lynn praised Anyanwu as "an intelligent, resolute and powerful woman . . . ; again and again she tests, thwarts, and escapes [Doro's] control, forcing him to confront his own weaknesses and to adjust his plans to her choices and to her moral concerns." Tom Easton hailed the book in *Analog Science Fiction/Science Fact* as "warm, involving, [and] sympathetic," and recommended it as a candidate for a Nebula award, adding, "It's that good." "*Wild Seed* is a powerful story beautifully told," Margaret Anne O'Connor concluded in the *Dictionary of Literary Biography*, "and Anyanwu is the embodiment of the feminist ideal of compassionate exercise of power."

The 1977 novel *Mind of My Mind* provides the details of the forming of the Patternist culture, tracing the development of Doro's daughter Mary into a leader who eventually takes over his leadership role and becomes the first Patternmaster. When Mary is born, most Patternists are scattered across the globe, and many will never overcome situations of poverty, racism, or addiction to assume control over their powers. When Doro, recognizing Mary's high potential, gives her into the care of Anyanwu, here known as Emma, he unknowingly sets in motion his own destruction. Nevertheless, Linda G. Benson noted in *Twentieth-Century Young Adult Writers*, Mary's triumph over Doro is "an act with mythic resonances that establishes the violent means of succession to the position of Patternmaster."

"Butler's is a literature of survival." —*Ms.*

OCTAVIA E. BUTLER

The Pattern begins in an ages-long war of love—and power . . .

POPULAR LIBRARY 20537-7 $5.50 U.S.A. ($6.99 CAN)

WILD SEED

A Patternist novel by multiple Hugo and Nebula Award winner Octavia E. Butler, author of <u>Dawn</u> and <u>Adulthood Rites</u>

This 1980 novel, from Butler's "Patternist" series, explores the relationship between Doro, the shapeshifter Anyanwu, and the Patternmaster.

The Consequences of Power

Other novels in the "Patternist" series present "the future evolution of the human race into three warring groups," as Hoda M. Zaki described it in *Women's Review of Books.* The Patternists are set against two other groups, one of whom is created when an American spaceship returns to Earth carrying a disease which kills half of the Earth's people. Those who survive the disease are mutated yet superior beings called Clayarks, who are driven to further spread the disease. This crisis causes the Patternists to emerge from their self-imposed isolation to set up and govern a society that enables humanity to survive the Clayark crisis. They allow the third group, the Missionaries of Humanity—a religious group of mutes (people without mental powers) that believes the only correct human form is an unmutated one—to seek new homes on planets throughout the galaxy. The 1984 novel *Clay's Ark* details these events in relating the story of Asa Elias ("Eli") Doyle, the American space traveler who brought the Clayark disease to earth. Together with other survivors of the disease that he has spread and the mutant children the group have produced, Eli goes into hiding. Nevertheless, the disease spreads beyond their enclave. In the words of Algis Budrys in *Magazine of Fantasy and Science Fiction,* the "race of *homo sapiens* is doomed; what has been brought back from the stars is the end of human history." While *Fantasy Review* critic John R. Pfeiffer felt that *Clay's Ark* doesn't measure up to some of the author's earlier works, he concluded that "Butler's craft is now so strong that even one of her works of intermission is a delicious confection."

In *Survivor,* Butler explores the society of the Missionaries, seen through the eyes of Alanna, a young Afro-Asian "wild child" adopted by a white Missionary family who are to colonize a distant planet. Although Alanna's family has escaped the battle between Clayark and Patternist, they encounter a new pattern of conflict with their new home's two native tribes, the Tehkohn and Garkohn. After Alanna is kidnapped from her Garkohn residence and forced to live as a Tehkohn, she comes to appreciate the culture of her captors and to accept her Tehkohn husband. She is then placed in the center of tensions when she tries to convince the Missionary colonists to reassess their alliance with the Garkohn; as an outsider to all three cultures, she is in a unique position to judge all three. "The novel advocates power attained through the union of apparent opposites, a recognition of the positive power of differences among beings," O'Connor stated, while Benson likewise saw the novel as an expression of Butler's "use of alien contact as a metaphor for change."

While the first of the series to be published, 1976's *Patternmaster* relates events that come last in the Patternist saga. Far in the future, Earth society has evolved into a series of isolated, agrarian Houses which are protected by Patternist leaders from the attacks of nomadic Clayark tribes. In an almost-feudal structure, the Patternists rule over a caste of mutes who perform most of the tasks necessary to the society, including the raising of Patternist children. In this setting, the young Patternist Teray seeks to inherit the role of Patternmaster, in opposition to his brother Coransee but with the aid of a powerful woman named Amber. According to Foster, "The central conflict of the novel, the rivalry between the brothers, is symbolized by their attitudes toward this woman: Coransee desires to subjugate her and to benefit from her skills through ownership. Teray wants her to be free and hopes she will freely work with him." The eventual triumph of Teray over Coransee, who tries to control Amber and abuses the mutes, "makes clear that coercive relationships warp the powerful even as they debilitate the powerless," Benson asserted. Despite the deeper themes running through the work, *Patternmaster* is an entertaining read: a *Publishers Weekly* reviewer noted that this story "of love, chase and combat is consistently attention-holding."

As Foster emphasized, black female characters stand out in the "Patternist" series. In *Patternmaster,* Amber is "a significant and complex individual who functions as a symbol, a catalyst, and a mentor" and tips the scales in the struggle between brothers to inherit the Pattern by teaching Teray "humane tendencies." In *Mind of My Mind,* Mary defeats her father's leadership and "defines the limits of and represents an alternative to Doro's power." Finally, *Survivor*'s Alanna Verrick, a human raised by Missionaries, comes to accept her Hao husband, a fur-covered, blue alien. Rather than focusing on "racial conflict or even racial tension," Foster wrote, "Butler explores the future implications of racism and sexism by focusing upon relationships between powerful persons who are various types of Other."

Akin, a young "construct" who is part human, part alien, is kidnapped by a band of sterile humans in this 1988 tale, part of the "Xenogenesis" series.

Between writing the books in the "Patternist" series, Butler also produced a mainstream novel that was published in 1979 as *Kindred.* Butler explained to See in her interview why she decided to write this book: "I had this generation gap with my mother. She was a maid and I wished she wasn't. I didn't like seeing her go through back doors. . . . If my mother hadn't put up with all those humiliations, I wouldn't have eaten very well or lived very comfortably. So I wanted to write a novel that would make others feel the history: the pain and fear that black people have had to live through in order to endure."

Kindred does just that: its protagonist, Dana, a young, struggling black writer, experiences life as

a slave when she is transported from contemporary times to the early nineteenth century to save a white ancestor, her several-times-great-grandfather Rufus. As Beverly Friend related in *Extrapolation,* Dana makes "six trips into the past, called each time by Rufus's near encounter with death. Each return Dana makes to the present is triggered by the possibility of her own death. Once she returns during a hideous beating; another time she causes the return by desperately slitting her own wrists." On her third visit, Dana is transported back in time while in her husband Kevin's embrace, and he is pulled into the past with her. As Kevin is white, they cannot live together as husband and wife in this past world. By accident, Dana is transported home without him, and when she returns to the past again—eight days later for her but five years for him—Rufus prevents her from contacting Kevin. Although Dana escapes to look for her husband, as Friend writes, "she is caught. Nothing in her twentieth-century education or experience had prepared her to succeed."

Later, Rufus rapes Dana's ancestor, thus ensuring Dana's future birth. Finally, when Dana kills Rufus, she is transported back to the future, losing her left arm in the process. According to O'Connor, "it is the contrasts—and perhaps even more, the similarities—between Dana's life in contemporary California and her experiences in the stratified plantation culture of the early nineteenth century that create the plot interest in this unusual novel." In addition to presenting deep themes, however, *Kindred* is an entertaining read. *Magazine of Fantasy and Science Fiction* contributor Joanna Russ described the story as "exciting and fast-moving and the past occurs without a break in style—a technique that makes it more real—even down to characters' speech." "*Kindred* transcends the science fiction genre," Pfeiffer asserted in *St. James Guide to Science Fiction Writers,* adding that "it deserves comparison with Alex Haley's *Roots* and Margaret Walker's *Jubilee,* and it is a worthy homage to authentic slave narratives such as that by Frederick Douglass."

Exploring the Nature of Humanity

Butler returned to traditional futuristic science fiction with the books in the "Xenogenesis" series. The story begins with *Dawn (Xenogenesis I),* which takes place after the Earth's population has been almost entirely destroyed by nuclear war. Lilith

Iyapo awakes to find herself on the living ship of the Oankali, an alien race of traders who travel the galaxy exchanging genetic material with other species in processes that alter both races forever. The Oankali offer Lilith the chance to redeem humanity from its self-destruction by teaching other individuals to allow union with the Oankali—an offer she herself is ambivalent about accepting. She eventually agrees, however, and is bonded to the Oankali ooloi Nikanj, a member of the third sex that performs genetic manipulation. While not answering all questions that Butler raises, the book's portrayal of the bond between Lilith and Nikanj "is so touching and so essentially right, that it transcends all else," Laurence

In an economically and environmentally devastated future America, Lauren Olamina, an empath who feels other people's pain, leads a small group through dangerous country in this 1993 novel.

Coven wrote in *Washington Post Book World*. In *Analog: Science Fiction/Science Fact*, reviewer Tom Easton hailed the author's look at the nature of humanity and reproduction, noting that as the series develops "we may recognize that Butler has gifted SF with a vision of possibility more original than anything we have seen since Clarke's *Childhood's End*."

In *Adulthood Rites (Xenogenesis II)* Lilith's son, Akin, an infant human-Oankali construct with the intelligence of an adult, is kidnapped by the humans who have refused to cooperate with the genetic merger and cannot bear children of their own. To his surprise, Akin is not immediately rescued from his kidnappers, and so begins to learn and identify with this holdout human society. Because Akin looks more like his human parents than his Oankali ones, the physical changes in him as he matures make him the focus of the hopes and fears of his captors. His struggle to understand human society and later readjust to his hybrid world make compelling reading, Easton stated in *Analog*: "For all the alienness of Akin's being, so marvelously portrayed, the reader identifies with his personal problems." And a *Publishers Weekly* critic likened Butler's work to that of Toni Morrison as the novel's "moving bitter truths emerge about the obligations and constraints of family and people."

The trilogy concludes with *Imago (Xenogenesis III)*, which tells the story of the first human-Oankali construct who is an ooloi, the third Oankali sex which unites the male and female. Since Oankali and human-Oankali constructs do not settle on a specific sex until they metamorphose sometime in their twenties, Jodahs is not really prepared when it begins to develop ooloi characteristics, particularly after it is separated from its family. During its travels, however, it comes to accept its destiny and even finds human mates who are fertile if defective. While *Washington Post Book World* contributor Ted White found the book an "anticlimactic" conclusion to the trilogy, due to Jodahs's extraordinary abilities, *Locus* reviewer Faren Miller enjoyed the "fully realized genetic and cultural heritage" which backs the character. Miller noted that Jodahs is "bizarrely talented, miraculous, deeply alien, yet human as well, both repellent and fascinating—even seductive. The same terms serve to describe *Imago*." Benson hailed the entire "Xenogenesis" trilogy for its exploration of how "violence will always underlie and define the human condition, unless the hierarchical element [of society] is bred out."

Like the Earth in the "Xenogenesis" series, the world in the *Parable of the Sower* has been devastated. Yet this time it is economic collapse and environmental depletion which have led to the decline of civilization in the early twenty-first century. Lauren, the black, teenage daughter of a minister, narrates her story in diary entries and poems. Lauren suffers from "hyperempathy," a condition that causes her to feel the pain of others around her. This affliction, along with her religious upbringing, leads her to develop a new religion she calls "Earthseed." Based on the idea that "God is Change," Earthseed promotes education, forethought, adaptability, and a belief that space colonization is the natural reproductive adulthood of humanity. After her own deteriorating neighborhood in Southern California is destroyed and her father is killed, Lauren travels nearly 700 miles up the coast of California gathering other homeless travelers who gradually come to regard her as a leader. *Parable of the Sower*, which has been marketed as a mainstream novel rather than science fiction, received praise from several critics. As Gary K. Wolfe wrote in a *Locus* review: "Butler makes us empaths, too: we feel the fear and pain of all the little catastrophes." Another *Locus* contributor, Faren Miller, described Earthseed as "simply the most emotionally *and* intellectually appealing religion I've encountered in nearly four decades of reading sf." Gerald Jonas concluded in the *New York Times Book Review* that *Parable of the Sower* is a "gripping tale of survival and a poignant account of growing up sane in a disintegrating world" that "succeeds on multiple levels."

Butler has offered science fiction readers a fresh perspective and has taken up issues traditional writers have neglected. Yet while Butler's contribution to science fiction is unmistakable, novels like *Kindred* and *Parable of the Sower* have brought her voice a wider audience than just fans of that particular genre. As O'Connor asserted in the *Dictionary of Literary Biography*, "Feminists and critics of Afro-American literature write admiringly of her handling of issues of gender and race," while "general readers find that these novels . . . present compelling stories of all-too-human beings." Winner of a 1995 MacArthur fellowship (known as the "genius grant"), Butler is also known for several award-winning short stories;

these works are collected in *Bloodchild: Novellas and Stories*, along with several personal reminiscences about her writing that a *Publishers Weekly* critic calls "a refreshing look into Butler's writing process" that helps to reveal "what excites and motivates this exceptionally talented writer."

Her devotion to writing science fiction hasn't been easy, Butler revealed in *Essence*, as for a long time nearly all the other genre writers around her were white men and she had no role models to help

---

If you enjoy the works of Octavia E. Butler, you may also want to check out the following books and films:

Chinua Achebe's books on the Igbo people, including *Things Fall Apart* (1958) and *Arrow of God* (1964).
Arthur C. Clarke, *Childhood's End*, 1953.
Stanislaw Lem, *Solaris*, 1961.
Sheri S. Tepper, *The Gate to Women's Country* (1988).
Joan D. Vinge, *Psion*, 1982, and *Catspaw*, 1988.
Alien Nation, Twentieth Century–Fox, 1988.

---

boost her confidence. She has persevered, however, and has become an example herself who sometimes speaks on her role as a black woman writing science fiction. Despite her success, she has in the past been asked, "What good is science fiction to Black people?" To which she replies: "What good is science fiction's thinking about the present, the future and the past? What good is its tendency to warn or to consider alternative ways of thinking and doing? What good is its examination of the possible effects of science and technology, of social organization and political direction?" She concluded: "At its best, science fiction stimulates imagination and creativity. It gets reader and writer off the beaten track, off the narrow, narrow footpath of what 'everyone' is saying, doing, thinking—whoever 'everyone' happens to be this year. And what good is all this to Black people?"

■ Works Cited

Review of *Adulthood Rites*, *Publishers Weekly*, May 6, 1988, p. 98.

Benson, Linda G., "Octavia E. Butler," *Twentieth-Century Young Adult Writers*, 1st edition, St. James Press, 1994, pp. 94-95.

Review of *Bloodchild: Novellas and Stories, Publishers Weekly*, August 21, 1995, pp. 50-51.

Budrys, Algis, review of *Clay's Ark, Magazine of Fantasy and Science Fiction*, August, 1984, pp. 34-35.

Butler, Octavia E., "Birth of a Writer," *Essence*, May, 1989, pp. 74, 79, 132-34.

Coven, Laurence, "Genetic Invention," *Washington Post Book World*, June 28, 1987, p. 10.

Easton, Tom, review of *Wild Seed, Analog Science Fiction/Science Fact*, January 5, 1981, p. 168.

Easton, Tom, review of *Dawn, Analog Science Fiction/Science Fact*, December, 1987, pp. 182-83.

Easton, Tom, review of *Adulthood Rites, Analog Science Fiction/Science Fact*, December, 1988, pp. 165-66.

Foster, Frances Smith, "Octavia Butler's Black Female Fiction," *Extrapolation*, spring, 1982, pp. 37-49.

Friend, Beverly, "Time Travel as a Feminist Didactic in Works by Phyllis Eisenstein, Marlys Millhiser, and Octavia Butler," *Extrapolation*, spring, 1982, pp. 50-55.

Jonas, Gerald, review of *Parable of the Sower, New York Times Book Review*, January 2, 1994, p. 22.

Lynn, Elizabeth A., "Vampires, Aliens, and Dodos," *Washington Post Book World*, September 28, 1980, p. 7.

Miller, Faren, review of *Imago, Locus*, April, 1989, p. 15.

Miller, Faren, review of *Parable of the Sower, Locus*, December, 1993, pp. 17, 19, 60.

O'Connor, Margaret Anne, "Octavia E. Butler," *Dictionary of Literary Biography*, Volume 33: *Afro-American Fiction Writers after 1955*, Gale, 1984, pp. 35-41.

Review of *Patternmaster, Publishers Weekly*, June 14, 1976, p. 104.

Pfeiffer, John R., "Latest Butler a Delicious Confection," *Fantasy Review*, July, 1984, p. 44.

Pfeiffer, John, "Octavia E. Butler," *St. James Guide to Science Fiction Writers*, 1st edition, St. James Press, 1996, pp. 145-147.

Russ, Joanna, review of *Kindred, Magazine of Fantasy and Science Fiction*, February, 1980, pp. 96-97.

See, Lisa, "PW Interviews: Octavia E. Butler," *Publishers Weekly*, December 13, 1993, pp. 50-51.

White, Ted, "Love with the Proper Stranger," *Washington Post Book World*, June 25, 1989, p. 8.

Wiloch, Thomas, review of *Parable of the Sower, Bloomsbury Review*, May/June, 1994, p. 24.

Wolfe, Gary K., review of *Parable of the Sower, Locus*, April, 1994, pp. 19, 52.

Zaki, Hoda M., "Fantasies of Difference," *Women's Review of Books*, January 1, 1988, pp. 13-14.

■ For More Information See

BOOKS

Contemporary Literary Criticism, Volume 38, Gale, 1986, pp. 61-66.

Law, Richard, and others, *Suzy Charnas, Joan Vinge, and Octavia Butler*, Borgo Press, 1986.

Smith, Jessie Carney, editor, *Notable Black American Women*, Gale, 1992, pp. 144-47.

PERIODICALS

Black American Literature Forum, summer, 1984, pp. 78-87.

Booklist, May 1, 1989, p. 1511.

Emerge, June, 1994, p. 65.

Essence, April, 1979; May, 1995, p. 198.

Janus 4, winter, 1978-79, pp. 28-29.

Kirkus Reviews, May 15, 1976, p. 612; April 15, 1977, p. 453.

Kliatt, May, 1995, p. 12.

Los Angeles Times, January 30, 1981.

Magazine of Fantasy and Science Fiction, February, 1990, p. 41.

Ms., March, 1986; June, 1987.

Science Fiction Studies, March, 1995, p. 47.

Thrust: SF in Review, summer, 1979, pp. 19-22.

Voice of Youth Advocates, October, 1987, p. 174.

—*Sketch by Diane Telgen*

Patricia Calvert

■ Personal

Also writes under pseudonym Peter J. Freeman; born July 22, 1931, in Great Falls, MT; daughter of Edgar C. (a railroad worker) and Helen P. (a children's wear buyer; maiden name, Freeman) Dunlap; married George J. Calvert (in insurance business), January 27, 1951; children: Brianne L., Dana J. *Education:* Winona State University, Minnesota, B.A., 1976, graduate study, 1976—. *Politics:* Liberal Democrat. *Religion:* Unitarian-Universalist. *Hobbies and other interests:* Reading, hiking, observing wildlife.

■ Addresses

Home—Foxwood Farm, 6130 County Rd., #7 S.E., Chatfield, MN 55923. *Office*—Mayo Clinic, 200 Southwest First St., Rochester, MN 55901.

■ Career

St. Mary's Hospital, Great Falls, MT, laboratory clerk, 1948-49; General Motors Acceptance Corp.,

clerk typist, 1950-51; Mayo Clinic, Rochester, MN, cardiac laboratory technician, 1961-64, enzyme laboratory technician, 1964-70, senior editorial assistant in section of publications, 1970—; Institute of Children's Literature, instructor, 1987—. *Member:* American Medical Writers Association, Children's Reading Round Table, Society of Children's Book Writers and Illustrators, Society of Midland Authors.

■ Awards, Honors

Best book award, American Library Association (ALA), juvenile fiction award, Society of Midland Authors, and juvenile award, Friends of American Writers, all 1980, and award for outstanding achievement in the arts, Young Women's Christian Association (YWCA), 1981, all for *The Snowbird;* Mark Twain Award nomination, Missouri Association of School Libraries, 1984, for *The Money Creek Mare;* Maude Hart Lovelace Award nomination, 1985, for *The Stone Pony;* Junior Library Guild selection and ALA best book for young adults, both 1986, both for *Yesterday's Daughter;* William Allan White Award, 1987, for *Hadder MacColl;* "Best of 1990" award, Society of School Librarians International, 1991, for *When Morning Comes;* Junior Library Guild selection, 1993, for *Picking Up the Pieces.*

■ Writings

YOUNG ADULT FICTION

The Snowbird, Scribner, 1980.

The Money Creek Mare, Scribner, 1981.
The Stone Pony, Scribner, 1982.
The Hour of the Wolf, Scribner, 1983.
Hadder MacColl, Scribner, 1985.
Yesterday's Daughter, Scribner, 1986.
Stranger, You and I, Scribner, 1987.
When Morning Comes, Macmillan, 1989.
The Person I Used to Be, Macmillan, 1993.
Picking Up the Pieces, Scribner, 1993.
Bigger, Scribner, 1994.
Writing to Richie, Scribner, 1994.

OTHER

(Editor) *The Communicator's Handbook: Techniques and Technology*, Maupin House, 1990.

Contributor to *Developing Reading Efficiency*, edited by Lyle L. Miller, 4th edition, Burgess, 1980. Also contributor, sometimes under pseudonym Peter J. Freeman, of more than one hundred articles and stories to magazines, including *Highlights for Children, Friend, Junior Life, Grit, National Future Farmer*, and *Jack and Jill*.

■ Sidelights

"By the time I was ten years old, I knew that what I wanted to be most in life was a writer," recalled Patricia Calvert in *Something about the Author* (*SATA*). The circumstances of her childhood—she spent her early years with her family in a cabin in the rugged mountains of Montana—provided Calvert with ample opportunities to read and listen to the stories her mother told her and her brother. "It was our good fortune to have a mother who was a lively story-teller," noted Calvert in *SATA*. "She never tired of telling us sad and funny (and often outrageous!) tales about her own childhood. In addition, my mother read to us almost every evening by the light of a smoky kerosene lamp—not the traditional classics that most children hear, but a crazy assortment of detective, adventure, and love stories from such popular magazines as *Liberty* and *Saturday Evening Post*." It was on those evenings at the foot of her mother's bed, the lamplight glowing and flickering warmly around the room, that Calvert fell in love with stories. "I was stricken," she later said in an essay for *Something about the Author Autobiography Series* (*SAAS*). "I became hopelessly infected with the magic of words. I never recov-

ered." This passion for stories eventually manifested itself in a series of award-winning novels written for the young adult audience.

Calvert's parents were only eighteen years old when they married. Wed during the height of the Great Depression, the couple struggled to make ends meet, and they were forced to live with a variety of relatives during their first months of marriage. In May of 1932, though, Calvert's father, Fred Freeman, came upon an abandoned miner's cabin during a casual hike past Big Timber Creek, an area in Montana's Little Belt mountain range. "The cabin, constructed nearly forty years before, was windowless; its puncheon floor had rotted away; rats and mice were its only inhabitants. The surrounding countryside, however, once the scene of gold-and-silver mining activity during the 1890s, was lively with wild game, and the nearby creeks were full of slim, silver trout," recalled Calvert in *SATA*. "In such a place, my father reasoned, a man and his family might live off the land—and so, in October 1933, he moved a wife, a two-year-old daughter, and an infant son into that inhospitable cabin and set about to make it livable."

In many ways Calvert's childhood was an idyllic one, for she woke every morning to the beautiful mountains and forests that surrounded their home. She grew to recognize and appreciate the numerous wild animals that shared the land with them as well. Deer, bears, bobcats, coyotes, beavers, porcupines, and wolverines all made their home in the Little Belt mountains. Even as a child of five or six, Calvert learned how to fish, and she and her brother spent endless hours exploring area mine shafts, woods, and berry patches. "It was a magic world for any child, one in which lodge-pole pines grew like arrows toward a sky that seemed always blue. When I was older I had a sassy little horse named Redbird to ride, a collie named Bruno to keep me company, and a calico cat named Agamemnon to sleep at the foot of my bed," Calvert remarked in *SAAS*.

Struggles with Dyslexia

In 1937 the Freeman family relocated to less isolated realms so that the children could attend public school (though they still spent large blocks of time back at Big Timber Creek in subsequent years). School proved difficult for their young daughter, however, for she suffered from dyslexia, a reading disability. "My parents and teachers had no idea why I seemed to be so slow in first grade nor why I soon became somewhat of a discipline problem in the classroom. The truth is that within a few weeks of entering first grade I turned into the sort of annoying, pain-in-the-neck kid maybe you've met in school yourself," she admitted in *SAAS*. "With each day that passed I became more intensely frustrated over not being able to understand the lessons in our textbooks or what Mrs. Bowlin wrote in large letters on the blackboard." After reviewing Calvert's shaky performance that first year, the school decided to make her repeat first grade, but Calvert's mother insisted that she could teach her daughter how to read over the summer.

Mrs. Freeman subsequently laid out the ground rules for young Calvert, the principal one being that the radio was off-limits unless she agreed to her mother's schedule of tutoring. "I howled and yelped and pretended to fall over dead," described Calvert in *SAAS*, "but finally I agreed to sit with her." Using a set of homemade flash cards as a learning tool, the hard work eventually paid off, and Calvert gradually improved her reading skills.

By age ten Calvert was convinced that she wanted to be a writer, and it was at this time in her life that she penned her first stories. During her high school years she and her family lived in a small house that her father built outside of Great Falls. Each summer, though, Calvert returned with her family to Big Timber Creek, a haven of cool forests, towering mountains, and bright meadows. On one occasion, a high school boy named George Calvert rode his motorcycle all the way out to Big Timber Creek to see her, a testament to the attraction that the two of them felt for one another.

Calvert attended college at the University of Montana, a place that seemed huge and intimidating to the freshman, who had lived most of her life in rural surroundings. She made a number of lifelong friends, though, and did well in her studies. "Although my passion was words and although I knew for sure I wanted to be a writer someday, I enrolled in a four-year program for medical technologists at the university; I believed I could get a job more easily with that sort of education," she explained in *SAAS*.

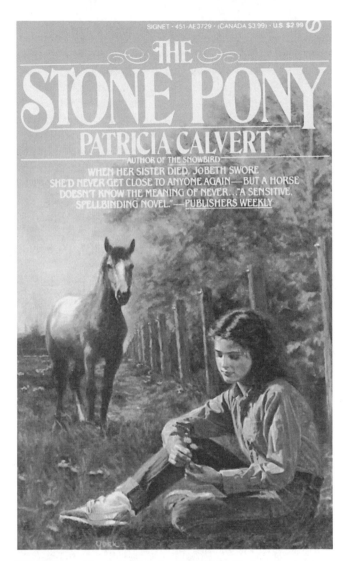

When her sister, Ashleigh, dies, JoBeth learns to care for Ashleigh's horse in this 1982 story.

In 1950 the United States became involved in the Korean War, and George Calvert, Patricia's sweetheart, was called to serve. "It was a scary time, full of uncertainty and fear but also rich with excitement and adventure, and we did what young people in such circumstances have done in so many other troubling times," Calvert said in *SAAS*. "We ran away to get married." George Calvert was subsequently stationed at an air force base in Valdosta, Georgia, and it was there that the couple had their first daughter, Brianne. Less than two years passed before the Calverts added another daughter, Dana, to the family.

The Calvert family eventually settled in Minnesota after Calvert's husband was discharged from the military. With Brianne and Dana in grade school, Calvert worked as an editorial assistant at the Mayo Clinic in Rochester, Minnesota. During this time Calvert continued to nurture her long-time interest in writing, and a number of her stories were published in such magazines as *Junior Life*, *Highlights for Children*, *Friend*, and *American Farm Youth*, but she became convinced that she would never have the time or opportunity to write a novel. One summer day she gathered together all the story fragments and ideas and poems and essays that she'd written over the years and poured them into the flames of a backyard fire. "I destroyed my dearest dreams, believing (mistakenly) that motherhood and wifehood couldn't be combined with authorhood," she wrote in *SAAS*.

Country Return Spurs Writing

As the years passed, Calvert's love of fiction flourished despite her sorrowful conviction that she would never write a novel of her own. Her daughters eventually married and began families, and she and her husband began to investigate the possibility of returning to the sort of country environment that Calvert had enjoyed as a child. They bought a small, forty-acre farm in southeastern Minnesota, which they named Foxwood. "We turned our acres into a wildlife preserve where deer, fox, and raccoon could wander where they wished," Calvert related in *SATA*. Back in the country, where the sounds of traffic and telephones and other neighborhood noises gave way to the honking of geese and the soothing ruffling of forest winds, Calvert felt old desires stir to life once more. "I converted an old chicken coop into a place to write, and when I did I returned to scenes from my childhood and to those half-forgotten tales told to me by my mother about her own childhood," continued Calvert in *SATA*.

Calvert's first book, which she titled *The Snowbird*, is an historical novel set in the 1880s. Its primary characters are a thirteen-year-old girl named Willie (Willana) Bannerman and her younger brother TJ, who are forced to join their Uncle Randall and his wife Belle in Dakota territory after their parents perish in a fire. Willie has a difficult time coming to terms with her loss, but she comes to love Belle and the young white filly, called Snowbird, that she helps raise. Life on the plains is not easy, though, and Willie endures additional hardships over the course of the novel.

"For ever so long," Calvert remarked in *SAAS*, "it seemed to me as if that first book would never find itself between hard covers, that it would never be published, that a girl named Willie Bannerman would forever be merely a figment of my imagination. Although I had once hoped to be in print—and rich and famous, naturally!—by the time I was twenty-five, I was forty-nine years old when *The Snowbird* was published by Scribner's in 1980."

Calvert's second young adult novel, *The Money Creek Mare*, was published in 1981. It was followed

> "If I have entertained readers with my novels, that's what I intended to do. If I have informed their hearts, that's what I hoped might happen."

a year later by *The Stone Pony*, which, like her first two books, features a horse that plays an important role in the novel's plot. In 1983 Calvert published *The Hour of the Wolf*, which is set against the backdrop of the famous Alaskan Iditarod sled dog race and tells the story of young Jake Mathiessen's efforts to come to terms with the death of a close friend and his own earlier suicide attempt. Two years later Calvert's second historical novel was published. *Hadder MacColl* is a story of eighteenth-century life on the Scottish Highlands during the Jacobite Rebellion. Its title character, the fourteen-year-old daughter of a Highland chieftain, shares her father's fierce loyalty to Charles Edward Stuart, who hopes to reclaim the Scottish throne from the English. Her older brother Leofwin, however, is unenthusiastic about the forthcoming clash, a stance that leads Hadder to speculate whether his academic studies have made him soft. *Horn Book* reviewer Mary M. Burns noted that "after the battle, in which her brother is killed, she finally perceives that his premonitions were not a coward's way out but rather a rational assessment of possibilities. . . . Patricia Calvert has revivified the memories of those tragic days and skillfully integrated a wealth of historical detail into a well-paced narrative."

School Library Journal reviewer Ann W. Moore similarly described *Hadder MacColl* as "a well-crafted, exciting, enthralling story—her best novel so far."

Readers came to recognize that Calvert's books, while often full of adventure, also attempt to address issues and concerns of special interest to teenagers. "If I have entertained readers with my novels, that's what I intended to do," Calvert commented in *Twentieth-Century Young Adult Writers.* "If I have informed their hearts, that's what I hoped might happen. One of the best letters I ever received was from a boy in a state far from mine who wrote: 'I never thought much about my own life until I read your book.'"

Calvert's sixth novel, *Yesterday's Daughter,* was published in 1986. Its primary character, sixteen-year-old Leenie, leads a peaceful existence on her grandfather's fishing camp in Georgia. Her life, though, is rocked by a visit from her mother, who has not seen her daughter since she was an infant. Zena Sutherland, in a *Bulletin of the Center for Children's Books* review of *Yesterday's Daughter,* called the book a well-written effort, while at the same time cautioning that it was "more dependent on contrivance than other stories by Calvert." *Voice of Youth Advocates* reviewer Ruth Creech, however, praised the author's characterizations and noted that the book's "prevailing emotion is love; the attitude respect. Leenie's coming of age is special."

Calvert's next young adult novel, *Stranger, You and I,* explores the depth of a friendship between Hughie, a smart and perceptive teenage boy, and Zee, who suddenly finds herself pregnant by another boy who refuses to accept responsibility for his actions. *Stranger, You and I* enjoyed a strong critical reception upon its release for its sensitive treatment of the issue of teenage pregnancy. *Horn Book* reviewer Margaret A. Bush, noting that "Calvert is a practiced hand at developing likable characters in greater depth," called the novel "a touching story of everyday people who survive failed dreams and hurts and fears through shadings of friendship, caring, and responsibility."

By the late 1980s Calvert's career as a writer of young adult novels was well-established, and there was no indication that her prolific writing pace might slow. As she indicated in *SATA,* "I am everlastingly fascinated by that country from which we are all emigrants: the land of childhood—and

that is the reason why my fiction is for (and about) children." In 1989 she published *When Morning Comes,* the story of Cat Kincaid, a streetwise and promiscuous fifteen-year-old girl who has run away from a nightmarish family life. Reviewers praised Calvert's unflinching portrayal of the hazards of the streets, and noted that the character of Cat—a convincing combination of vulnerabilities and strengths—is drawn with a deft hand.

If you enjoy the works of Patricia Calvert, you may also want to check out the following books and films:

Judi Angell, *Tina Gogo,* 1978.
Sue Ellen Bridgers, *Notes for Another Life,* 1981.
Alden R. Carter, *Up Country,* 1989.
Cynthia Voight, *Dicey's Song,* 1982.
Alan & Naomi, Columbia Tristar, 1992.

In 1993 Calvert saw the release of two of her novels, *The Person I Used to Be* and *Picking Up the Pieces.* The latter book details a teenage girl's struggle to come to terms with an injury that has relegated her to a wheelchair for the rest of her life. A *Publishers Weekly* reviewer pointed out that the novel is "exceptionally powerful, endowed with the grace of the human spirit," while Pat Katka, writing for *School Library Journal,* called *Picking Up the Pieces* "a sensitive and gritty story." As Katka explained, "the theme is not original, but the depiction of Megan's world—the constant battle with bladder infections, the frustrating struggles with once routine activities, the haunting awareness of the situation's permanence—is vivid and moving."

A year later two more Calvert novels were published. In the first of these tales, *Bigger,* the author returned to the historical novel format. Set during the final days of the Civil War, *Bigger* relates the adventures of twelve-year-old Tyler and Bigger, an abused dog that the boy adopts, as Tyler searches for his father, a member of a band of renegade Confederate soldiers. Several of the events that take place during the journey led critics to question the realism of the novel, but they also pointed to *Bigger*'s basic strengths. Reviewer Susan Ackler noted in *Voice of Youth Advocates* that "the book is well written with an interesting cast of characters and shows some aspects of the Civil

War seldom found in youth literature." *Booklist* reviewer Chris Sherman similarly remarked that "Calvert's story has many tantalizing elements: Tyler is likable and realistically portrayed, the book raises some provocative issues, and the ending is sad but satisfying."

Calvert's second novel of 1994 was *Writing to Richie*, a story concerning two brothers, David and Richie, and the grief and rage that David feels when young Richie dies from an acute allergic reaction. *Booklist* reviewer Carolyn Phelan echoed the thoughts of some other critics when she wrote that "Calvert has created several intriguing characters, but the brevity of the novel and the breathless pace of the plot leave too little time for their development."

Calvert, though, has compiled a strong body of work since the release of *The Snowbird* back in 1980, and she shows no inclination to retire from the world of storytelling. "For me," she remarked in *SAAS*, "writing has truly become a habit of the heart, of looking deep inside myself as well as into the center of others. It has become a way of trying to be a better, more responsible person. Oh, yes, I still want to entertain an audience and to spin a good yarn—but most of all I enjoy climbing inside my own head and rummaging through the notes and jottings and partly finished manuscripts that litter the dusty tables and shelves in that large, sunny writing room right behind my eyes."

■ Works Cited

Ackler, Susan, review of *Bigger, Voice of Youth Advocates*, April, 1994, p. 24.

Burns, Mary M., review of *Hadder MacColl, Horn Book*, March/April, 1986, p. 206.

Bush, Margaret A., review of *Stranger, You and I, Horn Book*, January/February, 1988, p. 67.

Calvert, Patricia, comments in *Something about the Author*, Volume 45, Gale, 1986, pp. 54-56.

Calvert, Patricia, essay in *Something about the Author Autobiography Series*, Volume 17, Gale, 1994, pp. 27-40.

Calvert, Patricia, remarks in *Twentieth-Century Young Adult Writers*, edited by Laura Standley Berger, Gale, 1994.

Creech, Ruth, review of *Yesterday's Daughter, Voice of Youth Advocates*, December, 1986, p. 213.

Katka, Pat, review of *Picking Up the Pieces, School Library Journal*, June, 1993, p. 126.

Moore, Ann W., review of *Hadder MacColl, School Library Journal*, October, 1985, p. 180.

Phelan, Carolyn, review of *Writing to Richie, Booklist*, December 15, 1994, p. 752.

Review of *Picking Up the Pieces, Publishers Weekly*, May 3, 1993, pp. 310-11.

Sherman, Chris, review of *Bigger, Booklist*, April 1, 1994, p. 1433.

Sutherland, Zena, review of *Yesterday's Daughter, Bulletin of the Center for Children's Books*, December, 1986, p. 63.

■ For More Information See

BOOKS

Gallo, Donald R., editor, *Speaking for Ourselves, Too*, National Council of Teachers of English, 1993.

PERIODICALS

Bulletin of the Center for Children's Books, November, 1985; December, 1987.

Horn Book, July/August, 1994.

Publishers Weekly, November 13, 1987; October 27, 1989.

School Library Journal, January, 1995.

Times Educational Supplement, July 31, 1987.

Voice of Youth Advocates, February, 1990; August, 1993.*

—Sketch by Kevin Hillstrom

Pam Conrad

■ Personal

Born June 18, 1947, in New York, NY; died of cancer, January 22, 1996, in Rockville Centre, Long Island, NY; daughter of Robert F. (a teacher) and Doris (a businesswoman; maiden name, Dowling) Stampf; married Robert R. Conrad (a designer), June 25, 1967 (divorced, 1982); children: Johanna, Sarah. *Education:* Attended Hofstra University, 1977-79; New School for Social Research, B.A., 1984. *Hobbies and other interests:* "I like needlework, quilting, crocheting, and knitting, pug dogs, country music, Ray Charles, jogging, reading, the seashore (including boats, fish, seashells and sand) and the plains (including big skies, fossils, corn, and coal trains)."

■ Addresses

Agent—Maria Carvainis, Maria Carvainis Agency, Inc., 235 West End Ave., New York, NY 10023.

■ Career

Writer, 1979–96. Teacher of writing courses at Queens College, New York. *Member:* Authors Guild, Society of Children's Book Writers and Illustrators.

■ Awards, Honors

Society of Children's Book Writers grant, 1982; Western Writers of America Spur Award, American Library Association (ALA) notable book and best book for young adults citations, Society of Children's Book Writers Golden Kite Award honor book citation, National Council for Social Studies and the Children's Book Council notable trade book in the field of social sciences citation, National Cowboy Hall of Fame Western Heritage Award, and Child Study Association of America's children's books of the year citation, all 1985, International Reading Association Children's Book Award, *Boston Globe-Horn Book* Award honor book, Women's National Book Association Judy Lopez Memorial Award, and Society of Midland Authors' outstanding books about the Midwest or by Midwestern authors citation, all 1986, and ALA *Booklist* "Best of the '80s" books for children citation, all for *Prairie Songs*.

ALA recommended book for the reluctant young adult reader citation, 1987, and International Reading Association young adult choices citation, 1988, both for *Holding Me Here*; ALA best book for young adults citation, 1987, for *What I Did for Roman*; ALA *Booklist* children's editors' choices citation, 1988, for *Staying Nine*; ALA best books for young adults citation, ALA *Booklist* children's editors' choices citation, Western Writers of America Spur Award for best western juvenile, and National Council for the Social Studies and Children's Book Council notable children's trade book in social studies citation, all 1989, and International Reading Association teachers' choices citation, 1990, all for *My Daniel*; ALA notable children's book citation, and *New York Times* notable book citation, both 1989, and International Reading Association and Children's Book Council children's choice citation, 1990, all for *The Tub People*; *Boston Globe-Horn Book* Award honor book, 1990, and Mystery Writers of America Edgar Award, 1991, both for *Stonewords: A Ghost Story.*

■ **Writings**

YOUNG ADULT BOOKS

Prairie Songs, illustrated by Darryl S. Zudeck, Harper, 1985.
Holding Me Here, Harper, 1986.
What I Did for Roman, Harper, 1987, published in England as *A Seal upon My Heart*, Oxford University Press, 1988.
Taking the Ferry Home, Harper, 1988.
My Daniel, Harper, 1989.
Stonewords: A Ghost Story, Harper, 1990.
Prairie Visions: The Life and Times of Solomon Butcher, illustrated by Zudeck, HarperCollins, 1991, new edition illustrated with photographs by Solomon Butcher, 1993.
Pedro's Journal: A Voyage with Christopher Columbus, August 3, 1492-February 14, 1493, illustrated by Peter Koeppen, Boyds Mills Press, 1991.
Our House: The Stories of Levittown, Scholastic, 1995.
Zoe Rising (sequel to *Stonewords: A Ghost Story*), HarperCollins, 1996.

JUVENILE BOOKS

I Don't Live Here!, illustrated by Diane de Groat, Dutton, 1983.
Seven Silly Circles (sequel to *I Don't Live Here!*), illustrated by Mike Wimmer, Harper, 1987.
The Tub People, illustrated by Richard Egielski, Harper, 1988.
Staying Nine, illustrated by Wimmer, Harper, 1988.
The Lost Sailor, illustrated by Egielski, HarperCollins, 1993.
The Tub Grandfather, illustrated by Egielski, HarperCollins, 1993.

Molly and the Strawberry Day, illustrated by Mary Szilagyi, HarperCollins, 1994.
Dollface Has a Party, illustrated by Brian Selznick, HarperCollins, 1994.
Pumpkin Moon, Harcourt, 1994.
The Rooster's Gift, illustrated by Eric Beddows, HarperCollins, 1995.
Animal Lingo, illustrated by Barbara B. Falk, HarperCollins, 1995.
Call Me Ahnighito, illustrated by Egielski, HarperCollins, 1995.
Old Man Hoover's Dead Rabbit, illustrated by Mark English, HarperCollins, 1996.

OTHER

Contributor of essays and articles to periodicals, including *Horn Book*, *Publishers Weekly*, *McCall's*, *Newsweek*, *Newsday*, and the *New York Times*.

■ **Sidelights**

Pam Conrad began taking her career as a children's author seriously when her husband left her. As a mother of two children, she knew she needed a career that would support her family. Instead of letting her difficult circumstances control her life, though, Conrad used the tragedies and joys she experienced as inspiration for her fictional works. It is this realism and detail that made Conrad a leading children's author. Her 1985 novel *Prairie Songs* launched her into the national spotlight and won numerous awards. Steven Lillington wrote in *Books for Your Children* that Conrad "is one of the brightest talents to emerge in the last few years."

Conrad was born in Brooklyn, New York, in 1947. Her parents were very young when she entered the world and the family grew up in an apartment near her grandparents; Conrad even went to the same school her mother had attended years earlier. Living so close to her grandparents, Conrad formed strong bonds with both her grandmother (Nanny) and her grandfather (PopPop), and when the family moved to Long Island she was sad because she knew she would miss them. However, Conrad's fears turned out to be unjustified. "I was sad to leave Nanny, but it turned out that we saw her a lot," she recalled in an autobiographical essay for *Something about the Author Autobiography Series* (SAAS). "She called on the telephone every day and we saw her every

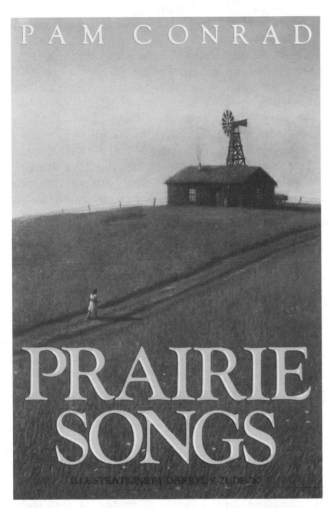

P A M   C O N R A D

PRAIRIE SONGS

ILLUSTRATIONS BY DARRYL S. ZUDECK

Louisa is enchanted when a doctor from New York City and his wife move near her home on the Nebraska prairie in this award-winning 1985 work.

Sunday. Either we would drive to Queens to visit her and PopPop and have Sunday dinner, or they would drive out to visit us."

In addition to having close relationships with her grandparents, Conrad remembered that she enjoyed learning how to read with the Dick and Jane books. "Before my eyes, squiggles on a page turned to sounds, to words, and then a story. I was smitten." She became a voracious reader, and often tried her hand at writing. Her mother had a rule that when one of the children had a fever, they had to stay home; Conrad used these sick days very productively. "I discovered very early that when I did have a fever I could write poetry, and that's what I would do to amuse myself," she wrote in *SAAS*. Influenced by A. A. Milne's *Winnie the Pooh* stories, she wrote poetry about tea parties and honey. For her gradu-

ation from elementary school, her parents made up a book of all her poems and named it "Tea by the Garden Wall." Conrad related in *SAAS* that her parent's present "was pretty impressive, but I was embarrassed. Being a poet was not a cool thing to be in 1959."

When Conrad entered junior high school she continued to write poetry, but found a different motivation. "I found that falling in love had the same effect as having a fever," she described in *SAAS*. In eighth grade, she decided to audition for admission to the High School of Performing Arts. Conrad had been dancing since a very early age, and she honed her skills for the audition. This hard work paid off when she was admitted into the school. "Going to school in New York City was an entirely new experience. I went from walking across a field to get to school to taking a subway into Times Square," she related in *SAAS*.

Creating "Nelephants"

Conrad worked hard at her dancing, but soon decided that she felt uncomfortable performing in front of an audience. Her senior year, she struck up an acquaintance with a young man who was working to be an illustrator. He had an assignment to illustrate a children's book, and Conrad helped him out by writing a story about two "nelephants" who fall in love. Upon graduation, Conrad decided not to pursue a career in dancing and instead went to work at an exercise studio. One of the clients of the studio was a children's book editor for a local publishing house. Conrad mentioned to her that she had written a children's book and the editor offered to look it over, giving it back to Conrad with a few suggestions. It could have meant an early break for Conrad; however, she wrote in *SAAS* that "I had a young person's arrogance in those days, and didn't really know how to rewrite, so I never followed up on her suggestions. I often think how if I had been paying attention, I could have started my career in children's books much earlier than I eventually did!"

In the meantime, Conrad married her high-school illustrator friend. In order to avoid getting drafted to fight in the Vietnam War, her husband joined the Air Force, forcing the couple to move to Denver for his training. Conrad was at a loss; life in Colorado was so different from her life in New

York. But she and her husband soon met new people who introduced them to the area, including the plains of Nebraska. "Imagine a New York City girl, used to bright lights, sitting on a front porch in Nebraska, late at night, without a star or a moon in the sky," Conrad mused in *SAAS*. These Nebraska days and nights were the beginnings of many of Conrad's later writings. "Something began to stir inside me," she explained in *SAAS*. "It would be years before I knew what it was."

After a few years, the couple moved to Texas, a state which suited Conrad better than Colorado. "Suddenly I was happy. I loved it. We lived in a trailer on a piece of land backed up against a

In this 1988 novel, two teenage girls, one the daughter of a recovering alcoholic, the other of a cocaine-abusing mother, share a summer together on a resort island.

horse pasture," Conrad described in *SAAS*. It was in this new state that Conrad became pregnant and then later miscarried during the midst of preparations for the new baby. The grief that followed prompted Conrad to revisit writing poetry, something she had not done for a long time.

Shortly thereafter Conrad's husband received his discharge orders from the Air Force and they moved back to New York. The couple adopted a year-old black child and Conrad was ecstatic with her new role as a mother, a role one that looked as if it might expand when she became pregnant again shortly after the adoption. This time she carried the baby to term, but it lived for only a short time after birth. Once again, Conrad was heartbroken, but on her third attempt she delivered a healthy baby girl.

After a few years of being a full-time mother, onrad went back to college, and it was here that she found her true calling. "The first thing I realized as I began taking classes was that I loved to write, and that if I were to pick a career, it would have to be something to do with writing," she recalled in *SAAS*. Focusing her early writing efforts on romance novels, which she knew offered a decent living, Conrad's first writings experienced little success. Then she took a class on writing for children, a genre that instantly clicked with her. As she went further into her studies of children's books Conrad focused on the author Beverly Cleary, reading and studying her books. "I read as many Cleary books as I could get my hands on and then I wrote a book I called 'Gazebo Stories,'" related Conrad in *SAAS*. After being rejected by many publishers, the book was finally published in 1983 with the title *I Don't Live Here!* The story is about Nicki Bennet and the anger she feels toward her parents after a move in which she has to leave behind her best friend.

After the book was published, Conrad's husband left the family and they were divorced. She knew that she would have to turn her ambition for writing into a full-blown career. "What had begun as a spirited search for a career now turned to a definite need to make a living. I began trying to write picture book manuscripts as well, about little people living on the edge of a bathtub, about a little girl losing a tooth, about anything I could think of. I wrote every day, and I studied children's books," Conrad continued in *SAAS*.

Return to the Prairie

Memories and ideas about things she had seen in Nebraska gelled to form the idea for Conrad's second book, *Prairie Songs* (1985). The novel's setting is the wide and open prairie of Nebraska, where a contented Louisa resides in a sod house with her family. The local doctor's wife, named Emmeline, is a beautiful and well-bred woman from New York City. She is having a difficult time adjusting to the rigors of pioneer life; nevertheless, she becomes the idol of young Louisa. Emmeline becomes pregnant, and seems to lose all her vigor with the strain of childbearing and living on the prairie. When she loses her baby in childbirth, she loses her sanity as well. "I had a story to tell—about a woman who moves from New York to the West, much as I had—and goes mad," Conrad recalled in the *Sixth Book of Junior Authors and Illustrators*. "But the story was too painful for me to write from her point of view. It wasn't till I found a child's voice to tell the story that it began to flow and *Prairie Songs* was written. Since them I have found my young adult novels begin with settings."

Prairie Songs was met with much critical praise, winning recognition and several awards. Janet Hickman, writing in *Language Arts*, praised both Conrad and her work, describing the combination as "a satisfying book and a promising new author." In a *Horn Book* review, Anita Silvey wrote that *Prairie Songs* "is a quiet, gentle, yet moving re-creation of another period and another way of life."

For her next work, Conrad returned to a contemporary setting. In *Holding Me Here* (1986), Robin Lewis is the child of divorced parents. One day, her mother lets another woman stay at their house, and by snooping in the boarder's diary, Robin starts to think that this woman abandoned her two children. Later the truth is found out—the mysterious woman needed to leave her alcoholic husband. A *Publishers Weekly* reviewer called the writing in *Holding Me Here* "strong and clear," adding that it "draws one into the story." The novel is based on a true story in Conrad's life. "One night an old friend of mine had called me from the train station. She had been with a man who beat her and she needed a place to hide. . . . She stayed a few days, until he found her, and then she left," Conrad described in *SAAS*.

"*Holding Me Here* is also the first book in which I dealt with alcoholism. Many members of my family have struggled with this disease and it has made a great impact on my life," Conrad also related in her essay for *SAAS*. "I know many children live with it daily and my heart always goes out to them because I know how difficult it is. I have been there." Conrad further explored the topic of alcoholism in *Taking the Ferry Home* (1988). In this novel, two girls, Ali and Simone, become best friends. They soon learn that they have something in common—Ali's father is a recovering alcoholic and Simone's mother is using cocaine.

Silvey wrote about *Taking the Ferry Home* in *Horn Book*, praising Conrad's skill in depicting addiction in families: "Rarely have the disease of alcoholism and its effect on families been so well drawn in a book for young readers." A *Kirkus Reviews* contributor similarly found the book "moving and memorable," and a *Publishers Weekly* reviewer related that "Conrad's story resonates with truth and caring."

In the 1989 release *My Daniel* Conrad revisited her familiar Nebraska setting. The novel begins with Julia Summerwaite's arrival in New York City to visit her grandchildren, Ellie and Stevie. Her agenda is to take the grandchildren to the Natural History Museum. Julia then relates to them the story of how she and her brother Daniel had found some of the dinosaur bones (back on their farm in Nebraska) that are on display at the museum. A *Horn Book* contributor asserted that although *My Daniel* is "ambitious in concept and uneven in execution," it "is built around an absorbing story." In a *Voice of Youth Advocates* review, Rosemary Moran pointed out that "the beauty of the prairie as well as the rugged life of those who lived there is eloquently evoked."

The Scary Stuff

In response to her daughter's interest in scary stories, Conrad wrote *Stonewords: A Ghost Story* (1990). This novel is about present-day Zoe, who finds that the hundred-year-old ghost Zoe Louise is living in her grandparents' house. Through the use of a magical back staircase, Zoe is able to enter Zoe Louise's life as a ghost. Calling *Stonewords: A Ghost Story* "an eerie and gripping time fantasy," Margaret A. Chang commented in

The Chrisman sisters stand outside their Nebraska sod house in this photo from *Prairie Visions: The Life and Times of Solomon Butcher.*

School Library Journal: "The spare, vivid prose sustains the suspense, drawing readers inexorably toward a climax as satisfying as it is unexpected." And a *Horn Book* contributor concludes that "the story is truly compelling. How each child slips in and out of her own time is skillfully and convincingly described."

In 1991, Conrad tackled a nonfiction book that is based on the life of Solomon Butcher, a man who photographed prairie settlers in the late nineteenth century. Butcher was an eccentric man who seemed to wander from profession to profession with no noticeable plan. He wanted to be a prairie farmer, but he was too lazy for the difficult work. Instead, he dedicated many years of his life to photographing and interviewing pioneers in Nebraska. Conrad unearthed his research years later and wrote this detailed biography—*Prairie Visions: The Life and Times of Solomon Butcher.* Alex

Harris, writing in the *New York Times Book Review*, concluded that Conrad "re-creates the photographer and lets him show that history can happen in front of our eyes. She provides the improbable hero Solomon Butcher to teach us that history is alive."

In *Our House: The Stories of Levittown* (1995), Conrad traces the history of a suburban town in New York by fictionalizing the stories of the residents of one house. Through the stories of children, Conrad describes a rich landscape that shows how Levittown moved from being a potato field to its current state. A *Publishers Weekly* reviewer wrote that Conrad's "abilities to fuse fact with fiction and connect the past with the present are nothing less than remarkable." Writing in *Horn Book*, another critic called Conrad's book "rich in connotative details, the collection is an invitation to remember."

Over the course of her career Conrad used the details of her own life throughout her writings. When she first discovered she had breast cancer it was a difficult truth for her to confront, but in the end it strengthened her conviction to her writing. "It was a terrible thing to go through, but when I didn't die I realized how wonderful my life is. And how much I love the work I do," she wrote in *SAAS*. The illness, which eventually took her life in 1996, became another of the difficult issues in her life, all of which helped make her fiction more realistic. Divorce, dealing with alcoholism in the family, and troubles with the children were all issues intimately connected to her

---

If you enjoy the works of Pam Conrad, you may also want to check out the following books and films:

Bruce Brooks, *No Kidding*, 1989.
Kathryn Lasky, *The Bone Wars*, 1988.
Glendon Swarthout, *The Homesman*, 1988.
Paul Zindel, *The Effects of Gamma Rays on Man-in-the-Moon Marigolds*, 1971.
Lonesome Dove, Cabin Fever Entertainment, 1989.

---

life, and all surfaced as themes in her books. "Each of my books is finely connected to the life I lead. It has been that way right from the start and it is safe to assume that my life will always be woven into the pages of my books," she continued in *SAAS*, concluding that "the truth is everything in my life is my material, and I write books. I am a writer."

■ **Works Cited**

Chang, Margaret A., review of *Stonewords: A Ghost Story*, School Library Journal, May, 1990, p. 103.

Conrad, Pam, essay in *Sixth Book of Junior Authors and Illustrators*, edited by Sally Holmes Holtze, H. W. Wilson, 1989.

Conrad, Pam, essay in *Something about the Author Autobiography Series*, Volume 19, Gale, 1995, pp. 113-31.

Harris, Alex, review of *Prairie Visions: The Life and Times of Solomon Butcher*, New York Times Book Review, September 1, 1991, p. 23.

Hickman, Janet, review of *Prairie Songs*, Language Arts, January, 1986, pp. 85-86.

Review of *Holding Me Here*, Publishers Weekly, June 27, 1986, p. 95.

Lillington, Steven, review of *A Seal upon My Heart*, Books for Your Children, summer, 1988, p. 19.

Moran, Rosemary, review of *My Daniel*, Voice of Youth Advocates, June, 1989, p. 98.

Review of *My Daniel*, Horn Book, May, 1989, pp. 374-75.

Review of *Our House: The Stories of Levittown*, Horn Book, November-December, 1995, p. 740.

Review of *Our House: The Stories of Levittown*, Publishers Weekly, September 25, 1995, p. 57.

Silvey, Anita, review of *Prairie Songs*, Horn Book, January-February, 1986, p. 57.

Silvey, Anita, review of *Taking the Ferry Home*, Horn Book, May-June, 1988, pp. 356-57.

Review of *Stonewords: A Ghost Story*, Horn Book, September, 1990, p. 600.

Review of *Taking the Ferry Home*, Kirkus Reviews, June 1, 1988, p. 825.

Review of *Taking the Ferry Home*, Publishers Weekly, June 10, 1988, p. 84.

■ **For More Information See**

BOOKS

Children's Literature Review, Volume 18, Gale, 1989.
Twentieth-Century Young Adult Writers, St. James Press, 1994.

PERIODICALS

Newsweek, December 4, 1989.
Times Literary Supplement, November 20, 1987.
Women's Record, November, 1985.

■ **Obituaries**

PERIODICALS

School Library Journal, March, 1996, p. 103.*

—Sketch by Nancy Rampson

Berlie Doherty

■ Personal

Surname is pronounced "*Doh*-er-ty"; born November 6, 1943, in Liverpool, England; daughter of Walter Alfred (a railway clerk) and Peggy (Brunton) Hollingsworth; married Gerard Adrian Doherty, 1966; children: Janna, Tim, Sally. *Education:* University of Durham, B.A. (with honors), 1964; University of Liverpool, postgraduate certificate in social science, 1965; University of Sheffield, postgraduate certificate in education, 1978. *Hobbies and other interests:* Opera, ballet, music of all kinds, singing, theatre, walking in the countryside.

■ Addresses

Home—38 Banner Cross Rd., Sheffield, Yorkshire S11 9HR, England. *Agent*—Gina Pollinger, 222 Old Brompton Rd., London, England.

■ Career

Leicestershire Child Care Services, Leicester, England, social worker, 1966-67; homemaker, 1967-78; English teacher in Sheffield, England, 1978-80; schools broadcaster for British Broadcasting Corporation (BBC)-Radio, Sheffield, 1980-82; full-time writer, 1983—. Writer-in-residence at various schools and libraries. Member of Yorkshire Arts Literature Panel, 1988-90; chair of Arvon Foundation at Lumb Bank, 1989—. *Member:* Writers Guild of Great Britain, Northern Association of Writers in Education (deputy chair, 1988-89), Arvon Foundation.

■ Awards, Honors

Carnegie Medal, British Library Association, 1986, Burnley/National Provincial Children's Book of the Year Award, 1987, and *Boston Globe-Horn Book* Honor Award, 1988, all for *Granny Was a Buffer Girl*; award from Television and Film Awards, New York, 1988, for *White Peak Farm*; Carnegie Medal, 1991, for *Dear Nobody.*

■ Writings

FOR CHILDREN

Tilly Mint Tales, illustrated by Thelma Lambert, Methuen, 1984.
Paddiwak and Cosy, illustrated by Teresa O'Brien, Methuen, 1988, Dial, 1989.
Tilly Mint and the Dodo (also see below), illustrated by Janna Doherty, Methuen, 1989.

Snowy, illustrated by Keith Bowen, HarperCollins, 1992.

(Reteller) *Old Father Christmas: Based on a Story by Juliana Horatia Ewing,* illustrated by Maria Teresa Meloni, Barron's, 1993.

Willa and Old Miss Annie, illustrated by Kim Lewis, Candlewick Press, 1994.

The Magic Bicycle, illustrated by Christian Birmingham, Crown, 1995 (published in England as *The Magical Bicycle*).

FOR YOUNG ADULTS

How Green You Are! (short stories; also see below), illustrated by Elaine McGregor Turney, Methuen, 1982.

The Making of Fingers Finnigan (short stories), illustrated by John Haysom, Methuen, 1983.

White Peak Farm (also see below), Methuen, 1984, Orchard, 1990.

Children of Winter (also see below), illustrated by Ian Newsham, Methuen, 1985.

Granny Was a Buffer Girl (also see below), Methuen, 1986, Orchard, 1988.

Tough Luck, Hamish Hamilton, 1988.

Spellhorn, Hamish Hamilton, 1989.

Dear Nobody, Hamish Hamilton, 1991.

Walking on Air (poetry), illustrated by J. Doherty, HarperCollins, 1993.

Street Child, Orchard, 1994.

The Snake-Stone, Orchard, 1996.

FOR ADULTS

Requiem (novel; also see below), M. Joseph, 1991.

The Vinegar Jar, St. Martin's, 1996.

TELEVISION AND RADIO PLAYS

The Drowned Village, BBC-Radio 4, 1980.

Requiem, BBC-Radio 4, 1982.

The White Bird of Peace, BBC-Radio 4, 1983.

A Case for Probation (also see below), BBC-Radio 4, 1983.

Miss Elizabeth, BBC-Radio 4, 1984.

Fuzzball, BBC-TV, 1985.

Sacrifice, BBC-Radio 4, 1985.

The Mouse and His Child (adapted from Russell Hoban's work of the same title), BBC-Radio 4, 1986.

White Peak Farm (serial), BBC-TV, 1988.

Dream of Unicorns, BBC-Radio 4, 1988.

Children of Winter, BBC-Radio 4, 1988.

Granny Was a Buffer Girl, BBC-Radio 4, 1990.

There's a Valley in Spain, BBC-Radio 4, 1990.

Dear Nobody, BBC-Radio 5, 1993.

STAGE PLAYS

Smells and Spells (two-act), produced in Sheffield, England, 1978.

Howard's Field (one-act), produced in Sheffield, 1979.

A Growing Girl's Story (one-act), produced in Hartlepool, England, 1980.

The Amazing Journey of Jazz O'Neil, produced in Hull, England, 1984.

Rock 'n' Roll Is Here to Stay (one-act), produced in Sheffield, 1984.

Return to the Ebro (one-act), produced in Manchester, England, 1986.

Tilly Mint and the Dodo, produced in Doncaster, England, 1986.

A Case for Probation, published in *Studio Scripts,* edited by David Self, Hutchinson, 1986.

How Green You Are!, published in *Drama 1,* edited by John Foster, Macmillan, 1987.

Matthew, Come Home, published in *Drama 2,* edited by Foster, Macmillan, 1987.

Tribute to Tom, published in *Drama 3,* edited by Foster, Macmillan, 1988.

Home, published in *Stage Write,* edited by Gervase Phinn, Unwin Hyman, 1988.

Who Wants Gold (two-act), produced in Newcastle-under-Lyme, England, c. 1993.

Work represented in anthologies, including *School Poems,* Oxford University Press, 1986, and *Best Short Stories 1989.* Contributor to magazines and newspapers, including *Arts Yorkshire, Times Educational Supplement, Stand,* and *Critical Quarterly.* Author of numerous series for local radio.

■ Adaptations

Several of Doherty's works have been adapted onto audiocassette by Chivers Press, including *Granny Was a Buffer Girl,* 1988, and *Tilly Mint Tales,* 1991.

■ Work in Progress

Walking on Air, a book of poetry for younger children; a storybook for beginning readers for Walker Books.

■ Sidelights

Berlie Doherty's works range from picture books such as *Paddiwak and Cosy* to adult novels like *Requiem* and *The Vinegar Jar*. However, she is probably best known for her award-winning books for young adults. Doherty has twice received Great Britain's prestigious Carnegie Medal, in 1986 for *Granny Was a Buffer Girl*, a generational portrait of a family living near Sheffield, England, and in 1991 for *Dear Nobody*, about the way two teenagers react to an unplanned pregnancy. *Magpies* contributor Agnes Nieuwenhuizen, in an interview with the author, lists some of Doherty's major themes in her books: "Unlocking the secrets of the past, family and family connections, colour, landscape, domestic detail, the inner life, the search for identity and the precise nature of the bond between mother and child."

Doherty's relationship with her parents provided inspiration for some of her books. She was born in Liverpool, England, on November 6, 1943—in the middle of World War II. Her father worked as a railway clerk and maintained a close relationship with the younger of his two daughters. The author's mother was a more distant figure. "She was nearly forty when I was born, and often ill," Doherty writes in her *Something about the Author Autobiography Series* (SAAS) entry. "She died in her mid-seventies, and I always regret the fact that I never really talked to her." "If I have inherited anything from her," the author declares, "it is my love of daydreaming. She loved to sit in the firelight and watch the flickering of flames and the shadows they made on the walls. Years later she gazed at the television set in the same way, watching the flickering patterns there, for hours on end, daydreaming." "My mother was very shy of strangers," Doherty continues, "and would sometimes cross the road rather than have to talk to people when she was out shopping. Yet, as a young woman, she had been an exhibition ballroom dancer. My father put a stop to that because, as she put it, he had two left feet, and the only dancing I ever saw her doing was round the kitchen when she was in a good mood. An old man who had known her as a young woman told me recently that she had always been the life and soul of the party."

"From my father I inherited stories," Doherty explains in *SAAS*. Although he spent his life as a railway clerk, Walter Alfred Hollingsworth was also a frustrated writer. "When I was a child I remember my father writing," Doherty recalls in an interview for *Something about the Author* (SATA). "He loved writing poetry and short stories so it was always a very familiar and comforting thing to see him typing away on the typewriter in the corner of the room." "My father used to type out my stories and send them in for me (though very soon I learnt how to type for myself)," Doherty concludes in her *SAAS* entry. "He wanted success for me . . . he was a writer too, in the sense that he loved writing and was compelled to do it."

A Catholic Schooling

Doherty spent her earliest years in a public school, but in the 1950s she won a scholarship to a private, Catholic convent school. "At school I was a relatively poor child among many very rich girls," Doherty states in her *SAAS* entry. "I had to lose my Liverpool accent in order to survive. I had to keep my nails clean, and have my hair tied back in plaits. And at night, instead of playing out, I had homework to do. To my friends in the street, who all went to a local school, it was the ultimate betrayal. They never forgave me for it." "I loved the chapel," Doherty recalls in *SAAS*, "with its sweet smells of polish and incense and flowers, and the jewelled patterns of light cast by the stained glass windows, the tiptoeings of the nuns as they came and went, the susurrations of their prayers. I must have spent hours there, at peace with myself and daydreaming, and I understand now that it must have looked like prayer, and that my natural love of solitude and introspection must have made me seem a very holy child."

"It must have soon become very clear that I had no vocation to be a nun, because the matter was never referred to again," she continues in *SAAS*. "My commitment was to other things." After she was "invited to join the choir, and became the soloist," the author explains, "from then on singing and music became my passion." "I wanted to write, and I wanted to sing," Doherty concludes. "My life has turned out in such a way that it has been possible to do both, and I know how lucky I am, though I never became the singer of my dreams, and my writing had to wait a long time before I put my mind to it properly." Doherty drew on her experiences in the convent school for several books, most notably *Requiem*,

How Green You Are! and *The Making of Fingers Finnigan.*

Doherty completed her primary education in Liverpool and launched herself on a career as a musician. "I sang as a duo then with a boyfriend and we performed as floor singers in some of the famous Liverpool folk clubs, haunting the footsteps of the Spinners and Liverpool/Irish groups," she states in *SAAS*. "This was in the sixties, when folk music was at its height." Even when she went off to the University of Durham she stayed extremely active in music, singing light opera, madrigals, and in choirs. It was at the University of Durham that she met her future husband Gerard Doherty, who shared her interest in music. "We got married when he was still a student in his fourth year. I had gone from Durham to Liverpool to do a post-graduate course," Doherty recalls in *SAAS*, "then came to Leicester as a social worker." "We spent every minute of our spare time arranging, learning, rehearsing, and sometimes composing songs," she remembers. "It seems now like another life, something that happened to somebody else."

"And now my life took a huge revolution," Doherty reveals in her *SAAS* entry. "I struggled to make independence work, to learn to be an individual." Her marriage to Gerard Doherty in 1966 was followed by a year with Leicester Child Care Services as a child care officer. In 1967 she retired to work at raising her three children. Over the next ten years her marriage began to suffer, and she and her husband eventually separated. "It was the darkest period of my life," Doherty recalls, "and I deeply sympathise with anyone who enters the same black waters. I had months of counseling, and emerged from all that as a writer." "I needed a career, and I needed it to fit in with my children's school hours," she explains. "Teaching was the only thing I could think of." Doherty earned a post-graduate certificate in education in 1978 and began teaching in a Sheffield school system.

A Musician Turns to Writing

Doherty's education certificate revived her interest in writing. "[I] was interested to see that there was an option to do some creative writing," she states in *SAAS*. "The tutor asked us to write a 1500-word story, and he said the subject was to

be Black and White. My thoughts flew to the black-and-white habits that the nuns at school had worn." Drawing on her experience in the Catholic girls' school, Doherty "wrote a short story called 'Requiem,' about the death of the nun who had taught singing at my convent school." "Writing it had unlocked something in me, and it was a kind of emotional truth," she reveals. "The story was about coming through a psychological barrier; so had the writing of it been. But also what was important about it was the joy I had felt when I was writing it, as if I was touching some arcane part of my inner life."

The composition of "Requiem" opened new vistas for the author. "The tutor liked the story, and recommended I should try to sell it," Doherty states in *SAAS*. "I was very excited. I showed it to a friend, a playwright, and he said, whatever you do, don't push this back in a drawer." "I had no idea where to send it," she confesses, "but I knew they sometimes broadcast stories on our local radio station, so I took it there." The producer, a man named Dave Sheasby, bought the broadcast rights to the story and requested that Doherty write ten more stories for radio broadcast. "Nothing, in the whole of my writing career, seeing my work on television and on the stage, winning two Carnegie Medals," she concludes, "nothing has given me more joy than that first letter of acceptance gave me."

In 1980, Doherty left the classroom and took the position of schools radio broadcaster. "The two years I spent as a seconded teacher to BBC-Radio Sheffield, for school broadcasts, were invaluable," she told *Contemporary Authors* (*CA*). The stories that she wrote for broadcast were collected in her first two books, *How Green You Are!* and *The Making of Fingers Finnigan.* Doherty told her *SATA* interviewer that these two works "very, very much explored" her own childhood, and added in her *CA* sketch, "These books reflect my own background in a small, seaside town." Both are set near Liverpool on Britain's west coast and feature a group of four average teenagers—Bee, Julia, Kevin, and Marie—who live fairly ordinary lives. "Each chapter of [*How Green You Are!*] is a separate episode," writes A. Thatcher in the *Junior Bookshelf*, "but it interlinks into a vividly written and strongly characterized picture of their lives, their friends and relatives, people who live in the street, and their schools."

Stories on the Air

In the title story of *How Green You Are!*, Julie repeats Doherty's own experience by winning a scholarship to a rich "snob" Catholic school for girls. At first her friends are angry—they mock her green school uniform—but soon, says Thatcher, "they find out that she has not changed." In *The Making of Fingers Finnigan*, the friends join with adults "in an attempt to save the decrepit swimming pool," declares *Junior Bookshelf* reviewer R. Baines, "and fund raising activities for this project continue intermittently throughout the book." The title episode tells how Julie's little brother Robert gets locked in a local movie house and has to be set free by Finnigan, a local small-time crook.

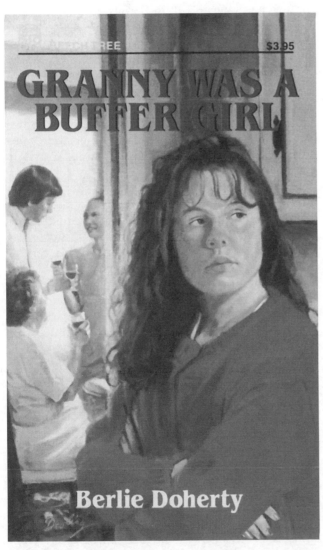

The stories about the love her family has for each other, told as Jess prepares to leave for college, make up this 1986 work, recipient of the Carnegie Medal.

"Bee, Kevin, Julie and the rest of their friends," states Lucinda Fox in the *School Librarian*, "could easily be the children you might expect to meet in your own neighborhood."

"Writing for radio determined my style and it is still my favourite medium," Doherty says in her *Magpies* interview with Nieuwenhuizen. "I learned that each chapter has to work on its own and has to be satisfying as a unit. Clear, strong voices are important too. I started off by asking myself what young people want to find when they go through the door into the secret garden that a writer creates. I decided that maybe what they most wanted to find was themselves, or someone very like themselves, doing the kind of things that they do, or would love to do if they had the chance." In radio, she reveals to her *SATA* interviewer, "the writer can go anywhere and so can the listener. The world inside your head is perhaps the greatest—it is obviously the greatest imaginative world there is . . . as long as the language is strong enough and vivid enough that you're going to take your reader with you, you're going to invoke an emotional response and you're going to create the color."

The experiences of young people growing up form the basis for her next two books, *White Peak Farm* and *Children of Winter*. They share other elements in common as well. "*White Peak Farm* is set in nearby Derbyshire, which I love," the author told *CA*, "as is *Children of Winter*, a story of the plague year." Like *How Green You Are!* and *The Making of Fingers Finnigan*, *White Peak Farm* consists of a series of interrelated stories about a farm family. Jeannie Tanner, the young narrator, tells the story of how her family copes with the rhythms of the farm and the problems that arise from everyday life. Jeannie's experiences lead her to the realization "that it is not permanence that is the heart of life," explains a *Publishers Weekly* reviewer, "but rather a steady stream of changes, big and small."

"Much of the life of the stories," writes *Times Educational Supplement* reviewer Geoff Fox, "stems from the tension between the emerging young people and the claims of both the land and a brooding patriarch of a father (*not* a stock character)." Jeannie's grandmother moves to a hospice for the terminally ill, her sister Kathleen elopes with the son of a neighbor, and her brother Martin chooses art school over the family farm. Finally, Mr. Tanner himself is permanently crippled in an accident involving a tractor and has to surrender control of the farm to his wife. "In the end," concludes Trev Jones in the *School Library Journal*, "all is not-so-neatly resolved through love and family bonding." The novel, states Nancy Vasilakis in *Horn Book*, "is a bittersweet meditation on the effects of people and place on the individual." "The richness of the novel's imagery and thematic content and the finely-textured ambiguities of its characterizations," she concludes, "will leave readers with sweet, lingering memories."

Children of Winter differs from *White Peak Farm* because it incorporates the fantasy element of time travel. In the story, a family hiking through the countryside is caught in a storm and seeks shelter in an old barn where centuries earlier a couple had sheltered their children to save them from the effects of the plague. When the modern-day children, Catherine, Patsy, and Andrew, are left alone by their parents, time is altered. "The time-slip is made possible," writes Margery Fisher in *Growing Point*, "because Catherine Tebbutt is a sensitive, dreamy girl, ready to respond to the influence of the old barn where they shelter from the storm and to the spirit of an earlier Catherine Tebbutt." Catherine and her small brother and sister "emerge to join a sadly depleted village group in celebrating the end of the terror." "The book may serve a two-fold purpose," states Lucinda Fox in the *School Librarian*: "for escape reading, or as a vivid picture of what might have happened to a family in plague-stricken England." Doherty also mixes fantasy elements in several later volumes, including her young adult novel *Spellhorn* and her books for younger readers *Tilly Mint Tales* and *Tilly Mint and the Dodo*.

Carnegie Awards

"*Granny Was a Buffer Girl* reflects the loss of the steel industry of Sheffield, my adopted city," Doherty told *CA*, "but is more importantly a book for teenagers about aspects of love: a difficult and essential subject to explore." Like *White Peak Farm*, it is an intergenerational family story, but the family in question is urban rather than rural. The narrator, Jess, is about to leave home for a year studying in France. She brings her family together and listens to their stories about their love for each other. "In each generation there is love rewarded and love betrayed," writes a *Kirkus Review* critic: "the contrasts and parallels enrich the meaning of all." Her grandparents Bridie and Jack defy their religious differences when they fall in love and marry in spite of their parents' opposition. Her own parents have to confront the slow sickness and death of Jess's brother Danny, who suffered from a wasting disease.

"Not expecting her to understand him, Grandad Albert tells seventeen-year old Jess that Love doesn't have much to do with kissing and cuddling," states *School Librarian* contributor Dorothy Atkinson. "What it does have to do with is the substance of this story: family loyalties, disappointments, great griefs, and brief, vivid happiness." Her grandmother Dorothy recalls how she worked in Sheffield's world-famous cutlery industry as a "buffer girl," cleaning and polishing silverware. She reveals that, although the factory owner's son had been a suitor, she chose her husband Albert—a common steelworker—because of the timing of his proposal. "Such pieces of distant family folklore, and the more recent death of her young brother," explains a *Publishers Weekly* reviewer, "give Jess the courage to embrace changes in her life head-on." The British Library Association honored *Granny Was a Buffer Girl* with its Carnegie Medal in 1986.

Street Child and *Tough Luck* return to the world of schoolchildren. *Street Child* is reminiscent of "Charles Dickens's novels," reveals a *Publishers Weekly* contributor. "Homelessness is the central topic of this grim and gripping novel set in Victorian England." The book tells the story of Jim Jarvis, an orphan condemned by poverty to wander the streets of London in the 1860s. "Unlike Dickens, Doherty doesn't romanticize Jim's hard times," writes a *Kirkus Reviews* critic. "His trials are soberingly realistic, his encounters with those who wish they could help him poignantly brief." Jim's story has a happy ending, however: he is adopted by Thomas John Barnardo, a wealthy Irishman who founded and maintained schools and homes for destitute children in Victorian London. *Tough Luck* is set in a modern classroom and looks at the problems of several teenage students. The problems are as varied as the student body: Twagger, whose mother is missing and who consistently skips school as a consequence; Sprat, whose mother left home after an unexpected pregnancy; and Nasim, a Pakistani student who had begun to settle in when she was summoned home to complete an arranged marriage. Doherty "refuses to make her adults into easy caricatures," declares Geoff Fox in the *Times Educational Supplement*. A *Junior Bookshelf* reviewer states, "This book, rooted in experience, is told straightforwardly and with truth."

Doherty won her second Carnegie Medal for *Dear Nobody*, about two teenagers, Helen and Chris, who conceive a child. The story is told largely from Chris's point of view. He wants to marry Helen, but she has other plans. "I wanted to look seriously and genuinely at love because that's a major part of what being a teenager is about," Doherty declares in her *SATA* interview. Helen and Chris learn about themselves and their families in the turmoil that follows. As her pregnancy advances, Helen withdraws from Chris and begins to concentrate on her unborn child, to whom she addresses a series of letters—the "dear nobody" of the title. Chris encounters the mother who deserted him years before; Helen learns that her own mother was born out of wedlock. The two teenagers are reunited after the birth of their daughter. Helen and Chris, Doherty explains, "never totally separate . . . it's a journey towards their own parents. It's a way for them to find out as much as they can about their own parents—to come to an understanding about what *parenthood* means."

Doherty chose a distinctly individual approach to a problem theme. "I wanted it to speak directly to teenagers about something that is very important to them: love," she states in *SAAS*. "Most of all, I wanted to speak to boys. If there is any justification at all in writing and selling books for teenagers it is that it gives them a place to find themselves, the inner, emotional self, taking that exciting and bewildering and sometimes distressing journey towards adulthood." "The subject matter is one that every teenager wonders and worries about," Doherty tells Nieuwenhuizen. "How to step away from the familiar territory of childhood and strike out alone. I wanted to write a love story, not a romance. Helen needs to make her own decision. To reach this point, she needs to face a number of trials, overcome a number of obstacles. She was my version of the hero. Her journey is not a cosmic one, but a personal one."

Critics largely celebrated Doherty's accomplishment in *Dear Nobody*. "Told as a flashback, in some of the loveliest, most lyrical prose to be found in YA fiction," says *School Library Journal* contributor

In this 1991 novel, teenagers Helen and Chris must confront the issues surrounding her unwanted pregnancy.

Alice Casey Smith, "Helen and Chris narrate the consequences of one night's unprotected passion that changes the course of their lives forever." "Doherty's excellent writing, combined with the unusual dual point of view from the narration and the letters," declares a reviewer in the *Bulletin of the Center for Children's Books*, "makes this a richly nuanced examination of a familiar situation." "Doherty realistically depicts two nice young people who care for each other as they struggle to cope with the consequences of their incaution," *Booklist* reviewer Stephanie Zvirin states. "While the story outline is all too familiar, Doherty sets her version of it apart by plunging into her characters' emotions in a way that will move you to tears."

"Don't concentrate on one kind of writing," Doherty advises aspiring writers in her *Magpies* interview, "and write a little bit every day. Writing is rather like learning an instrument. You need to limber up, perhaps by writing in a diary. You need to keep the 'word muscles' going. Every day, something happens that is worth writing about— jot it down." People who want to be authors, she tells the *SATA* interviewer, ought to "write and write and to love writing. To write about anything and everything. To keep a notebook, to make writing part of their daily life whether or not they call it a diary or a journal. To just pour every-

---

If you enjoy the works of Berlie Doherty, you may also want to check out the following books and films:

Janni Howker, *Isaac Campion*, 1986.
John Neufeld, *Sharelle*, 1983.
Gary Paulsen, *The Winter Room*, 1989.
Gayle Pearson, *One Potato, Tu: Seven Stories*, 1992.
Places in the Heart, Twentieth-Century Fox, 1984.

---

thing out, to keep going back to things. To take an idea that they've written about and bring it out again and rework it—never to think of something as being finished." "Sometimes children say to me, What would you do if you didn't write?' and the answer, now, is that I don't know," Doherty declares in *SAAS*. "I can't imagine doing anything else."

■ Works Cited

Baines, R., review of *The Making of Fingers Finnigan, Junior Bookshelf*, December, 1983, p. 242.
Review of *Dear Nobody, Bulletin of the Center for Children's Books*, January, 1993, p 143.
Doherty, Berlie, sketch in *Contemporary Authors*, Volume 131, Gale, 1991, pp. 152-53.
Doherty, Berlie, essay in *Something about the Author Autobiography Series*, Volume 16, Gale, 1993, pp. 111-26.
Doherty, Berlie, interview in *Something about the Author*, Volume 72, Gale, 1993, pp. 48-53.
Fisher, Margery, review of *Children of Winter, Growing Point*, May, 1985, p. 4432.

Fox, Geoff, review of *White Peak Farm, Times Educational Supplement*, September 7, 1984, p. 29.
Fox, Geoff, "Through Teenage Eyes," *Times Educational Supplement*, June 5, 1987, p. 61.
Fox, Lucinda, review of *How Green You Are!, School Librarian*, September, 1982, p. 232.
Fox, Lucinda, review of *Children of Winter, School Librarian*, March, 1986, p. 45.
Review of *Granny Was a Buffer Girl, Kirkus Reviews*, January 1, 1988, p. 53.
Review of *Granny Was a Buffer Girl, Publishers Weekly*, January 29, 1988, p. 431.
Jones, Trev, review of *White Peak Farm, School Library Journal*, March, 1990, pp. 234-35.
Nieuwenhuizen, Agnes, "Berlie Doherty: Daydreams and Things That Matter," *Magpies*, July, 1995, pp. 10-13.
Smith, Alice Casey, review of *Dear Nobody, School Library Journal*, October, 1992, p. 140.
Review of *Street Child, Kirkus Reviews*, October 15, 1994, p. 1406.
Review of *Street Child, Publishers Weekly*, September 19, 1994, p. 71.
Thatcher, A., review of *How Green You Are!, Junior Bookshelf*, August, 1982, pp. 150-51.
Review of *Tough Luck, Junior Bookshelf*, August, 1987, p. 177.
Review of *White Peak Farm, Publishers Weekly*, March 30, 1990, p. 63.
Vasilakis, Nancy, review of *White Peak Farm, Horn Book*, July/August, 1990, p. 461.
Zvirin, Stephanie, review of *Dear Nobody, Booklist*, October 1, 1992, p. 329.

■ For More Information See

BOOKS

Chambers, Nancy, editor, *The Signal Selection of Children's Books 1988*, Thimble Press, 1989.
Children's Literature Review, Volume 21, Gale, 1990.
Twentieth-Century Children's Writers, 3rd edition, St. James Press, 1989.

PERIODICALS

Booklist, October 1, 1992, p. 329.
Books for Keeps, June, 1987, p. 3; July, 1987, p. 11.
Bulletin of the Center for Children's Books, March, 1988, p. 133; March, 1996, p. 224.
Horn Book, August, 1987, p. 177; May/June, 1988; July/August, 1990, pp. 461-62; May/June, 1996, p. 339.
Junior Bookshelf, December, 1984, p. 254.

Kirkus Reviews, August 15, 1992, p. 1059.

Publishers Weekly, September 7, 1992, p. 97.

School Librarian, December, 1984; November, 1989, p. 159; November, 1993, p. 162.

School Library Journal, October, 1992, p. 140.

Spectator, December 11, 1993, pp. 45-46.

Times Educational Supplement, January 18, 1985; February 13, 1987, p. 48; November 11, 1988; September 1-7, 1989, p. 957.

Times Literary Supplement, December 16, 1988, p. 1406.

Voice of Youth Advocates, June, 1988, p. 84; October, 1990, p. 216; June, 1996, pp. 94-95.*

—Sketch by Kenneth R. Shepherd

Clint Eastwood

■ Personal

Full name, Clinton Eastwood, Jr.; born May 31, 1930, in San Francisco, CA; son of Clinton and Ruth Eastwood; married Maggie Johnson, 1953 (divorced, 1980), married Dina Ruiz (a television broadcaster), March 31, 1996; children: (first marriage) Kyle, Alison; (with actress Frances Fisher) Francesca Ruth. *Education:* Attended Oakland Technological High School and Los Angeles City College, 1953-54. *Politics:* Republican. *Hobbies and other interests:* Jazz music.

■ Addresses

Office—Malpaso Productions, 4000 Warner Boulevard, Burbank, CA 91522.

■ Career

Film actor, director, and producer; founder and owner, Malpaso Productions, 1969—. Appeared as Rowdy Yates in the television series *Rawhide*, CBS, 1959-66. Also appeared in episodes of several tele-

vision shows, including *The West Point Story*, ABC, 1957, *Wagon Train*, NBC, 1957, *Maverick*, ABC, 1959, *Mr. Ed*, CBS, 1962, and *Crazy about the Movies*, Cinemax, 1993; appeared in several television specials, including *James Stewart: A Wonderful Life*, PBS, 1987, *The Presidential Inaugural Gala*, CBS, 1989, *The Siskel and Ebert Special*, CBS, 1990, *Clint Eastwood's Favorite Films*, Cinemax, 1993, *Here's Looking at You, Warner Bros.*, TNT, 1993, and *Clint Eastwood Talking with David Frost*, PBS, 1993. Director of an episode of *Amazing Stories*, NBC, 1985. Performed on the single "Smokin' the Hive" with Randy Travis, 1990. Mayor of Carmel, CA, 1986-88; owner of Hog's Breath Inn, Carmel, CA; former lumberjack in Oregon, steel-furnace stoker, and gas pumper. Member of the National Council on the Arts, 1973. *Military service:* U.S. Army, Special Services, 1950-54. *Member:* Directors Guild of America, Screen Actors Guild, American Film Institute, American Federation of Television and Radio Artists.

■ Awards, Honors

Golden Globe Award, world film favorite—male, Hollywood Foreign Press Association, 1971; People's Choice Awards, favorite motion picture actor, 1981, 1984, 1985, and 1987; named Chevalier des Lettres by the French government, 1985; shared Golden Apple Star of the Year Award, Hollywood Women's Press Club, 1985; People's Choice Award as an "all-time favorite," 1988; Cecil B. De Mille Award, Hollywood Foreign Press Association, 1988; Orson Welles Award, best directorial achievement—English language, 1988, and Golden Globe Award, best director, Hollywood Foreign Press Association, 1989, both for *Bird;* Hasty Pudding Man of the Year Award, Hasty Pudding Theatricals, 1991; Golden Globe Award, best director, Academy Awards, best director and best picture, and Academy Award nomination, best actor, all 1992, all for *Unforgiven;* named NATO/ShoWest Director of the Year, city of Los Angeles, 1993; Irving G. Thalberg Memorial Award, Academy of Motion Picture Arts and Sciences, 1995.

■ Films

DIRECTOR

Play Misty for Me, Universal, 1971.
Breezy, Universal, 1973.
High Plains Drifter, Universal, 1973.
The Eiger Sanction, Universal, 1975.
The Outlaw Josey Wales, Warner Bros., 1976.
The Gauntlet, Warner Bros., 1977.
Bronco Billy, Warner Bros., 1980.
(And producer) *Firefox,* Warner Bros., 1982.
(And producer) *Honkytonk Man,* Warner Bros., 1982.
(And producer) *Sudden Impact,* Warner Bros., 1983.
(And producer) *Pale Rider,* Warner Bros., 1985.
(And producer) *Heartbreak Ridge,* Warner Bros., 1986.
(And producer) *Bird,* Warner Bros., 1988.
(And producer) *White Hunter, Black Heart,* Warner Bros., 1990.
(And producer) *Unforgiven,* Warner Bros., 1992.
A Perfect World, Warner Bros., 1993.
The Bridges of Madison County, Warner Bros., 1995.

PRODUCER

Tightrope, Warner Bros., 1984.
The Dead Pool, Warner Bros., 1988.

EXECUTIVE PRODUCER

Thelonius Monk: Straight, No Chaser, Warner Bros., 1988.
(And director) *The Rookie,* Warner Bros., 1990.

ACTOR

Lab technician, *Revenge of the Creature,* Universal, 1955.
First Saxon, *Lady Godiva,* Universal, 1955.

First pilot, *Tarantula,* Universal, 1955.
Jonesy, *Francis in the Navy,* Universal, 1955.
Will, *Never Say Goodbye,* Universal, 1956.
Jack Rice, *The First Travelling Saleslady,* RKO, 1956.
Dumbo, *Escapade in Japan,* Universal/RKO, 1957.
Keith Williams, *Ambush at Cimarron Pass,* Twentieth Century-Fox, 1958.
George Moseley, *Lafayette Escadrille* (also known as *Hell Bent for Glory*), Warner Bros., 1958.
The Man With No Name, *A Fistful of Dollars* (also known as *Per Un Pugno Di Dollari*), United Artists (UA), 1964.
The Man With No Name, *For a Few Dollars More* (also known as *Per Qualche Dollaro in Piu*), UA, 1967.
Joe, *The Good, the Bad, and the Ugly* (also known as *Il Buono, It Brutto, Il Cattivo*), UA, 1967.
Lieutenant Morris Schaffer, *Where Eagles Dare,* Metro-Goldwyn-Mayer (MGM), 1968.
Jed Cooper, *Hang 'em High,* UA, 1968.
Walt Coogan, *Coogan's Bluff,* Universal, 1968.
Husband, *The Witches* (also known as *Le Streghe* and *Les Sorcieres*), Lopert, 1969.
Pardner, *Paint Your Wagon,* Paramount, 1969.
Kelly, *Kelly's Heroes* (also known as *The Warriors*), MGM, 1970.
Hogan, *Two Mules for Sister Sara,* Universal, 1970.
John McBurney, *The Beguiled,* Universal, 1971.
Dave Garland, *Play Misty for Me,* Universal, 1971.
Harry Callahan, *Dirty Harry,* Warner Bros., 1971.
Title role, *Joe Kidd,* Universal, 1972.
The Stranger, *High Plains Drifter,* Universal, 1973.
Harry Callahan, *Magnum Force,* Warner Bros., 1973.
John "Thunderbolt" Doherty, *Thunderbolt and Lightfoot,* UA, 1974.
Jonathan Hemlock, *The Eiger Sanction,* Universal, 1975.
Title role, *The Outlaw Josey Wales,* Warner Bros., 1976.
Harry Callahan, *The Enforcer,* Warner Bros., 1976.
Ben Shockley, *The Gauntlet,* Warner Bros., 1977.
Philo Beddoe, *Every Which Way But Loose,* Warner Bros., 1978.
Frank Morris, *Escape from Alcatraz,* Paramount, 1979.
Bronco Billy McCoy, *Bronco Billy,* Warner Bros., 1980.
Philo Beddoe, *Any Which Way You Can,* Warner Bros., 1980.
Mitchell Gant, *Firefox,* Warner Bros., 1982.
Red Stovall, *Honkytonk Man,* Warner Bros., 1982.
Harry Callahan, *Sudden Impact,* Warner Bros., 1983.
Wes Block, *Tightrope,* Warner Bros., 1984.
Lieutenant Speer, *City Heat,* Warner Bros., 1984.

The Preacher, *Pale Rider*, Warner Bros., 1985.
Sergeant Thomas "Gunny" Highway, *Heartbreak Ridge*, Warner Bros., 1986.
Harry Callahan, *The Dead Pool*, Warner Bros., 1988.
Tommy Noak, *Pink Cadillac*, Warner Bros., 1989.
John Wilson, *White Hunter, Black Heart*, Warner Bros., 1990.
Nick Pulovski, *The Rookie*, Warner Bros., 1990.
William Munny, *Unforgiven*, Warner Bros., 1992.
Red Garnett, *A Perfect World*, Warner Bros., 1993.
Frank Horrigan, *In the Line of Fire*, Columbia, 1993.
Robert Kincaid, *The Bridges of Madison County*, Warner Bros., 1995.

Also appeared in *Star in the Dust*, 1956.

OTHER

Author of film songs, including "How Much I Care," *Heartbreak Ridge*, Warner Bros., 1986; "Claudia's Theme," *Unforgiven*, Warner Bros., 1992; and "Big Fran's Baby," *A Perfect World*, Warner Bros., 1993. Also contributor of music to the films *Tightrope* and *Pale Rider*.

■ Sidelights

"You get trapped by an image, but I've overcome it to some degree," commented Clint Eastwood in a *Gentleman's Quarterly* (*GQ*) interview with Bernard Weinraub. "What the hell! You make an impact in a certain kind of role and everyone thinks you're that person. That's fine. It's nice in a way—you've set out to do what you want to do. But I don't carry a .44 Magnum around. . . . I've fought my way out of the genre."

Still, as *Cosmopolitan* writer Michael Segell noted, "Eastwood invites comparison to the rugged, laconic tough guys he's played during thirty-plus years of filmmaking. A loner with conservative working-class values . . . he admits to sharing a few traits of temperament with some of the maverick characters he's come to be identified with: Dirty Harry, The Man With No Name, William Munny (the hero of *Unforgiven*), and other moral avengers whose gritty independence pushes them to the fringes of society." Over the course of his acting and directing career, Eastwood has become entrenched as a true icon of American film on the strength of these roles.

One of the movie world's most enduringly popular figures since he first burst on the scene in the mid-1960s in *A Fistful of Dollars*, Eastwood's critical reputation has undergone a fascinating metamorphosis over the years. His work in Sergio Leone's Man-With-No-Name trilogy (*A Fistful of Dollars*, *For a Few Dollars More*, and *The Good, the Bad, and the Ugly*) and his portrayal of lone-wolf police detective Harry Callahan in the Dirty Harry movies prompted bitter denunciations from many prominent critics, who branded the violent films as amoral, sexist, and fascist in tone.

As the years passed, though, and Eastwood's body of work grew, a re-evaluation of the merits of his acting and directing abilities took place. Robert E. Kapsis noted in *Society* that as far back as the mid-1980s critics such as Vincent Canby confessed that they were rethinking their opinions on Eastwood. As quoted by Kapsis, Canby wrote, "I'm just now beginning to realize that, though Mr. Eastwood may have been improving over the years, it's also taken all these years for most of us to recognize his very consistent grace and wit as a filmmaker." Kapsis subsequently remarked that "this critical re-evaluation occurred partly because Eastwood apparently made all the right career moves in reshaping his reputation. He would often select properties that challenged his earlier macho image without the constraint of a critical discourse hostile to such efforts. Also critics, writing during the less radical 1980s, could acknowledge that the charge that Eastwood was a 'fascistic' director was a vast overstatement."

The changing tide of opinion regarding the quality of Eastwood's work as an actor and director crystallized with the 1992 release of *Unforgiven*, a Western which received Academy Awards for Best Picture and Best Director (and a Best Actor nomination for Eastwood as well). Reviewers hailed the film as a masterpiece, pointing especially to Eastwood's portrayal of William Munny, a formerly violent man ashamed of his past who takes up his guns one last time. Critics noted how the dark tale destroyed much of the mythology built up around Western heroes. (Ironically, earlier Eastwood films such as *A Fistful of Dollars*, *The Outlaw Josey Wales*, and *High Plains Drifter* had contributed greatly to such myths.) *Film Comment* writer Henry Sheehan spoke for many when he contended that "*Unforgiven* is the harsh, brilliant culmination, indeed consummation, of themes, motifs, characterizations, and critical attitudes that have evolved in Clint Eastwood's Westerns for more than thirty years."

Early Years Marked by Traveling

Eastwood was born on May 31, 1930, in San Francisco. He grew up in post-Depression California, and his parents were often forced to move the family in their search for work. Eastwood's father worked at various times as a salesman, pipe fitter, and defense-industry worker, and his blue-collar work ethic was passed on to his son and daughter. "I guess I was what they now call a latchkey child," Eastwood recalled in his conversation with Weinraub. "My parents were working-class people. They both worked a lot. They were very caring. . . . My father believed nothing came to nothing. You had to work like hell."

After his father secured a steady job in Oakland, Eastwood was able to settle in at one school for his high school years. He graduated from Oakland Technical High School and moved on to a series of jobs. He pumped gas, hauled lumber,

In the 1971 film *Dirty Harry*, Eastwood introduced perhaps his most famous character, maverick cop Harry Callahan.

worked in factories, and fought fires for the Forest Service before being drafted at the age of twenty. Eastwood was stationed at the Fort Ord army base in Monterey, California, where he spent much of his time working as a lifeguard. It was during his stay at Fort Ord that Eastwood became acquainted with a group of soldiers who wanted to be actors.

After his discharge from the service in 1953, Eastwood enrolled at Los Angeles City College and set about trying to make some inroads in Hollywood. He also married Maggie Johnson, with whom he eventually had two children—Kyle and Alison. In 1955 Eastwood was signed by Universal Studios for $75 a week as a contract player, and he quickly tallied up a string of bit roles in B-pictures. "I'd always play the young lieutenant or the lab technician who came in and said, 'He went that way' or 'This happened' or 'Doctor, here are the X-rays' and he'd say, 'Get lost, kid,' I'd go out and that would be the end of it," he told an interviewer for *Show*. Universal finally dropped Eastwood after eighteen months, and he was forced to make ends meet as a mechanic and garbage man.

In 1959, though, Eastwood secured the role of Rowdy Yates in *Rawhide*, a popular television series. During a break in the shooting for the show in 1964, Eastwood accepted an offer to star in *A Fistful of Dollars*, a movie being shot in Spain by Italian director Sergio Leone. "In the TV Western," Eastwood told Weinraub, "I was playing a good guy, and I kept thinking, Wouldn't it be great to play the hero sort of like the villain is normally played and give the villain some heroic qualities?" Eastwood convinced Leone to drop a great deal of the dialogue in the original script, stripping his character down to a terse, menacing mystery man with ice in his veins and a penchant for gallows humor. Sheehan noted that "this deliberately unsettling humor quickly became a hallmark of (most) Eastwood performances, accomplished with expressions as whittled-down as a suspicious shift of the eyes."

Eastwood reprised the role as the Man With No Name in two subsequent films, *For a Few Dollars More* and *The Good, the Bad, and the Ugly*. Leone's violent trilogy struck a chord with audiences in Europe (where the movies were first released) and the United States, and, as Peter Buskind suggested in *Premiere*, "established the formula for the

Eastwood western: the Man with No Name squinting in the fierce midday sun, laconic, cool, and laid-back but remorseless and vengeful at the same time, coming from nowhere, going nowhere, without a past, without a future."

Eastwood proved adept at capitalizing on his immensely popular screen persona. In 1968 he returned to the United States to star in *Hang 'Em High*, the first of several violent Westerns (including *Coogan's Bluff*, *Two Mules for Sister Sara*, and *Joe Kidd*) in which the actor played characters that resembled, at least to some extent, the vengeful and implacable gunslinger of the Leone epics.

The Arrival of Dirty Harry

In 1971 Eastwood weighed in with his first directorial effort. *Play Misty for Me* concerns a popular disc jockey (played by Eastwood) who is being stalked by a psychotic female fan. Skillfully rendered and executed, the film received positive reviews for the most part, but Eastwood's debut in the director's chair was quickly obliterated in the public's eye by the controversy that surrounded the release of *Dirty Harry*. This film was the first of a series of films in which Eastwood played the role of "Dirty" Harry Callahan, an embittered San Francisco police detective who tracks murderers and drug dealers with a vigilante zeal that puts him at odds with bureaucrats and a justice system that is portrayed as ineffectual and uncaring. The Dirty Harry films were directed by Don Siegel, who, along with Leone, was a key mentor to Eastwood during the actor's early film career.

Dirty Harry proved tremendously popular with the ticket-buying public, but many reviewers savaged the film (and its sequels). Influential *New Yorker* critic Pauline Kael charged that the movie was fascist in tone and deeply immoral. Hers was by no means the only voice leveling such accusations. When asked by *Psychology Today* contributor Stuart Fischoff about the social commentary in *Dirty Harry* and the other films featuring Harry Callahan (*Magnum Force*, *The Enforcer*, *Sudden Impact*, and *The Dead Pool*), Eastwood responded, "I approached it from the uncomplicated point of view. That it was an exciting detective story but it also addressed the issue of the victims of violent crime. In the 1960s and early '70s, it was very fashionable to address the plight of the criminals instead

of the victims. Dirty Harry came along and it seemed like it was ahead of its time." *New York Times Magazine* writer John Vinocur similarly argued that "what *Dirty Harry* did in the 1970s was to outrun an American political phenomenon by close to a decade. In the series involving the rebellious detective, Eastwood caught a mood of blue-collar discontent with a country portrayed in the films as being run by bureaucrats, sociologists, appeasers and incompetents. American society's deepest incapacity, the Dirty Harry films said, was in failing to protect the normal lives of its normal people."

Eastwood has been a prolific artist throughout his career, and the 1970s were no exception. In addition to the Dirty Harry movies, he starred in and directed *The Eiger Sanction* (1975) and *The Gauntlet* (1977), and returned to the mythical West in *High Plains Drifter* (1973) and *The Outlaw Josey Wales* (1976). Both of the films were directed by Eastwood, and there were reviewers who detected promising elements in the works. Commenting on *High Plains Drifter*, Sheehan remarked that "Eastwood displays a . . . startling stylistic maturity in his first Western feature." *The Outlaw Josey Wales*, meanwhile, was touted as "an attempt to socialize, to humanize, The Man With No Name," according to *American Film* writer Dave Kehr, who went on to contend that Eastwood had created a work of "grandeur" and "moral seriousness."

The late 1970s and early 1980s also saw some dramatic changes in Eastwood's personal life. In 1977, after twenty-four years of marriage, he left his wife and began seeing actress Sandra Locke, who subsequently appeared in a number of his films. His divorce was finalized in 1984, and Johnson received $25 million as part of the settlement.

By the early 1980s, it was clear that Eastwood intended to use his box office muscle to experiment, to investigate roles and stories that did not hinge on the actor's usual portrayal of some flinty-eyed dispenser of retribution. In 1980 Eastwood directed and starred in *Bronco Billy*, in which the title character leads "an impoverished cowboy circus through the back roads of the Midwest in a decidedly corny fable about idealism and perseverance," wrote Doug Brod and Steve Daly in *Entertainment Weekly*. "A sentimental, arch and harmlessly good-natured" film, according to

Newsweek's David Ansen, *Bronco Billy* still stands as one of Eastwood's favorites. Two years later he released another sentimental movie, *Honkytonk Man,* in which he portrays a dying country singer touring during the Depression.

The Political Arena

The film that really got people's attention, though, was *Tightrope.* *Time* reviewer Richard Schickel called Eastwood's performance as tough police detective Wes Block a fascinating one because "he has dared to play *into* type, to bring to the surface certain disturbing aspects of his Dirty Harry character." Schickel remarked that Eastwood's decision to play a detective who in several ways resembles the murderer he is hunting down "represents a provocative advance in the consciousness, self and social, of Eastwood's one-man genre."

In 1985 Eastwood returned to the West with *Pale Rider,* in which he plays a mysterious preacher who delivers innocents from greedy strip miners.

The following year, however, it was Eastwood's fledgling political career that made headlines. In 1986 he campaigned for and won the mayor's office in Carmel-by-the-Sea, California, a small coastal village in the northern part of the state where the actor had lived since the early 1960s. Once installed as the new mayor, he initiated changes to the town's zoning laws and tackled the inevitable paperwork that accompanies the assumption of such a public office. *Time* contributor Paul A. Witteman noted that Eastwood "takes a kind of bemused pleasure in the minor crises that bedevil any small-town mayor. 'If someone had told me two years ago that I'd be spending time in someone else's garage, deciding if it could be moved three inches to the north,' he says ruefully, 'I would have said he'd lost it.'"

The actor declined to run for re-election after his term expired in 1988. "I'm not a good politician," he told Segell. "I could get along with people, but to sit there and fudge the truth all the time or omit things or say you're going to do something and know you're not going to do it—well, that's

Eastwood received the Academy Award for best director for his 1992 western, *Unforgiven.*

not me." Eastwood continued to make his home in Carmel into the mid-1990s, though, and residents confirm that Eastwood is far more likely to be found drinking beers with blue-collar golf buddies from the town than sipping martinis in Hollywood.

Passion for Jazz Seen in *Bird*

In 1988 Eastwood directed *Bird*, a film based on the life of legendary jazz musician Charlie Parker, a self-destructive genius who remains one of the jazz world's pre-eminent figures. A long-time jazz fan, Eastwood tackled the project enthusiastically. "When I was growing up in San Francisco there was a big classic-jazz revival in the Bay Area. I used to go to Hambone Kelly's, lie about my age, stand in the back and listen to Lu Watters and Turk Murphy play New Orleans jazz," recalled Eastwood in an interview with *Newsweek*'s Jack Kroll. "I played piano, I played a little cornet, I listened to a lot of rhythm and blues on radio. I think I was really a black guy in a white body."

Besides allowing Eastwood to indulge his passion for jazz music, *Bird* further solidified his rapidly growing standing as a director of merit. Reviewing the film for the *New Republic*, Stanley Kauffmann remarked that "Eastwood has been highly praised for his direction because, though he has directed before, people seem to be surprised that he knows a lot about films. In fact he's an old hand who has worked with many old hands." As a result, said Kroll, "*Bird* is an extraordinary work, made with honesty, insight and unmistakable love for the subject. . . . The movie is visual bebop, exultant and sorrowful, just like the music." For his part, Eastwood told *Film Quarterly* interviewer Ric Gentry that "of Charlie Parker's relatives and friends who've seen it, they're all moved by it and even a little spooked by it, that they were watching something they lived and they recognized as characteristic of what happened to them, and what Charlie Parker was like. I guess I'm as proud of that as I am of anything."

In 1989 Eastwood's thirteen-year relationship with actress Sandra Locke came to an end. Eastwood, who had initiated the breakup, was subsequently hit by Locke with a palimony lawsuit that featured several unsavory charges. Newspaper tabloids were quick to pounce on the acrimony, and

Eastwood was shaken by the resulting bad publicity. They eventually settled the suit out of court, agreeing not to discuss the arrangements. Eastwood began seeing actress Frances Fisher, with whom he had a daughter, Francesca (he and Fisher split up in the mid-1990s).

By the dawn of the 1990s Eastwood had settled on a movie-making formula that seemed beneficial both for him and Warner Brothers (Eastwood has long had a non-contractual, handshake agreement with the company). He still appeared in action-adventure films for the studio, invariably dispatching criminals and other unpleasant individuals with his trademark efficiency, but his work in those films also allowed him to freely pursue his own projects without worrying about their commercial viability. One of these projects was 1990's *White Hunter, Black Heart*, a fictionalized portrayal of famous movie director John Huston of *African Queen* fame. Many reviewers found it to be a flawed film, but they also recognized that, as *People* contributor Ralph Novak said, "Eastwood has had the courage to address a real and difficult phenomenon—the coexistence of artistic genius and personal immaturity in the same person." *Rolling Stone* reviewer Peter Travers praised his efforts as well, writing that Eastwood's performance, "like the movie, is a high-wire act that remains fascinating even when it falters." Eastwood himself professed to Weinraub that he enjoyed making the film, in part because the obsessive Huston was so unlike himself. "And yet I totally agree with one of his favorite lines," he said. "'When you make a film, you must forget anybody is ever going to see it. Just make it. Just stay true to it.' I believe that."

Eastwood Makes *Unforgiven*

While films like *Bird* and *White Hunter, Black Heart* suggested that Eastwood's filmmaking vision was growing increasingly complex and interesting, it was not until the 1992 release of *Unforgiven* that many reviewers conceded that the long-time actor was also a director of considerable skill. The film's story line concerns William Munny, an aging gunfighter-turned-farmer with small children who lives a life of grinding poverty. Munny, accompanied by his old partner and a young punk, sets out to collect the bounty on two cowboys who viciously slashed a prostitute. Munny and his party subsequently run afoul of Little Bill Daggett,

A psychopath threatens to kill the President of the United States in the 1993 thriller *In the Line of Fire,* featuring Eastwood as an aging Secret Service agent who is haunted by the memory of John F. Kennedy's assassination.

a jovial and sadistic sheriff. At the same time, Munny grapples with his dark past and his promise to his dead wife to forsake his previous life of violence.

Reviewers marveled at the complexity of *Unforgiven* and Eastwood's ability to realize his vision of the film. "In his long, many-chambered career, Clint Eastwood has exhibited both genuine talent and commercial cynicism," wrote *New York* critic David Denby. "In the Dirty Harry films and some of the thrillers, Westerns, and cop movies he directed himself, he easily exploited the American love of shooting-gallery violence. Under his pitiless monetary gaze, the bodies fell by the hundreds. And yet sterner impulses were obviously working in him—an obsession with isolated, tormented men. . . . [In *Unforgiven*] he has created a work of surprising moral complexity, a mordant yet sustained and even-flowing work of art." *Newsweek* reviewer David Ansen, meanwhile—a vehement critic of Eastwood's early films—wrote

that "the deeper *Unforgiven* plunges into violence, the more powerfully Eastwood reveals his disgust for the false mythology of the Western hero. A lot of violent movies have pushed an anti-violent message, but there's no taint of hypocrisy in Eastwood's methods here." *Unforgiven*, he concluded, is "a stunning, dark Western that may stand as actor/director Eastwood's summation of the form."

Unforgiven was honored with numerous awards, including Best Picture and Best Director Academy Awards, and Eastwood confirmed that it was a film that he was determined to make. "*Unforgiven* became a very important film for me, because it sort of summed up my feelings about certain movies I participated in," he told Fischoff. "Movies where killing is romantic. And here was a chance to show that it really wasn't so romantic."

A year later Eastwood directed (and co-starred with) Kevin Costner in *A Perfect World*, which tells the story of a sheriff's pursuit of an escaped convict in early 1960s America. While *A Perfect World* did not enjoy the same level of popular or critical acclaim that Eastwood's previous film had experienced, the director noted that its subject matter was the same. "I don't want to make family values the sole thing in *Perfect World*," he told *Entertainment Weekly*'s Anne Thompson, "but one of its big concerns is how violent acts rot your soul. It's the theme of *Unforgiven*—the young boy glamorizes being a killer until he finds out what it does to him, when he has a taste of it, something the character William Munny understood all along but couldn't communicate."

Another 1993 film in which Eastwood appeared—*In the Line of Fire*—was tremendously successful at the box office. Kapsis noted that Eastwood's "portrayal of a character haunted by his failure of having prevented President Kennedy's assassination thirty years earlier transforms a fairly conventional chase film into one of the most satisfying thrillers in recent years." In 1995 Eastwood appeared in and directed yet another blockbuster, *The Bridges of Madison County*. The film, which was based on the best-selling novel by Robert James Waller, also starred Meryl Streep.

Eastwood in the Director's Chair

During the filming of *The Bridges of Madison County*, Streep was exposed for the first time to Eastwood's famously economical and laid-back movie making style (he brings in nearly all of his films under budget). She thus joined the swelling ranks of actors and actresses who have lauded the atmosphere that Eastwood creates on the sets of the films he directs. "I feel the director's job, besides picking a script, is casting the right people," Eastwood told *Time*'s Richard Schickel. "But then after that, the real responsibility is to make those people feel at home. Set an atmosphere where everybody is extremely relaxed and there's no tension. Coming from acting, you know what rattles people, what rattles you. You have to set a tone and just demand a certain amount of tranquility."

Eastwood's film crew has remained intact over much of the past twenty years, an indication that they are comfortable with one another. Indeed, Eastwood is known for hanging out with the crew rather than retreating to his trailer during filming breaks on the set. "I really don't think he *knows*

he's Clint Eastwood," a friend told Weinraub. "I don't think he knows his power. We work in a world here where people think they're stars and demand chauffeur-driven limousines or private helicopter trips or behave like megalomaniacs. Here's a guy who gets in his pickup truck and drives himself to work, drives himself to the airport. No entourage. No bullshit."

Eastwood shows no inclination to retire from the world of cinema, either as an actor or director, and he continues to investigate new roles and stories that offer challenges. "If you lose enthusiasm, it shows, and no cosmeticizing will cover it up," he told Thompson. "It's what's beyond the eyes. It has nothing to do with how a person looks. I've had my ups and downs, but I've never lost it."

If you enjoy the works of Clint Eastwood, you may also want to check out the following books and films:

Joseph Wambaugh, *The Choirboys*, 1975.
Larry McMurtry, *Lonesome Dove*, 1985.
The French Connection, Twentieth-Century Fox, 1971.
Lethal Weapon, Warner Brothers, 1987.
The Searchers, Warner Brothers, 1956.

Eastwood's critical reputation has seen peaks and valleys as well, but as Gentry noted, an examination of Eastwood's films "reveals a dramatically diverse but thematically consistent body of work. Moreover, his independent, usually rootless characters may be presented with varying degrees of aesthetic depth, but there is an undeniable seriousness and passion to someone who makes films so prolifically." This passion, though, has been but one factor in the consolidation of Eastwood's unique and enduring place in American movies. As Kehr remarked, Eastwood "has fashioned a mythic image, drawing on elements both personal (the distinctive voice, glance, stride) and cultural (the American legends of the West, of individualism versus the law) to create the best-defined, most resonant screen persona in contemporary American cinema."

■ Works Cited

Ansen, David, "Bloody Good and Bloody Awful," *Newsweek*, August 10, 1992, p. 52.

Ansen, David, "Clint Goes Soft," *Newsweek*, June 23, 1980, p. 77.

Brod, Doug, and Steve Daly, "Direct from Clint," *Entertainment Weekly*, December 10, 1993, p. 24.

Buskind, Peter, "Any Which Way He Can," *Premiere*, April, 1993, p. 52.

Denby, David, "How the West Was Lost," *New York*, August 24, 1992, pp. 119-20.

Fischoff, Stuart, "Clint Eastwood & the American Psyche—A Rare Interview," *Psychology Today*, January/February, 1993, p. 38.

Gentry, Ric, "Clint Eastwood: An Interview," *Film Quarterly*, Spring, 1989, pp. 12-23.

Kapsis, Robert E., "Clint Eastwood's Politics of Reputation," *Society*, September/October, 1993, p. 68.

Kauffmann, Stanley, "Leaning on Lives," *New Republic*, October 31, 1988, pp. 26-28.

Kehr, Dave, "A Fistful of Eastwood," *American Film*, March, 1985, pp. 63-67.

Kroll, Jack, "Clint Makes Bird Sing," *Newsweek*, October 31, 1988, pp. 68-71.

Novak, Ralph, review of *White Hunter, Black Heart*, *People*, October 8, 1990, pp. 14-15.

Schickel, Richard, "The Gams and Guns of August," *Time*, August 27, 1984, p. 64.

Schickel, Richard, "The Cowboy and the Lady," *Time*, June 5, 1995, pp. 62-64.

Segell, Michael, "Clint Eastwood: The Man behind the Myth," *Cosmospolitan*, August, 1993, p. 154.

Sheehan, Henry, "Scraps of Hope: Clint Eastwood and the Western," *Film Comment*, September/October, 1992, pp. 17-27.

Show, February, 1970.

Thompson, Anne, "Eastwood's World," *Entertainment Weekly*, December 10, 1993, p. 22.

Travers, Peter, "The Past Picture Show," *Rolling Stone*, October 18, 1990, p. 45.

Vinocur, John, article in *New York Times Magazine*, February 24, 1985.

Weinraub, Bernard, "Even Cowboys Get Their Due," *Gentleman's Quarterly* (*GQ*), March, 1993, pp. 213-17, 286.

Witteman, Paul A., "No More Baby Kissing," *Time*, April 6, 1987, p. 34.

■ For More Information See

BOOKS

International Dictionary of Films and Filmmakers: Directors, 3rd edition, Gale, 1996.
Newsmakers, Gale, 1993.

PERIODICALS

Commentary, March, 1994.
Esquire, June, 1995.
Film Comment, September/October, 1992, pp. 12-14.
Good Housekeeping, July, 1995.
Journal of Popular Film, Fall, 1982.
Nation, July 5, 1980.
New Yorker, January 23, 1984; August 12, 1985; July 12, 1993; June 19, 1995.
Rolling Stone, June 29, 1995; August 24, 1995.
Sight and Sound, October, 1992.
Time, November 29, 1993.
Vogue, February, 1993, p. 220.*

—Sketch by Kevin Hillstrom

Allan W. Eckert

■ Personal

Born January 30, 1931, in Buffalo, NY; son of Edward Russell and Ruth (Roth) Eckert; married Joan Dowling, May 14, 1955 (divorced May, 1975); married Gail Ann Hagemann Green, April, 1976 (divorced June, 1978); married Nancy Cross Dent, 1978; children: (first marriage) Julie Ann, Joseph Matthew. *Education:* Attended University of Dayton, 1951-52, and Ohio State University, 1953-54. *Politics:* Uncommitted. *Religion:* Agnostic. *Hobbies and other interests:* Exploring uncharted areas of jungle or wilderness, collecting butterflies, moths, beetles, and other insects (collection includes over twenty-five thousand specimens), as well as fossils, mineral specimens, and other nature objects, collecting rare books (collection exceeds fifteen thousand volumes), observing nature, fishing.

■ Addresses

Home and office—655 Arlington Rd., Bellefontaine, OH 43311. *Agent*—William Reiss, John Hawkins & Associates, Inc., 71 West 23rd St., Ste. 1600, New York, NY 10010-4102.

■ Career

Writer. Prior to 1955, worked as postman, private detective, fireman, plastics technician, cook, dishwasher, laundryman, salesman, chemist's assistant, trapper, commercial artist, draftsman, and at some fifteen types of factory work and farming; National Cash Resister Co., Dayton, OH, associate editor of *NRC Factory News*, 1955-56; *Dayton Journal-Herald*, Dayton, at various times outdoor editor, nature editor, police reporter, columnist, and feature writer, 1957-60. Member of board of trustees, Dayton Museum of Natural History, Dayton, 1963-65; founder and board chairperson of Lemon Bay Conservancy (now Allan W. Eckert Conservancy), Englewood, FL; member of board of directors, Charlotte County (FL) Civic Association. Consultant to LaSalle University, Chicago, and Writer's Digest, Inc., Cincinnati, OH. *Military Service:* U.S. Air Force, 1948-52, became staff sergeant. *Member:* Outdoor Writers Association (board member, 1962-64), Society of Magazine Writers, Authors League of America, Authors Guild, American Society of Gem Cutters, Gemological Institute of America.

■ Awards, Honors

Pulitzer Prize nominations, 1964, 1965, 1967, 1968, 1970, and 1992; Ohioana Book Award, 1968, for *The Frontiersmen*; Friends of American Writers Awards, 1968, for *Wild Season* and *The Frontiers-*

men; Emmy Award, outstanding program achievement, National Academy of Television Arts and Sciences, 1968-69, for *Wild Kingdom*; Newbery Honor Book Award, American Library Association, 1972, Recognition of Merit, George C. Stone Center for Children's Books, 1975, and Austrian Juvenile Book of the Year Award, 1977, all for *Incident at Hawk's Hill*; Ph.D., Bowling Green State University, 1985; Second Annual Silver Arrow Humanitarian Award, Scioto Society, 1987; commended as Kentucky Colonel, Governor of the State of Kentucky, 1987. Some of Eckert's books have been *Reader's Digest* Condensed Book Club selections.

■ Writings

JUVENILE BOOKS

Bayou Backwaters (nature novel), illustrated by Joseph Cellini, Doubleday, 1967.

The Dreaming Tree (novel), Little, Brown, 1968.

The Crossbreed, illustrated by Karl E. Karalus, Little, Brown, 1968.

The King Snake (nature novel), illustrated by Franz Altschuler, Little, Brown, 1968.

Blue Jacket: War Chief of the Shawnees (biographical fiction), Little, Brown, 1968.

In Search of a Whale (nature novel), illustrated by Cellini, Doubleday, 1969.

Incident at Hawk's Hill (novel), illustrated by John Schoenherr, Little, Brown, 1971.

Savage Journey (novel), Little, Brown, 1979.

Song of the Wild (novel), Little, Brown, 1980.

Johnny Logan: Shawnee Spy, Little, Brown, 1983.

The Dark Green Tunnel ("Mesmerian Annals" series), illustrated by David Weisner, Little, Brown, 1984.

The Wand: The Return to Mesmeria ("Mesmerian Annals" series), illustrated by Weisner, Little, Brown, 1985.

DOCUMENTARY FICTION

The Great Auk, Little, Brown, 1963, published as *The Last Great Auk*, Goodchild Publishers, 1984.

The Silent Sky: The Incredible Extinction of the Passenger Pigeon, Little, Brown, 1965.

Wild Season (nature study), Little, Brown, 1967.

The Court-Martial of Daniel Boone, Little, Brown, 1973.

HISTORICAL NARRATIVES

A Time of Terror: The Great Dayton Flood, Little, Brown, 1965.

A Sorrow in Our Heart: The Life of Tecumseh, Bantam, 1992, limited edition published as *Sorrow of the Heart: The Life of Tecumseh*, 1992.

Men at War: Tecumseh, Smithmark Publishers, 1994.

That Dark and Bloody River: Chronicles of the Ohio River Valley, Bantam, 1995.

"WINNING OF AMERICA" SERIES

The Frontiersmen, Little, Brown, 1967.

Wilderness Empire, Little, Brown, 1968.

The Conquerors, Little, Brown, 1970.

The Wilderness War, Little, Brown, 1978.

Gateway to Empire, Little, Brown, 1982.

Twilight of Empire: A Narrative, Little, Brown, 1988.

NONFICTION

The Writer's Digest Course in Article Writing, Writer's Digest, 1962.

The Writer's Digest Course in Short Story Writing, Writer's Digest, 1965.

The Owls of North America: All the Species and Subspecies Described and Illustrated, illustrated by Karl E. Karalus, Doubleday, 1973, new edition, 1975, reprinted as *The Owls of North America, North of Mexico: All the Species and Subspecies Illustrated in Color and Fully Described*, Weathervane, 1987.

The Wading Birds of North America: All the Species and Subspecies Described and Illustrated, illustrated by Karalus, Doubleday, 1979, published as *The Wading Birds of North America (North of Mexico)*, Weathervane, 1987.

Earth Treasures: Where to Collect Minerals, Rocks, and Fossils in the United States, Volume 1: *The Northeastern Quadrant*, Volume 2: *The Southeastern Quadrant*, Volume 3: *The Northwestern Quadrant*, Volume 4: *The Southwestern Quadrant*, Harper, 1985-87.

NOVELS

The HAB Theory (science fiction), Little, Brown, 1976.

The Scarlet Mansion, Little, Brown, 1985.

OTHER

Tecumseh! (play), Little, Brown, 1974.
Whattizzit? Nature Pun Quizzes (humor), Landfall
Press, 1981.

Also author of more than 200 television scripts for
the series *Wild Kingdom* and of screenplays, including *The Legend of Koo-Tan*, 1971, *Wild Journey*, 1972,
The Kentucky Pioneers, 1972, and *George Rogers
Clark*, 1973. Contributor of more than 200 articles
to periodicals, including *Field & Stream*, *Reader's
Digest*, and *Saturday Evening Post*. Some of Eckert's
work has been translated into thirteen languages.
The Allan W. Eckert Collection was established at
Mugar Memorial Library, Boston University, 1965;
another Allan W. Eckert Collection, containing historical documents, manuscripts, and other pieces,
was established at the Filson Historical Society
Club, Louisville, KY, 1994.

■ Work in Progress

The World of Opals, tracing the history of the precious gemstone, including deposits worldwide, lore
and mythology of the opal, values, cutting techniques, and other data; two more novels in the
"Mesmerian Annals" series, *The Phantom Crystal*
and *The Witching Well*.

■ Adaptations

Incident at Hawk's Hill was adapted into a two-
part television movie by Walt Disney Productions.

■ Sidelights

Combining thorough research and factual details
with literary techniques such as dialogue and narration, Allan W. Eckert brings to life the world of
nature in his documentary fiction and recreates the
adventures and people of the past in his historical narratives. Able to capture the time and place
he is describing, Eckert's own excitement for his
subject matter makes for well-told stories that both
entertain and inform his readers. These same elements are transferred to his juvenile novels, which
include *Blue Jacket: War Chief of the Shawnees, Incident at Hawk's Hill*, and *Savage Journey*, as well as
the "Mesmerian Annals" nature and ecology series of fantasy novels. Having written such a va-

riety of books, Eckert sees only more opportunities in the future: "I fully anticipate that some
other wonderfully interesting thing will have captured my attention," he relates in an autobiographical essay for *Something about the Author
Autobiography Series* (*SAAS*). "It may be something
entirely apart from anything I have ever attempted
before—the chances are good, in fact, that it *will*
be—and once more I'll be off and running on the
research trail as I attempt to track down all the
information I can find or experience about it."

Although he was born in Buffalo, New York,
Eckert spent the majority of his childhood in the
Chicago area. His family was poor, but even
though he lived in the slums Eckert did not feel
deprived; he had known no other way of life. "I
was a child with an intense love of nature, which
is rather strange, since the Chicago slums was
hardly a place for developing an interest in wildlife," he explains in *SAAS*. "Yet, I remember
crawling about in the gangways between build-
ings or in vacant lots, overturning boards and
pieces of tin and other debris and studying the
creatures I found beneath—mice, worms, spiders,
centipedes, etc."

Things only got worse for Eckert and his family
when his father died shortly after his sixth birthday. "My mother had a difficult time providing
for my brother and me, but even though we did
not have much more than the bare necessities for
survival, she instilled us with good manners and
morals and gave us plenty of love and care," he
remembers in *SAAS*. She later met and married
Austin Rexroat, and Eckert moved to his house
in the country outside of Chicago. There were all
kinds of insects, birds, mammals, and other creatures for him to examine. His stepfather gave him
his first rifle for a birthday present, and taught
him how to use it safely.

Hitchhiking Adventures

All this nature study gave Eckert a desire to see
the rest of the country and the many wonders it
had to offer. "The notion grew on me that I
wanted to see a lot more of the United States,
especially areas that differed from where we lived,
and so I began to pester my mother to allow me
to go off on my own, as soon as school finished
for the summer, and hitchhike to distant places,"
recalls Eckert in his autobiographical essay. Hitch-

hiking was much safer at this time, and although Eckert's mother first said no, he was finally allowed to go after a lot of begging and a promise to send a postcard every other day; he also had to be back in time for the new school year. "I packed a duffle bag, a few changes of clothes, a few books to read, some writing materials, my fishing rod, and my little single-shot .22 rifle and started to hitchhike toward the northwest—toward Canada," writes Eckert in *SAAS.* "My mother had stuck a five-dollar bill to my stomach with adhesive tape for emergency use, if necessary. I was nine years old."

This first trip brought only good experiences for Eckert: all the people who picked him up were kind and interested in his adventure, he slept in old barns or made a little camp in the woods, and he ate roots and herbs with the fish he caught and the little animals he shot down. Reaching the Lake of the Woods region in Manitoba, Canada, he decided to spend his summer there. "I spent my days wandering about, mostly away from anywhere that people were, watching wildlife and studying the ways of nature," he describes in *SAAS.* "I caught plenty of fish to eat, and I was quite good with my rifle, so I rarely went hungry that whole summer long. It was a wonderful time, and I had many interesting adventures and learned a great deal about nature and survival." Having ignited a wanderlust spirit within himself during this first trip, Eckert continued to spend his summers this way all the way through high school. By the time he graduated he had traveled through the then forty-eight states of the United States, all of the lower provinces of Canada, and the Northern part of Mexico.

"The many different people I met and the closeness I shared with nature gave me a very good foundation for what I would eventually become— a writer—even though that goal was not firmly fixed in my mind at the time," Eckert asserts in his autobiographical essay. It was not until he was a junior in high school that Eckert even realized that people actually made money and supported themselves as writers. "I guess, when you come right down to it, I always wanted to be a writer," he continues in *SAAS.* "I loved to write, but I didn't realize one could actually make a living at it; to me, writing was simply great fun and a way of expressing myself and my ideas better than I could in conversation." Once he knew he could

make money doing something he loved to do, "the die was cast and I decided I would really become a professional writer," Eckert adds in *SAAS.* "I started writing in earnest, with the idea of selling what I wrote, and began submitting my manuscripts to publishers everywhere."

Eckert's early interests in nature and animals became the main focus of these many writings. The writers that influenced him were those who dealt with similar subject matter—Ernest Thompson Seton, a self-taught naturalist who learned from observation, and William Beebe, a scientist who brought natural history subjects to life in his writings. "So, with these authors to influence me, little wonder that I decided to become a writer, with the emphasis on nature," Eckert relates in *SAAS.* "And so I wrote . . . and wrote . . . and wrote. Unfortunately, though I by then had a substantial background for writing pieces on nature, I had no actual training in the mechanics of writing and how best to direct my writing. . . . I simply wrote and submitted . . . and received rejection after rejection. It was often quite discouraging but, fortunately, I had a very stubborn streak and would not give up, feeling that somehow, some way, someday I would make it as a writer."

By the time Eckert finished high school he had been writing for two years without selling anything. The family was still too poor to send him to college, so he enlisted in the United States Air Force in hopes of attending college with funds from the GI Bill. During the next four years Eckert continued his writing during his off-duty hours, often under difficult circumstances. "At night, when the barracks lights would have to be turned off, I would go to the latrine, where a single 60-watt bare bulb hung from the ceiling, but at least it was light," he recalls in *SAAS.* "There I would sit on a toilet and continue to write, often until the wee hours of the morning." Taking his discharge while stationed in Dayton, Ohio, Eckert enrolled at Ohio State University in Columbus, trying to stay close to a woman he was dating. Instead of enrolling in courses to further his writing career, though, Eckert decided to become a veterinarian. For two years he worked and went to school full-time while trying to continue writing. Experiencing difficulty in some of the required veterinarian courses and becoming extremely burned out, Eckert quit school at the end of these two years and moved to Dayton to be with his fiancee.

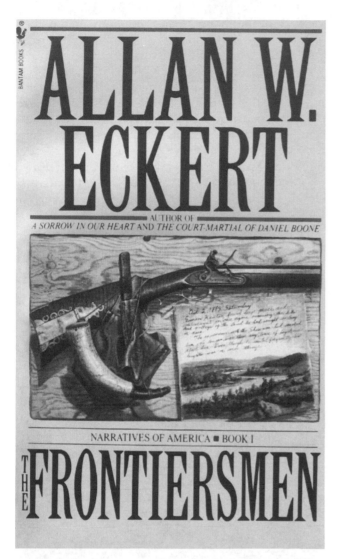

This 1967 historical narrative focuses on the lives of frontier explorer Simon Kenton and his rival, the Shawnee Indian leader Tecumseh.

While living in Dayton Eckert went through a series of jobs, including private detective, fireman, artist and illustrator, taxicab driver, stockman, and dishwasher. "Each new job I undertook held my interest only for so long as it took to learn the ropes, and then the very routine of the work would become overpoweringly boring and I would resign and move on to another field," explains Eckert in *SAAS*. Finally landing a job at the *Dayton Journal-Herald* daily newspaper, Eckert was able to write for a living, but he also continued his own writing, adding to his shoe boxes full of rejection slips. Realizing that he should have published something by this point, Eckert finally decided to look at his own writing from an objective standpoint. When he did, he found that it was lacking in direction. He had only been writing for himself. He began to examine the short stories and articles that were being published in magazines in regard to construction and audience. "Those writings were very specifically aimed at a certain readership; my own writing had been directionless and thus never quite made it for any particular periodical," Eckert points out in *SAAS*. "I guess I wasn't too bright; it had only taken me a dozen years to learn to be critical of my own writing."

Rewrites End Rejections

With this new insight, Eckert went back to his manuscripts and rewrote them with the a specific audience in mind, giving his writing the slant it needed. "My first sale, after having received 1,147 rejections over the preceding twelve years, came in 1958—a full-length article bought by *Field & Stream*," remembers Eckert in *SAAS*. The following two years brought more of the same—sales of articles, short stories, and poetry to several major periodicals. "I continued revising and rewriting all those so-often-rejected pieces and wound up selling them as well. Every last one of them!" he continues in *SAAS*. By 1960, Eckert was earning as much in free-lance sales as he earned in a year at the newspaper, so he quit his job and began writing full-time. Despite the fact that he continued to sell a steady stream of pieces to magazines, money began to dwindle; most of the magazines Eckert sold to paid on publication instead of on acceptance. "Gradually the money began coming in and financial matters eased," he relates in *SAAS*. "It was becoming fun, not only to research and write new pieces, but to rewrite the old ones and make them salable."

There was one short story in particular, though, that Eckert could not sell. Entitled "The Valiant Migration," the story described the final migration of a flock of auks (a penguin-like bird) just before they became extinct. "This short story had been rejected by over thirty magazines, although almost without exception the rejection, instead of a standard printed form, would arrive as a personal letter from the editor who would say how much he or she enjoyed the story, but just couldn't make it fit into their magazine's format," observes Eckert in *SAAS*. At this point, in early 1963, Eckert decided to turn the story into a short book that followed the life of the last auk on earth. It took him only five days to expand his story into *The Great Auk,* which begins with the birth of the auk, follows it into adulthood, describing its natural history, and ends with the final migration and the auk's death.

Eckert sent the manuscript to a literary agent with whom he had previously corresponded, and it was first sold to *Reader's Digest* as a condensed book and then to Little, Brown. Published in 1963, *The Great Auk* was well-received—Marian Sorenson maintains in the *Christian Science Monitor* that Eckert, "in a beautifully written book, personally involves the reader in the tragedy of the extinction of a whole species." This first success prompted Little, Brown to ask Eckert for another book along the same lines, which he provided in *The Silent Sky,* an account of the life and history of the passenger pigeon. But when asked for yet another similar account, Eckert feared that he would become categorized and instead offered a book on the great 1913 flood of Dayton, Ohio. *A Time of Terror* chronicles this natural disaster by focusing on both the historical facts as well as the people involved; "the result is a vividness and immediacy that will capture and hold readers of all ages," asserts Robert H. Donahugh in *Library Journal.*

Historical Controversy

With such a successful book career underway, Eckert began to phase out his magazine articles and short stories. But it was one of his early articles that gave him the idea for the book that both created a new genre and raised controversial questions among historians. Originally starting out as an historical novel, *The Frontiersmen* soon grew into a biography focusing on Simon Kenton, an adventurous member of the American frontier, and his main adversary, the Shawnee Indian leader Tecumseh. History was a dull subject to Eckert as a child, but as he researched his topics he found much information that was exciting and interesting. "I wondered why historians seemed to think it necessary to make history such a dull subject," he explains in *SAAS.* "I decided I wouldn't do that; that I would write in a narrative style, trying to embody all the better qualities of the novel form while at the same time retaining the veracity of straight historical writing."

In his attempt to blend these two forms of writing, Eckert filled *The Frontiersmen* with dialogue,

as well as the thoughts and emotions of the characters as the historical events unfolded. "I termed this form of writing 'historical narrative' and wrote it chronologically, with no forecasting of events to come, in such a manner that, by utilizing the better elements of the novel form for excitement, pace, and continuity, while at the same time striving to remain reliable as an accurate depiction of the history it embraces, the reader might, as with a good novel, feel himself drawn into the current events and be able to identify closely with the characters," explains Eckert in *SAAS.* The dialogue he gives these characters is what he terms reconstituted dialogue—it is found in original documents written as straight commen-

A BANTAM STARFIRE BOOK

INCIDENT AT HAWK'S HILL

A NOVEL BY ALLAN W. ECKERT

THE MOVING AND TRIUMPHANT TALE OF A BOY'S SURVIVAL IN THE WILD

Based on an actual event, this acclaimed 1971 novel follows the adventures of a young boy who is adopted by a female badger after he becomes lost on the prairie.

tary. "But in the straight documentation are couched the keywords that legitimately allow such information, if the effort is made, to be returned to vibrant and meaningful dialogue that remains accurate to the intent and direction of what is occurring at any given time to the character of the individual making the utterance," Eckert asserts in *SAAS*.

This first historical narrative was criticized by some historians because of this dialogue and its other narrative techniques, but its success in making history more interesting and accessible paved the way for Eckert to publish five more similar books and create "The Winning of America" series. In a review of the second book in the series, *Wilderness Empire*, *Christian Science Monitor* contributor James Nelson Goodsell writes that the book is "readable and fascinating," concluding: "History need not be dull as Mr. Eckert proves. But whether such an approach is ideal is open to question." In a later review of the next book in the series, *The Conquerors*, Goodsell praises this same approach, stating that "the use of 'hidden dialogue' enhances the story and one puts the book down feeling that this concession to the novel has not hurt the story one whit." And a *Publishers Weekly* contributor asserts in a review of *Twilight of Empire* (sixth in the series): "Reading Eckert is like listening to a master storyteller: he presents his materials in vivid detail, using the novelist's technique to enhance dramatic events."

While his career was branching into a variety of different adult genres, Eckert also began writing books for young readers. About a year after the publication of *The Great Auk*, he was approached by the producers of the television series *Wild Kingdom* to write two juvenile novels based on previous episodes. The first, *Bayou Backwaters*, tells the story of the wildlife and plants that coexist through the balance of nature in the swampy bayou country of Louisiana. Because of Eckert's "eye for detail, his sense of the rhythms of the natural world, his feeling for its beauty and balance, *Bayou Backwaters* is a celebration of life in all its forms," observes Robert Berkvist in the *New York Times Book Review*. *In Search of a Whale* is similar to Eckert's adult nature stories, following the voyage of a scientific ship as it sets out to capture a young pilot whale for further study. A *Science Books* contributor points out that *In Search of a Whale* "is a well-written action narrative with plenty of excitement."

Nature and History for the Young

Following the progression of his adult book career, Eckert moved from nature novels to historical stories for his young audience. A character that first appeared in *The Frontiersmen* is, in fact, the main focus of Eckert's 1968 novel *Blue Jacket: War Chief of the Shawnees*. The greatest war chief of his tribe, Blue Jacket was actually part of a family of settlers on the Virginia frontier before being captured by the Shawnees. Adopted into the tribe, Blue Jacket slowly rose in power as his courage and intelligence developed. He eventually became the tribe's war chief and led his people into battle against the whites. Jane Manthorne, writing in *Horn Book*, describes Eckert's documentary novel *Blue Jacket* as maintaining "a precise fidelity to the facts of history," adding that the story is "terse, brooding in its revelation of white man's greed."

At this point, Eckert's varied career took another unexpected turn when he was asked to write a few episodes for *Wild Kingdom*. These scripts were so well-liked that Eckert was asked to write the rest of the scripts for the season. "Though I wasn't really keen about writing more television scripts, the money was so good that it didn't take a great deal of coaxing to make me agree to do more," relates Eckert in *SAAS*. "The upshot was that even though I was continuing to write my own books, for the next ten years I also wrote all the *Wild Kingdom* shows, plus scattered others in subsequent years, until eventually, when new productions were finally halted, I had written well over two hundred *Wild Kingdom* half-hour scripts."

Among the novels Eckert wrote while busy with *Wild Kingdom* is his Newbery Honor-winning young adult novel *Incident at Hawk's Hill*. Published in 1971, this nature tale brought Eckert a new following of younger readers. He relates in *SAAS*: "I have received literally thousands of letters over the years from children who are enthralled with the story of the little six-year-old boy who becomes lost in the vast prairies of Manitoba and is adopted by a badger who has just lost her litter of pups." In another young adult nature novel, *Savage Journey*, Eckert tells the story of thirteen-year-old Sarah Francis as she accompanies her father on an archeological dig in the Amazon jungle. When every member of the party dies, Sarah must brave the jungle alone as she attempts to return to civilization.

"Having so much enjoyed writing various books for young readers," writes Eckert in *SAAS*, "I then began a projected series of a dozen children's fantasies patterned after *The Chronicles of Narnia* by C. S. Lewis, except mine were set in modern times in the United States and, instead of being religious allegories, there were allegories of nature and ecology." The first two books of the "Mesmerian Annals" series, *The Dark Green Tunnel* and *The Wand: The Return to Mesmeria*, feature twins Barnaby and Lara as they first come across the land of Mesmeria while visiting their cousin William in the Florida Everglades. When the three children

---

If you enjoy the works of Allan W. Eckert, you may also want to check out the following books:

Midas Dekkers, *Arctic Adventure*, 1987
C. S. Lewis, *The Complete Chronicles of Narnia*, 1986.
Scott O'Dell, Elizabeth Hall, *Thunder Rolling in the Mountains*, 1992.
Gary Paulsen, *The Island*, 1988.

---

enter this new land they encounter evil King Thorkin, who killed their father and who fears that they will bring about the end to his rule. By the end of their battle Barnaby and Lara have become rulers of the kingdom. The twins return to their own world, but they find themselves transported back to Mesmeria when they lose their way in an airport. In this second adventure, the evil sorcerer Krumpp has become ruler of Mesmeria. The twins set off on a dangerous journey to free their Mesmerian friends who have been locked up by Krumpp and to win back the kingdom that is rightfully theirs.

In a review of *The Dark Green Tunnel*, a *Booklist* contributor observes that "Eckert's nature descriptions, strange characters, and fast-paced adventure contribute much to the fantasy, which, although quite scary in parts, ends with the children safe and secure." And Deborah Felder, writing in the *New York Times Book Review*, maintains that *The Wand* "is a satisfying fantasy," adding: "It has just about everything a good fantasy ought to have: bright, enterprising, likable children; noble, heroic adults; all manner of exotic, imaginatively named creatures, some lovable, others loathsome; a be-

neficent sorceress and a wicked sorcerer; gentle humor; a colorful, compelling setting; wonderful illustrations; and a plot of high adventure culminating in eventual triumph for the forces of good."

The adventures of Eckert's characters continue; so does his writing career. As he looks back over the course of it he asks himself in *SAAS*: "If I were a youngster again, knowing what I know now, would I enter another profession? Absolutely not. . . . I know of no other profession where one has such complete freedom to go wherever one wishes, live wherever one cares to, experience whatever one wishes to experience, and which can so frequently and delightfully change direction and interests; nor do I know of any other profession that, in the end result, is so fully and completely gratifying in the knowledge that one has left something of value behind, contributed something that may continue to benefit the world long after one is gone. What greater sense of fulfillment in one's life could there be?"

■ Works Cited

Berkvist, Robert, review of *Bayou Backwaters*, *New York Times Book Review*, June 30, 1968, p. 26.

Review of *The Dark Green Tunnel*, *Booklist*, April 1, 1984, pp. 1114-15.

Donahugh, Robert H., review of *A Time of Terror*, *Library Journal*, March 15, 1965, p. 1319.

Eckert, Allan W., essay in *Something about the Author Autobiography Series*, Volume 21, Gale, 1995, pp. 103-20.

Felder, Deborah, review of *The Wand: The Return to Mesmeria*, *New York Times Book Review*, January 19, 1986, p. 29.

Goodsell, James Nelson, "Should History Read Like Fiction?," *Christian Science Monitor*, October 23, 1969, p. 15.

Goodsell, James Nelson, "In Living History: How the Wilderness Was Won," *Christian Science Monitor*, May 13, 1971, p. 11.

Review of *In Search of a Whale*, *Science Books*, May, 1970, p. 53.

Manthorne, Jane, "Red, Black, and White," *Horn Book*, April, 1969, p. 193.

Sorenson, Marian, "Noble Bird," *Christian Science Monitor*, October 31, 1963, p. 7.

Review of *Twilight of Empire*, *Publishers Weekly*, August 26, 1988, p. 71.

■ For More Information See

BOOKS

Contemporary Literary Criticism, Volume 17, Gale, 1981.

PERIODICALS

Booklist, March 1, 1992, p. 1193.
Library Journal, February 15, 1992, p. 178.
Publishers Weekly, June 15, 1984, p. 83; January 1, 1992, p. 42.
School Library Journal, January, 1986, p. 66.*

—Sketch by Susan Reicha

Louise Fitzhugh

for *Harriet the Spy; New York Times* Choice of Best Illustrated Books of the Year citation, 1969, and Brooklyn Art Books for Children citation, both for *Bang, Bang, You're Dead; Children's Book Bulletin* award, 1976, for *Nobody's Family Is Going to Change;* Emmy Award for children's entertainment special, 1979, for "The Tap Dance Kid."

■ Personal

Born Louise Perkins Fitzhugh, October 5, 1928, in Memphis, TN; died of an aneurism, November 19, 1974, in New Milford, CT; daughter of Millsaps (an attorney and government official) and Louise (Perkins) Fitzhugh. *Education:* Attended Southwestern College, Florida Southern College, Bard College, and New York University; studied painting at Art Students League, in Bologna, Italy, and at Cooper Union. *Hobbies and other interests:* Playing the flute, tennis, dancing.

■ Career

Author, illustrator, and artist. *Exhibitions:* Oil paintings exhibited at various galleries, including Banfer Gallery, New York City, 1963.

■ Awards, Honors

New York Times Outstanding Book of the Year citation, 1964, American Library Association Notable Book citation, and Sequoya Award, both 1967, all

■ Writings

SELF-ILLUSTRATED, EXCEPT AS NOTED

(With Sandra Scoppettone) *Suzuki Beane,* Doubleday, 1961.
Harriet the Spy, Harper, 1964.
The Long Secret, Harper, 1965.
(With Scoppettone) *Bang, Bang, You're Dead,* Harper, 1969.
Nobody's Family Is Going to Change, Farrar, Straus, 1974.
I Am Five, Delacorte, 1978.
Sport, Delacorte, 1979.
I Am Three, illustrated by Susanna Natti, Delacorte, 1982.
I Am Four, illustrated by Susan Bonner, Delacorte, 1982.
I Know Everything about John and He Knows Everything about Me, illustrated by Lillian Hoban, Doubleday, 1993.

OTHER

Also author of text of *I Am Six;* author of plays and adult novels.

■ Adaptations

Nobody's Family Is Going to Change was adapted as "The Tap Dance Kid" for television and broadcast on NBC-TV's "Special Treat" series, 1978; as a film, Learning Corporation of America, 1978; and as a play, first produced on Broadway at Broadhurst Theater, 1983 (winner of two Tony Awards); *Harriet the Spy* was released by Paramount in 1996, featuring Rosie O'Donnell as Harriet's mentor, Ole Golly.

■ Sidelights

"SOME PEOPLE ARE ONE WAY AND SOME PEOPLE ARE ANOTHER AND THAT'S THAT," observed Louise Fitzhugh's best-known character, Harriet M. Welsch, in the ground-breaking young-adult novel *Harriet the Spy*. Calling this statement the "moral" of Fitzhugh's writing, Perry Nodelman noted in *Dictionary of Literary Biography* that "like Harriet . . . Fitzhugh had an unfailing interest in the oddities of people, an uncanny ability to describe them in words and pictures." During her brief career, Fitzhugh wrote and illustrated several controversial yet enduringly popular stories about eccentric children struggling to cope with the rigidity of the adult world. "Fitzhugh's mastery in writing witty dialogue, her gift for creating memorable characters, and her moral honesty in relentlessly depicting psychologically realistic portraits of contemporary American children," Anita Moss wrote in *Twentieth-Century Children's Writers*, "have earned for her a lasting place in children's literature."

Distaste for the South

Fitzhugh was born in Memphis, Tennessee, in 1928. Her father was an attorney and held an important position in the state government, so her family was fairly well off. Fitzhugh enjoyed reading from an early age, and she began writing her own stories at the age of eleven. During her childhood, she also learned to play the flute and developed a lifelong love of music, dancing, and tennis.

Despite growing up with many advantages, however, Fitzhugh did not consider her childhood a particularly happy time. Her bad feelings about it came, in large part, from the racial tension and bigotry she witnessed around her. As her editor and friend Ursula Nordstrom recalled in *Dictionary of Literary Biography*, "There were many things in Louise's well-born southern upbringing that she did not like, including her horrified remembrance of teenage friends who, after a date, decided it would be fun to go down to 'coon town' and throw rocks at the heads of young Negro boys and girls. She got out of the South as soon as she could, and concentrated on losing every single trace of her southern accent—and prejudices."

Fitzhugh attended several colleges in New York and Florida, majoring in literature. Her interest in art gradually became more important, however, so she ended up leaving school six months before

An intelligent, eccentric girl keeps a secret notebook filled with her observations of family and friends in this groundbreaking 1964 novel.

earning her degree. She then studied painting at two prominent art schools in New York City, Cooper Union and the Art Students League. During the mid-1950s, she also spent six months in Europe and a year in Italy studying art. Fitzhugh became an accomplished artist, and her realistic oil paintings were exhibited at several galleries beginning in 1963.

Though she spent a great deal of time pursuing her interest in art, Fitzhugh continued to write during these years, mostly adult fiction and plays that were never published. Her start in children's literature came in 1961, when she co-wrote and illustrated *Suzuki Beane* with Sandra Scoppettone. This book tells the story of a hip young girl who lives with her beatnik parents in Greenwich Village. Suzuki, along with her square friend Henry, eventually realizes that most adults are set in their ways and unable to change. Fitzhugh's illustrations "present a satiric portrait gallery of early 1960s types—beatniks, society poets, dancing teachers," according to Nodelman. "Like all her drawings, they use a strong, definite line to wickedly unmask human silliness."

Impact of *Harriet the Spy*

Fitzhugh's humorous illustrations for *Suzuki Beane* attracted some attention from reviewers, but she still encountered obstacles in publishing her first individual effort—*Harriet the Spy*. She received little financial support from her family, so she needed to convince a publisher to give her an advance to write the book, which is often a difficult task for an unproven writer. Fitzhugh hired an agent to submit an early draft of the manuscript—which later became the contents of Harriet's notebook—to publishers. An editor at Harper and Row recognized the book's potential, gave Fitzhugh an advance, and helped her to expand the book to its final form.

Harriet the Spy, published in 1964, follows the adventures of an eleven-year-old girl who wants to be a famous writer. For practice, Harriet methodically spies upon the people in her neighborhood and writes down her painfully honest observations about them in a secret notebook. Along her spy route, Harriet is exposed to all the unpleasant aspects of adult life. Harriet always follows precisely the same routine, including eating a tomato sandwich for lunch every day at the same time for five years. Although Harriet comes from a wealthy family, she receives little guidance from her parents. Her father is an overworked advertising executive and her mother is always busy with social activities, so Harriet is often lonely. For support and understanding, she relies upon her nursemaid, Ole Golly.

Although she is intelligent and imaginative, Harriet dislikes school because she has trouble accepting the weaknesses she sees in her classmates. She records often-unkind thoughts about them, like "IF MARION HAWTHORNE DOESN'T WATCH OUT SHE'S GOING TO GROW UP INTO A LADY HITLER," in her notebook. Harriet's carefully arranged life begins to unravel when Ole Golly leaves to get married. Soon after, Harriet's friends discover her secret notebook, read everything she has written about them, and give her the silent treatment. Though she tries to take things in stride, Harriet begins to fall apart emotionally. Only after she attends sessions with a psychotherapist, receives a supportive letter from Ole Golly, and finds a productive outlet for her writing in the school newspaper does she begin to recover. Harriet comes to the realization that people are the way they are, and that sometimes it is necessary to sacrifice the absolute truth in order to spare people's feelings.

Though Fitzhugh relates the story in third person, she also includes numerous entries from Harriet's notebook, which give the reader a detailed picture of Harriet's thought processes. In a review for the *Bulletin of the Center for Children's Books*, Zena Sutherland described Harriet as "a little girl whose fierce candor and rebellious pride make it hard for her to get the love and approval she so desperately needs." Calling *Harriet the Spy* "a remarkable book," Maggie Stern of *Horn Book* stated that "through Harriet one sees the process of life, the human struggle. From unawareness to awareness—from order to chaos to new order."

Harriet the Spy "excited a great deal of controversy" when it was first published, according to Nodelman. "While the book is anything but realistic in style, it does discuss perfectly ordinary things that were not ordinarily discussed in children's books in the early 1960s. Reviewers hated its supposedly unchildlike cynicism and its obvious lack of faith in the supposed delights of childhood innocence. . . . But like many pioneering books, it was and continues to be an immense success with young readers." Some reviewers claimed that Harriet's behavior was antisocial, and worried that young people might be tempted to emulate her. Others found Fitzhugh's exaggerated characterizations of adults shocking. In some schools, the book was deemed unsuitable for children and censored. Despite the controversy, however, Fitzhugh's book paved the way for young-adult fiction that presented a realistic—though not always pleasant—view of society. "Fitzhugh has proven that contemporary, realistic fiction of psychological and philosophical depth is a viable possibility for children," Virginia L. Wolf stated in *Children's Literature*. "*Harriet the Spy* is a milestone and a masterpiece of children's literature—perhaps *the* masterpiece of the mid-twentieth century."

Promising Career Cut Short

Due to her sudden death from an aneurism in 1974, Fitzhugh's career as an author of books for young people lasted only thirteen years. Besides *Harriet the Spy*, she published only one young-adult novel and two picture-book collaborations with Sandra Scoppettone during her lifetime. Fitzhugh had several other projects underway at the time of her death, however, so her body of work also includes two more young-adult novels and several more picture books that were published posthumously.

Fitzhugh's follow-up effort to *Harriet the Spy* was *The Long Secret*, published in 1965. It is usually regarded as a sequel to the earlier book, though it is told primarily from the perspective of Harriet's painfully shy classmate, Beth Ellen Hansen. The story takes place on Long Island during the summer, as both girls spend time at their families' cottages. Beth Ellen struggles to relate to her wealthy, self-absorbed parents, who have basically abandoned her to pursue their own interests. Meanwhile, Harriet works to find out who has been leaving mysterious, nasty notes for the townspeople. At the end of the story, it is revealed that mousy Beth Ellen is responsible for the notes, which provide a release for her anger and a means of communicating with other people. "Fitzhugh returns to characters from an earlier novel we thought we knew completely, and reveals unexpected facets both of their lives and of their personalities," Nodelman observed. "*The Long Secret* is a subtle and energetic novel, as good in its own way as *Harriet the Spy*."

This controversial 1974 novel, published just a week after Fitzhugh's death, focuses on issues like discrimination and women's rights.

Fitzhugh continued to invite controversy with *The Long Secret* by including a frank discussion of the formerly taboo topic of menstruation. Beth Ellen spends a whole day feeling ill, and she later admits to Harriet that she has had her period for the first time. Fitzhugh's editor, Ursula Nordstrom, described her reaction to reading this section of the book in *Dictionary of Literary Biography*: "When I came to the page where the onset of Beth Ellen's first menstrual period occurred, and it was written so beautifully, to such perfection, I scrawled in the margin, 'Thank you, Louise Fitzhugh.' It was the first mention in junior books of this tremendous event in a girl's life."

Fitzhugh's third young-adult novel, *Nobody's Family Is Going to Change*, was published one week after her death in 1974. Nodelman called it her "most earnest and most paradoxical novel—a savage attack on the rigidity of conventional values that expresses no faith that change is possible," noting that Fitzhugh's "earlier insistence on respect for individuality here becomes a general attack on discrimination of all sorts." The story centers around Emma Sheridan, an overweight, eleven-year-old black girl who wants to be a successful lawyer like her father. Her younger brother, Willie, has a talent for dancing and hopes to dance professionally one day. Unfortunately, their father is a domineering man who believes that girls should be lawyers' wives rather than lawyers, and that dancing is for sissies. At first the siblings struggle to gain their father's approval, but later they re-

---

If you enjoy the works of Louise Fitzhugh, you may also want to check out the following books:

Michael Behrens, *At the Edge*, 1988.
Harry Mazer and Norma Fox Mazer, *Bright Days, Stupid Nights*, 1992.
Rhea Beth Ross, *The Bet's On, Lizzie Bingham!*, 1988.
Donald E. Westlake, *Trust Me on This*, 1988.

---

alize that he will not change, and that they should not have to. At the end of the book, when Emma's father tells her that "any woman who tries to be a lawyer is a damned fool," she replies, "That . . . is your problem."

Like Fitzhugh's earlier books, *Nobody's Family Is Going to Change* aroused some controversy. For example, the novel includes a character who is a transvestite, and at one point Emma admits feeling a basic dislike for people with white skin. Nevertheless, it was very popular with readers and was adapted as a television special, a film, and an award-winning Broadway musical under the title "The Tap Dance Kid."

Fitzhugh's last young adult novel was *Sport*, published in 1979. It relates the adventures of Harriet's best friend, an ordinary boy who has just inherited $32 million from his grandfather. Sport copes in comic fashion with the return of his world-traveling mother—whom Nodelman called "a pure force of unmitigated, self-regarding evil"—and looks forward to the impending marriage of his father to a kind, sweet, loving woman named Kate. Compared to Fitzhugh's other works,

Nodelman said that *Sport* "seems unfinished and rather thin," though he noted that Fitzhugh "simply chose not to emphasize the psychological aspects of the situation here. Instead, she makes things deliciously lurid."

Fitzhugh's Lasting Influence

Fitzhugh's controversial novels anticipated both the trend toward realism in young-adult fiction and the alienation many young people feel in modern society. As Moss explained, "Fitzhugh's works resonate with social consciousness and with just indignation against human selfishness, greed, and ignorance. She sometimes creates grotesque characterizations, apparently in an attempt to shock her readers into an awareness that middle-class, affluent children may be lost in the wilderness, the emotional and moral chaos of contemporary urban life."

Even though *Harriet the Spy* was published more than thirty years ago, its themes have continued to ring true for young readers. "Despite the fading contemporaneity of Fitzhugh's writing," Nodelman stated, "her novels still cleverly express the differences between individuality and eccentricity, and between what one owes others and what one deserves oneself. As her treatment of once-controversial issues becomes less shocking, Fitzhugh's merit as a tough-minded satirist becomes more apparent."

■ Works Cited

Fitzhugh, Louise, *Harriet the Spy*, Harper, 1964.

Fitzhugh, Louise, *Nobody's Family Is Going to Change*, Farrar, Straus, 1974.

Moss, Anita, "Louise Fitzhugh," *Twentieth-Century Children's Writers*, St. James Press, 1989, pp. 346-48.

Nodelman, Perry, "Louise Fitzhugh," *Dictionary of Literary Biography*, Volume 52: *American Writers for Children since 1960: Fiction*, Gale, 1986, pp. 133-42.

Stern, Maggie, "A Second Look: *Harriet the Spy*," *Horn Book*, August, 1980.

Sutherland, Zena, review of *Harriet the Spy*, *Bulletin of the Center for Children's Books*, December 1964, p. 53.

Wolf, Virginia L., "*Harriet the Spy*: Milestone, Masterpiece?" *Children's Literature*, 1975, pp. 120-26.

■ For More Information See

BOOKS

Children's Literature Review, Volume 1, Gale, 1976, pp. 71-73.
Contemporary Authors, New Revision Series, Volume 34, Gale, 1991, pp. 131-32.
Something about the Author, Volume 45, Gale, 1986, pp. 74-79.
Wolf, Virginia L., *Louise Fitzhugh,* Twayne, 1991.

PERIODICALS

Elementary English, October, 1974, pp. 963-70.
Lion and the Unicorn, fall, 1977, pp. 77-90.
Publishers Weekly, November 8, 1993, pp. 74-75.
Washington Post Book World, September 21, 1986, p. 12.

■ Obituaries

PERIODICALS

New York Times, November 21, 1974.
Publishers Weekly, December 2, 1974.*

—Sketch by Laurie Collier Hillstrom

Ernest J. Gaines

■ Personal

Full name, Ernest James Gaines; born January 15, 1933, in Oscar, LA (some sources cite River Lake Plantation, near New Roads, Pointe Coupee Parish, LA); son of Manuel (a laborer) and Adrienne J. (Colar) Gaines; married Dianne Saulney (an attorney), May 15, 1993. *Education:* Attended Vallejo Junior College, California; San Francisco State College (now University), B.A. 1957; graduate study at Stanford University, 1958-59.

■ Addresses

Office—Department of English, University of Southwestern Louisiana, P.O. Box 44691, Lafayette, LA 70504. *Agent*—JCA Literary Agency, Inc., 242 West 27th St., New York, NY 10001.

■ Career

Denison University, Granville, OH, writer in residence, 1971; Stanford University, Stanford, CA, writer in residence, 1981; Whittier College, CA, visiting professor, 1983, writer in residence, 1986; University of Southwestern Louisiana, Lafayette, professor of English and writer in residence, 1983—. *Military service:* U.S. Army, 1953-55. *Member:* Fellowship of Southern Writers.

■ Awards

Wallace Stegner Fellow, Stanford University, 1957; Joseph Henry Jackson Award, San Francisco Foundation, 1959, for "Comeback" (short story); National Endowment for the Arts Award, 1967; Rockefeller grant, 1970; Guggenheim fellowship, 1971; Black Academy of Arts and Letters Award, 1972; Commonwealth Club of California fiction gold medal, 1972, for *The Autobiography of Miss Jane Pittman*, and 1984, for *A Gathering of Old Men*; Louisiana Literature Award, Louisiana Library Association, 1972, for *The Autobiography of Miss Jane Pittman*; honorary doctorate of letters from Denison University, 1980, Brown University, 1985, Bard College, 1985, and Louisiana State University, 1987; award for excellence of achievement in literature, San Francisco Arts Commission, 1983; D.H.L., Whittier College, 1986; literary award, American Academy and Institute of Arts and Letters, 1987; John D. and Catherine T. MacArthur Foundation fellowship, 1993; National Book Critics Circle Award for fiction, 1994, for *A Lesson before Dying*.

■ Writings

FICTION

Catherine Carmier, Atheneum, 1964.

Of Love and Dust, Dial, 1967.

Bloodline (short stories), Dial, 1968.

A Long Day in November (for children; originally published in *Bloodline*), illustrated by Don Bolognese, Dial, 1971.

The Autobiography of Miss Jane Pittman, Dial, 1971.

In My Father's House, Knopf, 1978.

A Gathering of Old Men, Knopf, 1983.

The Sky Is Gray (story; originally published in *Bloodline*), Creative Education (Mankato, MN), 1993.

A Lesson before Dying, Knopf, 1993.

A collection of Gaines's manuscripts are held at the Dupree Library, University of Southwestern Louisiana, Lafayette.

■ **Adaptations**

The Autobiography of Miss Jane Pittman was made into an Emmy-winning television movie by Columbia Broadcasting System (CBS-TV), 1974; the story "The Sky Is Gray" was filmed for public television, 1980; *A Gathering of Old Men* was made into a television movie, CBS-TV, 1987. *A Lesson before Dying* is available on cassette, and has been optioned for a television movie.

■ **Work in Progress**

Three novellas.

■ **Sidelights**

"When we moved to California I was lonely, so I went to the library and began to read a lot of fiction," Ernest J. Gaines told Paul Desruisseaux in the *New York Times Book Review.* It was the late 1940s, and fifteen-year-old Gaines had just come with his family from Louisiana to enjoy the greater opportunities that could be found in a more integrated state. "But the books I read did not have my people in them, no Southern blacks, Louisiana blacks. Or if they did it was by white writers who did not interpret things the way I would have. So I started writing about my people." From that first determination, Gaines has written several acclaimed short stories and novels—including *The Autobiography of Miss Jane Pittman,* the inspiration for a popular television movie—which have brought the history, culture, and people of his childhood home to life for countless readers and students.

Born in 1933 on a sugar cane plantation in Oscar, Louisiana, Gaines was the eldest of several children, and grew up in an extended family of aunts, uncles, and cousins who all lived in the "quarter" behind the main plantation house. "We didn't have running water, and my responsibility from the time I was eight years old was to get the water," the author recalled to Scott Jaschik in the *Chronicle of Higher Education.* At nine he was digging potatoes for fifty cents a day, and "by the time I was eleven or twelve I was going out with my father to saw wood." Gaines was a lively, intelligent child, and enjoyed learning even though his schooling was limited to the five or six months between harvest and planting seasons. Recognized throughout the plantation for his aptitude, Gaines was often asked to read and write letters for many of the older people in the community.

Many of these people also came to visit his great-aunt, Augusteen Jefferson, who cared for Gaines and his siblings even though she had been disabled since birth. Unable to walk, Gaines's Aunt Augusteen crawled to get around; she cooked, cleaned, and even tended the garden. Her house was a social center of the plantation community, with family and friends coming to visit and share stories. Sitting with his aunt and hearing these tales gave the author a firm grounding in the black oral tradition which now informs his fiction. "Anytime someone asks me who had the greatest influence on me as an artist or a man, I say she had," Gaines said in an *Essence* interview. Aunt Augusteen was later to serve as the inspiration for Gaines's most memorable character, the resilient and spirited former slave, Miss Jane Pittman.

Opportunities were limited for a bright young black man in rural Louisiana, and so when his mother and stepfather moved to the San Francisco area, Gaines chose to join them. "Had I remained in Louisiana two more years," the author explained to Bob Summer in *Publishers Weekly,* "I would have been broken and become bitter." Instead, Gaines graduated from high school and attended junior college with an eye towards becoming a published author. At nineteen, he attempted his first novel. "I must have used the cheapest paper I could find, because we couldn't afford anything else," he told Summer. "I cut the paper in half, the size of a book, and typed on both sides, single space. I thought it was pretty good. I wrapped it in brown paper, tied a string around it, and sent the thing off. It came back, of course."

Russian Novels Provide Models

After serving in the army for two years, Gaines returned to college, enrolling at San Francisco State University. His formal studies gave him few models for his own writing; as he told Jaschik, "I didn't read a single black author there. The only black character I knew was Othello, and he had been written by a white guy 300 years earlier." His reading had led him to the works of Russian novelists such as Ivan Turgenev and Leo Tolstoy,

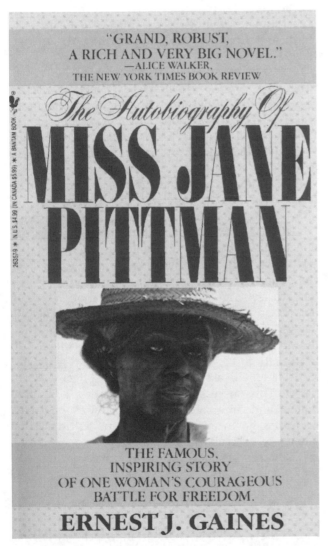

"GRAND, ROBUST, A RICH AND VERY BIG NOVEL."
—ALICE WALKER, THE NEW YORK TIMES BOOK REVIEW

The Autobiography Of
MISS JANE PITTMAN

THE FAMOUS, INSPIRING STORY OF ONE WOMAN'S COURAGEOUS BATTLE FOR FREEDOM.

ERNEST J. GAINES

A 110–year–old African American woman recounts her experiences from the slave era to the civil rights movement of the 1960s in this award-winning 1971 novel.

however, and he used their stories about country people and peasant life as an example. By the time he graduated in 1957, he had published his first story, won a creative writing fellowship to attend Stanford University, and found an agent to represent him. He began writing novels on the advice of a critic who said they were more marketable than stories, and in 1964 published his first book. Developed from his teenage attempt at a novel, *Catherine Carmier* "took me five years to finish and gave me a lot of trouble," Gaines related to Bernard Magnier in the *UNESCO Courier*. "But all the time I was learning how to write."

The first of Gaines's books to be set in the fictional area of Bayonne, Louisiana, *Catherine Carmier* relates the story of Jackson Bradley, an educated young black man who returns home and rekindles a doomed romance with Catherine, a black Creole woman. Both young people are battling conflicting loyalties: Jackson's learning has led him to question his aunt's beliefs and expectations, while Catherine's father opposes her relationship with Jackson because he is not of Creole heritage. Feeling out of place, Jackson seeks to rekindle his relationship with Catherine; in the process, he makes an unpleasant discovery about her father and eventually fights and beats him. The ending is ambiguous, as Keith E. Byerman points out in the *Concise Dictionary of American Literary Biography*: "Either [Jackson] has lost Catherine or, the deepest irony, he has succeeded in his quest, but at the price of his freedom." Although *Catherine Carmier* did not bring him immediate success, Gaines continued writing both stories and novels.

His next book, 1967's *Of Love and Dust*, explores plantation life more fully through a series of interracial romances and conflicts set in the 1940s. The narrator, Jim Kelly, is a middle-aged black man entrusted with supervising the rebellious young Marcus, who has been charged with a stabbing. While Jim has promised Marcus's godmother he will help the youth adapt to plantation life, he encounters resistance from his ward, particularly when Sidney Bonbon, the farm's white overseer, assigns Marcus a series of unfair tasks. Marcus seeks revenge by courting Bonbon's black mistress, and when he is rejected turns instead to Bonbon's wife Louise, who accepts him as a way to punish her husband's infidelity. Despite the black community's protests—Marcus's actions could endanger all of the area's black men if he were discovered—the illicit relationship turns into a genuine love. The lovers are eventually betrayed by the plantation owner Hebert, leaving Marcus dead, Louise insane, and Bonbon and his mistress banished. Jim, because of his knowledge of the events, must also leave, but has learned "that risk is necessary if one is going to live in dignity," as Byerman writes. "Jim acknowledges this lesson when he refuses to accept Hebert's offer of a recommendation. . . . Unlike Jackson of *Catherine Carmier*, Jim has hope at the end of the novel because he has found something to believe in—himself."

Of Love and Dust was fairly well-received, making Gaines successful enough to publish a short story collection, *Bloodline*, in 1968. The author made minor revisions to one of these stories, *A Long Day in November*, and published it as a book for children in 1971. It is a chilly fall morning when six-year-old Sonny's parents argue; his mother leaves angrily and his father spends the day searching for a way to win her back. Sonny narrates the tale of this difficult day, which includes an embarrassing incident at school; "Sonny's observations, fantasies and problems are very real," Marilyn Sachs states in the *New York Times Book Review*. The critic praises Gaines for his "wonderfully funny" portrayal of a poor black family, adding that he "includes those small, human details that so many authors neglect."

Book World contributor Digby B. Whitman similarly observes that "people, talk, and action are wholly credible" in *A Long Day in November*, and adds that "the simple, halting language makes for extraordinary realism and tenderness." While Mary M. Burns believes that it will take a "sophisticated" reader to grasp the "subtle nuances of characterization, the skilled uses of contrast, and the superbly realized setting," she notes in her *Horn Book* review that mature readers will find "a well-wrought story which is very real and touchingly human." A *Publishers Weekly* writer likewise remarks that the book may be more appealing to adults than children, but concludes that "there is no reason why older readers could not enjoy this truly remarkable story."

Miss Jane Pittman Tells Her Story

The year that Gaines produced *A Long Year in November* was also the year he brought out his breakthrough novel, *The Autobiography of Miss Jane Pittman*, a book which *Iowa Review* contributor Jerry H. Bryant called "one of the finest novels written since World War II in America and a distinguished contribution to our national literature." In the novel, Miss Jane relates the story of her life, from when she is freed from slavery as a young girl to her participation in a civil rights demonstration when she is 110 years old. Her experiences echo the history of African Americans in the South, a history Gaines heard firsthand from his Aunt Augusteen and others. When people came to visit his aunt, the author related to Desruisseaux, "I'd be there to serve them icewater, or coffee. There was no radio, no television, so people *talked* about everything, even things that had happened 70 years earlier. I learned about storytelling by listening to these people talk," he continued. "The idea behind 'Miss Jane Pittman' was based on things I'd heard as a child, and from the life I come from, the plantation."

"*The Autobiography of Miss Jane Pittman* is history rewritten and sifted through the mind of a talented novelist," Addison Gayle, Jr. writes in *The Way of the New World: The Black Novel in America*. In recollections taped by a young historian, Miss Jane tells of the arrival of Union troops to her Louisiana home; her emancipation and trip northward, when most of her fellow travellers are murdered by Klansmen; her settling down on a Louisiana plantation, her marriage, and her adoption of the orphan Ned; Ned's return home after a Northern education, when he is assassinated for challenging white racism; and her joining the modern civil rights movement after another bright, outspoken young man is killed for what he believes. "Never mind that Miss Jane Pittman is fictitious, and that her 'autobiography,' offered up in the form of taped reminiscences, is artifice," Josh Greenfeld asserts in *Life*. "The effect is stunning." This success is due to Gaines's skill with dialect and language, as Bryant claims: "So successful is he in *becoming* Miss Jane Pittman, that when we talk about her story, we do not think of Gaines as her creator, but as her recording 'editor.'"

What distinguishes Gaines's story of black persecution from similar novels, according to many critics, is the restrained manner in which he tells it. "Gaines does not avoid having Jane report white atrocities, but he does not allow her to use the propagandistic and sociological stridency that char-

This 1974 television adaptation of *The Autobiography of Miss Jane Pittman,* featuring a highly acclaimed performance by Cicely Tyson, won nine Emmy Awards.

acterizes so many earlier novels," Bryant observes. In *Miss Jane Pittman,* Alice Walker writes in the *New York Times Book Review,* "racists are dangerous, unstable, vicious individuals, but never that alone. They are people, fully realized in Gaines's fiction." "Gaines does not make the revolution happen by surreal rhetoric," Melvin Maddocks similarly remarks in his *Time* review. "He simply watches, a patient artist, a patient man, and it happens for him." As the author explained to Magnier, his work has a more subtle tone because "I write from my own viewpoint. I don't see the world as Jimmy Baldwin or Richard Wright did. I may not have suffered racism as directly as either one of those men did, and I haven't lived in large cities as they did . . . but we have fought for the same causes." In his writing, Gaines noted, "I'm doing what the others are doing, just more quietly." As Gayle explains, in Miss Jane's story "is symbolized the odyssey of a race of people; through her eyes is revealed the grandeur of a people's journey through history."

Other novels examine historical themes in a similarly subtle fashion; as Larry McMurtry writes in the *New York Times Book Review,* "it is the force of Mr. Gaines's character and intelligence, operating through this deceptively quiet style, that makes his fiction compelling." The 1978 novel *In My Father's House,* for instance, "will attract . . . those readers interested in the nonviolent vs. violent activism question," Ellen Lippmann writes in *School Library Journal.* Set in 1969, following the assassinations of Malcolm X, Robert Kennedy, and Martin Luther King, Jr., the novel follows the chaos created in the life of Reverend Phillip Martin, a local civil rights leader, when the illegitimate son he abandoned thirty years before unexpectedly turns up. Robert X, as he calls himself, is an emotionally damaged young man who has come to confront his father with his neglect. Robert's sudden appearance forces Phillip to revisit the actions of his past, from when he failed to support his lover Johanna and their children, to his discovery of his faith, to his establishing a new family with his wife Alma. In his quest to finally take responsibility for the past, however, Phillip overlooks the present, abdicating his duties within his community and eventually losing his newly found son to a violent end.

"This is a powerful, deeply probing novel," Mel Watkins asserts in the *New York Times Book Review*. Although it contains a few flaws, the critic adds, "this is a solid contribution to the impressive oeuvre of one of America's finest Southern writers." According to McMurtry, throughout the novel Gaines reveals "an individual, a marriage, a community and a region, but with such an unobtrusive marshalling of detail that we never lose sight of the book's central thematic concern: . . . a father's abandonment of his children and the terrible and irrevocable consequences of such an abandonment." It was this concern that inspired the novel, Gaines told Mary Ellen Doyle in *Melus*. *In My Father's House* was "a book I had to write because I was haunted by the idea." He further explained: "The father and son were separated when they were brought to this country over three centuries ago. The white man did not let them come together during slavery, and they have not been able to reach each other since."

The results of enduring a lifetime of racism are similarly portrayed in *A Gathering of Old Men*; when Beau Boutan, a white Cajun work boss, is found shot in a black man's yard, nineteen elderly black men and a young white woman all claim responsibility for the murder in order to thwart the expected lynch mob. Complicating matters are the changing attitudes of some of the Cajun community; the dead man's brother, for instance, has been part of a successful interracial football team and now refuses to take part in any racial violence. Thus the racist local sheriff, instead of leading the vigilante party, is forced to listen as each of the men relates his reasons for wanting the murdered man dead. Gaines's "portraits of the aged men taking a stand against their oppressors—some of them for the first time in their long lives—are beautiful and painful," Gregory Maguire writes in *Horn Book*. Although the situation ends in violence, it represents progress, as former victims stand up for their rights and former vigilantes are brought to justice.

One of the strengths of the book, according to *Voice of Youth Advocates* contributor Penny Parker, is Gaines's ability to bring the reader into the story and the minds of the characters "without losing interest in the events, nor even suspecting what will occur." While the book has a contemporary setting, the critic concludes, as Gaines reveals his characters' stories "we are swept into a maelstrom that began many, many years before." Through these various narratives, Reynolds Price notes in the *New York Times Book Review*, the author "has built, with large and single-minded skills, a dignified and calamitous and perhaps finally comic pageant to summarize the history of an enormous long waste in our past—the mindless, mutual hatred of white and black, which, he implies, may slowly be healing."

Of Lessons and Justice

A 1940s setting is the basis for another examination of race and injustice, in the National Book Critics Circle Award-winning novel a *Publishers Weekly* critic says "may be [Gaines's] crowning achievement." In *A Lesson before Dying*, a barely literate young black man named Jefferson is an unwitting witness and only survivor of a robbery of a white store owner. Despite his defense attorney's claims that executing the young man for the shopkeeper's murder would be tantamount to killing a "hog," Jefferson is condemned to death. Outraged by the portrayal of her godson as an unthinking animal, Miss Emma convinces teacher Grant Wiggins to prepare Jefferson to die like a man. Despite Wiggins's reluctance—both Jefferson's ignorance and the white system's condescension make him uncomfortable—he inspires the young man to succeed through the writing of a journal. Gaines "admirably manages to sustain the somber tone of the issues confronting the black citizens of Bayonne," *New York Times Book Review* contributor Carl Senna states, adding that "it is a tribute to Mr. Gaines's skill that he makes the conflicts convincing."

Praising the author's unusual ability to capture the everyday manners and prejudice of the time, *Time* critic R. Z. Sheppard adds that few writers "have [Gaines's] dramatic instinct for conveying the malevolence of racism and injustice without the usual accompanying self-righteousness." As Jonathan Yardley explains in his *Washington Post Book World* review, "It is not that Gaines is incapable of anger. . . . Rather it is that he has the breadth and depth of mind to understand that generalizations are always suspect, that one must look at individual humans instead of stereotypes if there is to be any hope of understanding them." "Gaines' masterpiece is about what Ralph Ellison and William Faulkner would call the morality of connectedness, of each individual's responsibility to his community, to the brotherhood beyond his self," Charles R. Larson concludes in Chicago *Tribune Books*. "This majestic, moving novel is an instant classic, a book that will be read, discussed and taught beyond the rest of our lives."

Gaines has said that he sees no end to the inspiration he finds in his Louisiana heritage, and likely will continue to write about the South. "Before Alex Haley called it *Roots*, I was trying to do something like that, to write about our past, where we come from," Gaines told Doyle in *Melus*. He further explained: "I'm trying to write

---

If you enjoy the works of Ernest J. Gaines, you may also want to check out the following books and films:

Maya Angelou, *I Know Why the Caged Bird Sings*, 1970.
Toni Morrison, *Song of Solomon*, 1977.
Ivan Turgenev, *Fathers and Sons*, 1862.
Dead Man Walking, Polygram Pictures, 1995.
The Piano Lesson (from August Wilson's play), CBS–Video, 1995.
A Soldier's Story, Columbia, 1984.

---

about a people I feel are worth writing about, to make the world aware of them, make them aware of themselves. They've always thought literature is written about someone else, and it's hard to convince them that they are worthy of literature. I keep repeating this over and over, to convince them." In addition, the author revealed that "my aim in literature is to develop character, not only the character in the book, but my character as well as yours, so that if you pick up the book, you will see something you feel is true, something not seen before, that will help develop your character from that day forward."

■ Works Cited

Bryant, Jerry H., "From Death to Life: The Fiction of Ernest J. Gaines," *Iowa Review*, winter, 1972, pp. 106-20.
Burns, Mary M., review of *A Long Day in November*, *Horn Book*, April, 1972, p. 153.
Byerman, Keith E., "Ernest J. Gaines," *Concise Dictionary of American Literary Biography*, Volume 6: *Broadening Views, 1968-1988*, Gale, 1989, pp. 96-109.
Desruisseaux, Paul, "Ernest Gaines: A Conversation," *New York Times Book Review*, June 11, 1978, pp. 13, 44-45.
Doyle, Mary Ellen, interview with Gaines in *Melus*, summer, 1984, pp. 59-81.
Gaines, Ernest, interview in *Essence*, August, 1993, p. 52.
Gayle, Addison, Jr., *The Way of the New World: The Black Novel in America*, Doubleday, 1975, pp. 294-300.
Greenfeld, Josh, review of *The Autobiography of Miss Jane Pittman*, *Life*, April 30, 1971, p. 18.
Jaschik, Scott, "A New Star in the Canon," *Chronicle of Higher Education*, May 11, 1994, pp. A23-A24.
Larson, Charles R., "End as a Man," *Tribune Books* (Chicago), May 9, 1993, p. 5.
Review of *A Lesson before Dying*, *Publishers Weekly*, March 1, 1993, p. 38.
Lippmann, Ellen, review of *In My Father's House*, *School Library Journal*, November, 1978, p. 81.
Review of *A Long Day in November*, *Publishers Weekly*, August 23, 1971, p. 81.
Maddocks, Melvin, "Root and Branch," *Time*, May 10, 1971, pp. K13-K17.
Magnier, Bernard, interview with Gaines in *UNESCO Courier*, April, 1995, pp. 5-7.
Maguire, Gregory, review of *A Gathering of Old Men*, *Horn Book*, December, 1983, pp. 739-40.
McMurtry, Larry, "Reverend Martin's Son," *New York Times Book Review*, June 11, 1978, p. 13.
Parker, Penny, review of *A Gathering of Old Men*, *Voice of Youth Advocates*, April, 1984, p. 30.
Price, Reynolds, "A Louisiana Pageant of Calamity," *New York Times Book Review*, October 30, 1983, p. 15.
Sachs, Marilyn, review of *A Long Day in November*, *New York Times Book Review*, February 13, 1972, p. 8.
Senna, Carl, "Dying Like a Man," *New York Times Book Review*, August 8, 1993, p. 21.
Sheppard, R. Z., "An A-Plus in Humanity," *Time*, March 29, 1993, pp. 65-66.
Summer, Bob, "PW Interviews: Ernest J. Gaines," *Publishers Weekly*, May 24, 1993, pp. 62, 64.
Walker, Alice, review of *The Autobiography of Miss Jane Pittman*, *New York Times Book Review*, May 23, 1971, pp. 6, 12.
Watkins, Mel, review of *In My Father's House*, *New York Times*, July 20, 1978, p. C19.

Whitman, Digby B., review of *A Long Day in November, Book World,* November 7, 1971, Part II, p. 6.

Yardley, Jonathan, "Nothing but a Man," *Washington Post Book World,* March 28, 1993, p. 3.

■ For More Information See

BOOKS

Beavers, Herman, *Wrestling Angels into Song: The Fictions of Ernest J. Gaines and James Alan McPherson,* University of Pennsylvania Press, 1994.

Contemporary Literary Criticism, Gale, Volume 3, 1975, Volume 11, 1979, Volume 18, 1981, Volume 86, 1995.

Dictionary of Literary Biography, Gale, Volume 2: *American Novelists since World War II,* 1978, Volume 33: *Afro-American Fiction Writers after 1955,* 1984.

Dictionary of Literary Biography Yearbook: 1980, Gale, 1981.

Estes, David C., editor, *Critical Reflections on the Fiction of Ernest J. Gaines,* University of Georgia Press, 1994.

O'Brien, John, editor, *Interview with Black Writers,* Liveright, 1973.

Simpson, Anne K., *A Gathering of Gaines: The Man and the Writer,* University of Southwestern Louisiana, Center for Louisiana Studies, 1991.

Twentieth-Century Young Adult Writers, 1st edition, St. James Press, 1995.

Wooton, Carl, and Marcia Gaudet, editors, *Porch Talk with Ernest Gaines: Conversations on the Writer's Craft,* Louisiana State University Press, 1990.

PERIODICALS

Bulletin of the Center for Children's Books, February, 1972, p. 91.

Horn Book, October, 1978, p. 546.

Kliatt, spring, 1984, p. 8.

Los Angeles Times Book Review, May 30, 1993, p. 11.

Publishers Weekly, March 8, 1971, p. 64.

New Statesman, September 2, 1973, pp. 205-06.

Saturday Review, May 1, 1971, p. 40.

School Library Journal, July, 1993, p. 110.

Times Literary Supplement, March 16, 1973, p. 303.

Voice of Youth Advocates, October, 1993, p. 216.

Washington Post Book World, June 18, 1978, p. E5.

OTHER

Louisiana Stories: Ernest Gaines (television documentary), WHMM-TV, 1993.*

—Sketch by Diane Telgen

Nancy Garden

actress and lighting designer, taught at various levels, and done freelance editorial work for various publishers. Gives talks at schools and libraries to children on writing and speaks at writer's conferences for adults. *Member:* Society of Children's Book Writers and Illustrators, PEN American Center.

■ Personal

Born May 15, 1938, in Boston, MA; her father served as an executive with the Rhode Island Seminar on Human Relations, National Conference of Christians and Jews, and her mother, Elisabeth (maiden name, Yens) Garden, was a psychologist and social worker. *Education:* Columbia University, B.F.A. from School of Dramatic Arts, 1961, M.A. from Teacher's College, 1962. *Hobbies and other interests:* Gardening, weaving, hiking, running, cross-country skiing, traveling.

■ Addresses

Home—Carlisle, MA, and West Tremont, ME.

■ Career

Scholastic Magazines, New York City, began as assistant editor, became associate editor, 1966-70; Houghton Mifflin Co., Boston, MA, editor, 1971-76; writing teacher, freelance writer, and book reviewer, 1976—. Has also worked in theater as an

■ Awards, Honors

Annie on My Mind was selected as a 1982 *Booklist* Reviewer's Choice, and was on the 1982 American Library Association (ALA) Best Books list and the 1970-83 ALA Best of the Best list; *Fours Crossing* was on the 1983-84 William Allen White Award Master List.

■ Writings

FICTION

What Happened in Marston, illustrated by Richard Cuffari, Four Winds, 1971.
The Loners, Viking, 1972.
Maria's Mountain, illustrated by Barbara Brascove, Houghton, 1981.
Annie on My Mind, Farrar, Straus, 1982.
(Adaptor) *Favorite Tales from Grimm*, illustrated by Mercer Mayer, Four Winds, 1982.
Prisoner of Vampires, illustrated by Michele Chessare, Farrar Straus, 1984.
Peace, O River, Farrar, Straus, 1986.

Lark in the Morning, Farrar, Straus, 1991.
My Sister, the Vampire, Knopf, 1992.
Prisoner of Vampires, Farrar, Straus, 1993.
My Brother, the Werewolf, Bullseye Books, 1994.
Dove and Sword, Farrar, Straus, 1995.

"FOURS CROSSING" SEQUENCE

Fours Crossing, Farrar, Straus, 1981.
Watersmeet, Farrar, Straus, 1983.
The Door Between, Farrar, Straus, 1987.

"MONSTER HUNTERS" SERIES

Mystery of the Night Raider, Farrar, Straus, 1987.
Mystery of the Midnight Menace, Farrar, Straus, 1988.
Mystery of the Secret Marks, Farrar, Straus, 1989.
Mystery of the Kidnapped Kidnapper, Minstrel, 1994.
Mystery of the Watchful Witches, Minstrel, 1994.

NONFICTION

Berlin: City Split in Two, Putnam, 1971.
Vampires, Lippincott, 1973.
Werewolves, Lippincott, 1973.
Witches, Lippincott, 1975.
Devils and Demons, Lippincott, 1976.
Fun with Forecasting Weather, Houghton, 1977.
The Kids' Code and Cipher Book, Linnet, 1981.

■ Work in Progress

The Joining, a fourth volume in the "Fours Crossing" sequence.

■ Adaptations

What Happened in Marston was adapted for television and broadcast by the American Broadcasting Company (ABC) as an "ABC After School Special" under the title *The Color of Friendship*; *Annie on My Mind* was adapted for television and first broadcast by the British Broadcasting Corporation (BBC) in 1992.

■ Sidelights

Nancy Garden's books for young people vary between the realistic and the fantastic. *What Happened in Marston* tells of racial problems in 1960s New York. *Annie on My Mind* is an examination of two girls and the discovery of their feelings for each other. Other volumes look at topics such as *Vampires, Werewolves, Witches,* and *Devils and Demons.* "I write for young people because I like them," Garden once wrote in *Contemporary Authors*, "and because I think they are important. Children's books can be mind-stretchers and imagination-ticklers and builders of good taste in a way that adult books cannot, because young people usually come to books with more open minds. It's exciting to be able to contribute to that in a small way."

"I suppose the fact that I was an only child played a big part in my becoming a writer," Nancy Garden declares in an autobiographical essay in *Something about the Author Autobiography Series (SAAS)*. Garden was born in Boston, Massachusetts, in 1938, to a Red Cross executive of Sicilian ancestry, and his wife, a trained social worker with parents of German descent. Both of her parents strongly influenced Garden's thinking. "When I was growing up," Garden relates in *SAAS*, "Dad used to tell me that a girl could do anything a boy could do, but that in order to get recognized, she had to do it twice as well. I could do anything I wanted, he'd say, if I worked hard enough at it." "Mum was a strong woman, both physically and emotionally," Garden continues. "She was my best friend while I was growing up, my confidante, and my rock. I could talk about almost anything with her, and she always encouraged me to think for myself." Almost as influential was Garden's great-aunt Anna. "She had been born in Germany . . . [and] had no children of her own, but she brought up my mother and her brother and sister," Garden explains. "She understood children and dogs as did few adults, and had unending patience with both."

"We moved a lot when I was a child," Garden explains in *SAAS*, "partly because of my father's job with the American Red Cross and partly because of the housing shortage that followed World War II." Although she was born in Boston, Garden's family moved to New York City, then to Cambridge and Concord, Massachusetts. Garden spent her early school years in Scarsdale, New York, and then moved to nearby White Plains before finally settling in Providence, Rhode Island, in 1947. Her uprooted early life meant that she had to make new friends often. Like many authors, Garden spent a lot of time reading. She recalls first encountering A. A. Milne's adventures of Christopher Robin and Winnie-the-Pooh, and Robert Lawson's *Rabbit Hill* while living in Scarsdale.

"I was sick a lot, too, and that meant I often had to amuse myself," Garden writes in *SAAS*. "Since I loved to read and had always been read to by my parents, this wasn't hard, nor was it much of a step from reading to acting out what I read and making up stories based on my favorite characters." The same summer that she moved to White Plains, New York, the author continues, she came

> *"... I believe any challenge to any book endangers the First Amendment. Still, I entered this battle with equal measures of fear, rage, and eagerness—and sometimes a desire for it all to go away so I could work on my next book."*

down with scarlet fever. "I spent most of our time in White Plains being sick, recovering, and then being sick again," Garden states in *SAAS*, "for I ran around too much when I was finally allowed out, and had a relapse." She spent the time reading Anna Sewell's *Black Beauty* and reenacting scenes from Rudyard Kipling's *The Jungle Books*. Garden also declares in *SAAS* that she "discovered another wonderful author—Hugh Lofting—and his lovable character, Dr. Doolittle."

Garden recalls other influences on her writing, including stories from World War II and the fears of the emerging Cold War. "I can still see the *Life* magazine photos of mass graves in the concentration camps," Garden relates in *SAAS*, "and I know that like many other World War II children, I lived in terror of the atom bomb. The world could end at any moment; life could end, and there was nothing anyone—even grown-ups—could do about it. People have asked me why so many of my books deal with death in some way; perhaps this is why." *Berlin: City Split in Two,*

Garden's first non-fiction book, tells about one of the consequences of the war: the division of Germany's capital city between the occupying forces of the Soviet Union and the Western Allies—the U.S., France, and Great Britain.

Call of the Stage

When she entered Lincoln School, a private institution run by the Society of Friends (the Quakers) in the early 1950s, Garden found a new interest. "At Lincoln I discovered theater, and realized that I wanted to be an actress," Garden explains in *SAAS*. "It was an obsession with me, akin to what I imagine a religious vocation is like for a girl of the same age." While she attended Lincoln School, Garden met her best friend and future companion Sandra Scott, and began a career performing in professional summer stock theater in Peterborough, New Hampshire. Her experiences there showed up in some of her fiction; *Mystery of the Secret Marks* is partly based on some strange fires that occurred while she was performing in the Hilltop Theater, a summer stock program, outside Baltimore, Maryland. "Was it arson? We never really knew, but one member of the acting company was let go, as was a young odd-jobs man, and the fires stopped," Garden recalls.

These experiences, among others, helped Garden decide to enroll in the Columbia School of Dramatic Arts in New York City, where she worked in lighting design and directed community theater. She had "done pretty well as an actress, both in college and in stock," Garden states in *SAAS*, "and I loved acting dearly, but I felt directing was more creative. Also, I was a character actress, and since many character parts are of older people, and there are plenty of older people around to play them, there's a lot of unbeatable competition around for a young character actor or actress in the professional theater." "After a while, though, it became clear that I was going to have trouble supporting myself in theater," she continues, "and so . . . I decided to go to Columbia Teachers College and major in speech." She received her Master's degree in 1962.

After completing her studies Garden settled in Brooklyn Heights and began teaching at Hunter College. However, her Hunter job was only part-time; and she had to work in an insurance office to make up the lost income. The company failed,

NANCY GARDEN

Annie on My Mind

aerial fiction

In this controversial young adult novel, two young women discover the joys and fears of their first homosexual relationship.

Garden relates in *SAAS*, but while she was there she made two new friends, Barbara Seuling and Winnette Glasgow. "While we were all at the insurance company," she states, "Barb and I discovered we were both 'interested' in children's books, she as an illustrator and me as a writer. We collaborated on a book called *Aloysius P. Bookworm*, in which we made, I think, every mistake a young writer and illustrator can possibly make." The book was never published. "We learned an enormous amount from those mistakes," Garden concludes, "and now that we both know some of the pitfalls to avoid, we're thinking of collaborating again, both as writers this time." In the 1960s, Garden began working as an editor for an editorial service. "We had a good time," she writes, "but we also tried to do our best for our poor clients, and we did manage to learn, from our work and from each other, a fair amount about writing and editing."

Celtic and Occult Fantasy

After a few years as an editor Garden took an extended trip to Europe with a friend, Renee Cafiero. "It was largely through visiting Wales and Scotland and reading about both that I began to learn about Celtic lore," Garden states in *SAAS*, "which led directly to my books about the made-up village of Fours Crossing, New Hampshire." *Fours Crossing,* according to *Horn Book* reviewer Paul Heins, concerns the "strange happenings caused by a religious rift in the community at the time of its settlement in the seventeenth century." The protagonist, Melissa Dunn, travels with her grandmother to Fours Crossing to live after the death of her mother. The townspeople preserve many of the traditional Celtic customs of their ancestors, including welcoming the spring season by carrying an evergreen tree around the village. The year that Melissa and her grandmother arrive, however, winter lingers on and spring refuses to come. In company with her friend Jed, Melissa discovers that an old hermit is preventing the onset of springtime through magic spells. "He is convinced," writes *School Library Journal* contributor Virginia Golodetz, "that the people must be punished for growing lax in following the Old Ways." The hermit captures Jed and Melissa and holds them prisoner in his root cellar. Finally Melissa manages to break the hermit's hold on the seasons and releases spring to the town.

The sequel to *Fours Crossing,* titled *Watersmeet,* continues Melissa's adventures. Although the hermit's power has been broken, the release of spring has caused the flooding of the village. A newcomer, named Rhiannon, also brings dissent to the community. Many of the villagers—including, for a time, Jed—believe that she is allied with the hermit. Melissa is one of the few that believe in Rhiannon's innate goodness and the positive effects of her power. "A succession of events," writes *Horn Book* reviewer Mary M. Burns, "provides a battleground for conflict between the old ways and the new as the hermit manipulates ancient rituals and contemporary fears into an attack on stable community institutions."

Garden continues the story of Fours Crossing in *The Door Between.* Melissa has discovered that she is the descendant of the true Keepers of the Old Ways—the job that the mad hermit has hitherto claimed. With the aid of Jed, her dog Ulfin, and her sparrowhawk Llyr, Melissa has to travel to the world of the dead to defeat the hermit and merge the Old Ways with the new. "Melissa wins the hermit over with a new-found compassion and maturity," declares a *Publishers Weekly* reviewer. Despite some reservations—reviewers noted that it was difficult for readers unfamiliar with the earlier volumes to follow the story line—critics generally praised Garden's "Fours Crossing" series. "Melissa is a resourceful character," declares a *Booklist* writer, "and readers of the first two books won't want to miss the third saga in this projected quartet."

With the "Fours Crossing" novels underway, Garden launched the "Monster Hunters" series. Like Melissa's adventures, the stories of the "Monster Hunters" tell about preteens—Brian, Mumbles, and Dark—confronting the occult. In the first volume, *Mystery of the Night Raiders,* Brian launches an investigation of a series of mysterious cattle deaths on his grandparents' Vermont farm. Brian, a mystery fan; Mumbles, a budding scientist; and Dark, an athlete, are unprepared "for the possibility that something supernatural is behind the deaths of the cows," writes a *Publishers Weekly* reviewer, "until it looks as if Brian has become the next dish on a vampire's menu." The second volume in the series, *Mystery of the Midnight Menace,* looks at the possibility that one of Brian's classmates is in fact the werewolf that has been terrifying Central Park. "This is a creepy, moody piece for lovers of the genre," declares JoEllen Broome in *Voice of Youth Advocates,* "and big chuckles for the more skeptical among us."

Garden has also explored the problem of the undead in several non-series titles, including *Prisoner of Vampires* and *My Sister, the Vampire.* Preteen Alexander Darlington has an enthusiasm for vampires—until he actually meets one in the person of Radu. Radu, "a red-lipped specter of a man who has a taste for rare roast-beef sandwiches," according to a *Booklist* contributor, haunts the basement of a small library where Alexander is doing research for his project on the undead. Radu gains a power over Alexander and uses him to victimize Alexander's older sister Peggy. "Thanks to Alexander's brave friend Mike and a wise old

neighbor, Mrs. Potter," writes a *Publishers Weekly* critic, "the villain is done in and the prisoners are saved." "It's a chilling, gorey and absurdly funny story with perfectly suited black-and-white illustrations," declares Trev Jones in the *School Library Journal.* "Horror fans will love it."

If you enjoy the works of Nancy Garden, you may also want to check out the following books:

Jean Ferris, *Looking for Home,* 1989.
Deborah Hautzig, *Hey, Dollface,* 1978.
R. L. Stine, *Goodnight Kiss,* 1992.
Robert Swindells, *A Serpent's Tooth,* 1989.
Jane Yolen, *Werewolves: A Collection of Original Stories,* 1988.

My Sister the Vampire tells the story of three siblings—Tim, Sarah, and Jenny—who are left alone at their family's summer home in Maine. Strange events haunt their time, dampening their pleasure at being on their own. "Hundreds of bats invade the house," explains Lyle Blake Smythers in *School Library Journal;* "the girl in the neighboring cabin is wasting away, haunted by disturbing dreams; and Sarah seems to be developing the same symptoms." Eventually the children, together with Emily's brother John, confront the mysterious new owners of nearby Spool Island and bring the matter to a close. "Sure to be popular with those who like to be scared but not terrified," concludes Sally Estes in *Booklist.*

Sex and Growing Up

Garden's best-known book, however, has little to do with the occult. *Annie on My Mind* is the story of two girls who fall in love with each other. The story begins with the adult Annie and Liza reflecting on their relationship while attending college on opposite coasts. It chronicles their meeting at a New York museum and the discovery of their relationship by school officials. At the end of the volume, in a positive reinforcement of individual values and choices, the two girls reaffirm their feelings for one another. Critics praised Garden's treatment of adolescent homosexuality. Mary K. Chelton writes in *Voice of Youth Advocates* that the book's "writing is clear, consistent, at times lyrical, but best of all gut-level believable." *School Library Journal* contributor Roger D. Sutton declares that Garden "gives the relationship a solid resonance that until now has been absent from this genre."

Because of its subject matter, *Annie on My Mind* became the subject of a federal court case in 1995. The school board of Olathe, Kansas, voted to remove *Annie on My Mind* from the school even though no students or parents had complained about the book over the decade it had been on the library's shelves. In 1993, when a gay rights group called Project 21 donated a copy of *Annie on My Mind* to the Olathe school library, the board, dominated by members who believed that homosexuality was wrong, directed the library to remove the book from circulation. In response, the American Civil Liberties Union, on behalf of some students, their parents, and a science teacher, filed suit in federal court, claiming that the school board had violated their constitutional rights of free speech and due process. According to a *Kansas City Star* reporter, "School officials replied that they were exercising their right to choose material for students and their right not to succumb to the agenda of a special interest group."

Garden testified at the trial, as did Olathe media specialists and members of the Olathe school board. In November, 1995, United States District Judge Thomas Van Bebber ruled that "the book was unconstitutionally removed from the shelves," and the Olathe school board decided not to appeal the decision, though they did announce plans to revise their book selection process. *Annie on My Mind* has since been returned to school library shelves. In a *Voice of Youth Advocates* article titled "*Annie* on Trial: How It Feels To Be the Author of a Challenged Book," Garden stated, ". . . I believe any challenge to any book endangers the First Amendment. Still, I entered this battle with equal measures of fear, rage, and eagerness—and sometimes a desire for it all to go away so I could work on my next book." She added, ". . . we must stand firmly together in our resolve to protect the amendment that protects us and that allows people in this country free access to all ideas. *Annie* won, but there are other battles still to fight."

"Garden's *Annie on My Mind*," declares Roger D. Sutton in the *Bulletin of the Center for Children's Books*, "was a groundbreaker in its romantic treatment of a gay theme." *Lark in the Morning*, the critic continues, "is notable in that it presents a gay relationship as just one (and a subordinate one, at that) story element." *Lark in the Morning* tells of Gillian Harrison, seventeen years old and in a committed relationship with her best friend, Suzanne. Gillian arrives at her parents' summer home in Pookatasset, Rhode Island only to find that the place has been burglarized and a number of items—including her diary, which spells out the details of her relationship with Suzanne—have been taken. Gillian sets out to recover her lost property and soon uncovers the culprits: two young runaways from an abusive home, Jackie and Lark, who are hiding in an old hut nearby. Gillian takes Lark into her confidence, coaxes her out of her suicidal depression, and begins a plan to get them to their aunt's home in New Hampshire—even though she has to lie to her family, her friend Brad, and the authorities. "By interweaving the issues of child abuse, suicide, runaways, and homosexuality with ethical questions regarding helping 'outlaws' and lying . . . in order to protect others," writes *School Library Journal* contributor Dona Weisman, "Garden offers readers much food for thought." "Garden, author of the remarkable *Annie on My Mind*," declares Rebecca Sue Taylor in *Voice of Youth Advocates*, "again creates an honest and realistic look at love, truth, and responsibility."

Peace, O River is also a "problem book," but it echoes the themes that Garden examined back in *What Happened in Marston*. In it, states *New York Times Book Review* contributor Merri Rosenberg, "Nancy Garden uses the contemporary issue of nuclear waste to propel what is essentially a thinly veiled tale about class and social status." It tells the story of 16-year-old Kate Kincaid, who has returned to her childhood home of River View, Massachusetts, after her father's heart attack. River View, which is an affluent neighborhood, has a long-standing feud with its companion town of Hastings Bay, a blue-collar area. Recently the rumor of a nuclear waste dump to be located in the area has made the feud worse. Kate and her new friend from Hastings Bay, Pippa Brown, try to end the bad feelings. However, the anger spills over into the local high school. Kate's brother is attacked and beaten; Pippa is nearly raped, and Kate's old friend Jon drowns in the river. Jon's death finally ends the feud. "The novel's main interest," states a *Booklist* reviewer, "lies in the conflicts about ideas—is it 'heartless' to care more for the general good than for family and friends?

Is it 'bossy' to try to change things? Does total pacificism always make sense, locally and globally?" The book, declares a *Horn Book* critic, "is a valiant attempt to help teenagers understand the tremendous difficulties faced by those who would seek to solve difficult problems through direct nonviolent intervention."

In *Dove and Sword*, a historical novel set in fifteenth-century France, Garden takes a different slant on the problem novel by looking at the pros and cons of war. The book tells the story of Joan of Arc through the eyes of a friend, Gabrielle, who is taken with Joan's inspirational voices and violent death. Garden provides a modern perspective on the events leading up to Joan's martyrdom. "This is a fascinating and well-written historical novel," writes Ann W. Moore in *School Library Journal*, "filled with rich details, evocative descriptions, and interesting characters." Garden's "strategically plotted novel," declares a *Publishers Weekly* critic, "achieves the highest goals of historical fiction—it vivifies the past, robustly and respectfully, then uses its example to steer the audience toward a more courageous future."

Garden writes in *SAAS* that she regards writing as a wonderful occupation. "What nicer requirements could there be for a career? Think of it: when you curl up with a book on a rainy day; when you visit a new place or meet a new person; when you feel sorrow or joy, you're not just being lazy or having fun or living life as anyone might live it—you're also, even if you're not aware of it, *working*. What joy!"

■ **Works Cited**

"Board Tells Reason for Banning Book," *Kansas City Star*, October 5, 1955, p. C4.

Broome, JoEllen, review of *Mystery of the Midnight Menace*, *Voice of Youth Advocates*, February, 1989, p. 284.

Burns, Mary M., review of *Watersmeet*, *Horn Book*, October, 1983, pp. 580-81.

Chelton, Mary K., review of *Annie on My Mind*, *Voice of Youth Advocates*, August, 1982, p. 30.

Review of *The Door Between*, *Publishers Weekly*, July 24, 1987, p. 187.

Review of *The Door Between*, *Booklist*, November 1, 1987, p. 476.

Estes, Sally, review of *My Sister, the Vampire*, *Booklist*, July, 1992, p. 1931.

Garden, Nancy, essay in *Something about the Author Autobiography Series*, Volume 8, Gale, 1989.

Garden, Nancy, sketch in *Contemporary Authors, New Revision Series*, Volume 30, Gale, 1990, p. 147.

Garden, Nancy, "*Annie* on Trial: How It Feels To Be the Author of a Challenged Book," *Voice of Youth Advocates*, June, 1996.

Golodetz, Virginia, review of *The Door Between*, *School Library Journal*, December, 1987, pp. 99-100.

Heins, Paul, review of *Fours Crossing*, *Horn Book*, August, 1981, pp. 431-32.

Jones, Trev, review of *Prisoner of Vampires*, *School Library Journal*, February, 1985, pp. 73-74.

Moore, Ann W., review of *Dove and Sword*, *School Library Journal*, November, 1995, p. 119.

Review of *Mystery of the Night Raiders*, *Publishers Weekly*, November 13, 1987, p. 71.

Review of *Peace, O River*, *Horn Book*, January/February, 1986, pp. 91-92.

Review of *Peace, O River*, *Booklist*, March 1, 1986, p. 973.

Review of *Prisoner of Vampires*, *Publishers Weekly*, January 25, 1985, p. 94.

Review of *Prisoner of Vampires*, *Booklist*, April 1, 1985, p. 1119.

Rosenberg, Merri, review of *Peace, O River*, *New York Times Book Review*, March 2, 1986, p. 29.

Smythers, Lyle Blake, review of *My Sister, the Vampire*, *School Library Journal*, September, 1992, p. 252.

Sutton, Roger D., review of *Annie on My Mind*, *School Library Journal*, August, 1982, p. 125.

Sutton, Roger D., review of *Lark in the Morning*, *Bulletin of the Center for Children's Books*, June, 1991, p. 236.

Weisman, Dona, review of *Lark in the Morning*, *School Library Journal*, June, 1991, pp. 124-25.

■ **For More Information See**

BOOKS

Gallo, Donald R., editor and compiler, *Speaking for Ourselves, Too*, National Council of Teachers of English, 1993.

Something about the Author, Volume 77, Gale, 1994, pp. 69-72.

Twentieth-Century Young Adult Writers, St. James, 1994, pp. 233-34.

PERIODICALS

ALAN Review, winter, 1996.

Bulletin of the Center for Children's Books, May, 1981, p. 170; December, 1982, p. 66; November, 1983, p. 48; October, 1987, p. 27.

Horn Book, December, 1983, p. 580; March/April, 1996, p. 206.

Publishers Weekly, June 7, 1991, p. 676; July 6, 1992, p. 56.

School Library Journal, September, 1983, p. 134; November, 1987, pp. 104-05; December, 1988, p. 103.

Voice of Youth Advocates, February, 1984, p. 338; June, 1986, p. 78.*

—Sketch by Kenneth R. Shepherd

Alan Garner

■ Personal

Born October 17, 1934, in Congleton, Cheshire, England; son of Colin (a decorator) and Marjorie (a tailor) Garner; married Ann Cook, 1956 (marriage dissolved); married Griselda Greaves, 1972; children: (first marriage) one son, two daughters; (second marriage) one son, one daughter. *Education:* Attended Magdalen College, Oxford. *Hobbies and other interests:* Archaeology and the history and folklore of Cheshire.

■ Addresses

Home—"Toad Hall," Blackden-cum-Goostrey, Cheshire CW4 8BY, England.

■ Career

Writer. *Military service:* Served two years in the Royal Artillery; became second lieutenant.

■ Awards, Honors

Carnegie Medal commendation, 1965, for *Elidor;* Carnegie Medal, 1967, and *Guardian* Award for children's fiction, 1968, both for *The Owl Service;* Lewis Carroll Shelf Award, 1970, for *The Weirdstone of Brisingamen: A Tale of Alderly;* selected as a highly commended author by the Hans Christian Andersen Award committee of the International Board on Books for Young People, 1978; first prize, Chicago International Film Festival, 1981, for *Images;* Mother Goose Award, 1987, for *A Bag of Moonshine;* Phoenix Award, Children's Literature Association of America, 1996, for *The Stone Book.*

■ Writings

FICTION

The Weirdstone of Brisingamen: A Tale of Alderly, Collins, 1960, published as *The Weirdstone: A Tale of Alderly,* F. Watts, 1961, revised edition, Penguin, 1963, Walck, 1969.
The Moon of Gomrath (sequel to *The Weirdstone of Brisingamen*), Collins, 1963, Walck, 1967.
Elidor, illustrated by Charles Keeping, Collins, 1965, Walck, 1967.
The Old Man of Mow, photographs by Roger Hill, Collins, 1966, Doubleday, 1970.
The Owl Service, Collins, 1967, Walck, 1968.
Red Shift, Collins, 1973, Macmillan, 1973.
The Breadhorse, illustrated by Albin Trowski, Collins, 1975.
Alan Garner's Fairy Tales of Gold (contains *The Golden Brothers, The Girl of the Golden Gate, The Three Golden Heads of the Well,* and *The Princess and the Golden Mane*), four volumes, illustrated

by Michael Foreman, Collins, 1979, one-volume edition, Philomel, 1980.

"STONE BOOK QUARTET" SERIES

The Stone Book, etchings by Michael Foreman, Collins (London), 1976, Collins (New York), 1978.

Tom Fobble's Day, etchings by Foreman, Collins (London), 1977, Collins (New York), 1979.

Granny Reardun, etchings by Foreman, Collins (London), 1977, Collins & World, 1978.

The Aimer Gate, etchings by Foreman, Collins (London), 1978, Collins (New York), 1979.

The Stone Book Quartet (contains *The Stone Book, Granny Reardun, The Aimer Gate,* and *Tom Fobble's Day*), Collins (New York), 1983, Dell, 1988.

PLAYS

Holly from the Bongs: A Nativity Play (music by William Mayne; produced in Goostrey, Cheshire, England, 1965; revised version with music by Gordon Grosse produced in Manchester, England, 1974), photographs by Roger Hill, Collins, 1966, revised version published in *Labrys 7* (Frome, Somerset, England), 1981.

The Belly Bag, music by Richard Morris, produced in London, 1971.

Potter Thompson (music by Crosse; produced in London, 1975), Oxford University Press, 1975.

To Kill a King (television play; broadcast, 1980), published in *Labrys 7*, 1981.

The Green Mist (dance drama), published in *Labrys 7*, 1981.

Also author of plays, *Lurga Lom*, 1980, and *Sally Water*, 1982. Author of screenplays, including *Places and Things*, 1978, and *Images*, 1981. Author of radio plays, including *Have You Met Our Tame Author?*, 1962, *Elidor*, 1962, *The Weirdstone of Brisingamen*, 1963, *Thor and the Giants*, 1965, revised, 1979, *Idun and the Apples of Life*, 1965, revised as *Loki and the Storm Giant*, 1979, *Baldur the Bright*, 1965, revised, 1979, and *The Stone Book, Granny Reardun, Tom Fobble's Day*, and *The Aimer Gate*, all 1980. Author of television plays, including *The Owl Service*, 1969, *Lamaload*, 1978, *Red Shift* (with John Mackenzie), 1978, *To Kill a King* ("Leap in the Dark" series), 1980, and *The Keeper*, 1982.

OTHER

(Editor) *A Cavalcade of Goblins*, illustrated by Krystyna Turska, Walck, 1969, published in En-gland as *The Hamish Hamilton Book of Goblins: An Anthology of Folklore*, Hamish Hamilton, 1969, also published as *A Book of Goblins*, Penguin, 1972.

(Compiler) *The Guizer: A Book of Fools*, Hamish Hamilton, 1975, Greenwillow, 1976.

The Lad of the Gad (folktales), Collins, 1980, Philomel Books, 1981.

(Reteller) *Alan Garner's Book of British Fairy Tales*, illustrated by Derek Collard, Collins, 1984, Delacorte, 1985.

(Reteller) *Jack and the Beanstalk*, Collins, 1985, illustrated by Julek Heller, Delacorte, 1992.

A Bag of Moonshine (folktales), illustrated by Patrick James Lynch, Delacorte, 1986.

(Reteller) *Once Upon a Time, Though It Wasn't in Your Time, and It Wasn't in My Time, and It Wasn't in Anybody Else's Time* (folktales; contains "The Girl and the Geese," "The Fox, the Hare, and the Cock," and "Battibeth"; originally published in England), illustrated by Norman Messenger, Dorling Kindersley, 1993.

Member of editorial board of "Detskaya Literatura," Moscow. Manuscripts collected at Brigham Young University, Provo, UT.

■ Sidelights

When Alan Garner was a child, he almost died three times. A very sickly boy, he suffered variously from spinal and cerebral meningitis, pleurisy, pneumonia, and diphtheria, at times so ill that he could neither speak nor move. It was on these occasions that, although he was not technically dead, the doctors at the time felt there was no hope for him and told his parents that, even if their son recovered, his brain would be severely damaged. But the young Garner had other ideas: he eventually recovered from his illnesses, went on to school at Oxford, and became an award-winning author. Respected for his knowledge of folklore and mythology, Garner is best known for such fantasy novels as *Elidor, The Owl Service,* and *Red Shift*, as well as his "Stone Book" quartet. With works such as these, he "was throughout most of the 1960s and '70s the most talked-about children's author in Britain," related Michael Dirda in the *Washington Post Book World*.

Although Garner is often classified as a fantasy writer for young audiences, his work has undergone an evolution over the years that exceeds the limitations of any one genre. It can more accurately be said that he is an author fascinated by time and place and the history and folklore that go with them, an author who, as he himself said, as quoted in Frank Eyre's *British Children's Books in the Twentieth Century*, only "uses fantasy as crutch." This is not to say Garner takes the easy way out—far from it. With each book he has demanded more from his readers, so that, by the time he wrote *Red Shift*, critics were questioning whether or not he should still be classified as a children's writer. "I write for myself and for no other audience," Garner declared in *Speaking for Ourselves: Autobiographical Sketches by Notable Authors of Books for Young Adults*. "Yet, for some reason that I do not understand, I am read with far greater passion, intelligence, and commitment by young people than by adults. Is that strange?"

A Sense of Time and Place

Garner credits his long childhood illness as being the inspiration for his view of time, which permeates so much of his work. "For most children, I know now, time drags," he wrote in *Horn Book*. "That is because inertia is uncommon and days are filled with events. But where a child has only inertia, time must not rule. And I played with time as if it were chewing gum, making a minute last an hour, and a day compress to a minute. I had to. . . . I switched myself off. And the universe opened. I was shown a totality of space and time." Garner's interest in place has its roots in his family. He was born in Congleton, Cheshire, near the Keuper and Bunter Triassic sandstones, an eroded, six-hundred-foot-high hill that the locals called "the Edge." Garner's family and ancestors were all craftsmen, miners, and stonecutters who had a great respect for this land, where legend had it that King Arthur was buried behind a rock called the Iron Gates. But Garner, who was the first in his family to receive a higher education, also gained a scientific awe of Alderly Edge. "For me the Edge both stopped and melted time," he continued in *Horn Book*. "I knew enough geology to become amazed. I could trace the tidal vortex in the strata: the print of water swirling for a second under the pull of wind and moon and held for two hundred million years."

Garner's early education was achieved in sporadic steps because of his health. A meek child, he described himself in *Speaking for Ourselves* as "a

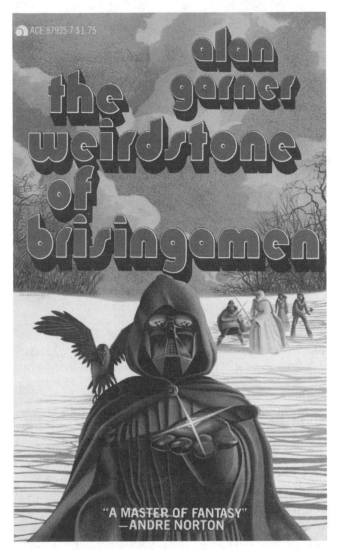

ACE 87935-7 $1.75

alan garner
the weirdstone of brisingamen

"A MASTER OF FANTASY"
—ANDRE NORTON

Recipient of the 1970 Lewis Carroll Shelf Award, this 1960 novel of the eternal struggle between good and evil, steeped in legend, folklore, and Celtic mythology, is the author's first book.

physical coward . . . [who] had a lot of practice at running away." He eventually turned this into an advantage, however, by becoming a talented track athlete. In fact, he became so good that his school coach believed he could make it to the Olympic semifinals. But Garner quit track because he did not believe in competition and because he wanted to pursue a career that did not end when a person turned thirty and was too old to keep up physically. After his two years of compulsory military service, Garner attended university.

"[By] the time I went to Oxford University I knew that I was heading in the wrong direction," he wrote in *Speaking for Ourselves*. Garner studied

Homeric archaeology at Magdalen College and later took up British mythology. He enjoyed mythology because it made him feel closer to his native land, but, at the same time, his education was causing a rift between him and his family, who felt that his learning was distancing him from them. As he told Justin Wintle and Emma Fisher in an interview for *Pied Pipers: Interviews with the Influential Creators of Children's Literature,* this caused a "traumatization within the family resulting in a total failure of communication, absolute social breakdown, collapse." In addition to this reason, Garner left Oxford after two years because he questioned the necessity of studying the Classics, and because he felt formal study would diminish his interaction with the land and its myths.

Apprentice Works

So Garner left school at the young age of twenty-two to start a career as a writer. After four years of effort, he still had not published a book, but in 1960 his first novel, *The Weirdstone of Brisingamen: A Tale of Alderly,* was published by Collins in London. This book, along with Garner's next work, *The Moon of Gomrath,* have been compared to the fantasies of J.R.R. Tolkien because they borrow heavily from mythology and folklore (although Garner's work is more influenced by Celtic mythology than the Scandinavian and English elements found in Tolkien), but they are also considered apprentice works. Both novels are set in Garner's native Cheshire—indeed, in his own backyard near Alderly Edge—and feature the same two protagonists, siblings Susan and Colin. In *The Weirdstone of Brisingamen* the children, who are staying with some friends who live on a Cheshire farm, meet a wizard named Cadellin Silverbrow from an alternate and magical world called Fundindelve. Cadellin tells them they have been chosen to find the weirdstone of Brisingamen, which must be used to awaken the enchanted knights who are the only ones who can fight the evil spirit Nastrona. *The Moon of Gomrath* brings Susan, Colin, and Cadellin back, aided by Atlendor the elf lord and a dwarf named Uthecar, to battle Brollachan—a formless, speechless, black spirit—and the witch-queen Morrigan. This time, instead of the weirdstone, Susan has the magical Mark of Fohla to help fight their evil foes.

Reviewers of these novels were quick to draw parallels with two other famous fantasy writers.

Favorably comparing Garner to fellow English authors J.R.R. Tolkien and Lloyd Alexander, *School Library Journal* critic Michael Cart added, "Yet Garner's voice is uniquely his own: his novels in general are less diffuse, more controlled, and, in a sense, darker and more sophisticated." But, despite the fact that *The Weirdstone of Brisingamen* received a 1970 Lewis Carroll Shelf Award, many critics found flaws in these early works. In a completely opposing assessment of Cart's review, Eyre commented that the two books "are marred by uncertainty in their organisation, roughness in the writing and a general sense of unsureness of touch." Zena Sutherland, writing in the *Bulletin of the Center for Children's Books,* further averred that Garner's combination of real and fantasy worlds was "not completely successful." And a *Junior Bookshelf* reviewer thought the author littered his plot with "too many characters and too many names, and while some of the latter are mellifluous and haunting, others are ugly and confusing."

A common criticism of *The Weirdstone of Brisingamen* is that Susan and Colin are two-dimensional—and therefore unbelievable and unsympathetic—characters whose only purpose is to serve the plot. A *Times Literary Supplement* writer described Susan and Colin as "rather negative. They are people to whom things happen." Eyre simply commented that Garner's young protagonists "are not fully realised and do not come alive." Interestingly, Garner has not tried to deny that his early work was imperfect, and he even admitted that *The Weirdstone of Brisingamen* was "a fairly bad book," according to John Rowe Townsend in his *A Sense of Story: Essays on Contemporary Writers for Children.*

In retrospect, however, the time Garner spent on his first two novels was not in any way wasted, for in them the author planted the seeds for his future successes. *The Weirdstone of Brisingamen* and *The Moon of Gomrath* address a theme that Garner would continue to develop throughout his career: how a geographical place, including all its history, myths, folklore, and legends, have a profound effect upon our present-day lives. In his first works, Garner emphasizes the more magical aspects of a place—specifically, his native Cheshire—because of his professional interest in the mythology, and so his novels were naturally more inclined toward the fantasy genre. As he developed as a writer, however, he leaned less and less upon these fantastic elements like a "crutch." As a *Times Literary Supplement* critic noted, "To read this author's books straight through in their order of writing gives the reader a sense of the distances he has travelled."

Bringing Fantasy and Reality Together

Elidor was the first significant step in this evolution: whereas in his first two novels the fantasy land of Fundindelve remains separate from our world, in *Elidor* Garner begins to draw the two together. Again, the story involves children who find themselves in another reality that relies on the author's knowledge of mythology and legend.

> *"I write for myself and for no other audience. Yet, for some reason that I do not understand, I am read with far greater passion, intelligence, and commitment by young people than by adults. Is that strange?"*

When the Watson children—Roland, Helen, Nicholas, and David—wander into a bombed-out section of Manchester, they stumble into the ruins of a church where the fabric of reality has been weakened, and they suddenly find themselves meeting the wizard-minstrel Malebron in the doomed land of Elidor. The children—whose appearance in that world has been foretold as the event that augurs the return of light to the wasted four kingdoms—are given four objects (a sword, a stone, a cauldron, and a spear) that contain the virtues of that land. They then return home, where they hide the treasures to protect them until they can be used to vanquish Elidor's enemies. Once they are back, however, the magical objects turn into ordinary rubbish, but they are charged with a kind of static electricity that wreaks havoc upon the modern technology of this world. Other events, such as the appearance of a wounded unicorn, make it clear that Elidor can interact with this world. This has forbidding implications, for Malebron has warned the children that "the death

of Elidor would not be without echo in your world."

In *Elidor*, observed Eleanor Cameron in the *Wilson Library Bulletin*, "are the first hints of Garner's captivation by the idea of past, present, and future existing in a timeless moment which comes to fuller fruition in *The Owl Service*." Writing in his book *The Marble in the Water: Essays on Contemporary Writers of Fiction for Children and Young Adults*, David Rees pointed out how this theme relates to the part of the story in which the Watson children find the link to the parallel Elidor in a part of Piccadilly that is being bulldozed. *Elidor* "has something interesting to say . . . about the position and importance of myth in a modern context, about the power and significance of place. The derelict church and the cobbled working-class streets of Manchester, with their years of private and public history swept away by the bulldozer in the name of progress, are portrayed convincingly, particularly when paralleled with the blighting of the world of Elidor." Or, as the *Times Literary Supplement* critic phrased this problem, the "rich worlds upon which the mind can draw . . . are in danger of being destroyed by modern ways of thinking and living."

Uncompromising Complexity

Unlike his first two novels, Garner has his *Elidor* characters spend most of their time in Manchester, with the world of Elidor being rarely viewed by the reader. With *The Owl Service*, the plot device of children voyaging to another fantastic land is completely abandoned, and the author instead chooses to further develop his idea of the link between the past and present of a place that was first glimpsed in *Elidor*. Garner based *The Owl Service*, which won the 1967 Carnegie Medal, on a story from the Welsh epic *The Mabinogion*. This legend takes place in the valley of Ardudwy centuries ago, when Blodeuwedd, the wife of Lleu Llaw Gyffes who was magically created for him out of the flowers of the land, is unfaithful to her husband when she has a love affair with the dark lord Gronw Pebyr. Lleu Llaw Gyffes, filled with jealous rage, kills Gronw Pebyr, and Blodeuwedd is turned into an owl as punishment.

Garner had the idea of using a dinner service as a plot device when he saw a set of plates decorated with a floral pattern. The owner had traced the pattern and rearranged the pieces until they looked like an owl. In *The Owl Service* teenaged Alison discovers a similar service and becomes obsessed with it when she sees the owl within the flowers in the pattern. In this way the spirit of Blodeuwedd is released and possesses Alison to reenact the love triangle that has been tragically repeated for generations, once including her own dead father. Caught up in the legend are Gwyn, the Welsh boy whose mother is the housekeeper for Alison's family, and Roger, the son of Alison's new stepfather. Tensions between the three grow until the cycle is broken when Roger is able to get over his own jealousy and hatred for Gwyn to see a new pattern in the service, thus releasing them all from repeating the sad legend. As Cameron explained, "Only through a fresh 'seeing' of the design can both Blodeuwedd's and Alison's release be affected after continuing discoveries by Gwyn and Roger concerning the past."

The vehicle for the tension in the story is not only the legend-inspired love triangle but also a conflict brought about by class differences in the characters: Roger and Alison are middle-class English, Gwyn is lower-class Welsh. As Tony Watkins explained in *Good Writers for Young Readers*, "Interwoven into [the] central theme are other themes: the challenge of an intelligent and vital working-class boy to the accepted and somewhat effete middle-class conventions and proprieties; and the humiliating, potentially explosive situation whereby the Welsh cannot afford to keep their own houses and lands but must sell out to the English." Also important to the tale is how the children's parents, particularly Alison's domineering mother, take control of their children, thus making it difficult for them to lead their own independent lives and take a new course that will steer them clear of their fate. Interestingly, while Garner makes Gwyn the more well-rounded, sympathetic character and Alison and Roger are "vapid and superficial," according to Cameron, it is Roger who ultimately saves them from the legend's curse.

A number of critics have had difficulty accepting this resolution to the story. As Bob Dixon phrased it in his book *Catching Them Young: Political Ideas in Children's Fiction*, Garner "foists upon the reader an ending which just doesn't seem to grow out of the rest of the book, at all. He gives us the unlikable, selfish prig, Roger, as hero, and passes over Gwyn, who has been more attuned to the

legendary background of the book all along. Garner has tried to pass over this class prejudice by saying that it's Gwyn's illegitimacy which makes him 'incapable of coping with the epic quality of the situation.' Thankfully, it's very much to be doubted whether anyone else will share such a weird and destructive view." On the other hand, while Rees agreed that the book's ending "is not a strength" it is, nevertheless, "right intellectually." Alison cannot be saved by Gwyn, the critic explained, because Alison "is too trapped and crushed; she can never be herself . . . , dominated as she is by her revolting mother," and Gwyn is just as flawed as Alison. Rees conceded, though, that "the author should not have asked us to be so much on Gwyn's side emotionally; it leads inevitably to confusion, to a sense of letdown." *Growing Point* critic Margery Fisher, how-

A legend of a tragic triangle from the Welsh *Mabinogion* is reenacted through successive generations in this haunting fantasy which won the Carnegie Medal in 1967.

ever, had no such qualms when she wrote that the story's ending was perfectly appropriate: "It is the last irony of a subtle book that [Alison's] safety is achieved finally not by the sensitive, tormented Welsh boy but by brash, unimaginative Roger. The book shows how people change under stress—shows it in a novelist's manner, with none of the limitations of 'writing for children.'"

Despite problems like this, many critics considered *The Owl Service* to be a work deserving the Carnegie. Townsend, for one, declared that the book is "the most remarkable single novel to appear on a children's list in the 1960s." The critic also remarked, "To my mind *The Owl Service* shows a new maturity and authority; it is the work of a man who has mastered his craft and knows just what he is about."

Red Shift

Garner continued to develop his literary skill with *Red Shift*, which was published six years after *The Owl Service*. Even more technically complex than its predecessor, *Red Shift* takes place in three different time periods in England: post-Roman times, the civil war, and modern-age 1973. The main plot takes place in modern times. Tom is the central character, a sensitive, intelligent teenager whose domineering mother is reminiscent of Alison's in *The Owl Service*. Tom is in love with Jan, who is about to move to London. But the two young lovers manage to arrange a rendezvous at a rail junction called Crewe station. For a time, their relationship blossoms until Tom's mother interferes, planting little seeds of doubt in Tom's mind that eventually cause him to believe Jan is being unfaithful, which, by the novel's conclusion, destroys his love for her.

Linked with this plot are the two historical subplots, which feature Macey of the Roman Ninth Legion and Thomas, who is caught up in a massacre during the time of Oliver Cromwell. Both Thomas and Macey are having relationships that are threatened by interfering characters, and Garner causes the transitions between these periods to occur "by using painful moments in the characters' experiences to break through the time barrier, as though pain were a kind of telepathic switching gear," as Aidan Chambers explained it in *Horn Book*. They are also connected by a Stone

Age axe, which seems to offer a kind of magical protection to those who find it and which Tom—through a weakness in his character nurtured by his mother—gives away at the end of the novel, thus sealing his fate. Garner parallels Tom's prob-

---

If you enjoy the works of Alan Garner, you may also want to check out the following books and films:

John Christopher, *The City of Gold and Lead*, 1967.
Berlie Doherty, *Granny Was a Buffer Girl*, 1988.
Jean Thesman, *The Rain Catchers*, 1991.
Rosemary Wells, *Through the Hidden Door*, 1987.
Time Bandits, Paramount, 1986.

---

lems with Thomas and Macey's. "All act out the timeless dilemma of striving for honesty and permanence in love and of trying to come to terms with its reality in a universe of perpetual flux," wrote Michael Benton in *Children's Literature in Education*. The commonalities of the three co-plots are made all the more apparent by the author's technique of coalescing the three time periods so that, as the plots progress, the stories move closer and closer together, until, as Chambers described it, "the three faces merge into one color, one time, one place, one set of people, one meaning." This happens, according to Ursula K. Le Guin in *Foundation*, when "the pain [which causes the time shifts] becomes intolerable, and the three times become one."

Through this technique, Garner demonstrates "the significance of place and the insignificance of time," described Benton. But what the author is trying to say thematically has been open to some debate. "If a novel is supposed to be news about people," wrote *Best Sellers* contributor Clara M. Siggins, "the news [in *Red Shift*] is garbled." She later added that "this novel leaves the reader puzzled, even exasperated." Taking a clue from the book's title, which refers to the effect observed by astronomers when viewing galaxies retreating in every direction as the universe expands, Chambers speculated that the theme concerns "the impossibility of reconciliatory contact," or perhaps simply the need for one to distance him or herself from pain in order to better understand it.

Critics in general have recognized the technical brilliance of *Red Shift*, and some reviewers have noticed improvements over its predecessor. One *Times Literary Supplement* critic, for example, wrote that both *Red Shift* and *The Owl Service* address "themes of fundamental importance . . . but [*Red Shift*] is better structured and more carefully written." However, many reviewers found the book—which consists almost entirely of dialogue—too complex to be understandable by most readers, especially younger audiences. "Some readers become frustrated by hunting for clues in the text and feel that they are missing the hidden key that will unlock it for them," commented Robert Protherough in *Twentieth-Century Young Adult Writers*. Chambers, more directly to the point, remarked that with *Red Shift*, "Garner has given up any pretense of writing for children and is now writing entirely to please himself and those mature, sophisticated, literate readers who care to study his work."

Garner Achieves a Writer's Vision

About his audience, Garner commented in *The Signal Approach to Children's Books: A Collection* that if "a child can read with a totality of experience and the adult can too, that is a good children's book." This expectation, in the author's opinion, he accomplished better than ever before in his "Stone Book Quartet" series. He later told Chambers that "of all the work I've done so far, the only work which I would permanently want to hold on to is this quartet of four books, because what I set out to achieve, I surpassed." Critics of this set of four deceptively simple and short tales—*The Stone Book, Granny Reardun, The Aimer Gate,* and *Tom Fobble's Day*—agreed that the quartet was a crowning achievement in the author's career. Edward Blishen, for one, declared in *Books and Bookmen* that they are "beautiful books. Because of their rare clarity, and . . . exhilarations, they will be much loved by many children. But they're books for everybody. They are among those uncommon books that cause perfectly natural laughter and tears in a reader."

Each book is less than one hundred pages long and features members of a family living in the Cheshire village of Chorley. Together, the stories cover four generations from the middle of the nineteenth century to the time of World War II. Like Garner's own family, these people are crafts-

men, working as blacksmiths, miners, and clock makers. Though they don't have conventional plots, the tales dwell "on the truths of childhood . . . ," commented Ralph Lavender in the *Times Educational Supplement*. "One of these filed-down truths of human existence tells of the connectedness of things." In each book, a young character learns from the older generation to have a respect for good craftsmanship and for the family's Cheshire home. The sense of life's continuity—how each generation builds upon those that have come before it—is carried through each story, as items from the past reappear before the eyes of later generations: Mary in *The Stone Book* is lead to a Stone Age cave painting deep in a mine that reminds her how ancient the land is; Robert in *The Aimer Gate* finds his name written on a clock tower from a Robert of a previous generation; William's sledge runners in *Tom Fobble's Day* are made from a loom once owned by a previous William; and other instances such as these are scattered throughout the books.

The quartet is a significant departure for Garner. Up until their publication, his works had been getting more and more complex. But with the quartet, the author rediscovered the depth and elegance that simplicity can foster. "In the 'Stone Book Quartet,'" Townsend asserted, "the complications of showing-not-telling have been resolved with an artistry that is nothing short of breathtaking, a simplicity that engages everyone who can hear the voices of the characters on the page." The central theme of the books, which Townsend interpreted as Garner's lament for "the depreciation of human strength and skill, decline in the craftsmanship that comes from working elemental materials into artifacts of use and beauty," is made clearer by his more direct approach to the subject. "Where once [Garner's use of metaphor] was a stumbling block (at the end of *The Owl Service*, for example), now it has a diamond-like quality that makes us read his text as an exciting exploration in writing."

Garner has not written much original work since his quartet, many of his published works since that time being retellings or collections of fairy tales and folklore, but his contribution to children's literature will not be denied, even if he never publishes again. As Humphrey Carpenter asserted in his book *Secret Gardens: A Study of the Golden Age of Children's Literature*, "Alan Garner seems to stand at the culmination of the post-war movement in modern English children's writing." No longer using fantasy as a "crutch," Garner also managed to resolve the disparity between his classical education and his humble roots through his quartet. "*The Stone Book* is a glorious result of his personal resolution," Chambers concluded in another *Horn Book* article. "And in achieving it Garner has, to a significant extent, revised the standards by which writing for children, and for younger children especially, must now be judged in this country." Not bad for someone who was never supposed to survive childhood.

■ Works Cited

Benton, Michael, "Detective Imagination," *Children's Literature in Education*, March, 1974, pp. 5-12.

Blishen, Edward, "Garner's Quartet," *Books and Bookmen*, June, 1979, p. 57.

Cameron, Eleanor, "'The Owl Service': A Study," *Wilson Library Bulletin*, December, 1969, pp. 425-33.

Carpenter, Humphrey, *Secret Gardens: A Study of the Golden Age of Children's Literature*, Houghton Mifflin, 1985, pp. 210-23.

Cart, Michael, review of *The Weirdstone of Brisingamen: A Tale of Alderly, School Library Journal*, February, 1970, p. 86.

Chambers, Aidan, "Letters from England: Literary Crossword Puzzle . . . or Masterpiece?," review of *Red Shift, Horn Book*, October, 1973, pp. 494-97.

Chambers, Aidan, "Letter from England: A Matter of Balance," review of *The Stone Book, Horn Book*, August, 1977, pp. 479-82.

Dirda, Michael, "England, His England," *Washington Post Book World*, June 12, 1988, pp. 14-15.

Dixon, Bob, *Catching Them Young: Political Ideas in Children's Fiction*, Pluto Press, 1977, pp. 120-64.

Eyre, Frank, *British Children's Books in the Twentieth Century*, revised edition, Longman Books, 1979, pp. 79-156.

Fisher, Margery, "Special Review: 'The Owl Service,'" *Growing Point*, September, 1967, pp. 949-50.

Garner, Alan, "The Edge of the Ceiling," *Horn Book*, September/October, 1984, pp. 559-65.

Garner, Alan, *Elidor*, Walck, 1967.

Garner, Alan, in an interview with Aidan Chambers in *The Signal Approach to Children's Books: A Collection*, edited by Nancy Chambers, Scarecrow Press, 1980, pp. 276-328.

Garner, Alan, essay in *Speaking for Ourselves: Autobiographical Sketches by Notable Authors of Books for Young Adults*, edited by Donald R. Gallo, National Council of Teachers of English, 1990.

Lavender, Ralph, *Times Educational Supplement*, September 29, 1978, p. 29.

Le Guin, Ursula K., "No, Virginia, There Is Not a Santa Claus," *Foundation*, May, 1974, pp. 109-12.

Protherough, Robert, "Alan Garner," *Twentieth-Century Young Adult Writers*, St. James Press, 1994, pp. 236-38.

Rees, David, "Hanging in Their True Shapes: Alan Garner," *The Marble in the Water: Essays on Contemporary Writers of Fiction for Children and Young Adults*, Horn Book, 1980, pp. 56-67.

Siggins, Clara M., "Fiction: 'Red Shift,'" *Best Sellers*, December 1, 1973, p. 387.

Sutherland, Zena, review of *The Weirdstone of Brisingamen, Bulletin of the Center for Children's Books*, October, 1961, p. 29.

"Thursday's Child Has Far to Go," *Times Literary Supplement*, November 30, 1967, p. 1134.

"To the Dark Tower," *Times Literary Supplement*, September 28, 1973, p. 1112.

Townsend, John Rowe, *A Sense of Story: Essays on Contemporary Writers for Children*, Lippincott, 1971, pp. 108-19.

Watkins, Tony, "Alan Garner," *Good Writers for Young Readers*, edited by Dennis Butts, Hart-Davis, 1977, pp. 45-48.

Review of *The Weirdstone of Brisingamen, Junior Bookshelf*, December, 1960, pp. 363-64.

Wintle, Justin, and Emma Fisher, *The Pied Pipers: Interviews with the Influential Creators of Children's Literature*, Paddington Press, 1975, pp. 221-35.

■ For More Information See

BOOKS

Children's Literature Review, Volume 20, Gale, 1990, pp. 90-116.

Contemporary Literary Criticism, Volume 17, Gale, 1981, pp. 134-51.

Crouch, Marcus, *The Nesbit Tradition: The Children's Novel in England, 1945-1970*, Ernest Benn, 1972, pp. 112-41.

Crouch, Marcus, and Alec Ellis, editors, *Chosen for Children: An Account of the Books Which Have Been Awarded the Library Association Carnegie Medal, 1936-1975*, 3rd edition, Library Association, 1977, pp. 143-44.

Fisher, Margery, *Who's Who in Children's Books: A Treasury of the Familiar Characters of Childhood,* Holt, 1975, pp. 17-18.

Fisher, Margery, *Margery Fisher Recommends Classics for Children & Young People,* Thimble Press, 1986, p. 65.

Meek, Margaret, Aidan Warlow, and Griselda Barton, editors, *The Cool Web: The Pattern of Children's Reading,* Bodley Head, 1977, pp. 291-93.

Moss, Elaine, *Part of the Pattern: A Personal Journey through the World of Children's Books,* Greenwillow Books, 1986, pp. 45-165.

PERIODICALS

Children's Literature in Education, June, 1992, pp. 83-92.

Growing Point, March, 1967, p. 864; January, 1976, pp. 2783-84; November, 1977, pp. 3207-09; March, 1980, p. 3648; March, 1985, pp. 4398-99; January, 1987, pp. 4726-27.

Horn Book, February, 1970, pp. 45-46; April, 1979, pp. 192-93, 224-28; October, 1979, pp. 533-34; June, 1980, pp. 328-31; April, 1982, p. 174.

Junior Bookshelf, December, 1960, pp. 363-64; December, 1965, pp. 360-61; February, 1967, p. 39; February, 1976, pp. 42-43; December, 1978, pp. 309-10; June, 1981, pp. 122-23; February, 1987, p. 28.

Kirkus Reviews, July 1, 1969, pp. 680-81; September 15, 1970, p. 1028; July, 1979, p. 740.

New York Times Book Review, July 22, 1979, p. 19.

Publishers Weekly, November 8, 1993, p. 75.

Saturday Review, November 24, 1979, p. 65.

School Librarian, June, 1981, p. 133; November, 1991, p. 130.

School Library Journal, October, 1968, pp. 166-67; December, 1969, p. 50; March, 1981, p. 132; December, 1985, p. 88; November, 1986, p. 76; March, 1994, p. 215.

Times (London), August 24, 1977, p. 16.

Times Educational Supplement, November 18, 1977, p. 42.

Times Literary Supplement, December 9, 1965, p. 1130; June 26, 1969, p. 688; July 11, 1975, p. 771; March 25, 1977, p. 360; December 2, 1977, p. 1413; September 29, 1978, p. 1081; November 30, 1984, p. 1381; November 28, 1986, p. 1346.

Village Voice, December 25, 1978, pp. 98-100.

Washington Post Book World, November 3, 1968, p. 12; November 9, 1986, p. 19.*

—Sketch by Janet L. Hile

Michael Hague

■ Personal

Full name, Michael Riley Hague; born September 8, 1948, in Los Angeles, CA; son of Riley Herbert (a truck driver) and Daisy Marie (King) Hague; married Susan Kathleen Burdick (an artist and author of children's books), December 5, 1970; children: Meghan Micaela, Brittany Michael, Devon Heath. *Education:* Art Center College of Design, BFA (with honors), 1972.

■ Addresses

Home—Colorado Springs, CO.

■ Career

Hallmark Cards, Kansas City, KS, illustrator, 1973-75; Current, Inc., Colorado Springs, CO, illustrator, 1975-77; author and illustrator of children's books, 1977—.

■ Awards, Honors

Dream Weaver was chosen for the American Institute of Graphic Arts Book Show (formerly known as Fifty Books of the Year), 1980; International Reading Association children's choices citation, 1982, for *The Man Who Kept House*; Colorado Children's Book Award, University of Colorado, 1984, and Georgia Children's Picture Storybook Award, University of Georgia, 1986, both for *The Unicorn and the Lake*; Parents' Choice Award for children's books, Parents' Choice Foundation, 1984, for *The Frog Princess*; *Aesop's Fables*, *The Legend of the Veery Bird*, and *Alice's Adventures in Wonderland* were all selected as children's books of the year, Child Study Association of America, 1985; Graphic Arts Award for best juvenile book, Printing Industries Association, 1986, for *A Child's Book of Prayers*.

■ Writings

SELF-ILLUSTRATED CHILDREN'S BOOKS

(Reteller with wife, Kathleen Hague) *East of the Sun and West of the Moon*, Harcourt, 1980.
(Reteller with K. Hague) *The Man Who Kept House*, Harcourt, 1981.
(Editor) *Michael Hague's Favorite Hans Christian Andersen Fairy Tales*, Holt, 1981.
(Editor) *Mother Goose: A Collection of Classic Nursery Rhymes*, Holt, 1984.
(Editor) *Aesop's Fables*, Holt, 1985.
A Child's Book of Prayers, Holt, 1985.
Unicorn Pop-Up Book, Holt, 1986.
Michael Hague's World of Unicorns, Holt, 1986.

(Editor) Robert Louis Stevenson, *The Land of Nod and Other Poems for Children*, Holt, 1988.

My Secret Garden Diary, Arcade, 1990.

Magic Moments: A Book of Days, Arcade, 1990.

Our Baby: A Book of Records and Memories, Arcade, 1990.

A Unicorn Journal, Arcade, 1990.

Teddy Bear, Teddy Bear: A Classic Action Rhyme, Morrow, 1993.

(Editor) *Sleep, Baby, Sleep: Lullabies and Night Poems*, Morrow, 1994.

Michael Hague's Family Christmas Treasury, Holt, 1995.

(Compiler) *The Owl and the Pussy-Cat, and Other Nonsense Poems*, North-South Books, 1995.

(Compiler) *The Book of Dragons*, Morrow, 1995.

ILLUSTRATOR; CHILDREN'S BOOKS

Ethel Marbach, *The Cabbage Moth and the Shamrock*, Star & Elephant Books, 1978.

Beth Hilgartner, *A Necklace of Fallen Stars*, Little, Brown, 1979.

Jane Yolen, *Dream Weaver*, Collins, 1979, revised edition, Philomel Books, 1989.

Deborah Apy, reteller, *Beauty and the Beast*, Green Tiger, 1980.

Eve Bunting, *Demetrius and the Golden Goblet*, Harcourt, 1980.

Julia Cunningham, *A Mouse Called Junction*, Pantheon, 1980.

Kenneth Grahame, *The Wind in the Willows*, Holt, 1980.

Lee Bennett Hopkins, editor, *Moments: Poems about the Seasons*, Harcourt, 1980.

Clement C. Moore, *The Night before Christmas*, Holt, 1981.

Marianna Mayer, *The Unicorn and the Lake*, Dial, 1982.

L. Frank Baum, *The Wizard of Oz*, Holt, 1982.

Margery Williams, *The Velveteen Rabbit; or, How Toys Became Real*, Holt, 1983.

Grahame, *The Reluctant Dragon*, Holt, 1983.

C. S. Lewis, *The Lion, the Witch, and the Wardrobe*, Macmillan, 1983.

Nancy Luenn, *The Dragon Kite*, Harcourt, 1983.

Jakob Grimm and Wilhelm Grimm, *Rapunzel*, Creative Education, 1984.

Kathleen Hague, *Alphabears: An ABC Book*, Holt, 1984, published with cassette, Live Oak Media, 1985.

Elizabeth Isele, reteller, *The Frog Princess: A Russian Tale Retold*, Crowell, 1984.

J. R. R. Tolkien, *The Hobbit; or, There and Back Again*, Houghton, 1984.

Lewis Carroll, *Alice's Adventures in Wonderland*, Holt, 1985.

Hague, *The Legend of the Veery Bird*, Harcourt, 1985.

Hague, *Numbears: A Counting Book*, Holt, 1986.

Hague, *Out of the Nursery, Into the Night*, Holt, 1986.

Frances Hodgson Burnett, *The Secret Garden*, Holt, 1987.

J. M. Barrie, *Peter Pan*, Holt, 1987.

Carl Sandburg, *Rootabaga Stories*, two volumes, Harcourt, 1988-89.

Charles Perrault, *Cinderella, and Other Tales from Perrault*, Holt, 1989.

Marianna Mayer, *The Unicorn Alphabet*, Dial, 1989.

William Allingham, *The Fairies: A Poem*, Holt, 1989.

Hague, *Bear Hugs*, Holt, 1989.

Thornton W. Burgess, *Old Mother West Wind*, Holt, 1990.

(With Joe Krush) Sandburg, *Prairie-Town Boy*, Harcourt, 1990.

Mary Norton, *The Borrowers*, Harcourt, 1991.

Jimmy Kennedy, *The Teddy Bears' Picnic*, Holt, 1992.

Oscar Wilde, *The Fairy Tales of Oscar Wilde*, Holt, 1993.

Andrew Lang, *The Rainbow Fairy Book*, Morrow, 1993.

Louisa May Alcott, *Little Women; or, Meg, Jo, Beth, and Amy*, Holt, 1993.

Hans Christian Andersen, *The Little Mermaid*, Holt, 1994.

Gerald Hausman, editor, *How Chipmunk Got Tiny Feet: Native American Animal Origin Stories*, HarperCollins, 1995.

William J. Bennett, editor, *The Children's Book of Virtues*, Simon & Schuster, 1995.

ILLUSTRATOR; CHRISTMAS CAROLS

We Wish You a Merry Christmas, Holt, 1990.

Jingle Bells, Holt, 1990.

Deck the Halls, Holt, 1991.

O Christmas Tree, Holt, 1991.

OTHER

Unicorn Calendar, Holt, 1989.

Michael Hague, Holt, 1994.

Also illustrator of several calendars, including a series based on C. S. Lewis's "Chronicles of Narnia" books.

■ Sidelights

Michael Hague is well known for his vivid, detailed illustrations of various fantasy and children's classic books. Creator of paintings for such works as *The Hobbit; or, There and Back Again* and the "Chronicles of Narnia" books, Hague claims to have known he possessed the ability to draw as far back as kindergarten. "My mother had been to art school in England and encouraged me greatly by bringing home art books from which I could copy paintings and drawings," Hague once commented. "She never gave me lessons. I knew as a child that I wanted to illustrate books. I was always reading and rendering illustrations of my own creations for the King Arthur books as well as making portraits of such baseball heroes as Duke Snider of the Los Angeles Dodgers."

Born in Los Angeles, California, in 1948, Hague grew up surrounded by books. "I *still* have a hard time accepting that Prince Valiant is not a real character from English history," professed Hague. Comic books and Disney books were among his favorites, and his most treasured book demonstrated how to draw and animate the Disney characters. "I'm still a great Disney fan—I hold documents as one of the first Mickey Mouse Club members," Hague stated. "To this day I remember an enormous man named Roy, a Disney animator often featured on the *Mickey Mouse Club* television show. I used to think to myself. 'One day he'll retire, and then. . . .'"

Hague had many friends as he was growing up and played many sports, his favorite being baseball. Although he didn't take any art classes while in high school, he did continue to draw throughout that time and dreamed of playing professional baseball, all the while realizing that he didn't possess the talent to do so. After high school Hague attended junior college for two years, transferring to the Art Center College of Design in Los Angeles. He first majored in illustration, hoping for a career in children's books. However, the college directed its illustration majors toward more lucrative careers, such as advertising, so Hague changed his major to painting, concentrating on life drawing. His wife Kathleen, now an author of children's books, was also a painting major, and the two married while still students.

While Hague retained a strong interest in illustrating children's books by the time he graduated, he was convinced that he could not earn a living at it and decided to teach. When he was unable to land a teaching position, Hague took a job as a card designer at Hallmark Cards and worked for two years in their Kansas City studio. "It was great to get paid for drawing every day," he recalled. Hague enjoyed the work but still refused to give up on the publishing industry. During his first week at Hallmark, he put together a portfolio and sent it out to numerous publishers. "Many of the comments I received early were quite discouraging," Hague noted. "Some editors said my work was 'too weird' for children. Many art directors sent back my portfolio with *no* comment. Silence was the worst response, and alas, the most frequent. How did I keep my morale up? I just assumed they were idiots. Dr. Seuss went to twenty-nine publishers before he had his first book published. After five years, I finally was offered illustration work and then it all seemed to come at once."

Publishers Take Notice

In December 1978, the art director of *Cricket* magazine offered Hague his first illustration job: a cover and an inside story for the publication. His first published book illustration was a pop-up book version of *Gulliver's Travels*. Meanwhile, Hague had relocated to Colorado Springs, Colorado, to work for Current, Inc., another greeting card company. "While I was working at Current I contacted Green Tiger Press," stated Hague. "To my delight, they asked what *I* would like to illustrate. The first thing that came to my mind was *Beauty and the Beast*, which they agreed to. My illustrations for the book were influenced by the Cocteau film. It took a long time before I had another opportunity to propose what *I* wanted to illustrate to a publisher. When you're getting started, it's the publishers who make suggestions, and illustrators tend to accept everything and anything. It still takes me a long time to say 'no' to a project that doesn't interest me. But after the publication and success of *The Wind in the Willows* in 1980, I was in a position to suggest books I like to illustrate."

Hague's maternal grandmother was born in 1908, only two years before *The Wind in the Willows* was published for the first time. "She can recall with delight her father reading aloud to her about the adventures of Mr. Toad and his friends," Hague

In 1984, Hague illustrated J. R. R. Tolkien's classic fantasy, *The Hobbit; or, There and Back Again.*

related. "The book was her father's favorite, and indeed became hers as well. My grandmother passed on a love of 'Willows,' as she refers to it, to my mother; and so when the story reached me it had already claimed three generations and captivated its fourth generation in me." The book's main characters—Mole, Ratty, Badger, and Mr. Toad—have inspired an immense following over the years. "With such a loyal and affectionate following, from young children to their great-grandparents, I felt a great responsibility in illustrating the book," explained Hague.

Previous editions of *The Wind in the Willows* had been illustrated by two of Hague's idols, Ernest Howard Shepard and Arthur Rackham, so when he was first asked to do the project he was "thrilled, honored, and a bit frightened. I love the book," maintained Hague. "I love the dependable Water Rat, the kindly Mole, the sturdy Badger, and especially Mr. Toad. And so it is, as when one is in love, one forgets all obstacles and fears. That is what happened to me. I've not tried to create a new visual style or interpretation of the story," continued Hague. "I have instead tried to infuse my illustrations with the same spirit Kenneth Grahame's magic words convey. There is, I think, a bit of Toad in all of us. Certainly there must have been some of Mr. Toad in me when I agreed to illustrate this book." *School Library Journal* contributor Susan Dooley found that Hague's pictures "wonderfully fulfill Grahame's nostalgic vision," and his characters especially are "faithful embodiments of Grahame's originals." The overall effect of these "meticulously and tenderly rendered" paintings, the critic concluded, is one of "joyous celebration." Jean Stronse, writing in *Newsweek*, felt that the artist's drawings "keep perfect full-color faith with the buoyant spirit of the classic tale."

The Creative Mind

Hague tries to imbue all his illustrations with the same essence the author or the story itself originally creates in his imagination. "I begin with character studies and try to capture on paper what I see in my mind's eye," explained Hague. And to avoid making a book monotonous, he places his characters in a variety of light sources. "Light is one of the elements which makes a painting real," he claimed, "especially when you are painting the fantastic. The more real a tree looks, or

the light appears, the more believable the fantasy elements will be. One can't afford to be vague when illustrating fantasy. Ninety per cent of a fantasy book should be based on the real world; you don't need many strange elements to make a story work. In a good illustration of a knight riding on a horse, for example, the viewer will ride over the next hill with him, even though the artist hasn't illustrated what's over there. It's not hard to animate or give gesture to fantasy creatures once you have principles of drawing. I try to make movement and gesture look believable, and one way to do that is to be sure that the backgrounds are realistic. It adds emphasis. Once again, I build a concrete world—not a fuzzy, dream-like place—where kids can see real sky or walls or cities. Then a dragon can become believable."

Making the unbelievable seem real is a particular talent of Hague's, and two of his favorite subjects are unicorns and dragons. In such works as *Michael Hague's World of Unicorns* and *A Unicorn Journal*, the artist brings to life the magical, horse-like creatures that can heal the sick and soar into the sky. In *School Library Journal*, Carolyn Noah called the former a good choice for "mature unicorn hobbyists," adding that Hague mixes "luminous and earthen colors" to "enhance the magical aura" of the pop-up book. About the same work, a critic in *Publishers Weekly* noted that Hague's "woodland pictures have a fluidity that goes well with the engineering." In 1995 Hague published *The Book of Dragons*, a collection of seventeen stories selected by the artist and accompanied by twenty color and sixteen black-and-white illustrations. The book offers such tales as "Bilbo Baggins and Smaug" by J. R. R. Tolkien, "The Adventures of Eustace" by C. S. Lewis, and "The Dragon and the Enchanted Filly," retold by Italo Calvino. Hague's dragons are often fearsome, menacing creatures; in one illustration, from "The Devil and His Grandmother" by the Brothers Grimm, a red-winged, purple-scaled dragon flies over the countryside, clutching three frightened men in his claws. According to a *Publishers Weekly* critic, Hague uses a "generous dollop of unabashedly romantic color plates awash with vibrant hues" to create a "first-rate collection."

Hague most often works in watercolor and gouache, adding ink outlines last, but he also uses pen-and-ink alone. His influences include a wide variety of styles, ranging from the art of the

Disney Studios to Japanese printmakers. "I particularly love the work of turn-of-the-century illustrators Arthur Rackham, W. Heath Robinson, N. C. Wyeth, and Howard Pyle," Hague commented, adding that he is "an avid collector of their books, as well as those of contemporary illustrators [Maurice] Sendak and Errol LeCain." Hague continued: "It's difficult to put my finger on what makes an illustration a classic. I think it has to do with a universal quality of the work—a special something that strikes a chord in people. I

If you enjoy the works of Michael Hague, you may want to check out the following books and films:

The works of artist and illustrator Arthur Rackham (1867–1939), including William Shakespeare's *A Midsummer–Night's Dream*, 1939; Charles Dickens's *A Christmas Carol*, 1915; Edgar Allan Poe's *Tales of Mystery and Imagination*, 1935; and Kenneth Grahame's *The Wind in the Willows*, 1940.

The works of painter and illustrator N. C. Wyeth (1882–1945), including Robert Louis Stevenson's *Treasure Island*, 1911; Jules Verne's *Mysterious Island*, 1918; James Fenimore Cooper's *The Last of the Mohicans*, and Henry David Thoreau's *Men of Concord*, 1919.

The Wizard of Oz, MGM, 1939.

---

wish I knew! I'd write a book on it—then we'd all write and illustrate classics!"

Illustrating the Classics

Another classic story that still exists in Hague is *The Wizard of Oz*. "When I was a child, there were three places I would have given anything to visit," he remembered. "One was England in the days of King Arthur; another was the Wild West of Hopalong Cassidy; the third, quite different, was the Wonderful Land of Oz. Arthur's England and Hoppy's West were confined to earthly borders. The landscape of Oz was as large or as small as I wished it to be. And, like Alice's Wonderland, it was populated with such extraordinary creatures that I knew anything might happen there. It was

a place where the laws of our universe seldom applied." His desire to visit the land of Oz never waned over the years, so Hague enthusiastically accepted the job of painting his own Oz. "I count myself as one of the most fortunate of beings," he proclaimed. "For as an artist I have not only the pleasure but the duty to daydream. It is part of my work. I have been a contented daydreamer all of my life, often to the exasperation of those around me. While creating the illustrations for *The Wizard of Oz*, I would slip away. My hands went about their business while my mind walked among the Quadlings and the fierce Kalidahs." Hague's version of the classic drew positive reviews; a contributor to *People* commended the "attractive reissue" featuring the artist's "winsome new drawings."

Hague later illustrated another fantasy epic, J. R. R. Tolkien's *The Hobbit; or, There and Back Again.* The book, which follows the adventures of Bilbo Baggins, a hobbit, the wizard Gandalf, and a troupe of dwarves as they attempt to retrieve stolen treasure, was a challenge for the artist. "I wanted to take a new approach to Bilbo. It seemed to me that earlier hobbits all looked the same. I didn't want my hobbits to have pointed ears, which, in fact, are not mentioned in the text. I felt if Tolkien had wanted readers to imagine his hobbits with pointed ears, he certainly would have said so. I decided to make the hobbits appear more like children, sort of like aged children, rather than dwarves." Gene LaFaille, reviewing *The Hobbit* in the *Wilson Library Bulletin*, found that Hague's drawings "offer fine detail without being busy" and "add much pleasure and increase the reader's interest in the story, especially in the stirring battle scenes." And Faith McNulty in the *New Yorker* termed the work a "beautifully illustrated edition."

Hague claims to have no special tricks when it comes to illustrating, if something doesn't look right to him he merely plays around with it until it does, often by changing the perspective. "Sometimes I'll have a bad day, when nothing seems to come easy," observed Hague. "People ask me how long it takes to do a painting, and I can't really say because it changes from painting to painting from day to day. I've done some paintings in one day, others in two weeks. I couldn't say why that is." And while working on his illustrations, Hague creates for himself, not for a particular audience: "When I illustrate, I don't think about kids, or

Hague's illustrations enlivened "The Tree's Wife," a tale from Jane Yolen's 1979 fantasy work *The Dream Weaver*.

what age group the book is aimed toward. I don't like to generalize or second guess my audience. I try to please myself. I am still in touch with my childhood, with the child that still exists in me." Hague passed along these words to aspiring illustrators: "People play down luck, but my advice to young artists would be to draw all the time and get lucky. Fill up notebooks with drawings. Once you learn to draw you can do anything, but drawing is not simply technique. Your work must have meaning, it must have something behind it, something beyond technical skill."

Imagining and believing were important factors in Hague's childhood, and he maintains that they are "the only forms of magic left. When I was a kid, I thought that magicians actually did work magic—the power to cut a woman in two and put her back together again. As I got older I, of course, realized that these were optical illusions. After a while one draws a distinction between doing tricks and imagination. Our imagination is real magic. And while imagination may change in our increasingly technological world, it is still magic—it's what got us to the moon! Without it, we'd still be living in trees."

■ **Works Cited**

Review of *The Book of Dragons, Publishers Weekly,* September 4, 1995, p. 68.

Dooley, Susan, review of *The Wind in the Willows, School Library Journal,* November, 1980, pp. 74-75.

Hague, Michael, comments in *Something about the Author,* Volume 48, Gale, 1987.

LaFaille, Gene, review of *The Hobbit; or, There and Back Again, Wilson Library Bulletin,* February, 1990, p. 91.

McNulty, Faith, review of *The Hobbit; or, There and Back Again, New Yorker,* December 3, 1984.

Review of *Michael Hague's World of Unicorns, Publishers Weekly,* October 31, 1986, p. 67.

Noah, Carolyn, review of *Michael Hague's World of Unicorns, School Library Journal,* January, 1987, p. 64.

Stronse, Jean, review of *The Wind in the Willows, Newsweek,* December 1, 1980, p. 103.

Review of *The Wizard of Oz, People,* November 1, 1982, p. 10.

■ **For More Information See**

BOOKS

Holtze, Sally Holmes, editor, *Fifth Book of Junior Authors and Illustrators,* H. W. Wilson, 1983.

PERIODICALS

Booklist, June 1, 1994, p. 1815; August, 1994, p. 2046.

Books of Wonder News, November, 1988.

Horn Book Guide, April, 1981; July, 1990.

New York, December 12, 1988.

Publishers Weekly, January 20, 1989, p. 103; June 29, 1992, p. 61; July 18, 1994, p. 243.

School Library Journal, March, 1986; June-July, 1987; November, 1992, p. 112; October, 1993, p. 144; October, 1994, p. 110.

Times Educational Supplement, November 21, 1986.

Washington Post Book World, February 9, 1986.

Wilson Library Bulletin, May, 1987.*

—*Sketch by Thomas McMahon*

Nathaniel Hawthorne

■ Personal

Born Nathaniel Hathorne, July 4, 1804, in Salem, MA; died May 19, 1864, in Plymouth, NH; buried in Sleepy Hollow Cemetery, Concord, MA; son of Nathaniel (a seaman) and Elizabeth Clark (Manning) Hathorne; married Sophia Peabody, July 9, 1842; children: Una, Julian, Rose. *Education:* Graduated from Bowdoin College, Brunswick, Maine, 1825.

■ Career

Writer of novels and short stories. Editor of *American Magazine of Useful and Entertaining Knowledge,* Boston, 1836; weigher and gauger, Boston Custom House, 1839-40; surveyor of the Salem Custom House, 1846-49; appointed by President Franklin Pierce as U.S. Consul in Liverpool, England, 1853-57. Participant in the Brook Farm experiment in communal living, West Roxbury, MA, 1841-42.

■ Writings

NOVELS

Fanshawe, privately printed, anonymously, 1828, later published as *Fanshawe and Other Pieces,* Osgood, 1876.

The Scarlet Letter, Ticknor, Reed & Fields, 1850, new edition edited by Sculley Bradley and others, Norton, 1966.

The House of the Seven Gables, Ticknor, Reed & Fields, 1851, new edition edited by Seymour L. Gross, Norton, 1967.

The Blithedale Romance, Ticknor, Reed & Fields, 1852, new edition, Dell, 1960.

The Marble Faun; or, The Romance of Monte Beni, Ticknor & Fields, 1860, new edition edited by Richard Rupp, Bobbs-Merrill, 1971, published in England as *Transformation; or, The Romance of Monte Beni,* Smith, Elder, 1860.

UNFINISHED NOVELS

Septimius Felton; or, The Elixir of Life, Osgood, 1872.

The Dolliver Romance, and Other Pieces, Osgood, 1876, later published as *The Dolliver Romance, Fanshawe, and Septimius Felton* (with an appendix containing *The Ancestral Footstep*), Houghton, 1883.

Dr. Grimshawe's Secret, edited by Julian Hawthorne, Osgood, 1883, new edition edited by Edward H. Davidson, Harvard University Press, 1954.

SHORT STORIES

Twice-Told Tales, American Stationers' Co., 1837, revised and enlarged edition, Munroe, 1842, new edition edited by Wallace Stegner and illustrated by Valenti Angelo, Limited Editions Club, 1966.

Mosses from an Old Manse, two volumes, Wiley & Putnam, 1846, revised edition, Ticknor & Fields, 1854, reprinted, Books for Libraries, 1970.

Celestial Railroad, Skinner, 1847.

The Snow-Image, and Other Twice-Told Tales, Ticknor, Reed & Fields, 1851.

Legends of New England, Osgood, 1877.

Legends of the Province House, Osgood, 1877, also published as *Colonial Stories*, illustrated by Frank T. Merrill, Knight, 1897, later published as *In Colonial Days*, Page, 1906.

Tales of the White Hills (contains "The Great Stone Face," "The Great Carbuncle," and "The Ambitious Guest"), Osgood, 1877, also published as *The Great Stone Face, and Other Tales of the White Mountains* (with the addition of "Sketches from Memory"), Houghton, 1935.

STORIES FOR CHILDREN

The Gentle Boy: A Thrice-Told Tale, illustrated by Sophia Peabody, Wiley & Putnam, 1839.

Grandfather's Chair: A History for Youth, Peabody, 1841, revised and enlarged edition, Tappan & Dennet, 1842.

Famous Old People: Being the Second Epoch of Grandfather's Chair, Peabody, 1841.

Liberty Tree: With the Last Words of Grandfather's Chair, Peabody, 1841.

Biographical Stories for Children, Tappan & Dennet, 1842.

True Stories from History and Biography (contains *The Whole History of Grandfather's Chair* and *Biographical Stories for Children*), Ticknor, Reed & Fields, 1851.

A Wonder-Book for Girls and Boys, illustrated by Hammatt Billings, Ticknor, Reed & Fields, 1852, new edition illustrated by Dick Cuffari, Grosset & Dunlap, 1967.

Tanglewood Tales for Girls and Boys, Ticknor, Reed & Fields, 1853, new edition illustrated by Sheilah Beckett, Grosset & Dunlap, 1967.

Little Daffydowndilly, and Other Stories, Houghton, 1887.

The Whole History of Grandfather's Chair, or, True Stories of New England History, 1620-1803 (contains *Grandfather's Chair, Famous Old People*, and *Liberty Tree*), Houghton, 1896.

The Ghost of Dr. Harris, Tucker, 1900.

The Miraculous Pitcher, and Biographical Stories, edited by Margaret Hill McCarter, Crane, 1905.

A Wonder-Book [and] *Tanglewood Tales*, illustrated by Maxfield Parrish, Duffield, 1910.

The Seven Vagabonds, illustrated by Helen Mason Grose, Houghton, 1916.

The Golden Touch, illustrated by Valenti Angelo, Grabhorn Press, 1927, new edition illustrated by Paul Galdone, McGraw, 1959, also published as *The Tale of King Midas and the Golden Touch*, illustrated by Fritz Eichenberg, Limited Editions Club, 1952.

Pandora's Box, illustrated by Rafaello Busoni, Limited Editions Club, 1951, new edition illustrated by Paul Galdone, McGraw, 1967.

Pegasus, the Winged Horse, introduction by Robert Lowell, illustrated by Herschel Levit, Macmillan, 1963.

The Birthmark, and Other Stories, edited by Maxine Greene, Scholastic Book Services, 1968.

Young Goodman Brown, edited by Thomas E. Connolly, Merrill, 1968.

NONFICTION

(Editor) *Peter Parley's Universal History*, American Stationers' Co., 1837.

(Editor) *Horatio Bridge: Journal of an African Cruiser*, Wiley & Putnam, 1845, reprinted, Negro History Press, 1968.

The Life of Franklin Pierce, Ticknor, Reed & Fields, 1852, reprinted, Garrett Press, 1970.

Our Old Home: A Series of English Sketches, Ticknor & Fields, 1863.

COLLECTIONS

Passages from the American Notebooks of Nathaniel Hawthorne, edited by Sophia Peabody Hawthorne, Ticknor & Fields, 1868, new edition edited by Randall Stewart, published as *The American Notebooks of Nathaniel Hawthorne*, Yale University Press, 1932, reprinted, Folcroft, 1970.

Passages from the English Notebooks of Nathaniel Hawthorne, edited by S. P. Hawthorne, Fields, Osgood, 1870, new edition edited by Randall Stewart, published as *The English Notebooks of Nathaniel Hawthorne*, Modern Language Association of America, 1941, reprinted, Russell & Russell, 1962.

Passages from the French and Italian Notebooks of Nathaniel Hawthorne, edited by S. P. Hawthorne, Strahan, 1871, Osgood, 1872.

The Complete Works of Nathaniel Hawthorne, edited by George P. Lathrop, twelve volumes, Houghton, 1883, reprinted, Scholarly Press, 1970.

Tales, Sketches, and Other Papers, Houghton, 1883, reprinted, Books for Libraries, 1972.

Love Letters of Nathaniel Hawthorne, Society of the Dofobs, 1907, reprinted, with a foreword by C. E. Frazer Clark, Jr., NCR Microcard Editions, 1972.

Letters of Hawthorne to William D. Ticknor, 1851-1864, Carteret Book Club, 1910, reprinted, with a foreword by C. E. Frazer Clark, Jr., NCR Microcard Editions, 1972.

The Heart of Hawthorne's Journals, edited by Newton Arvin, Houghton, 1929, reprinted, University Microfilms, 1962.

Hawthorne as Editor: Selections from His Writings in "The American Magazine of Useful and Entertaining Knowledge," edited by Arlin Turner, Louisiana State University Press, 1941, reprinted, Kennikat Press, 1972.

Hawthorne's Short Stories, edited by Newton Arvin, Knopf, 1946, reprinted, 1961.

The Portable Hawthorne, edited by Malcolm Cowley, Viking, 1948, revised and enlarged edition, 1969.

Complete Short Stories of Nathaniel Hawthorne, Hanover House, 1959.

The Centenary Edition of the Works of Nathaniel Hawthorne, edited by William Charvat and others, Ohio State University Press, 1962-95.

Poems, edited by Richard E. Peck, Kingsport Press, 1967.

Great Short Works of Nathaniel Hawthorne, edited by Frederick C. Crews, Harper, 1967.

A Book of Mysterious and Fateful Stories, Gordon Press, 1991.

The Complete Novels & Selected Tales, Random House, 1993.

The Works of Nathaniel Hawthorne: House of Seven Gables, Scarlet Letter, Twice Told Tales, Longmeadow, 1994.

Contributor, often anonymously, to *The Token* (a Christmas annual), *New England Magazine, Democratic Review, Atlantic Monthly,* and other magazines and newspapers.

■ Adaptations

PLAYS

Maurice J. Valency, *Feathertop* (one-act), Dramatists Play Service, 1963.

Robert Brome, *Nathaniel Hawthorne's The Minister's Black Veil* (one-act), Eldridge Publishing, 1963.

Robert Brome, *Nathaniel Hawthorne's David Swan* (one-act), Eldridge Publishing, 1965.

Robert Brome, *Nathaniel Hawthorne's The Birthmark* (one-act), Eldridge Publishing, 1965.

I. E. Clark, *Pandora and the Magic Box,* Stage Magic Plays, 1968.

Edward J. Megroth, librettist, *Goodman Brown* (opera; music by Harold Fink), Lake Erie College Press, 1968.

Robert Lowell, *The Old Glory* (theater trilogy), Noonday Press, 1966, revised edition, Farrar, Straus, 1968.

MOVIES AND FILMSTRIPS

The Scarlet Letter (motion pictures), Fox Film Corp., 1917, Selznick Pictures Corp., 1920, Metro-Goldwyn-Mayer, 1926, Majestic Producing Corp., 1934, Cinergi, 1995.

The House of the Seven Gables (motion pictures), Universal, 1940, Teaching Film Custodians, 1946.

Swain (motion picture), Gregory J. Markopoulas and Robert C. Freeman, 1950.

The Great Stone Face (filmstrip), Encyclopaedia Britannica Films, 1956.

Twice-Told Tales (motion picture), United Artists, 1963.

Dr. Heidegger's Experiment by Nathaniel Hawthorne (motion picture), Encyclopaedia Britannica Educational Corp., 1969.

Young Goodman Brown (motion picture), Pyramid Films, 1972.

RECORDINGS

The Chimaera (read by Julie Harris), Spoken Arts, 1972.

King Midas and the Golden Touch (read by Julie Harris), Spoken Arts, 1972.

Jason and the Golden Fleece, from *Tanglewood Tales* (read by Cathleen Nesbitt), Caedmon, 1973.

Other recordings based on Hawthorne's works include *Tales,* read by Basil Rathbone (volumes 1 & 2, records or cassettes), Caedmon; *Tanglewood Tales: The Story of Pluto and Nesbitt,* read by Anthony Quayle (six cassettes, teacher's guide; or individual records and cassettes), Caedmon; *Tanglewood Tales: The Story of Theseus,* read by Anthony Quayle (six cassettes and teacher's guide; or individual records and cassettes), Caedmon.

The Scarlet Letter was adapted into a six-part series for WGBH-TV (Boston), 1978.

■ Sidelights

Nathaniel Hawthorne was fond of calling himself the "obscurist man of letters in America." Indeed, Edgar Allan Poe, with whom Hawthorne basically created the short story form in America, once said that Hawthorne was "*the* example, *par excellence*, in this country of the privately-admired and publicly-unappreciated man of genius." Although Hawthorne would become known as the father of the American novel and accepted as part of the canon of American literature, he lived a difficult life. Paid as little as $25 per short story, Hawthorne was forced to seek out a living as a surveyor for a time, only to lose the position to political patronage. His scandalous (at the time) book, *The Scarlet Letter,* may have given him some degree of celebrity status, but the book earned him only $1,500 from the American edition in his lifetime.

Yet Hawthorne persevered; his dimly lit peephole vision of the world may in fact have prepared him for just such a reception. A darkly melancholic man, yet one who disdained such melancholy in others, he was not surprised at such a reality. His novels and short stories mirror this dark image of the world in which past guilt comes to determine present lives, sin is a tie that binds, and a happy ending—save for *The House of the Seven Gables*—is not allowed. Hawthorne wished for the ability to write a cheerful book, but complained that the devil got in his ink-well instead. With the preface to his final novel, *The Marble Faun,* Hawthorne was still wishing for the lighter touch, for the ability to let some sunshine into his highly symbolic "romances," as he called his fiction. He praised the work of a writer such as Anthony Trollope over his own, and went so far as to say that, were he confronted with books like his own written by another author, he would not read them.

But millions have, and recognition of Hawthorne's skill as a novelist and writer of short stories and essays has endured the winds of fashion in literary criticism for well over a century. Almost 150 years after its publication, *The Scarlet Letter* is still required reading in the classroom and has even inspired a recent film rendition. In his introduction to a 1965 edition of *Twice Told Tales,* Francis R. Gemme noted that the collection of tales is "as penetrating, professional, and entertaining today as it was to readers in the 1830s." If anything, Hawthorne's tone of somber introspection resonates even more deeply in our age that in his own. "To see matters so blackly was Hawthorne's torment and his most serious limitation," wrote Frederick C. Crews in his 1967 introduction to *Great Short Works of Hawthorne.* "But it was also the basis of his greatness as an introspective writer."

New England Heritage

The darkness and introspection were part of Hawthorne's heritage. His first American paternal ancestor was Major William Hathorne, who settled in Boston in the 1630s, later moving on to Salem, Massachusetts, as one of the founding families of the town. Hawthorne described this ancestor in "The Custom House," an introductory sketch to *The Scarlet Letter,* as "a grave, bearded, sable-cloaked and steeple-crowned progenitor—who came so early, with his *Bible* and sword . . . and had all the Puritanic traits, both good and evil." Part of the downside of his Puritanism was William's persecution of the Quakers. William's son, Colonel John Hathorne, outdid his father in this regard, being an unrepentant magistrate during the Salem witch trials of 1692. From these two ancestors Hawthorne developed the idea of an ancestral curse that would play out in succeeding generations of a family. Hawthorne's grandfather was a sea captain who, during the Revolutionary War, sailed as a privateer and became the subject of a ballad, "Bold Hathorne."

Hawthorne's mother's family, the Mannings, were more men and women of the soil, yeomen who had come over from England about as early as the Hathornes. The Mannings, neither so ostentatious nor public as the Hathornes, were nonetheless solid citizens of New England. Nathaniel was born in Salem on Independence Day of 1804, into a prominent if not well-to-do family. His father, Nathaniel Hathorne, followed in the nautical tradition of the family, and as a sea captain, died of yellow fever in Dutch Guiana when his son was only four. Hawthorne's mother, Elizabeth, never recovered from the loss. She, her son, and her two daughters went to live in the Manning house in

Salem, and at her brother's residence at Raymond, Maine. It is said that the mother never shared a meal with the family after the death of her husband, and it is in this gloomy, almost Gothic atmosphere that the young Hawthorne grew up. The time spent in Maine was spent in nature, where Hawthorne could roam in the forest and around the shores of Lake Sebago, and it is here, he later said, that he acquired his habit of solitude. It was apparent from an early age that Hawthorne was not cut out for the land or for the sea, and the Mannings saw to his private education. Early writing came in the form of a family newspaper, "The Spectator," that Hawthorne hand-lettered. When it came time for college, the Manning family again saw to things: he was sent off to

Hawthorne's first collection of stories contained tales and sketches which had been previously published.

Bowdoin College in Maine and spent the next four years studying composition and languages. Though his marks were not excellent—Hawthorne graduated in the middle of his class—he did acquire two lasting components for his future life: a set of loyal and soon-to-be influential friends, and a course for his professional life. Of the first, there were the future poet Henry Wadsworth Longfellow, an early champion of Hawthorne's writings, and the future president, Franklin Pierce. Less well known was Horatio Bridge, an early benefactor of Hawthorne's. As for his choice of career, Hawthorne was reading widely of literary authors during his years in college, many of them not included in the curriculum. He had also begun writing tales as an undergraduate. So it was that the newly-named Hawthorne determined to become an author.

A Literary Apprenticeship

Learning of Hawthorne's ambitions, the Manning family once again came to his rescue, supporting him through the dozen years of his literary apprenticeship. After graduation in 1825, Hawthorne returned to the family home in Salem where he took up residence under the eaves in a room he would later call his "haunted chamber" for all the myriad characters and visions that came to him there. For twelve long years Hawthorne taught himself how to write, living a simple life, hidden away much of the time in his room or roaming the moonlit streets of Salem and recording the lonely scenes in his mind for later use in the stories he was crafting by daylight. Much that was written in this period was destroyed by Hawthorne, for it was fledgling work only, derivative and sketchy. Influenced by the Gothic tradition of Sir Walter Scott, Hawthorne's first novel, *Fanshawe*, is a tale of concealed identity, abduction and flight. It is set at a college quite similar to Bowdoin and Hawthorne himself paid the $100 to have it published, but quickly regretted the decision. Soon he withdrew the novel, and searched out copies that friends might have, all to be consigned to the flames. A fire at his publisher, Marsh & Capen, did much of this work for him, but some copies did survive, allowing a later edition to be published after Hawthorne's death. Hawthorne also worked on several stories at this time, "Tales of My Native Land" among them. Heavily stylized and derivative tales of adventure and mystery, many of these early stories also were destroyed. But increasingly, Hawthorne was beginning to find his own style and themes.

In 1830 Hawthorne published his first short story, "The Hollow of the Three Hills." In this narrative are already present many of the archetypical Hawthorne elements: the use of symbolism, the examination of the effects of guilt and sin on the human psyche, a fanciful plot whose particulars include a witch calling up remembered sounds of sorrow. Other earlier stories grouped together as "Provincial Tales" were sent out to an admirer of *Fanshawe*, Samuel Griswold Goodrich, publisher of *The Token*, an annual Christmas gift book. Though Goodrich did not take the collection, he used individual titles in *The Token* throughout the early 1830s. Hawthorne planned a third collection, "The Story Teller," using the narrative framework of a story teller who travels from New England to Detroit, telling various stories along the way. Partly inspired by the summertime trips Hawthorne had been taking with his Manning relatives since 1828, this collection, like earlier ones, was eventually broken up, its individual stories published in periodicals such as *New England Magazine* and *American Monthly*, as well as in *The Token*. But by 1836 Hawthorne had had enough of seclusion. Goodrich, publisher of *The Token*, was also a director of the *American Magazine of Useful and Entertaining Knowledge*, and in March of 1836 Hawthorne set off to Boston to embark on a new career—that of a magazine editor.

Hawthorne's editorship was short-lived, but for the half-year he was at the magazine, he and his sister Elizabeth wrote or excerpted the entire contents for each edition. It was more concentrated work than the young Hawthorne had to this time been accustomed to, but worst of all, his salary was not paid. Leaving the magazine, Hawthorne and his sister collaborated on a children's book, *Peter Parley's Universal History*, for a series published by Goodrich. It was his first taste of writing for children, and he found that he had a knack for it, returning to the format time and again throughout his career. Meanwhile, with a $250 advance against losses, his friend from college days, Horatio Bridge, persuaded Goodrich to bring out a collection of Hawthorne's short stories already published in *The Token* and in periodicals. An edition of 1,000 copies of these eighteen stories was published in March of 1937 under the title *Twice Told Tales*. It was Hawthorne's first literary success. Organized simply under the theme of stories that might be worthy of a second offering to the public, the tales were an eclectic hodge-podge, starting out with the patriotic "Gray Champion," which recalled the revolutionary days. Also included in the collection are some of his best early works, including "The Gentle Boy," with its sympathy for the Quakers persecuted by the Puritans, and "The Maypole of Merry Mount," in which the early Puritan colonists again come in for implied criticism as they try to squash the pagan reveries of the inhabitants of a nearby village. New England history and its drama of Puritan consciousness formed the core of many of these early stories, and with "The Minister's Black Veil," Hawthorne also introduces the technique of a central all-encompassing symbol later to be employed with *The Scarlet Letter*. The veil of the minister, Hooper, like Hester's scarlet letter, is symbolic of a shameful action; in Hooper's case he had killed a beloved friend by accident, and wishes to hide his face from other men. Thus the veil alienates Hooper, the protagonist, from his community, as does Hester's letter.

Though the stories were well received, sales only sufficed to pay off Bridge's security and earned Hawthorne little profit. Reviewers were more generous than the reading public, however. Henry Wadsworth Longfellow declared Hawthorne to be "a new star . . . in the heaven of poetry," in the *North American Review*, and others concurred, including writer and feminist Elizabeth Peabody, who in a *New Yorker* review of *Twice Told Tales* noted that Hawthorne had more genius than any other fiction writer of his time. Of course Peabody, like Longfellow, was not exactly a neutral judge. She and her sisters had been Hawthorne's neighbors in Salem and had recently moved back to the town and resumed the acquaintance. It was a relationship that would soon lead to an engagement between the frail and sensitive sister of Elizabeth Peabody, Sophia, and Hawthorne, much to the surprise of all concerned, including Elizabeth. Not one to hold a grudge, however, Elizabeth Peabody continued to champion Hawthorne, this time for a job as measurer of coal and salt in the Boston custom house, a post he held for two years beginning in 1839.

Experiments in Living

Hawthorne proved a competent customs officer and, for a man who had spent much of his life

Shortly after they were married in 1842, Hawthorne and his wife, Sophia, rented the "Old Manse," a house in Concord, Massachusetts, where they lived for three years.

cosseted from the realities that most men face daily, it was rewarding to know that he could hold his own. But his work left little time for writing. Some scholars estimate that he wrote only two adult sketches in the two years he was at the Boston customs, though he did produce a three-volume series of stories for children, *Grandfather's Chair*. Through the Peabody sisters he was kept abreast of new thought such as transcendentalism which was being propounded by articles in *The Dial* and by such literati as Emerson, Margaret Fuller, and Bronson Alcott. Indeed, it was this connection that finally persuaded Hawthorne to leave his job at the custom house. One of the men he met at the occasional discussions of the Transcendental Club was George Ripley, who, in 1840, established an experiment in communal living at West Roxbury, Massachusetts, known as Brook Farm. The idea behind the scheme was that members would share in the labor of the farm as well as its rewards. Such an arrangement was intended to leave members with

enough free time to pursue their artistic and literary dreams. Hawthorne invested $1,000 in the farm and advanced another $500 toward the construction of a house. He hoped to make this a home for himself and Sophia, and that their long engagement might finally be ended in marriage. However, Hawthorne was elected an officer of the community, and once again found that he had neither time nor privacy enough for his writing. Hard physical work was not especially to his liking, either, and within six months he left Brook Farm, never to recover his investment.

Soon after leaving the farm, he completed another children's book, *Biographical Stories for Children*. In 1842 he also published a second edition of *Twice Told Tales*, including 21 more stories than the first edition, though they had all been written before 1839. Notable among the new stories is "Endicott and the Red Cross," in which Hawthorne retells history, linking the tradition of Puritan defiance of royal authority to the American Revolution. Yet the writer leaves unresolved the conflict between the heroic defiance found in Puritanism and its religious intolerance. This second edition of *Twice Told Tales* prompted Edgar Allan Poe to declare in *Graham's Magazine* that "Mr. Hawthorne is a man of truest genius." Despite such praise, sales of the second edition fared not much better than the first. However, Hawthorne had begun to contribute articles and stories on a regular basis to the *Democratic Review,* and in a fit of optimistic belief that he could now support a family on his writing, he married Sophia Peabody on July 9, 1842 after a three-and-a-half-year engagement. The couple moved to Concord, taking up residence in a splendid old house known as the Old Manse. This was the beginning of a three-year idyll for the couple. Here Hawthorne was the neighbor of Emerson, Alcott, Fuller, and Thoreau, though he had reservations about the philosophy of transcendentalism. His Puritan background made him more pragmatic in his evaluation of humankind: Man for Hawthorne was a creature of limitations, but one which could choose. Emerson seemed to be too much in the clouds for Hawthorne, who took a liking to the more earthy Thoreau, noting in his journals that Thoreau was a "keen and delicate observer of nature."

Hawthorne continued to publish in the *Democratic Review,* and in March of 1844 a daughter, Una, was born to the couple. In 1845 plans were already afoot for collecting some twenty stories that Hawthorne had written during his marriage, to be entitled *Mosses from an Old Manse.* Three of the best known new stories from the collection are "The Birthmark," a representation of the fated tragic consequences of a noble though misguided search for perfection; "Rappaccini's Daughter," a complex story about the attempt of a man to change nature for his own purposes; and "The Artist of the Beautiful," an examination of the artistic life and its rewards. These stories deal in alchemy and science as well as with the ironic consequences of seemingly noble actions. In "The Old Manse," Hawthorne's introductory essay to the collection, he noted that "all that I had to show, as a man of letters, were these few tales and essays, which had blossomed out like flowers in the calm summer of my heart and mind." Although generally more formulaic than earlier short story collections, this work also includes two tales finished before 1830, "Roger Malvin's Burial" and "Young Goodman Brown," both now considered among his best short fiction. The latter story

has been read by critics as Hawthorne's anticipation of Freud in its exploration of the effects of a guilty secret on the unconscious mind. Brown, stumbling on a Black Mass led by the prominent people of Salem, decides that evil is the true nature of mankind; he is unable to accept the fact that sinfulness is part of the human condition. *Mosses from an Old Manse* was better received than *Twice Told Tales.* Poe again praised the author, and Herman Melville, in a *Literary World* review, lauded Hawthorne as a home-grown original: "And now, my countrymen, as an excellent author of your own flesh and blood—an unimitating, and perhaps, in his way, inimitable man—whom better can I commend to you, in the first place, than Nathaniel Hawthorne." Melville was also the

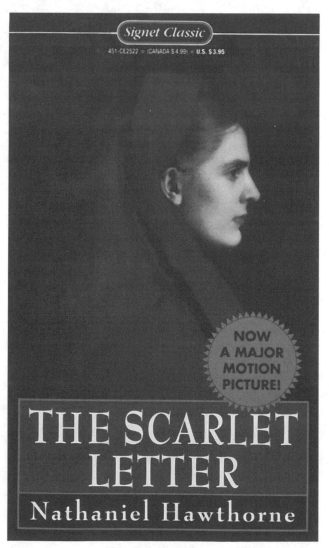

This 1850 work, considered Hawthorne's masterpiece, examines questions of morality and religion in the Puritan community of the seventeenth century.

first to single out the "great power of blackness" in Hawthorne which came from his concept of original sin. A future neighbor of Hawthorne's, Melville would dedicate *Moby Dick* to him.

Hawthorne also recorded in "The Old Manse" introduction that this would be "the last collection of this nature, which it is my purpose ever to put forth. Unless I could do better, I have done enough in this kind." True to his word, Hawthorne moved on after this collection. Though he did write the occasional short piece, and a further collection of short stories was brought out (most of which were written before 1837), Hawthorne's days as a writer of short stories came to an end with his sojourn at Concord. Ahead of him lay the great romantic novels of his maturity.

The Scarlet Letter

Before the publication of *Mosses from an Old Manse*, the Hawthornes moved from Concord back into the family home in Salem. This situation would last two years, through the birth of a son, Julian, and Hawthorne's appointment as surveyor to the port of Salem. Finally in the fall of 1847 the Hawthornes moved into their own home again, the meager $1,000 annual income from the surveyor position being supplemented by the lamp shades and screens Mrs. Hawthorne decorated and sold. This fragile security came to an end in June of 1849 when the Whigs defeated the Democrats in national elections and local politicians demanded that Democratic appointees be dismissed. Hawthorne's dismissal caused a controversy and divided the town of Salem, but eventually it stood. A month later his mother died, and it was with a bleak outlook that Hawthorne began work on what many critics and readers consider to be his masterpiece.

The work was based on a snippet of actual history Hawthorne had once heard: a young woman in Boston who was forced to wear the letter "A" on her bosom for an act of adultery. Intending to write a short story, Hawthorne was persuaded by the editor and publisher James T. Fields to turn it into a novel. And, once he had found his "pitch," as he put it, Hawthorne went about the writing quickly, completing *The Scarlet Letter*—called by some critics the greatest book written in the Western Hemisphere—on February 4, 1850. Essentially the story of how sin plays out among

various characters, *The Scarlet Letter* takes place in seventeenth-century Salem, an era and locale Hawthorne had often written about in his short fiction. The main characters are Hester Prynne, who at the outset of the novel is being punished for the sin of adultery by having to wear a letter "A" on her clothing; the Puritan minister, Arthur Dimmesdale, who is the secret lover whom Hester protects; Pearl, the illegitimate offspring of their union; and Roger Chillingworth, Hester's husband whom she had thought was lost at sea. Built around three dramatic scaffold scenes, the story proceeds from Hester's initial punishment to the arrival of Chillingworth and his vow to find the man who seduced his wife. A scholarly doctor, he makes Hester promise not to let anybody know that he is her husband, and his suspicions focus early on Dimmesdale. He takes rooms in the same house as the minister to worm his way into his confidence. Hester, meanwhile, comes to terms with her sin, turning a fault into piety. She accepts her own weakness and devotes herself to the community until many take the "A" to stand for "Able." Dimmesdale, on the other hand, is eaten by his guilt, unable to expiate it, while Chillingworth becomes totally possessed by hate and thus the worst sinner of them all. He hounds Dimmesdale until the minister makes a public confession—the final scaffold scene—after which the minister dies. This takes place just before Dimmesdale, Hester and the headstrong but loveable Pearl are due to sail away from Salem forever.

Less a story about adultery than about the effect of sin on the unconscious, *The Scarlet Letter* thus becomes a universal tale of mankind's struggle to deal with original sin or the sense of guilt that—according to Hawthorne's world view—afflicts us all. Hawthorne makes a clear distinction between sins of passion and those of principle or emotion, and Dimmesdale is allowed to perceive this as well, and acts as the author's spokesman: "We are not, Hester, the worst sinners in the world," Dimmesdale says. "There is one worse than even the polluted priest! That old man's revenge has been blacker than my sin. He has violated, in cold blood, the sanctity of a human heart. Thou and I, Hester, never did so."

Such sentiments made the book something of a scandalous success in its day. The citizens of Salem, however, were as interested in the introduction, "The Custom House," as they were in Hester's predicament. Intended to lighten the tone of the book, this sketch tells how the author supposedly found the manuscript as well as the scarlet letter in the custom house, left behind by a predecessor. But it also served to re-awaken the controversy over Hawthorne's unfair dismissal from the custom house. Another, perhaps inadvertent function of "The Custom House" was to define Hawthorne's stance vis-a-vis his fiction. He made the distinction between novel and romance, and noted that his book was of the latter type. Psychological or interior truth was the reality of a romance, unlike the novel, which demanded actualities. His type of book could walk a fine line between fiction and reality. It was a formula he would employ in the next three romances he wrote as well.

The Scarlet Letter earned Hawthorne a literary reputation, for it was with this book that a wide variety of critics began looking at his work. Never out of print since its publication in 1850, *The Scarlet Letter* has also continued to find favor with critics as the seminal American novel. As Arlin Turner characterizes it in *Dictionary of Literary Biography*, "few works in all literatures equal *The Scarlet Letter* in intensity, compression, and effective use of images and symbols." Indeed such images and symbols are to be found on almost every page, the overriding one being the letter "A" itself. An early advocate of Hawthorne's, E. P. Whipple, commented in the *Atlantic Monthly* that it was *The Scarlet Letter* which first made Hawthorne's "genius efficient by penetrating it with passion. . . . We seem to be following the guidance of an author who is personally good-natured, but intellectually and morally relentless." It is this relentless examination that keeps the book alive, that allows it to speak to readers over such a span of time. Praised by writers from Henry James to Trollope, Hawthorne first came to national and then international prominence with *The Scarlet Letter*; critics have labelled it everything from a book of moral advice to the first experiment in depth psychology, and over the years new layers have been uncovered in the book. Nearly 100 years after its publication, the critic Frederic I. Carpenter noted in *College English* that "from the first *The Scarlet Letter* has been considered a classic. It has appealed not only to the critics but to the reading public as well." Carpenter went on to measure the book's greatness in terms of the character Hester Prynne. Far from symbolizing the effects of sin, Prynne embodies for Hawthorne "the authentic American dream of a new life in the wilderness of the new world."

The Fruitful Decade

Hawthorne wrote in "The Custom House" that he wanted to become "a citizen of somewhere else," and that he wanted to raise his children away from Salem. In April, 1850, shortly after the publication of *The Scarlet Letter*, he moved his family to Lenox, Massachusetts, in the Berkshires, where his nearby neighbor was Herman Melville. Here his third child, Rose, was born in 1851, the same year that saw publication of three more books, two collections of short stories and the novel, *The House of the Seven Gables*. With *The Snow-Image, and Other Twice-Told Tales*, Hawthorne was through with the short story medium. The collection only had two newer pieces in it, one of them, "Ethan Brand," among his most famous tales. An aborted study for a novel, "Ethan Brand" tells a story of unpardonable sin through the eyes of a limeburner. A collection of children's stories, *A Wonder-Book for Girls and Boys*, also appeared that year, but it is Hawthorne's study of the sins of fathers which are passed on to succeeding generations as worked out in *The House of the Seven Gables* that was the year's major achievement. The story of the Pyncheon family, the book relates the curse that lies on the old house of the seven gables, lending it a tragic air. Two centuries earlier, a Pyncheon predecessor had fraudulently won the land the house is built upon when he sentenced an ancestral Maule to death for witchcraft. Maule's dying curse has stuck with the house since that time. In the current story, Clifford Pyncheon and his spinster sister Hepzibah live in the house, cut off from the outside world. Hepzibah has been forced to run a shop to support herself and her brother, recently let out of jail after serving a thirty year sentence for the murder of his uncle. Their relative, Judge Pyncheon, the last affluent member of the family, wants to have Clifford declared insane. Another cousin, Phoebe, is the one ray of light in the story, for she has been raised away from the house and its curse. A boarder, Holgrave, proves to be a Maule descendent, yet refuses to follow the vindictive family curse. In the end, Judge Pyncheon dies, the last victim of the curse, and is proved to have been responsible for Clifford's imprisonment and his subsequent loss of fortune. Holgrave wins Phoebe's hand, and love between the families has finally broken the curse.

Hawthorne personally thought *The House of the Seven Gables* a better piece of work than *The Scar-*

let Letter, and more characteristic of his mind. In fact, he reworked the last chapters to ensure that for once there would be a happy ending in his writing. The critic E. P. Whipple, while noting that this second romance has "less concentration of passion and tension of mind" than *The Scarlet Letter,* nevertheless saw a marvelous creation of sunshine and light in the character of Phoebe. "In this delightful creation," Whipple wrote, "Hawthorne for once gives himself up to homely human nature, and has succeeded in delineating a New-England girl, cheerful, blooming, practical, affectionate, efficient, full of innocence and happiness."

After only one year in Lenox, the Hawthornes again moved, first to West Newton near Boston, and then back to Concord where, with a degree of economic security, he was able to buy Wayside, a house originally belonging to Bronson Alcott. In the meantime, he had completed a third novel in as many years, *The Blithedale Romance,* based on his experiences at Brook Farm. Essentially a love triangle between the beautiful and wealthy Zenobia, the philanthropic but monomaniacal Hollingsworth, and the young and shy Priscilla, the story is narrated by the detached aesthete, Coverdale. Though Blithedale—the Brook Farm of Hawthorne's story—is a utopian community, it is not free from societal influences, passion included. In the book Hawthorne touches on themes ranging from the penal system to transcendentalism, and with the suicide of Zenobia occasioned by the love of Hollingsworth for Priscilla, the story comes to a tragic end. Once again the critic Whipple found genius in the work, especially in the manner in which Hawthorne does not try to "alter the destiny" of his characters. "They drift to their doom by the same law by which they drifted across the path of his vision," Whipple concluded.

The year 1852 saw the nomination of Hawthorne's old friend, Franklin Pierce, as Democratic candidate for president. Hawthorne wrote a campaign biography for the nominee, and after Pierce won the election, Hawthorne was rewarded with a consular post in Liverpool, England. Before departure, he published *Tanglewood Tales for Girls and Boys,* a companion to his earlier *Wonder-Book,* in both of which "Hawthorne's genius appears most lovable, though not in its deepest form," according to Whipple. Retellings of Greek mythology, the stories were written for children, but as Whipple noted, they "delight men and women as well."

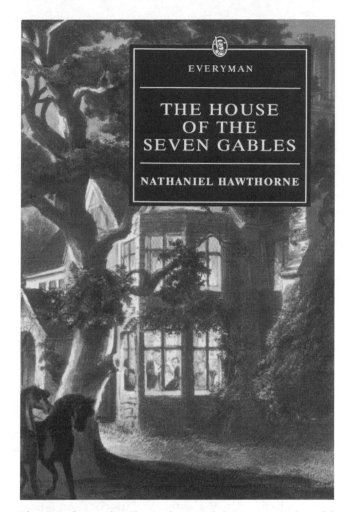

The Pyncheon family is haunted by a centuries-old curse placed on their house in this 1851 novel.

Hawthorne and his family sailed for Liverpool on July 6, 1853, and he served there until 1857, after which he and his family travelled throughout Europe, spending a year in Italy. During his consular years, Hawthorne wrote only journal entries, but while in Florence in 1858, he began a new work inspired by the museums of Italy and the time he had spent in Rome and Florence. The novel was outlined in Florence, and its first draft was completed in Rome—where his daughter Una almost died of fever—and finished in England. *The Marble Faun,* the fourth and last of Hawthorne's completed novels, is a re-enactment of the fall of man from innocence to knowledge, told through the characters of three Americans in Italy and the Italian, Count Donatello, who strongly resembles the famous faun of Praxiteles, a symbol of innocence for Hawthorne. The count is deeply in love with Miriam, a darkly lovely art student whose antecedents are shrouded in mystery. Kenyon, an

American sculptor, and Hilda, a blithe New England girl, are friends of Miriam's and thus of the Count's as well. However, Miriam seems to be under the power of a mysterious stranger, who Donatello finally kills. This act unites the two, but they do not know that Hilda has seen the murder. Destroyed by his guilt, his innocence lost, Donatello is finally taken by the police and convicted for his crime. Miriam, the temptress Eve of the tale, is left with her own guilt, while the innocent Hilda finds love with Kenyon.

Not considered one of his strongest romances, *The Marble Faun* relies, it has been noted, too heavily on symbol and allegory. However, in a retrospective of Hawthorne's career, the critic Whipple noted that Donatello "must be considered one of the most original and exquisite conceptions in the

---

If you enjoy the works of Nathaniel Hawthorne, you might also want to check out the following:

Washington Irving, *Rip Van Winkle*, 1819.
Arthur Miller, *The Crucible* (play), 1953.
Edgar Allan Poe, *The Tell-Tale Heart*, 1843.

---

whole range of romance," while the character Hilda introduces the sort of innocent American abroad which Henry James especially would later develop into a major thematic device. The book has also been called one of the finest guide books to Rome in all of fiction, for Hawthorne used large descriptive chunks of his journals in the writing.

The Final Years

Back in the United States after an absence of seven years, Hawthorne and his family once again took up residence at Wayside in Concord. He continued writing romances, though no further ones were brought to completion. Three fragments remain: *Dr. Grimshawe's Secret*, about an American's claim to an English inheritance; *Septimius Felton*, inspired by the idea for an elixir of life; and *The Dolliver Romance*. Hawthorne's English notebooks were published in 1862 in *The Atlantic Monthly*, collected in 1863 in *Our Old Home*, but failing health as well as despair at the onset of the Civil War clouded his last years. His stand, along with

Pierce, against the abolitionists cost him the respect of many of his old friends and neighbors in Concord. The war, he felt, was not worth fighting over slavery, but once begun it had to be prosecuted to victory. Yet the Union, he was sure, would be lost as a result.

Hawthorne's health continued to fail, but instead of visiting a doctor, he relied on visits to the seashore. He died at Plymouth, New Hampshire, in the early morning hours of May 19, 1864. His death did not end his publications, though most critics agree that such posthumous books and fragments are not indicative of his real power as a writer. He was championed by such critics as Whipple, Longfellow, and Poe in his lifetime, and after his death the banner was passed to Henry James, William Dean Howells, and Anthony Trollope, who in full length studies and magazine articles declared that Hawthorne was an American original and one of the fathers of the American novel. Hawthorne truly was a child of his age: he was deeply affected by his New England roots, both geographical and ancestral. The theme of sin and redemption runs through all his works, and his search beneath the surface of everyday life initiated an entire genre of introspective romantic fiction. His romances were not the sweeping realistic novels of Charles Dickens, but instead charted new territory in the world of emotions and the unconscious. If his novels and tales leave room for ambiguity, it is room for the reader to take part in the creation. By using compression and symbolism, Hawthorne was able to create worlds in his neutral ground between fiction and reality that are every bit as convincing as those found in any of the large realistic novels of his day. As George Perkins summed up Hawthorne's achievement in *Reference Guide to American Literature*, "Seldom have the modes of symbol and allegory been so effectively rendered in prose."

■ Works Cited

Carpenter, Frederic I., "Scarlet A Minus," *College English*, January, 1944, pp. 173-80.

Crews, Frederick C., "Introduction," *Great Short Works of Hawthorne*, Harper & Row, 1967, p. xii.

Gemme, Francis R., "Introduction," *Twice Told Tales*, Airmont Publishing Corporation, 1965, p. 6.

Hawthorne, Nathaniel, *The Heart of Hawthorne's Journals*, edited by Newton Arvin, Houghton, 1929.

Hawthorne, Nathaniel, *The Scarlet Letter*, Scholastic, 1961.

Hawthorne, Nathaniel, *Mosses from an Old Manse*, Books for Libraries, 1970.

Longfellow, Henry Wadsworth, review of *Twice Told Tales*, *North American Review*, July, 1837.

Melville, Herman, "Hawthorne and His Mosses," *Literary World*, August, 1850.

Perkins, George, "Nathaniel Hawthorne," *Reference Guide to American Literature*, 2nd edition, St. James Press, 1987, pp. 267-69.

Poe, Edgar Allan, review of *Twice Told Tales*, *Essays and Reviews*, edited by G. R. Thompson, The Library of America, 1984, pp. 577-88.

Turner, Arlin, "Nathaniel Hawthorne," *Dictionary of Literary Biography*, Volume One: *The American Renaissance in New England*, Gale, 1978, pp. 80-101.

Whipple, E. P., "Nathaniel Hawthorne," *Atlantic Monthly*, May, 1860, pp. 614-22.

■ **For More Information See**

BOOKS

Baym, Nina, *The Shape of Hawthorne's Career*, Cornell University Press, 1976.

Bridge, Horatio, *Personal Recollections of Nathaniel Hawthorne*, Harper, 1893.

Bunge, Nancy L., *Nathaniel Hawthorne: A Study of the Short Fiction*, Twayne, 1993.

Cantwell, Robert, *Nathaniel Hawthorne: The American Years*, Rinehart, 1948.

Clark, C. E. Frazer, Jr., *Nathaniel Hawthorne: A Descriptive Bibliography*, University of Pittsburgh Press, 1978.

Crews, Frederick C., *The Sins of the Fathers: Hawthorne's Psychological Themes*, Oxford University Press, 1966.

Dunne, Michael, *Hawthorne's Narrative Strategies*, University of Mississippi Press, 1995.

Fogle, Richard Harter, *Hawthorne's Fiction: The Light and the Dark*, University of Oklahoma Press, 1952.

Gale, Robert L., *A Nathaniel Hawthorne Encyclopedia*, Greenwood, 1991.

Gorham, Herbert, *Hawthorne: A Study in Solitude*, Doran, 1927.

Hawthorne, Julian, *Nathaniel Hawthorne and His Wife*, two volumes, Osgood, 1884.

Hawthorne, Julian, *Hawthorne and His Circle*, Harper, 1903.

Hoeltje, Hubert H., *Inward Sky: The Heart and Mind of Nathaniel Hawthorne*, Duke University Press, 1962.

James, Henry, *Hawthorne*, Harper, 1879.

Lathrop, Rose Hawthorne, *Memories of Hawthorne*, Houghton, 1897.

Levin, Harry, *The Power of Blackness: Hawthorne, Poe, and Melville*, Knopf, 1958.

Loggins, Vernon, *The Hawthornes: The Story of Seven Generations of an American Family*, Columbia University Press, 1951.

Male, Roy R., *Hawthorne's Tragic Vision*, University of Texas Press, 1957.

Martin, Terence, *Nathaniel Hawthorne*, Twayne, 1965.

Matthiesson, F. O., *American Renaissance: Art and Expression in the Age of Emerson and Whitman*, Oxford University Press, 1941.

Miller, Edwin Haviland, *Salem Is My Dwelling Place: A Life of Nathaniel Hawthorne*, University of Iowa Press, 1991.

Morris, Lloyd, *The Rebellious Puritan*, Harcourt, 1927.

Nathaniel Hawthorne: The Contemporary Reviews, edited by John L. Ido, Cambridge University Press, 1994.

Nathaniel Hawthorne's The Secret Letter, edited and with an introduction by Harold Bloom, Chelsea House, 1996.

Pearce, Roy Harvey, editor, *Hawthorne Centenary Essays*, Ohio State University Press, 1964.

Ricks, Beatrice, Joseph D. Adams, Jack O. Hazlerig, *Nathaniel Hawthorne: A Reference Bibliography, 1900-1971, with Selected Nineteenth Century Materials*, G. K. Hall, 1972.

Short Story Criticism, volume 3, Gale, 1989, pp. 152-97.

Stewart, Randall, *Nathaniel Hawthorne: A Biography*, Yale University Press, 1948.

Swann, Charles, *Nathaniel Hawthorne, Tradition and Revolution*, Cambridge University Press, 1991.

Turner, Arlin, *Nathaniel Hawthorne: An Introduction and Interpretation*, Barnes & Nobel, 1961.

Van Doren, Mark, *Nathaniel Hawthorne*, Viking, 1949.

Wagenknecht, Edward Charles, *Nathaniel Hawthorne: Man and Writer*, Oxford University Press, 1961.

Waggoner, Hyatt H., *Hawthorne: A Critical Study*, revised edition, Harvard University Press, 1963.

World Literature Criticism, volume 3, Gale, 1992, pp. 1592-1609.

PERIODICALS

Choice, November, 1965, p. 579; May, 1966, p. 209; June, 1968, p. 1442; June, 1978, p. 545; September, 1978, p. 868; June, 1979, p. 529; April, 1981,

p. 1098; January, 1983, p. 706; September, 1983, p. 96; December, 1985, p. 604; November, 1987, p. 474; March, 1988, p. 1094; January, 1991, p. 775.

Kliatt, Spring, 1978, p. 14; April, 1992, p. 10; Spring, 1993, p. 53; May, 1994, p. 51; July, 1994, p. 49.

Library Journal, February 15, 1972, p. 671; March 15, 1990, p. 90; November 15, 1991, p. 119.

New York Times Book Review, April 25, 1982, p. 3.

Times Literary Supplement, May 19, 1966, p. 456; May 26, 1966, p. 477; May 25, 1984, p. 592; May 22, 1987, p. 553.*

—Sketch by J. Sydney Jones

Lee Bennett Hopkins

■ Personal

Born April 13, 1938, in Scranton, PA; son of Leon Hall (a police officer) and Gertrude Thomas (a homemaker) Hopkins. *Education:* Newark State Teachers College (now Kean College of New Jersey), B.A., 1960; Bank Street College of Education, M.Sc., 1964; Hunter College of the City University of New York, Professional Diploma in Educational Supervision and Administration, 1967.

■ Addresses

Home—Kemeys Cove, Scarborough, NY 10510.

■ Career

Public school teacher in Fair Lawn, NJ, 1960-66; Bank Street College of Education, New York City, senior consultant, 1966-68; Scholastic, Inc., New York City, curriculum and editorial specialist, 1968-76; full-time writer and anthologist, 1976—. Lecturer on children's literature; host and consultant to children's television series, "Zebra Wings," Agency for Instructional Television, beginning 1976. Consultant to school systems on elementary

curriculum; literature consultant, Harper & Row, Text Division. *Member:* International Reading Association, American Library Association, American Association of School Librarians, Authors Guild of the Authors League of America, National Council of Teachers of English (member of board of directors, 1975-78; chair of 1978 and 1991 Poetry Award Committee; member of Commission on Literature, 1983-85; member of Children's Literature Assembly, 1985-88; Honorary Board Member of The Children's Literature Council of Pennsylvania, 1990—).

■ Awards, Honors

Outstanding Alumnus in the Arts award, Kean College, 1972; *To Look at Any Thing* was chosen as choice book of the 1978 International Youth Library exhibition, Munich, Germany; children's choice award, International Reading Association/Children's Book Council, 1980, for *Wonder Wheels*; honorary doctor of laws, Kean College, 1980; Phi Delta Kappa Educational Leadership Award, 1980; International Reading Association Manhattan Council Literacy Award, 1983; National Children's Book Week Poet, 1985; Silver Medallion, University of Southern Mississippi, 1989, for lifetime achievement in children's literature; *Don't You Turn Back, Rainbows Are Made, Surprises,* and *A Song in Stone* were chosen as American Library Association notable books; *Mama* was chosen as a National Council for Social Studies notable book; *Side by Side: Poems to Read Together, Voyages: Poems by*

Walt Whitman, and *On the Farm* were chosen as American Booksellers Pick-of-the-List books.

■ **Writings**

(With Annette F. Shapiro) *Creative Activities for Gifted Children*, Fearon, 1968.

Books Are by People, Citation Press, 1969.

Let Them Be Themselves: Language Arts Enrichment for Disadvantaged Children in Elementary Schools, Citation Press, 1969, 2nd edition published as *Let Them Be Themselves: Language Arts for Children in Elementary Schools*, 1974, 3rd edition, Harper, 1992.

(With Misha Arenstein) *Partners in Learning: A Child-Centered Approach to Teaching the Social Studies*, Citation Press, 1971.

Pass the Poetry, Please! Bringing Poetry into the Minds and Hearts of Children, Citation Press, 1972, revised edition, Harper, 1987.

More Books by More People, Citation Press, 1974.

(With Misha Arenstein) *Do You Know What Day Tomorrow Is? A Teacher's Almanac*, Citation Press, 1975, revised edition, Scholastic, 1990.

The Best of Book Bonanza (Instructor Book-of-the-Month Club selection), Holt, 1980.

The Writing Bug (autobiography), illustrated by Diane Rubinger, Richard C. Owen Publishers, 1992.

(Contributor) Alma F. Ada, editor, *A Chorus of Cultures Poetry Anthology: Developing Literacy Through Multicultural Poetry*, Hampton-Brown, 1993.

YOUNG ADULT NOVELS

Mama, Knopf, 1977.

Wonder Wheels, Knopf, 1979.

Mama and Her Boys, Harper, 1981.

CHILDREN'S BOOKS

Important Dates in Afro-American History, F. Watts, 1969.

This Street's for Me (poetry), illustrated by Ann Grifalconi, Crown, 1970.

(With Misha Arenstein) *Faces and Places: Poems for You*, illustrated by L. Weil, Scholastic Book Services, 1970.

Happy Birthday to Me!, Scholastic Book Services, 1972.

When I Am All Alone: A Book of Poems, Scholastic Book Services, 1972.

Charlie's World: A Book of Poems, Bobbs-Merrill, 1972.

Kim's Place and Other Poems, Holt, 1974.

I Loved Rose Ann, illustrated by Ingrid Fetz, Knopf, 1976.

A Haunting We Will Go: Ghostly Stories and Poems, illustrated by Vera Rosenberry, Albert Whitman, 1976.

Witching Time: Mischievous Stories and Poems, illustrated by Vera Rosenberry, Albert Whitman, 1976.

Kits, Cats, Lions, and Tigers: Stories, Poems, and Verse, illustrated by Vera Rosenberry, Albert Whitman, 1979.

Pups, Dogs, Foxes, and Wolves: Stories, Poems, and Verse, illustrated by Vera Rosenberry, Albert Whitman, 1979.

How Do You Make an Elephant Float and Other Delicious Food Riddles, illustrated by Rosekranz Hoffman, Albert Whitman, 1983.

Animals from Mother Goose, Harcourt, 1989.

People from Mother Goose, Harcourt, 1989.

COMPILER

I Think I Saw a Snail: Young Poems for City Seasons, illustrated by Harold James, Crown, 1969.

Don't You Turn Back: Poems by Langston Hughes, foreword by Arna Bontemps, Knopf, 1969.

City Talk, illustrated by Roy Arnella, Knopf, 1970.

The City Spreads Its Wings, illustrated by Moneta Barnett, F. Watts, 1970.

Me! A Book of Poems (Junior Library Guild selection), illustrated by Talavaldis Stubis, Seabury, 1970.

Zoo! A Book of Poems, illustrated by Robert Frankenberg, Crown, 1971.

Girls Can Too! A Book of Poems, illustrated by Emily McCully, F. Watts, 1972.

(With Misha Arenstein) *Time to Shout: Poems For You*, illustrated by L. Weil, Scholastic, Inc., 1973.

(With Sunna Rasch) *I Really Want to Feel Good about Myself: Poems by Former Addicts*, Thomas Nelson, 1974.

On Our Way: Poems of Pride and Love, illustrated by David Parks, Knopf, 1974.

Hey-How for Halloween, illustrated by Janet McCaffery, Harcourt, 1974.

Take Hold! An Anthology of Pulitzer Prize Winning Poems, Thomas Nelson, 1974.

Poetry on Wheels, illustrated by Frank Aloise, Garrard, 1974.

Sing Hey for Christmas Day, illustrated by Laura Jean Allen, Harcourt, 1975.

Good Morning to You, Valentine, illustrated by Tomie de Paola, Harcourt, 1976.

Merrily Comes Our Harvest In, illustrated by Ben Schecter, Harcourt, 1976.

(With Misha Arenstein) *Thread One to a Star,* Four Winds, 1976.

(With Misha Arenstein) *Potato Chips and a Slice of Moon: Poems You'll Like,* illustrated by Wayne Blickenstaff, Scholastic Inc., 1976.

Beat the Drum! Independence Day Has Come, illustrated by Tomie de Paola, Harcourt, 1977.

Monsters, Ghoulies, and Creepy Creatures: Fantastic Stories and Poems, illustrated by vera Rosenberry, Albert Whitman, 1977.

To Look at Any Thing, illustrated by John Earl, Harcourt, 1978.

Easter Buds Are Springing: Poems for Easter, illustrated by Tomie de Paola, Harcourt, 1979.

Merely Players: An Anthology of Life Poems, Thomas Nelson, 1979.

My Mane Catches the Wind: Poems about Horses, illustrated by Sam Savitt, Harcourt, 1979.

By Myself, illustrated by Glo Coalson, Crowell, 1980.

Elves, Fairies and Gnomes, illustrated by Rosekranz Hoffman, Knopf, 1980.

Moments: Poems about the Seasons, illustrated by Michael Hague, Harcourt, 1980.

Morning, Noon, and Nighttime, Too!, illustrated by Nancy Hannans, Harper, 1980.

I Am the Cat, illustrated by Linda Rochester Richards, Harcourt, 1981.

And God Bless Me: Prayers, Lullabies and Dream-Poems, illustrated by Patricia Henderson Lincoln, Knopf, 1982.

Rainbows Are Made: Poems by Carl Sandburg, illustrated by Fritz Eichenberg, Harcourt, 1982.

A Dog's Life, illustrated by Linda Rochester Richards, Harcourt, 1983.

The Sky Is Full of Song, illustrated by Dirk Zimmer, Charlotte Zolotow/Harper, 1983.

A Song in Stone: City Poems, illustrated by Anna Held Audette, Crowell, 1983.

Crickets and Bullfrogs and Whispers of Thunder: Poems and Pictures by Harry Behn, Harcourt, 1984.

Love and Kisses (poems), illustrated by Kris Boyd, Houghton, 1984.

Surprises: An I Can Read Book of Poems, illustrated by Meagan Lloyd, Charlotte Zolotow/Harper, 1984.

Creatures, illustrated by Stella Ormai, Harcourt, 1985.

Munching: Poems about Eating, illustrated by Nelle Davis, Little, Brown, 1985.

Best Friends, illustrated by James Watts, Charlotte Zolotow/Harper, 1986.

The Sea Is Calling Me, illustrated by Walter Gaffney-Kessell, Harcourt, 1986.

Click, Rumble, Roar: Poems about Machines, illustrated by Anna Held Audette, Crowell, 1987.

Dinosaurs, illustrated by Murray Tinkelman, Harcourt, 1987.

More Surprises: An I Can Read Book, illustrated by Meagan Lloyd, Charlotte Zolotow/Harper, 1987.

Voyages: Poems by Walt Whitman, illustrated by Charles Mikolaycak, Harcourt, 1988.

Side by Side: Poems to Read Together (Book-of-the-Month Club selection), illustrated by Hilary Knight, Simon & Schuster, 1988.

Still as a Star: Nighttime Poems, illustrated by Karen Malone, Little, Brown, 1989.

Good Books, Good Times, illustrated by Harvey Stevenson, Charlotte Zolotow/Harper, 1990.

Happy Birthday, illustrated by Hilary Knight, Simon & Schuster, 1991.

On the Farm, illustrated by Laurel Molk, Little, Brown, 1991.

Ring Out, Wild Bells: Poems about Holidays and Seasons, illustrated by Karen Baumann, Harcourt, 1992.

To the Zoo, illustrated by John Wallner, Little, Brown, 1992.

Pterodactyls and Pizza, illustrated by Nadine Bernard Westcott, Dell, 1992.

Through Our Eyes: Poems of Today, illustrated by Jeffry Dunn, Little, Brown, 1992.

Questions: An I Can Read Book, illustrated by Carolyn Croll, Harper, 1992.

Flit, Flutter, Fly, illustrated by Peter Palagonia, Doubleday, 1992.

Easter Buds Are Springing, Boyds Mills Press, 1993.

Extra Innings: Baseball Poems, illustrated by Scott Medlock, Harcourt, 1993.

It's about Time, illustrated by Matt Novak, Simon & Schuster, 1993.

Ragged Shadows: Poems of Halloween Night, Little, Brown, 1993.

April, Bubbles, Chocolate, illustrated by Barrett Root, Simon & Schuster, 1994.

My Country, 'tis of Thee, illustrated by Peter Fiore, 1994.

Been to Yesterdays: Poems of a Life, Boyds Mills Press, 1995.

Blast Off! Poems about Space, illustrated by Melissa Sweet, HarperCollins, 1995.

Good Rhymes, Good Times, illustrated by Frane Lessac, HarperCollins, 1995.

Pauses: Autobiographical Reflections of 101 Creators of Children's Books, HarperCollins, 1995.
Small Talk: A Book of Short Poems, illustrated by Susan Gaber, Harcourt, 1995.
Weather: Poems for All Seasons, illustrated by Melanie Hall, HarperCollins, 1995.
Opening Days: Sports Poems, illustrated by Scott Medlock, Harcourt, 1996.
School Supplies: A Book of Poems, illustrated by Renee Flower, Simon & Schuster, 1996.

OTHER

Also author of columns, "Poetry Place," in *Instructor* magazine, and "Book Sharing," in *School Library Media Quarterly*. Associate editor, *School Library Media Quarterly*, 1982—.

■ Sidelights

"Mrs. McLaughlin saved me; she introduced me to two things that had given me direction and hope—the love of reading and the theatre," children's author and poet Lee Bennett Hopkins confessed about his elementary schoolteacher in *Something about the Author Autobiography Series* (*SAAS*). With his teacher's help and encouragement, Hopkins went on to become a talented teacher, author, and compiler of children's verse collections. He has been termed the "Pied Piper" of poetry by others in the field.

Hopkins was born in Scranton, Pennsylvania, on April 13, 1938. It was during the Great Depression, and Hopkins's parents named him after Lee Bennett, the lead singer in one of the popular bands on the radio. His family was poor and struggling to make it financially. Yet, for the first ten years of his life, he and his two siblings lived in relative comfort surrounded by a loving extended family. In 1948, all of that changed. The family decided to uproot themselves and move to Newark, New Jersey, where it was rumored that work was easier to find. After a few years in the city where his parents changed jobs and apartments several times, Hopkins's parents decided to split up. Hopkins found himself attending school sporadically as he tried to balance the demands of his schoolwork with the increased demands from his home. It was during this time that he met Mrs. Ethel Kite McLaughlin, the woman who was to have so much influence on his life. "I remember not being interested in anything but sur-

vival during this period of my life," Hopkins wrote in *SAAS*.

One day during class, Mrs. McLaughlin recounted an evening at the theater in great detail. She had seen *Wish You Were Here*. "She related how actors and actresses danced and sang on stage. They even swam in a swimming pool!" Hopkins told *SAAS*. "I couldn't believe it." Hopkins was truly dumbfounded, never having been to any kind of live theater. But he had been an incredible film buff. "I wouldn't be able to even count the number of double features I sat through. If I could, I might well qualify for *The Guinness Book of World Records*," he told SAAS.

Oh, the Footlights!

His teacher had a sense that the overworked boy might have a need for a larger dream. So she suggested that he go to a professional theater production in Montclair, New Jersey. The entire trip, including transportation, cost $1.50. That was a real problem. His family was in such bad financial straits that the phone had been taken away and the electricity shut off because they couldn't pay the bills. Yet Hopkins knew that he would somehow find a way to go. "I decided I was *going* to get to the Paper Mill Playhouse, somehow! I read in the *Newark Star-Ledger* that they were having a contest called 'Babies Are Bright.' You had to send in a baby picture with a caption. I entered my young cousin's picture with a caption and won. The prize was ten dollars. Feeling like a millionaire because I now had the money to get to the theatre, I kept two dollars and gave the other eight dollars to my mother to help pay off some debts," Hopkins told *SAAS*.

Hopkins ended up going to see a production of *Kiss Me, Kate* at the playhouse. He was thrilled about the whole trip, even if he did have to sit in the last row of the balcony. This trip made Hopkins become an avid reader of plays, and each year he found a way to make it back to the Paper Mill Playhouse to see their shows. Hopkins's family moved to a subsidized housing project where they had a tiny apartment. It was a racially mixed building where all that they had in common was poverty. Hopkins, because he was the oldest child, continued to have extra responsibility with the family. He got a job and gave most of his money to his mother.

Fifty poems by such poets as Carl Sandburg, Emily Dickinson, Robert Frost, and Langston Hughes have been chosen and put in meaningful sequence by Hopkins in *Moments: Poems about the Seasons*.

Hopkins attended junior high school and high school where most of the students were poor minority children. He felt a little isolated because of his ethnicity. "Since the majority of the students were black, most social activities were out for me," he told *SAAS*. "Being white I stood out. It was the several other white students and I who were in the minority group." Even though Hopkins had become an avid reader, he did poorly in most of his classes. He detested the level of memorization and rote learning that was required. It was nearly impossible for him to grasp math. But his lack of success in the classroom did not deter him from his ultimate goal—becoming a teacher. Mrs. McLaughlin was Hopkins's role model and inspiration to become a teacher. When he graduated from school, he recounted in *SAAS*, "I knew I had to become a teacher and do for others what she had done for me."

After graduation, he applied to a local teacher's college and was pleasantly surprised that he got in. It was a difficult road, though, and he had to work several jobs just to pay the tuition. The first two years were difficult for him because of his lack of preparation in high school. He had to take remedial math courses, and he didn't do very well even in those. "It wasn't until I began majoring in education that I picked up. I loved methods courses and exploring child psychology. My grades improved greatly during these years. I went from a mediocre student to well-above average," Hopkins told *SAAS*.

Teacher, Teacher

Even though it was difficult to work and attend college, Hopkins still found time for trips into New York to see theater and films. When he was a senior in college he applied for a public school position in a wealthy area of New Jersey. Hopkins clinched the interview when the superintendent gave him a book of matches. "'This is all you have to teach with for the first three months in a sixth-grade classroom,' he said. 'What would you do?'" Hopkins related in *SAAS*. Within minutes, the creative Hopkins had given the superintendent several different ways to teach with only a book of matches. He got the job teaching sixth grade students immediately.

It was quite a change for Hopkins. He had been attending inner-city schools for a long time, and suddenly he was in one of the best public school systems in the state. Hopkins moved out of his shared apartment in the projects into a modest but beautiful garden apartment. Hopkins soon found that he really loved to teach and was very satisfied with his job. He continued his education by going to Bank Street College of Education through the help of a scholarship arranged by his principal.

After a few years of teaching, Hopkins was selected to become the school's resource teacher, a new position that involved organizing materials for all of the elementary teachers. While at this post Hopkins came up with the idea that poetry might help children with reading problems. "After all," Hopkins recalled in *SAAS*, "poetry was short, the vocabulary usually simple, often it was repetitive, and I've always maintained that many times the right poem can have as much impact in ten, twelve, or fourteen lines, that an entire novel can have." The idea was a success. "Poetry became 'the thing,'" Hopkins wrote in *SAAS*. "I used it in every way possible—in every subject area. Mother Goose rhymes served to create mathematical word problems; Carl Sandburg's 'Arithmetic' was read before mathematics lessons; a holiday wouldn't go by without sharing a Valentine's Day, Halloween, or Christmas poem."

During the late 1960s Hopkins went on to help disadvantaged children in Harlem as a consultant at Bank Street College of Education. Again he used poetry; the verse of black poets such as Gwendolyn Brooks and Langston Hughes became important educational tools for black youths. Unfortunately, when Martin Luther King, Jr., was assassinated on April 4, 1968, tensions between blacks and whites put pressure on Hopkins and

A companion volume to Hopkins's anthology on Carl Sandburg entitled *Rainbows Are Made,* this collection of fifty-three poems and excerpts by Walt Whitman provides a poetic biography of the creator of *Leaves of Grass.*

other whites working in Harlem to find work elsewhere. "The attitude of many black and white people in Harlem was becoming frightening as racial polarization became the norm and all whites were again an enemy. No matter what I knew or how I felt about these troubled times, I was *white,*" Hopkins told *SAAS*. A few days later Hopkins was hired as an editor for Scholastic, where he remained until 1976.

Though Hopkins's first books were completed while at Bank Street, his book-publishing career developed rapidly at Scholastic. The award-winning *Don't You Turn Back: Poems by Langston Hughes* spawned a succession of critically acclaimed verse collections for children. Recalling his days as a resource teacher, Hopkins realized the need for poetry collections that were focused thematically on seasons and holidays. He published the first book with this theme in 1974, *Hey-How for Halloween.* He continued with the popular *Sing Hey for Christmas Day* (1975), *Good Morning to You, Valentine* (1976), *Beat the Drum! Independence Day Has Come* (1977), and *Easter Buds Are Springing: Poems for Easter* (1979). In his *SAAS* entry, Hopkins described the key ingredients in his compilations. "Balance is important in an anthology. I want many voices within a book, so I rarely use more than three works by the same poet. I also try to envision each volume as a stage play or film, having a definite beginning, middle, and end. The right flow is a necessity for me. Sometimes a word at the end of a work will lead into the next selection. I want my collections to read like a short story or novel—not just as a hodgepodge of works thrown together aimlessly."

One of his more popular books does not contain poetry. In *Books Are by People* (1969), Hopkins interviewed close to 200 children's book authors and illustrators. He wrote the book partly to satisfy the children who had asked him, over the years, "'Are books written by *real* people?'" Hopkins wrote in *SAAS*. In the sequel, *More Books by More People* (1974), Hopkins interviewed 65 authors and illustrators.

Novels & Nature

In 1976, Hopkins tried his hand at writing a picture book. *I Love Rose Ann* is the story of unrequited love between two young people. It is an autobiographical rendering of one of Hopkins's young love experiences. The book is written from the standpoints of a young boy and Rose Ann (who does the rejecting). In *Mama* (1977), Hopkins attempted to write a picture book about a poor mother who has to steal to make ends meet in her family. But when he took it into his editor, she persuaded him to expand it into a novel. "I had never thought about writing a *novel*," Hopkins related in *SAAS*. "Where would I ever begin? I had no idea of what it took to write one chapter for a novel, let along an entire book. And how would I possibly find the time to write while holding a highly pressured position at Scholastic?"

After some soul searching, Hopkins made a huge decision. "I decided writing was the most important thing in my life and left Scholastic in 1976 to pursue the challenge of writing *Mama*. This also gave me the impetus to leave New York, to settle into a condominium in Westchester County— Kemeys Cove—a magical place, smack atop the Hudson River. Leaving New York City was odd. I had always been a city child. It took me quite a while to begin to know and enjoy the beauties of nature, which this area is so filled with. I really thought every bird was a pigeon!" After *Mama*, Hopkins wrote two more young adult novels: *Wonder Wheels* (1980), and *Mama and Her Boys* (1981). Both of these novels were highly autobiographical. *Wonder Wheels* was based on the story of Hopkins's girlfriend who was tragically murdered on his sixteenth birthday. *Mama & Her Boys* is the sequel to *Mama*. In this book, Mama finds a nice man to marry and she no longer needs to steal to make ends meet. In 1985, Hopkins went through an emotional personal encounter. His sister found their long-lost father. No one in the fam-

---

If you enjoy the works of Lee Bennett Hopkins, you may also want to check out the following books:

Ashley Bryan, *Sing to the Sun*, 1992.
Douglas Florian, *on the wing*, 1995.
Mark Jonathan Harris, *Came the Morning*, 1989.
Jane McFann, *One Step Short*, 1990.

---

ily had seen him for thirty-six years. "This led to a family reunion at my house sparked by my courageous mother," he recounts in *SAAS*. "The family picture came together again. Whenever I receive a note from my father which begins, 'My dear Son,' I think of the many years the family was apart and how much we all had missed."

From his perch near the Hudson River, Hopkins continues to produce well-received stories, novels, and verse collections for children. "I share land with raccoons and squirrels, and view breathtaking foliage. The commanding Hudson River can be seen from every window. All of this is quite a contrast to my childhood days spent in the city, on asphalt streets and cement sidewalks," Hopkins told *SAAS*. The pastoral setting has also had an effect on his writing: "If I hadn't witnessed the dramatic, changing seasons here," he wrote in *SAAS*. "I would never have compiled such volumes as *Moments: Poems about the Seasons* (1980) or *The Sky Is Full of Song* (1983)."

Though his projects vary, Hopkins remains best known for making accessible to children a wide range of poetry. Indeed, according to *Juvenile Miscellany*, "Hopkins' immersion in poetry, past and present, text and illustration, places him at the heart of children's literature." Hopkins himself noted in *Instructor* magazine that poetry "should come to [children] as naturally as breathing, for nothing—*no thing*—can ring and rage through hearts and minds as does this genre of literature."

■ Works Cited

Hopkins, Lee Bennett, essay in *Something about the Author Autobiography Series*, Volume 4, Gale, 1987, pp. 233-47.

Instructor, March, 1982.

Juvenile Miscellany, summer, 1989, p. 4.

■ For More Information See

BOOKS

Gallo, Donald R., *Speaking for Ourselves: Autobiographical Sketches by Notable Authors of Books for Young Adults*, National Council of Teachers of English, 1990.

Roginski, James W., *Behind the Covers: Interviews with Authors and Illustrators of Books for Children and Young Adults*, Libraries Unlimited, 1985.

PERIODICALS

Christian Science Monitor, June 29, 1983.

Horn Book, May/June, 1996, p. 366.

New York Times Book Review, April 8, 1979; October 5, 1986.

Washington Post Book World, May 11, 1980.*

—*Sketch by Nancy Rampson*

James A. Houston

■ Personal

Born James Archibald Houston, June 12, 1921, in Toronto, Ontario, Canada; came to the United States, 1962; son of James Donald (a clothing importer) and Gladys Maud (Barbour) Houston; married Alma G. Bardon, 1950 (divorced, 1967); married Alice Daggett Watson, December 9, 1967; children: (first marriage) John James, Samuel Douglas. *Education:* Attended Ontario College of Art, 1938-40, Ecole Grand Chaumiere, Paris, 1947-48, Unichi-Hiratsuka, Tokyo, 1958-59, and Atelier 17, 1961. *Religion:* Anglican. *Hobbies and other interests:* Fishing, sketching, glasswork.

■ Addresses

Home—24 Main St., Stonington, CT 06378 (winter); P.O. Box 43, Tlell, Queen Charlotte Islands, British Columbia, Canada VOT 1YO (summer). *Office*—717 Fifth Ave., New York, NY 10022.

■ Career

Author and illustrator. Canadian Guild of Crafts, Arctic advisor, 1949-52; Government of Canada,

West Baffin, Northwest Territories, first civil administrator, 1952-62; Steuben Glass, New York City, associate director of design, 1962-72, master designer, 1972—. Visiting lecturer at Wye Institute and Rhode Island School of Design; honorary fellow, Ontario College of Art. Chair of board of directors of Canadian Arctic Producers, 1976-77, and American Indian Art Center; member of board of directors of Canadian Eskimo Arts Council; president of Indian and Eskimo Art of the Americas; vice-president of West Baffin Eskimo Cooperative and Eskimo Art, Inc. Member of primitive art committee of Metropolitan Museum of Art. *Military service:* Canadian Army, Toronto Scottish Regiment, 1940-45; became warrant officer. *Exhibitions:* Canadian Guild of Crafts, 1953, 1955, 1957; Robertson Galleries, Ottawa, 1953; Calgary Galleries, 1966; Canadiana Galleries, Edmonton, 1977; Yaneff Gallery, Toronto, 1983, 1986; Steuben Glass, 1987; represented in collections of Glenbow-Alberta Museum of Art, Montreal Museum of Fine Arts, and National Gallery of Art, Ottawa. *Member:* Producers Guild of America, Writers' Union of Canada, Canadian Eskimo Arts Council, Canadian Arctic Producers, American Indian Arts Center, Indian and Eskimo Art of the Americas, Royal Society of Art (London; fellow, 1981), Explorers Club, Century Association, Grolier Club, Leash.

■ Awards

American Indian and Eskimo Cultural Foundation Award, 1966; Canadian Library Association Book of the Year awards, 1966, for *Tikta'liktak: An Es-kimo Legend*, 1968, for *The White Archer: An Es-kimo Legend*, 1980, for *River Runners: A Tale of Hardship and Bravery*, and runner-up, 1982, for *Long Claws: An Arctic Adventure*; American Library Association Notable Book citations, 1967, for *The White Archer*, 1968, for *Akavak: An Eskimo Journey*, and 1971, for *The White Dawn: An Eskimo Saga*; decorated officer of Order of Canada, 1972; D.Litt., Carleton University, 1972; Amelia Frances Howard-Gibbon award runner-up, 1973, for *Ghost Paddle: A Northwest Coast Indian Tale*; D.H.L., Rhode Island College, 1975; Vicky Metcalf award, 1977; Inuit Kuavati Award of Merit, 1979; D.F.A., Rhode Island School of Design, 1979; Vicky Metcalf Short Story award, 1980, for "Long Claws," in *The Winter Fun Book*; Canadian nominee, Hans Christian Andersen Award, 1987; Citation of Merit Award, Royal Canadian Academy of Arts, 1987; D.D.L., Dalhousie University, 1987; Max and Gretta Ebel Award, Canadian Society of Children's Authors, Illustrators, and Performers, 1989.

■ Writings

FOR YOUNG ADULTS; SELF-ILLUSTRATED

Tikta'liktak: An Eskimo Legend, Harcourt, 1965.
Eagle Mask: A West Coast Indian Tale, Harcourt, 1966.
The White Archer: An Eskimo Legend, Harcourt, 1967.
Akavak: An Eskimo Journey, Harcourt, 1968.
Wolf Run: A Caribou Eskimo Tale, Harcourt, 1971.
Ghost Paddle: A Northwest Coast Indian Tale, Harcourt, 1972.
(Editor) *Songs of the Dream People: Chants and Images from the Indians and Eskimos of North America*, Atheneum, 1972.
Kiviok's Magic Journey: An Eskimo Legend, Atheneum, 1973.
Frozen Fire: A Tale of Courage, Atheneum, 1977.
River Runners: A Tale of Hardship and Bravery, Atheneum, 1979.
Long Claws: An Arctic Adventure, Atheneum, 1981.
Black Diamonds: A Search for Arctic Treasure, Atheneum, 1982.
Ice Swords: An Undersea Adventure, Atheneum, 1985.
The Falcon Bow: An Arctic Legend, McElderry, 1986.
Whiteout, Key Porter, 1988.
The White Dawn: An Eskimo Saga, Harcourt, 1989.

Drifting Snow: An Arctic Search, McElderry, 1992.

FOR ADULTS; SELF-ILLUSTRATED

The White Dawn: An Eskimo Saga (novel), Harcourt, 1971.
Ghost Fox (novel), Harcourt, 1977.
Spirit Wrestler (novel), Harcourt, 1980.
Eagle Song (novel), Harcourt, 1983.
Running West (novel), Crown, 1989.
Confessions of an Igloo Dweller, Peter Davison, 1996.

FOR ADULTS; NONFICTION

Canadian Eskimo Art, Queen's Printer, 1955.
Eskimo Graphic Art, Queen's Printer, 1960.
Eskimo Prints, Barre Publishing, 1967.
Ojibwa Summer, photographs by B. A. King, Barre Publishing, 1972.

SCREENPLAYS

The White Dawn, Paramount, 1973.
The Mask and the Drum, Swannsway Productions, 1975.
So Sings the Wolf, Devonian Group, 1976.
Kalvak, Devonian Group, 1976.
Legends of the Salmon People, Devonian Group, 1977.
Art of the Arctic Whaleman, Devonian Group, 1978.
Ghost Fox, Sefel Pictures International, 1979.
Whiteout, Owl/TV Productions, 1987.

ILLUSTRATOR

Shoot to Live, Queen's Printer, 1944.
Alma Houston, *Nuki*, Lippincott, 1955.
Raymond de Coccola and Paul King, *Ayorama*, Oxford University Press, 1956, revised edition published as *The Incredible Eskimo*, Hancock House, 1986.
Tuktut/Caribou, Queen's Printer, 1957.
Elizabeth Pool, *The Unicorn Was There*, Bauhan, 1966.
(Designer) Alice Watson Houston, *America Was Beautiful*, Barre Publishers, 1970.
(And author of introduction) George Francis Lyon, *The Private Journal of Captain G. F. Lyon of H.M.S. Hecla, during the Recent Voyage of Discovery under Captain Parry, 1921-23*, Imprint Society, 1970.
Alice Watson Houston, *The American Heritage Book of Fish Cookery*, Scribner's, 1980.
Mary Jo Wheeler-Smith, *First Came the Indians*, Atheneum, 1983.

de Coccola and King, *The Incredible Eskimo*, Hancock House, 1986.

J. Kenneth Keatley, *Place Names of the Eastern Shore of Maryland*, Queen Anne Press, 1987.

OTHER

Contributor of short stories to periodicals. Houston's manuscripts are collected at the National Library of Canada, Ottawa.

■ Adaptations

Ghost Fox has been recorded on eight cassettes by Crane Memorial Library, 1978.

■ Sidelights

James A. Houston watched through one of the plane's windows as the isolated Arctic village came into view. Searching for adventure, the young man had been fortunate to secure a free ride on the little plane, which was being used to transport a doctor to the village of a boy who had been bitten by dogs. The pilot told Houston to expect a four-day layover before they returned to northern Ontario, a stretch of time that Houston hoped would allow him to explore the area, meet some of the native Inuit Eskimos, and work on his sketches. The plane landed and Houston disembarked. He was, according to his autobiography in *Something about the Author Autobiography Series* (*SAAS*), "more excited than I had ever been in all my life. Out on Hudson Bay, long skeins of heavy ice were drifting south from Foxe Basin. Behind me, the treeless tundra stretched as far as the eye could see. But best of all, crowding around me were short, sturdy, dark-tanned Inuit, laughing and flashing warm smiles as they spoke rapid Inuktitut, a rich and complex language." In a short time, however, the doctor appeared with the injured child and announced that they were leaving for a hospital. "'I'm not going,' I told him. 'I'll never have the chance to be here like this again. I've been looking for this place all my life.'" Houston watched the aircraft as it disappeared into the sky, then glanced around at the sum total of his possessions—a sleeping bag, a sketchpad, and a can of peaches. Houston had planned on a four-day visit; he had no idea that he would remain in the Arctic for the next twelve years.

Houston's experiences in the Eskimo and Indian villages of the Arctic proved to be a tremendous inspiration to him. "Inuit life has had a profound effect on me," Houston commented in *SAAS*. "I am surely the beneficiary of my long association with them. They allowed me into their lives and taught me how to view life in a way I had not formerly imagined. They taught me about the importance of kindness and generosity." When he finally left the Arctic in the early 1960s and moved to New York City to pursue a writing career, he was able to shape his memories of life in the north into a lengthy series of award-winning novels. Reviewing this body of work, critic Sheila Egoff remarked in *The Republic of Childhood: A Critical Guide to Canadian Children's Literature in English* that Houston has emerged as "not only . . . the most prolific spokesman for the Eskimo in children's literature, but the most artistic writer."

Encouraged to Explore and Imagine

Houston was born on June 12, 1921, in Toronto, Ontario. "I had the happiest childhood," he noted in the *New Yorker*. "I didn't have to overcome a damn thing." His mother encouraged him to explore the world of reading and develop his own writing and drawing abilities. His father, meanwhile, was a businessman who "used to make frequent trips across Canada to the Pacific," Houston recalled in *SAAS*. "When he returned, my sister and I could scarcely wait to jump into bed with him early the following morning. We would watch him make quick pencil drawings, and listen to him tell of Indian ceremonies he had seen and heard, and finally give us each a gift of intricately beaded moosehide moccasins."

Young Houston's friendship with Ojibwa Indians who lived near the family's summer cottage north of Toronto also contributed to his desire to explore far-off places and sharpened his love for the outdoors. Houston became especially close to Nels, an Ojibwa who "lived beyond the commercial corruptions of this world, as self-sufficient and well-protected as a porcupine," Houston noted in his autobiography. "Nels taught me to truly observe nature. . . . Those mornings that I went roaming with Nels over the land and lake I shall remember in vivid detail for the rest of my life. It seemed to me then that the only education I wanted or would ever need I could gain right there in that old, fish-smelling boat or stalking through the woods."

When Houston was eight years old, he came down with a case of scarlet fever. Quarantined from contact with other children for three long weeks, he immersed himself in the many books that his parents had bought for him. He was stunned one day when his mother told him that the government, which was concerned that other children might contract scarlet fever from contact with his books, had sent an official to their house to burn them. His mother gave him a book full of blank pages, though, so he could write and illustrate his own stories.

A year later, Houston was asked to illustrate a poem written by a girl of about his age for a Canadian magazine. He was thrilled when the magazine accepted his drawing, and even more excited when he discovered that he had received a three-dollar check for his efforts. "I knew then and there that drawing pictures and writing books would provide me with a shamefully joyous life of ease, and believe me, they always have," he said in *SAAS*.

At the age of ten, Houston enrolled at the Art Gallery of Ontario, a notable institution that helped him to further develop his artistic talents. The onset of World War II interrupted his education, however. He contributed five years of active service to the Toronto Scottish Regiment during the war, then traveled to Paris, France, to study drawing at Ecole Grande Chaumiere.

"Returning home to Toronto and Montreal," Houston recalled in *SAAS*, "I saw men dressed in bulky gray suits and young women in very tight girdles. I thought, there is something missing here. It's time to go north, to search for adventure, find new people to draw." This desire to explore the unknown led him to buy a one-way railroad ticket to Moosonee, a small town near James Bay in eastern Ontario. From there he took his life-changing plane ride to the Arctic, where he grew to love the people that thrived in that cold and harsh environment.

Houston was unfamiliar with the Inuit Eskimo culture, so he decided that he needed to be a fast learner. "At this time," Houston wrote in his autobiography, "I was just beginning my struggles with the Inuktitut language. Often, if I couldn't

RIVER RUNNERS

A Tale of Hardship and Bravery

JAMES HOUSTON

This gripping story of fifteen-year-old Andrew and his Indian friend Pashak setting up a fur-trading post in Naskapi Indian territory, based on true happenings, won the 1980 Canadian Library Association Book of the Year award.

act out a question, my sketchbooks saved me. When I needed to communicate, I could usually make some kind of drawing to help explain. . . . Much of the language I acquired was from their children. Later, when I was living on Baffin Island in summer tents or winter igloos, the children would jump on me in the early morning and teach me dozens of useful words."

During his stay in the Arctic, Houston served as the Game and Fisheries Department officer for the region and worked on a number of government projects. He also introduced printmaking to the Inuits. Still, he had time to immerse himself in the legends and myths of the Eskimo people, and he was fascinated by the richness and complexity of their oral storytelling tradition. "As an observer who would one day try to write such stories, how could I have dared to dream of any better opportunity than listening to the day-by-day adventures, myths, and legends of such people?" he wrote in *SAAS*.

Houston also met his wife during his stay among the Eskimos. In September 1950 he was interviewed by Alma Bardon, a reporter for the Montreal *Star*. They were married three months later and Bardon joined him in the Arctic. "Allie was divinely suited to Eskimo life," he commented in the *New Yorker*. Over time, though, the couple drifted apart. Houston's wife fell victim to postpartum depression after the birth of their second child. A subsequent nervous breakdown further frayed the union, and "the marriage never quite got back on its feet," wrote Mary D. Kierstead in the *New Yorker*. The two were divorced in 1967, "and Houston is clearly still saddened by whatever part he may have played in the erosion of what was once a sublimely happy marriage."

Writing about Arctic Culture

Once Houston had settled down in New York—the contrast between the cultures of the Arctic and the city was quite a shock—he tried to communicate his experiences with the Eskimos through his artistic talents in the areas of writing, drawing, and glass sculpture. "Whether creating in glass, drawings, or words, I try to reflect the historic Inuit vision of a world where man and nature are locked not in perpetual battle, but perpetual partnership," he said in his autobiography.

Houston first made a living as a designer of glass sculptures for Steuben Glass in New York. His drawings evoked striking images of the cold world he left behind, and he became the company's most prolific and successful designer. Initially, though, Houston was not as confident about his writing skills as he was about his drawing ability. After he related an Eskimo legend to Margaret McElderry, a well-known editor of children's books, she suggested that he tell the story in a book. Houston explained that while he would love to illustrate such a book, he didn't think he had the talent to write the story. McElderry convinced him to give it a try. "I wrote *Tikta'liktak* over one hard-working weekend," Houston recalled in *SAAS*, "and on the following weekend I did all the illustrations. That book won all kinds of im-

portant prizes, went into dozens of editions, and was translated into thirteen languages."

The success of *Tikta'liktak: An Eskimo Legend*, published in 1965, established Houston as a notable new writer of young adult fiction. The story, about an Inuit boy who struggles to survive after he finds himself adrift in the Arctic on an ice floe, highlights themes of human endurance and resourcefulness and mankind's relationship to the environment. "Survival is a theme that runs through much of [Houston's] fiction," noted Virginia L. Gleason in *Twentieth-Century Young Adult Writers*, "especially surviving the harsh environment of the Arctic winters in isolated locations where a person must depend on him or herself for everything: finding food, finding directions to travel, struggling against wild beasts and hostile people, and enduring chilling storms, all in places where there are few settlers and fewer signposts."

Houston's second self-illustrated book, *Eagle Mask: A West Coast Indian Tale*, was published in 1966. It relates the story of an Indian boy and his adventures as he grows to manhood. *The White Archer: An Eskimo Legend*, published a year later, tells of an Inuit boy named Kungo whose parents are killed and whose sister is abducted by Indian raiders in retaliation for the murder of an Indian by another Eskimo. Kungo vows revenge, but "at the crucial moment he realizes that he has unconsciously learned the value of compassion from two old people who cared for him, and his act of self-restraint leads to eventual reunion with his sister and reconciliation with his former enemies," commented John Robert Sorfleet in *Twentieth-Century Children's Writers*. "The morality is good, but unfortunately Kungo's change of heart is not entirely convincing." Helen B. Crawshaw, in her review for *Horn Book*, called *The White Archer* a "timeless, dramatically illustrated story" in which "the stark simplicity of the telling contrasts with the depths of the wisdom imparted."

Houston married Alice Watson late in 1967. The following year, he published *Akavak: An Eskimo Journey*, a novel telling of the journey of an Inuit boy who agrees to help his dying grandfather fulfill his wish to visit his brother before he dies. His grandfather's brother lives on the other side of an imposing mountain range, however, so the trip is a difficult one. "Though the grandfather dies as the trip is completed, it is not without passing on much of himself and the secrets of the mountains to Akavak, who proves himself during the journey," wrote Sorfleet. "The tale is stark and simple on the surface but very rich and emotionally rewarding underneath." *In Review: Canadian Books for Children* contributor Alice E. Kane agreed, writing that "the pictures and the simple narrative blend together with an unbearable intensity. . . . James Houston has an almost magical power of making the strange, hard world of the Eskimo believable to the city dweller and never more so than here."

If you enjoy the works of James Houston, you may also want to check out the following books and films:

Will Hobbs, *Bearstone*, 1990.
Walt Morey, *Death Walk*, 1992.
Scott O'Dell, *Black Star, Bright Dawn*, 1988.
Gary Paulsen, *Dogsong*, 1985.
Dances with Wolves, Orion Pictures, 1990.

The books written and illustrated by Houston during the early part of his career were primarily concerned with the native cultures of the Inuit Eskimos and various northern Indian tribes, but in the 1970s he shifted his emphasis somewhat; in works such as *River Runners: A Tale of Hardship and Bravery, Frozen Fire: A Tale of Courage, Black Diamonds: A Search for Arctic Treasure,* and *Ice Swords: An Undersea Adventure,* Houston writes about the relationships that develop between representatives of primitive cultures and those of the modern world.

In *River Runners,* for instance, a fifteen-year-old Scottish boy named Andrew and a Naskapi Indian boy known as Pashak meet at an isolated trading post in the far north. They join a group of Indian packmen on a dog-drawn toboggan trip to a distant trading outpost at Ghost Lake. Once they reach the outpost, though, the packmen leave and the boys are forced to endure a bone-chilling winter in a place where food and warmth are precious commodities.

Ghost Fox was one of the first of Houston's novels written for adults, although Houston has always felt that all of his books are accessible to a wide audience. "My stories are not really children's stories," he indicated in *Twentieth-Century Children's*

Writers. "They are simply northern stories that are suitable for both children and adults. I consider that my adult-length books are also suitable for children." *Ghost Fox*'s central character is a young Indian woman named Sara. Although kidnapped by another Indian tribe, she marries a member of the tribe. Given an opportunity to return to her original home, she decides to stay with the people with whom she has found happiness.

Running West, published in 1989, is one of Houston's best-known adult works. Set in the largely unexplored Hudson Bay Territory of the early eighteenth century, the novel recounts the love that develops between Thana, a Dene Indian woman, and William, a Scotsman. Kidnapped from her homeland by a cruel rival tribe at an earlier age, Thana is chosen to lead a band of fur traders that includes William to Dene country, where fur-bearing animals are plentiful. The journey proves dangerous, however, and many of the traders turn back in the face of marauding Indian tribes, bitter cold, and the threat of starvation. At journey's end, however, a pregnant Thana and William are married.

Another more recent novel by Houston, 1988's *Whiteout,* tells the story of a rebellious teenager from an urban neighborhood who is sent to stay with his uncle in an isolated village in the Arctic. A musically talented youth, the teenager develops an appreciation for his harsh but majestic surroundings that he is able to translate into his musical studies. In the process, he gains a greater understanding of his own ability and of the needs of those around him.

Recognized as an Authority

As a result of Houston's body of work, his support of Inuit art, and his scholarship in areas of Eskimo and Indian history and culture, he is recognized as an important contributor to efforts to understand Arctic life. T. F. Rigelhof, writing in the Toronto *Globe and Mail,* asserts that Houston is "probably the most popular and influential authority on Arctic culture that Canada has produced."

Houston continues to draw on his memories of Indian and Eskimo cultures and his love for the outdoors in his works, and remains an enthusiastic traveler. He and his wife spend their winters in an eighteenth-century house overlooking the

Atlantic Ocean in Stonington, Connecticut; they also own a river cottage on the north Pacific "among the Eagle and Raven clans of the Haida Indians," he wrote in *SAAS*. "There, I usually write or draw throughout the misty mornings and fly-fish for salmon or trout in the late afternoons. Standing beneath giant cedars in the very heart of nature with a glorious tidal river flowing around me, I try my best to make long casts, hoping to lure a record salmon or better still an original thought that leads me to another book or perhaps some new glass design."

■ **Works Cited**

Crawshaw, Helen B., review of *The White Archer: An Eskimo Legend, Horn Book,* October, 1967, p. 589.

Egoff, Sheila, *The Republic of Childhood: A Critical Guide to Canadian Children's Literature in English,* Oxford University Press, 1975.

Gleason, Virginia L., "James A. Houston," *Twentieth-Century Young Adult Writers,* St. James Press, 1994, pp. 298-300.

Houston, James, essay in *Something about the Author Autobiography Series,* Volume 17, Gale, 1994, pp. 135-55.

Kane, Alice E., review of *Akavak: An Eskimo Journey, In Review: Canadian Books for Children,* winter, 1969, pp. 26-7.

Kierstead, Mary D., "The Man," *New Yorker,* August 29, 1988, pp. 33-47.

Rigelhof, T. F., "Rites of Passage in the Arctic," *Globe and Mail* (Toronto), November 12, 1988.

Sorfleet, John Robert, "James A. Houston," *Twentieth-Century Children's Writers,* 3rd edition, St. James Press, 1989, pp. 468-70.

■ **For More Information See**

BOOKS

Children's Literature Review, Volume 3, Gale, 1978, pp. 83-88.

PERIODICALS

Booklist and Subscription Books Bulletin, December 1, 1966, p. 418.

Bulletin of the Center for Children's Books, November, 1972, p. 43.

Children's Literature: Annual of the Modern Language Association Seminar on Children's Literature and the Children's Literature Association, Volume 4, Temple University Press, 1975.

Horn Book, June, 1971, p. 287.

In Review: Canadian Books for Children, winter, 1967, p. 32; summer, 1971, p. 28.

New York Times Book Review, October 8, 1967, p. 38; November 5, 1972, p. 7.*

—Sketch by Kevin Hillstrom

Irene Hunt

1965, Dorothy Canfield Fisher Award, 1965, Clara Ingram Judson Memorial Award, 1965, Lewis Carroll Shelf Award, 1966, and American Library Association Notable Book citation, all for *Across Five Aprils*; Newbery Medal, 1967, and International Board on Books for Young People Honor List citation, 1970, both for *Up a Road Slowly*; Friends of Literature Award and Charles W. Follett Award, both 1971, both for *No Promises in the Wind*; Omar's Book Award, for *The Lottery Rose*; Certificate in Recognition of Contribution to Children's Literature, Twelfth Annual Children's Literature Festival, Central Missouri State University, 1980; Parents' Choice Award, 1985, for *The Everlasting Hills*.

■ Personal

Born May 18, 1907, in Pontiac, IL; daughter of Franklin Pierce and Sarah (Land) Hunt. *Education:* University of Illinois, A.B., 1939; University of Minnesota, M.A., 1946; graduate work at the University of Colorado, Boulder.

■ Addresses

Home—2591 Countryside Blvd., Clearwater, FL 33519.

■ Career

Oak Park Public Schools, Oak Park, IL, teacher of French and English, 1930-45; University of South Dakota, Vermillion, instructor in psychology, 1946-50; Cicero Public Schools, Cicero, IL, teacher, 1950-65, consultant and director of language arts, 1965-69; writer, 1964—.

■ Awards, Honors

Charles W. Follett Award, 1964, American Notable Book Award, 1965, Newbery Honor Book citation,

■ Writings

Across Five Aprils, Follett, 1964.
Up a Road Slowly, Follett, 1966.
Trail of Apple Blossoms, illustrated by Don Bolognese, Follett, 1968.
No Promises in the Wind, Follett, 1970.
The Lottery Rose, Scribner, 1976.
William, Scribner, 1978.
Claws of a Young Century, Scribner, 1980.
The Everlasting Hills, Scribner, 1985.

Also contributor to *The Writer's Handbook*, edited by A. S. Burack, 1973. Several of Hunt's manuscripts are in the Kerlan Collection of the University of Minnesota at Minneapolis.

■ Adaptations

No Promises in the Wind has been optioned for a motion picture.

■ Sidelights

"With her first book, *Across Five Aprils*," writes Clyde Robert Bulla in *Twentieth-Century Children's Writers*, "Irene Hunt established herself as one of America's finest historical novelists." In her works Hunt explores places and time periods ranging from 1860s Illinois to the Depression-era Rocky Mountains. Despite what *Bulletin of the Center for Children's Books* contributor Zena Sutherland calls her "historically authenticated" details, however, Hunt's strength lies in creating realistic characters learning to cope with their problems and maturing in the process. Her devotion to quality literature for children brought her a Newbery Medal honor citation in 1965 for her first book, *Across Five Aprils*, and her second book, *Up a Road Slowly*, won the award itself in 1967. "She has proven that she can write good books for children that please adults as well," states Philip A. Sadler in the *Dictionary of Literary Biography*, "and she has established an international audience."

Irene Hunt was born in Pontiac, Illinois—a small town about halfway between Springfield and Chicago—in 1907. When she was still quite young, however, her parents, Franklin and Sarah Hunt, moved to Newton, in the southeastern corner of the state. The family was living there in 1914, when her father died. Hunt and her mother relocated to her grandparents' farm nearby. She formed a close relationship with her grandfather, who had grown up during the Civil War and had a plentiful stock of stories about his childhood experiences. Hunt later drew on her grandfather's memories as the basis for *Across Five Aprils*. She based her second book, *Up a Road Slowly*, on her own experiences.

Hunt began her career not as a writer but as a schoolteacher. For fifteen years, from 1930 until 1945, she served as a teacher in French and English in the school system of Oak Park, a suburb of Chicago. She earned her bachelor's degree from the University of Illinois at Urbana in 1939, and went on to obtain a master's degree from the University of Minnesota in Minneapolis in 1946. Hunt taught psychology at the University of South Dakota in Vermillion for the next four years be-

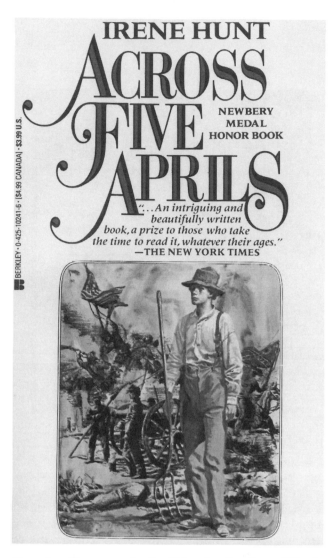

Covering five years in the life of a Southern Illinois family during the Civil War, this historically accurate account of a politically divided family was a 1965 Newbery Honor book.

fore returning to Illinois. From 1950 until her retirement in 1969 she taught in the school system in Cicero—another Chicago suburb. In her position as director of language arts Hunt found that good historical fiction for younger readers, which she felt was an effective teaching tool, was in short supply. *Across Five Aprils*, Sadler reveals, was "written to fit the needs of her students."

Across Five Aprils differs from other stories about the Civil War, such as Stephen Crane's *The Red Badge of Courage*, because the action of the war takes place, for the most part, elsewhere. The focus of the story is nine-year-old Jethro Creighton and how he grows and matures while the war goes on. "Jethro experiences the war through his relationships with his parents," writes Sadler: "his sisters, Jenny and Mary; his brothers, John and Bill; and his schoolmaster, Shadrach Yale." He has to learn to accept the fact that his brothers enlist to fight for different sides: John for the Union, Bill for the Confederacy. "The family respects their rights to act on their beliefs," Sadler states, "but because Bill's sympathies are with the Confederacy, the family is labeled 'Copperheads' and slated for retribution." "Once the pampered baby of the family," Patricia L. Bradley reveals in *Twentieth-Century Young Adult Writers*, "Jethro advances to adult status amid the disintegration of the family unit in which he had once felt security." In addition, he has to take up most of the responsibilities for the farm when his father suffers a heart attack. "At the end of the war," Sadler concludes, "Jethro, who has come to a knowledgeable understanding of it through letters and conversations, is taken east to school by Shadrach and Jenny, who are now married."

Hunt depicts the destruction and remaking of the Creighton family as a model of the destruction of the United States during the Civil War and the Reconstruction period. One major character, Jethro's cousin Ed, deserts from the Union Army and writes in desperation to President Lincoln for a pardon. Lincoln responds by offering to forgive all the deserters in Ed's party. "This story nobly emphasizes the futility of aggression," writes John Gillespie and Diana Lembo in *Juniorplots*. "The American Civil War with its drama is expertly presented through the lives of an ordinary family." "Hunt's research of historical details is impeccable," declares Bradley, "and her use of her grandfather's memories of his childhood during the war gives the reader a sense of great intimacy with the lives of the characters." Hunt has, according to a reviewer for *Booklist and Subscription Books Bulletin*, "in an uncommonly fine narrative, created living characters and vividly reconstructed a crucial period of history." "It is withal an intriguing and beautifully written book," states *New York Times Book Review* contributor John K. Bettersworth—"a prize to those who take the time to read it, whatever their ages."

A Story of Personal Growth

Up a Road Slowly, Hunt's second book, chronicles ten years in the life of Julie Trelling. Julie's mother dies when she is only seven years old. Her father and her beloved older sister, unable to care for her, send Julie to live with her Aunt Cordelia, a country schoolteacher. "Willful and adventurous," Bradley declares, "Julie clashes frequently with her aunt, a strict and duty-bound woman who nonetheless exerts a loving and powerful influence over Julie." Despite her early problems, Julie matures into a gracious young lady. "The Julie from 7 to 17 is an unusually intelligent girl who feels things deeply and is extremely sensitive to her environment," explains *Book Week* contributor Robin Gottlieb. "The adult Julie supposedly writing it all down can be perceptively articulate about young Julie's experiences without

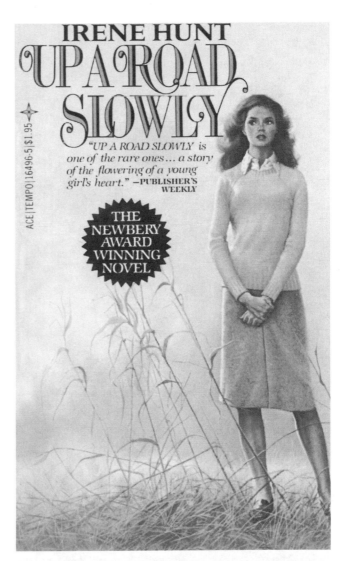

IRENE HUNT
UP A ROAD SLOWLY

"UP A ROAD SLOWLY is one of the rare ones... a story of the flowering of a young girl's heart." —PUBLISHER'S WEEKLY

THE NEWBERY AWARD WINNING NOVEL

ACE | TEMPO | 16496-5 | $1.95

This Newbery Award-winner is about self-willed, motherless Julie, brought up by her strict schoolteacher aunt, who learns the true meaning of love and family over the course of ten years.

the smallest jarring note." "Miss Hunt," claims Constantine Georgiou in *Children and Their Literature*, "relates with warmth and sympathetic insight the story of a young girl's growth to maturity."

Critics praised Hunt's depiction of her characters and her grasp of language and difficult themes in *Up a Road Slowly.* "Treating the story with a detached realism tempered with love," Sadler asserts, "Hunt introduces themes of jealousy, first love, parent-child and sibling relationships, foster-family relationships, and snobbishness and handles them in fresh new ways." Ruth Hill Viguers, writing in *Horn Book,* suggests that, while the characters in *Up a Road Slowly* "are no more unusual

This Depression-era story tells of two brothers on their own and their struggle for survival, both physical and emotional.

and varied than are most people's families and friends," Hunt "sees them so much more clearly . . . and gives them such vivid life that the reader is quickly and intensely interested in them." "She breaks new ground," concludes Sadler, "shattering old taboos in children's literature, to produce a book devoid of the artificiality and superficiality of many of the teenage novels of the time." "The author is adept at distinguishing the genuine from the spurious," writes a reviewer for *Virginia Kirkus' Service:* "Julie *is* a genuine character, and girls who go up the road with her will share in her growing up."

Like *Across Five Aprils, Up a Road Slowly* draws on Hunt's family history. It reflects her own experience growing up in relative isolation with only one parent after the death of the other. "Just as Hunt had been lonely, bewildered, and frightened upon the loss of her father," Sadler states, "another little girl . . . might, in her loneliness, wander into the woods quoting verses from Edna St. Vincent Millay or Shakespeare." Hunt, asserts *New York Times Book Review* contributor Dorothy M. Broderick, "brings off a difficult tour de force and turns personal reminiscence into art." Hunt herself acknowledged this debt in her Newbery acceptance speech, published in *Horn Book.* "Often children are troubled and in a state of guilt," Hunt wrote. "One can say to them, 'You are not unique. There is in all of us only a thin veneer of civilization that separates us from the primitive.'"

Trail of Apple Blossoms, Hunt's third book, drew for its inspiration on the American folk hero John Chapman, better known as Johnny Appleseed. The book "is not a biography, but a historical novel," Bulla reveals, "picturing Johnny Appleseed as he may have been—a heroic man with a reverence for life whose beneficent influence touched pioneer America." *Trail of Apple Blossoms* focuses not on Chapman's traditional planting and sowing of apple seeds, but on his reputation as a man of peace and a lover of life. The narrator of the story is Hoke Bryant, who is traveling with his parents and his two-year-old sister Rachel from their old home in Boston to a new place in the Ohio Country. During the trip, Rachel becomes ill and refuses to eat. The Bryants encounter Chapman, who uses his skills to coax Rachel into eating. He becomes a close friend of the Bryant family and his gentle philosophy inspires the adult Hoke to take up a career as a minister. "Irene Hunt," declares

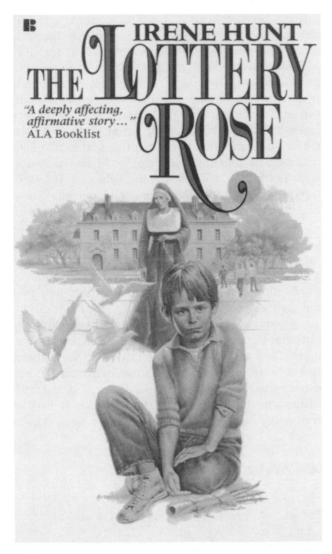

Published in 1976, this sensitive story of a boy abused by his alcoholic mother and brutal boyfriend was a rarity in its day.

Dorothy Broderick in the *New York Times Book Review,* "has written one of the best accounts of the gentle man who would harm neither man nor beast." Helen Armstrong, writing for *School Library Journal,* claims that Hunt "has endowed her subject with a spiritual quality which shines through the story."

Abuse, Love, and Family

In *No Promises in the Wind,* Hunt moves on to the twentieth century and the era of the Depression. The Grodowski brothers, Josh and his little brother Joey, flee their home and their negligent father. In the company of Howie, a friend, the two hop a freight train for the west. However, Howie slips beneath the wheels of a freight car and is killed. Josh and Joey travel on, finding both cold and comfort in their travels. "They are befriended by a kindly truck driver who treats them as his own sons," Sadler writes. "When Josh recovers from a serious illness, the boys leave their benefactor and continue on their wanderings. Joining a carnival group, they again find others who will share with them their meager substance as well as their love. . . . Even the hungry hoboes offer assistance to the boys." Eventually the boys return home and are reconciled with their repentant father. "With all the problems that exist today," Ruth Hill Viguers writes in *Horn Book,* "such an honest picture of one of our country's most tragic periods may give readers a wider perspective. It is a deeply moving story."

"The writer who takes on a subject like child abuse," writes author Betsy Byars in the *New York Times Book Review,* "faces a problem—whether to show the deed in all its headline horror or to soften it for young readers." *The Lottery Rose* is the story of Georgie Burgess, neglected by his alcoholic mother and abused by her boyfriend. "In a lottery held by the new owners of a local grocery story, Georgie wins a rose bush," Byars reveals. "Beautiful flowers . . . are the only meaningful things in his life, and he lavishes his concern on finding a place to plant his rose bush." After a particularly brutal beating Georgie is placed in a Catholic boarding school, where he encounters Mollie Harper who is in mourning for her husband and son. "In the passage of time," Sadler explains, "Georgie emerges from his withdrawn state." He makes friends with Mrs. Harper's surviving son Robin and, when Robin is lost in an accident, gains her acceptance. "Though the book may not be as strong a novel as her earlier ones," Sadler concludes, "Hunt does provide a touching treatment of a theme out of the ordinary at the time of the book's creation—the abuse of a small child—in a manner suitable for young readers."

William looks at interracial relationships on an intergenerational level. A young, pregnant white teenager named Sarah moves in next door to William's family. William's Mama, the head of the household, helps nurse Sarah through a hurricane strike and the birth of her child. When Mama dies of cancer, states Nancy P. Bailey in *School Library Journal,* "Sarah takes over as head of the family, refusing to let William and his sisters be placed in a foster home." "William recognizes that the situation and the home he has grown up in will never be the same again," Sadler concludes, "but he realizes that he must assume responsibility for the family." "The love and concern for human beings other than oneself are basic elements underlying the development of strong family relationships," explains *Horn Book* reviewer Mary M. Bush. "Through the skill with which the author delineates the characters, their ultimate triumph over multiple adversities is made believable, and each one emerges as a distinct personality."

If you enjoy the works of Irene Hunt, you may also want to check out the following books:

Chester Aaron, *Lackawanna*, 1986.
Clayton Bess, *Tracks*, 1986.
Isabelle Holland, *The Journey Home*, 1990.
Gilbert Morris, *The Last Confederate*, 1990.
Nadine Roberts, *With Love from Sam and Me*, 1990.

Hunt looks at feminist issues in *Claws of a Young Century*, the story of a young suffragette working for women's rights in the early years of the century. "On New Year's Eve, 1899, seventeen-year-old Ellen Archer has hopes of bringing change and progress into her life and into the lives of other women," writes *Horn Book* contributor Ann A. Flowers. She leaves her unenlightened father to live with her college-educated brother Alex, falls in love with his journalist friend Philip Wrenn, and becomes pregnant. Ellen and Philip marry, but separate and divorce so that Philip can work overseas as a foreign correspondent and Ellen can continue her campaign for women's rights. "Ellen goes to jail for her beliefs," explains Cyrisse Jaffee in *School Library Journal*, "and the brutal treatment she receives there proves fatal." "When Philip returns after sixteen years abroad to find Ellen dying," Sadler concludes, "they realize their love and that pride has kept them apart. He promises to continue her work for the ratification of the suffrage amendment."

The Enchanted Hills, Hunt's most recent book, is set in the Rocky Mountains during the 1930s. The protagonist is Jeremy Tydings, who has a learning disability. Alienated from his unfeeling father,

Jeremy finds solace in his relationship with his sister Bethany. When he realizes that Bethany is sacrificing her own life in order to care for him, he runs away. Jeremy finds shelter with an old hermit named Ishmael. "In the time he spends with Ishmael, Jeremy matures and grows in self-esteem," writes Barbara Chatton in *School Library Journal*. "After Ishmael dies, Jeremy returns to the cabin and embarks upon a project the two had dreamed of together and a difficult reconciliation with his father." "Their relationship . . . [is] delicately portrayed," Bulla states, "and reveal[s] some of Hunt's finest qualities."

Critics continue to celebrate Hunt's accomplishment in her novels. Hunt, Bradley states, "demonstrates her virtuosity as a storyteller by never duplicating her use of characters, setting, and plot within the genre of historical fiction. In addition, all of Hunt's novels consistently demonstrate other important elements such as poetic yet simple language and a delicate appreciation of the natural world." "Irene Hunt has a strong faith in the enduring qualities of courage, love, and mercy," Sadler concludes. "It is to reiterate this faith that she writes her books."

■ Works Cited

Review of *Across Five Aprils, Booklist and Subscription Books Bulletin,* July 1, 1964, p. 1002.

Armstrong, Helen, review of *Trail of Apple Blossoms, School Library Journal,* May, 1968, p. 79.

Bailey, Nancy P., review of *William, School Library Journal,* April, 1977, p. 77.

Bettersworth, John K., review of *Across Five Aprils, New York Times Book Review,* May 10, 1964, pp. 8, 10.

Bradley, Patricia L., "Irene Hunt," *Twentieth-Century Young Adult Writers,* St. James Press, 1994, pp. 312-14.

Broderick, Dorothy M., review of *Up a Road Slowly, New York Times Book Review,* November 6, 1966, pp. 8, 12.

Broderick, Dorothy M., review of *Trail of Apple Blossoms, New York Times Book Review,* April 14, 1968, p. 20.

Bulla, Clyde Robert, "Irene Hunt," *Twentieth-Century Children's Writers,* 3rd edition, St. James Press, 1989, pp. 481-82.

Bush, Mary M., review of *William, Horn Book,* October, 1977, pp. 540-41.

Byars, Betsy, review of *The Lottery Rose, New York Times Book Review,* May 16, 1976, pp. 16, 18.

Chatton, Barbara, review of *The Everlasting Hills, School Library Journal,* September, 1985, p. 134.

Flowers, Ann A., review of *Claws of a Young Century, Horn Book,* October, 1980, pp. 525-26.

Georgiou, Constantine, *Children and Their Literature,* Prentice-Hall, 1969, p. 379.

Gillespie, John, and Diana Lembo, *Juniorplots: A Book Talk Manual for Teachers and Librarians,* Bowker, 1967, pp. 181, 183.

Gottlieb, Robin, review of *Up a Road Slowly, Book Week,* November 6, 1966, p. 22.

Hunt, Irene, "Books and the Learning Process," *Horn Book,* August, 1967, pp. 424-29.

Jaffee, Cyrisse, review of *Claws of a Young Century, School Library Journal,* August, 1980, p. 77.

Sadler, Philip A., "Irene Hunt," *Dictionary of Literary Biography,* Volume 52: *American Writers for Children since 1960: Fiction,* Gale, 1986, pp. 202-08.

Sutherland, Zena, review of *Across Five Aprils, Bulletin of the Center for Children's Books,* July-August, 1964, p. 171.

Review of *Up a Road Slowly, Virginia Kirkus' Service,* November 15, 1966, p. 1188.

Viguers, Ruth Hill, review of *Up a Road Slowly, Horn Book,* February, 1967, p. 73.

■ For More Information See

BOOKS

Children's Literature Review, Volume 1, Gale, 1976.

Hopkins, Lee Bennett, *More Books by More People,* Citation Press, 1974.

Larrick, Nancy, *A Parent's Guide to Children's Reading,* 3rd edition, Doubleday, 1969.

PERIODICALS

Commonweal, May 24, 1968.

Horn Book, June, 1970.

New Yorker, December 14, 1968.

New York Times Book Review, November 6, 1966; March 19, 1967; April 14, 1968; April 5, 1970; May 16, 1976.

Publishers Weekly, March 13, 1967; March 22, 1976, p. 46.

School Library Journal, April, 1976, p. 74.

Writer, March, 1970.

Young Readers' Review, June, 1968.*

—Sketch by Kenneth R. Shepherd

Patricia MacLachlan

■ Personal

Born March 3, 1938, in Cheyenne, WY; daughter of Philo (a teacher) and Madonna (a teacher; maiden name, Moss) Pritzkau; married Robert MacLachlan (a clinical psychologist), April 14, 1962; children: John, Jamie, Emily. *Education:* University of Connecticut, B.A., 1962.

■ Addresses

Home—Williamsburg, MA. *Office*—Smith College, Department of Education, Northampton, MA 01063. *Agent*—c/o HarperCollins, 10 East 53rd St., New York, NY 10022.

■ Career

Bennett Junior High School, Manchester, CT, English teacher, 1963-79; Smith College, Northampton, MA, visiting lecturer, 1986—; writer. Lecturer, social worker, and teacher of creative writing workshops for adults and children. Children's Aid Family Service Agency, board member, 1970-80.

■ Awards, Honors

Golden Kite Award, Society of Children's Book Writers, 1980, for *Arthur, for the Very First Time;* Notable Children's Trade Book, National Council for Social Studies and the Children's Book Council, 1980, for *Through Grandpa's Eyes,* 1982, for *Mama One, Mama Two,* and 1985, for *Sarah, Plain and Tall;* American Library Association (ALA) Notable Book citation, 1980, for *Arthur, for the Very First Time,* 1984, for *Unclaimed Treasures,* 1985, for *Sarah, Plain and Tall,* and 1988, for *The Facts and Fictions of Minna Pratt;* Boston Globe-Horn Book Award Honor Book for Fiction, 1984, for *Unclaimed Treasures;* Horn Book Honor List citation, 1984, for *Unclaimed Treasures,* and 1985, for *Sarah, Plain and Tall;* Golden Kite Award, Scott O'Dell Historical Fiction Award, one of *School Library Journal's* Best Books of the Year, and one of the *New York Times* Notable Children's Books of the Year, all 1985, ALA Newbery Medal, Virginia Library Association Jefferson Cup Award, Christopher Award, and one of Child Study Association of America's Children's Books of the Year, all 1986, Garden State Children's Book Award from New Jersey Library Association, Charlie May Simon Book Award from the Elementary Council of the Arkansas Department of Education, and International Board on Books for Young People Honor List nominee, all 1988, all for *Sarah, Plain and Tall;* Parents' Choice Award, Parents' Choice Foundation, 1988, and *Horn Book* Fanfare 1989 citation, 1989, all for *The Facts and Fictions of Minna Pratt; Arthur, for the Very First*

Time, Cassie Binegar, Sarah, Plain and Tall, and *Seven Kisses in a Row* were all named Junior Library Guild selections.

■ Writings

JUVENILE NOVELS

Arthur, for the Very First Time, illustrated by Lloyd Bloom, Harper, 1980.
Moon, Stars, Frogs, and Friends, illustrated by Tomie de Paola, Pantheon, 1980.
Cassie Binegar, Harper, 1982.
Tomorrow's Wizard, illustrated by Kathy Jacobi, Harper, 1982.
Unclaimed Treasures, Harper, 1984.
Sarah, Plain and Tall, jacket illustration by Marcia Sewall, Harper, 1985.
The Facts and Fictions of Minna Pratt, Harper, 1988.
Journey, Delacorte Press, 1991.
Baby, Delacorte Press, 1993.
Skylark, HarperCollins, 1994.
All the Places to Love, illustrated by Mike Wimmer, HarperCollins, 1994.

PICTURE BOOKS

The Sick Day, illustrated by William Pene Du Bois, Pantheon, 1979.
Through Grandpa's Eyes, illustrated by Deborah Ray, Harper, 1980.
Mama One, Mama Two, illustrated by Ruth Lercher Bornstein, Harper, 1982.
Seven Kisses in a Row, illustrated by Maria Pia Marrella, Harper, 1983.
Three Names, illustrated by Alexander Pertzoff, HarperCollins, 1991.
What You Know First, illustrated by Barry Moser, HarperCollins, 1995.

OTHER

Skylark (teleplay), CBS-TV, 1993.

Also author of the teleplay for *Sarah, Plain and Tall,* broadcast as a *Hallmark Hall of Fame* presentation starring Glenn Close and Christopher Walken, 1991. Contributor to *Newbery Award Library II,* edited by Joseph Krumgold, Harper, 1988.

■ Adaptations

Arthur, for the Very First Time was adapted as a filmstrip with cassette, Pied Piper, 1984; *Sarah, Plain and Tall* was adapted as a filmstrip with cassette, Random House, 1986, and as a cassette, Caedmon, 1986, and as a television film starring Glen Close; *Mama One, Mama Two, Through Grandpa's Eyes,* and *The Sick Day* were adapted as a cassette, Caedmon, 1987; *Journey* was adapted for television as a Hallmark Hall of Fame presentation, Columbia Broadcasting System (CBS), 1995.

■ Sidelights

"First, let me say that as a child I made a conscious decision not to be a writer because I thought writers had all the answers," maintained Patricia MacLachlan in an interview with Ann Courtney for *Language Arts.* MacLachlan's writing career was thus put on hold for the first thirty-five years of her life. "I didn't begin writing stories as a child, as many writers did," she related in *Junior Library Guild.* "Probably it was because I was afraid of putting my own feelings and thoughts on a page for everyone to read. This still is a scary part of writing."

This fear of opening up in front of others is far from evident in the award-winning and critically praised juvenile novels MacLachlan writes. Her simple, compassionate stories, including *Sarah, Plain and Tall* and *The Facts and Fictions of Minna Pratt,* portray a cast of individualistic children on the brink of adolescence. And it is the graceful, lyrical style of MacLachlan's writing that makes these characters so real and so full of life as they experience the entire range of emotions associated with growing up. MacLachlan "shows a fine mastery of the difficult art of writing for preadolescents without flippancy, patronizing, or sentimentality," asserted Ethel L. Heins in *Twentieth-Century Children's Writers.*

Although she currently lives in the East, MacLachlan's roots are buried very deeply in the western prairie. Because she was "born in Wyoming and raised in Minnesota," explained MacLachlan in an interview with Marguerite Feitlowitz for *Something about the Author (SATA),* "the western landscape has always been a powerful force in my life, fueling my mind and imagination and giving me a sense of belonging to a particular place." In this sense, related MacLachlan in *Horn Book*, "I have this amazingly strong connection to the prairie. Each time I return I feel like I am home. The light on the land, the space enchants me. I carry around a bag of prairie dirt with me, like a part of my past."

MacLachlan's parents played a very important role in this past, for she was an only child and spent the majority of her youth in their company. A teacher since the age of nineteen, MacLachlan's father began his career on the prairie in a one-room schoolhouse. This background brought many books into the MacLachlan household, leading MacLachlan to later measure her life in terms of these books and at what age they were read. "*Little Women* marked a very specific period of my growing up. The same with *Charlotte's Web* and scores of other classics," recalled MacLachlan in her *SATA* interview with Feitlowitz.

The cello, for a short period, and then the piano occupied another large portion of MacLachlan's young life. "Her mother once told me that keeping Patty's skirt at a respectable level was what she remembered most about the cello playing," described MacLachlan's husband, Robert, in *Horn Book*. "Patty said only that the cello fell apart after a while, so they took it back to the school, and she focused on the piano. Her teacher had three pianos, and he used to let Patty decide which one she wanted to play. Most often she would choose the grand, with the mirror behind the keyboard. She would sometimes become distracted by the image of her own hands, lose track of the music, and wander a bit. The laissez-faire approach was quite helpful years later when, during a solo recital, she forgot the music in the middle of a Bach piece. 'I just made something up until I got to a place I remembered.'"

Making up stories was not as easy for MacLachlan, though, and after writing her first story, which consisted of three sentences, she vowed not to become a writer. "My teacher was not impressed," remembered MacLachlan in *Horn Book*. "I was discouraged, and I wrote in my diary: 'I shall try not to be a writer'. . . . It did not occur to me then that everything in my diary was fiction, carefully orchestrated and embroidered tales of an exciting life—an unreal life. Or was it? The question of what was real and what was not fascinated me, and I spent lots of time asking people, becoming a general annoyance. I surrounded myself with invented characters: kings and queens, brave men and cowards lived in my closet. I slipped into their skins, practicing, rehearsing to be the person I wished to be, the person I could be, the person I am."

As MacLachlan grew older and continued this search for self, she found herself following the path of her father and became an educator. While her children were still young, she also devoted her time doing publicity and interviewing possible foster mothers for the Children's Aid Family Service Agency. "And as my parents had done with me, I spent a lot of time reading with my kids," MacLachlan explained to Feitlowitz in her *SATA* interview. "When they became more independent, I felt a need to do something else—go to graduate school or go back to teaching, perhaps. It dawned on me that what I really wanted to do was to write. How would I ever have the courage, I wondered."

> *"The writing of a poem, a short story, or a picture book is like walking a tightrope; to go from beginning to end in bare-boned and memorable fashion takes much . . . control."*

Allowing herself only a few years to have something published before turning to another profession, MacLachlan acquired an agent and became a published author in one brief year. She attributes this quick success to living among other writers in the western Berkshires and to a writing class taught by Jane Yolen. "Writers need advocates," maintained MacLachlan in her *SATA* interview with Feitlowitz, "someone to help them along. Jane's help changed my life, and I try to do the same for my students."

One of MacLachlan's first advocates in the publishing world was her editor, Charlotte Zolotow. Upon receiving the manuscript for the picture book *Through Grandpa's Eyes*, Zolotow recognized MacLachlan's strengths. "It was filled with beautiful images, a poetic voice, and sensitive insights strung together like free verse," described Zolotow in her *Horn Book* dialogue with MacLachlan. The story itself relates how a young boy learns to see as his blind grandfather does during the course of a day. The close bond between John and his grandfather is evident as the two use their other four senses to eat and play the cello, among other things. "The high quality of this book deserves a long, close look," asserted Ruth W. Bauer in *Children's Book Review Service.* Natalie Babbitt, writing in the *New York Times Book Review,* pointed out: "Though the tone of this story is gentle and warm, it also has well-measured moments of humor, and is never sentimental." And a *Publishers Weekly* reviewer related that in *Through Grandpa's Eyes* "MacLachlan proves that a handicap need not be tragic. "

Picture Books Stretch to Novels

Despite her early success with picture books, both MacLachlan and Zolotow realized that a longer form was needed to encompass all that MacLachlan had to say; she needed more freedom and space for her thoughts to unfold. "Like so many beginning writers," admitted MacLachlan in her *Horn Book* dialogue with Zolotow, "I thought that perhaps shorter forms were the way to begin. When you became skilled at them, then you could do longer forms. What foolishness! Actually, for me the opposite is true. The writing of a poem, a short story, or a picture book is like walking a tightrope; to go from beginning to end in bare-boned and memorable fashion takes much more control." MacLachlan similarly related to Feitlowitz in her *SATA* interview: "It is more difficult to write a picture book than a novel. A good picture book is much like a poem: concise, rich, bare-boned, and multi-leveled. And the rhythm of image and text must create a sort of music. When I want to stretch into greater self-indulgence, I write a novel."

MacLachlan's first self-indulgent stretch into novels came in 1980 with the publication of *Arthur, for the Very First Time.* A quiet ten year old, Arthur must deal with change when he finds out his mother is pregnant and he is sent to stay with his Great-Aunt Elda and Great-Uncle Wilby for the summer. Farm life holds Arthur's interest, and he writes down his observations in his notebook as the months pass. He also eventually earns the

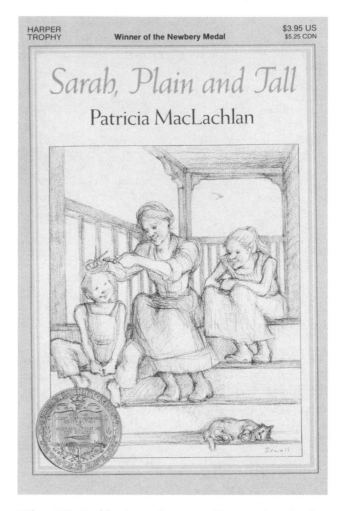

HARPER TROPHY

Winner of the Newbery Medal

$3.95 US
$5.25 CDN

Sarah, Plain and Tall
Patricia MacLachlan

When MacLachlan's mother was diagnosed as having Alzheimer's disease, the author applied her writing talents to preserving one of her mother's memories in this Newbery-winning 1985 story about a mail order bride.

respect of his new friend Moira when he stops thinking so much and is able to act courageously during an emergency situation. By the end of his stay, Arthur is much more self-confident and is able to deal with the imminent arrival of his new sibling. A *Publishers Weekly* contributor pointed out that in her first novel MacLachlan "describes a boy's awakening with moving and humorous touches." And Zena Sutherland, writing in the *Bulletin of the Center for Children's Books,* asserted that *Arthur, for the Very First Time* "has a deep tenderness, a gentle humor, and a beautifully honed writing style."

MacLachlan similarly deals with a child's resistance to change in her second novel, *Cassie Binegar.* Part of a large, disorganized, and happy family,

Cassie finds herself longing for the serenity found in her friend Mary Margaret's house. Growing up is suddenly a much more difficult task; Cassie is just beginning to really notice those around her. And at the core of most of her problems is a fear of change, a fear brought out when the family moves and her grandmother, among other relatives, comes to stay with the Binegars. In the end, though, it is Cassie's grandmother who teaches her to view things through other people's eyes to gain a greater understanding of things. "The writing style is elegant and evocative," stated Ann A. Flowers in *Horn Book.* Wendy Dellett, writing in *School Library Journal,* found the characters in *Cassie Binegar* to be "pleasant and kindly" and described MacLachlan's writing as "luminous and readable."

Both *Arthur, for the Very First Time* and *Cassie Binegar* "gave early evidence of the author's originality, compassionate and non-didactic approach, droll humor, and carefully chastened yet fluent style," related Heins in *Twentieth-Century Children's Writers,* adding: "Already evident too, was her preoccupation with intergenerational affinities and her idiosyncratic, unconventional characters." Arthur and Cassie, as well as John in *Through Grandpa's Eyes,* benefit from loving relationships with older relatives, gaining both insight and a higher level of maturity. "Older people have achieved an admirable tranquility and tend to be more tolerant and open than the rest of us," explained MacLachlan in her *SATA* interview with Feitlowitz. "They also seem more willing to explore beyond their own thinking, which is why the kids in my books will often have 'soulmates' who are in their sixties, seventies, and eighties."

Also an integral part of these novels, and probably all of MacLachlan's works, is an autobiographical element. "My books derive chiefly from my family life," revealed MacLachlan in her *SATA* interview, "both as a child with my own parents as well as with my husband and kids." These connections are not always evident to MacLachlan while she is actually writing, though. "When you write you reach back somewhere in your mind or your heart and pull out things that you never even knew were there," she maintained in *Junior Library Guild.* "This part of writing, my sons would agree, is like fishing for bait and catching a rainbow trout instead."

It was just such a discovery of past events and memories that formed the basis of *Cassie Binegar.*

These memories, however, remained in the author's subconscious until after the book was written. "When I was a child," MacLachlan remembered in her *Language Arts* interview with Courtney, "I spent a lot of time in hidden places observing and listening to conversations that I thought seemed very important—I was a listener. Cassie, of course, sits under this huge and ugly tablecloth listening to the conversations and watching feet. After my mother read the manuscript, she brought the tablecloth out and there it was and I hadn't realized that that was certainly me as Cassie underneath the table listening to things."

It was also something remembered from childhood that sparked the writing of *Sarah, Plain and Tall,* perhaps MacLachlan's most popular and critically acclaimed work. But the idea for the story was not instantly transformed into a book. "My writing rhythm has 'peaks and valleys,'" related MacLachlan in her *SATA* interview with Feitlowitz. "Sometimes we aren't meant to write and have to let our minds roam, instead. I find that much of my work comes to me when I'm 'not looking.'" In this sense, many of MacLachlan's books seem to magically appear. "Writing, for me," she explained in *Horn Book,* "is a process in which I watch an egg for years and then, when I least expect it, the shell breaks and a chicken steps out. No, not the whole chicken—more like one foot! *Sarah* was a very personal story, and the process of writing it was a personal process."

The end result of this personal process, *Sarah, Plain and Tall,* won MacLachlan the Newbery Award and also gave her a chance to write a teleplay; the book was made into a television movie starring Glenn Close as Sarah. The story is narrated by Anna, who has taken care of her father, younger brother, and their prairie home since her mother's death during childbirth. Both Caleb and Anna are excited when they find out their father, Jacob, has advertised for a bride and that Sarah is actually coming. Sarah agrees to a month's trial, leaving the sea of her hometown in Maine for the fields of the prairie. Despite her early reluctance, Anna soon gives in and loves Sarah as much as Caleb instantly does. And in the end Sarah decides to stay.

"My mother told me early on about the real Sarah," stated MacLachlan in an excerpt from her Newbery Medal acceptance speech printed in *Horn Book,* "who came from the coast of Maine to the prairie to become a wife and mother to a close family member. . . . So the fact of Sarah was there for years, though the book began as books often do, when the past stepped on the heels of the present; or backward, when something *now* tapped something *then.*" Shortly before two of her children were to leave for college, MacLachlan's parents took the family on a trip to the prairie where they, and MacLachlan, were born. This trip made the connection between the past and the present more evident to both MacLachlan and her mother, who was beginning to lose her memory because of Alzheimer's disease.

"When I began *Sarah,*" continued MacLachlan in her speech, "I wished for several things and was granted something unexpected. Most of all I wished to write my mother's story with spaces, like the prairie, with silences that could say what words could not. . . . But books, like children, grow and change, borrowing bits and pieces of the lives of others to help make them who and what they are. And in the end we are all there, my mother, my father, my husband, my children, and me. We gave my mother better than a piece of her past. We gave her the same that Anna and Caleb and Jacob received—a family."

Critics praise *Sarah, Plain and Tall* for its simplicity, its driving emotional force, and its strong characterizations and descriptions. "It is the simplest of love stories expressed in the simplest of prose," maintained Martha Saxton in the *New York Times Book Review,* adding: "Embedded in these unadorned declarative sentences . . . are evocations of the deepest feelings of loss and fear, love and hope." Trev Jones, writing in *School Library Journal,* praised MacLachlan's ability to create characters: "Through a simple sentence or phrase, aspects of each character's personality . . . are brought to light." And Margery Fisher contended in *Growing Point* that "not a word is wasted, not a nuance missed in the quiet tenor of a narrative which creates, seemingly without any effort, the family's world of sky and prairies and Sarah's remembered world of sea and sand."

Though her world may be dramatically dissimilar, Katherine, one of the characters MacLachlan creates in her 1982 picture book *Mama One, Mama Two,* plays a role similar to Sarah's. "The surface story is different in each of Patty's books," observed Zolotow in *Horn Book,* "but the same themes weave in and out. For instance, foster

mothers or stand-in mothers is one of the motifs in many of Patty's books, from *Mama One, Mama Two* to *Sarah, Plain and Tall.* . . . On the surface the books are totally unrelated, but there is a strong inner thread binding them to each other." In *Mama One, Mama Two,* Maudie and her foster mother, Katherine, tell the tale of how Maudie came to have two mothers. Taken away from her real mother, who suffers from severe depression, Maudie now lives with her Mama Two until

---

If you enjoy the works of Patricia MacLachlan, you might also want to check out the following books and films:

Patricia Calvert, *When Morning Comes,* 1989.
Paul Fleischman, *The Borning Room,* 1991.
Myron Levoy, *Pictures of Adam,* 1986.
Gary Paulsen, *The Cookcamp,* 1991.
My Life as a Dog, Paramount, 1985.

Mama One is well enough to come home. Sutherland, in the *Bulletin of the Center for Children's Books,* pointed out that in *Mama One, Mama Two* "the tone is candid, the approach positive." *Booklist* contributor Denise M. Wilms concluded that most children will be happy that Maudie has "a Katherine to look after her."

Characters Create Plots

It is also a rare child who does not develop a fondness for, and relate to, at least one of the many characters from MacLachlan's varied cast. These characters develop and grow slowly in her mind before they actually come to life on paper with a story to tell. "I start my books with a character," revealed MacLachlan in her *SATA* interview with Feitlowitz. "Plot was always my downfall until I learned that basically character and plot amount to the same thing. One grows from the other. As I get to know my characters they let me know what they need. . . . It's a fluid, organic, and even a little mysterious process. . . . I never work from an outline, and often I don't know how the story will end."

Just such a well-developed character is the focus of MacLachlan's first novel after winning the Newbery—*The Facts and Fictions of Minna Pratt.* Eleven-year-old Minna, teetering on the edge of adolescence, finds herself confronted with numerous changes as she strives and wishes to develop a vibrato. At the same time she is practicing her cello to attain this dream, Minna also longs for her eccentric mother, a writer, to be more like a "mother." And in the midst of all this appears Lucas Ellerby, a violinist who has the quiet and peaceful home Minna desires. Lucas, on the other hand, is fascinated with the unusual ways of Minna's family, and the two experience their first romance. "Patricia MacLachlan has created a wonderfully wise and funny story with such satisfying depths and unforgettable characters that one is reluctant to let it go," praised a *Horn Book* reviewer. Heather Vogel Frederick, writing in the *New York Times Book Review*, declared: "If writers of children's fiction were organized into a guild, the title of master craftsman would be bestowed upon Patricia MacLachlan. Her crisp, elegant prose and superb storytelling ability . . . grace her newest novel, *The Facts and Fictions of Minna Pratt*."

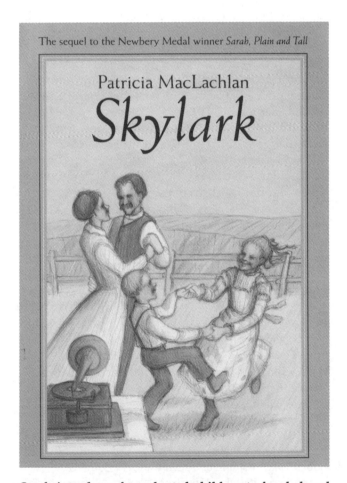

Sarah introduces her adopted children to her beloved sea in the 1994 sequel to *Sarah, Plain and Tall.*

MacLachlan continued to hone her realistic storytelling skills with two tales of loss—*Journey* and *Baby*. The first concerns a young boy of the same name and his attempt to deal with being abandoned by his mother. Journey and his sister Cat have always lived with their grandparents, but it is only recently that their mother left them. Each member of the family copes with the abandonment differently, and it is only after he is able to piece together some old photographs of his mother that Journey is able to find the love he seeks. Nancy Bray Cardozo wrote in the *New York Times Book Review* that "the language Ms. MacLachlan uses is beautiful, emotionally articulate. Journey speaks as though an eloquent adult is reminiscing about a childhood tragedy, the sadness still keenly remembered." *Baby* similarly is about a family dealing with tragedy; shortly after twelve-year-old Larkin's infant brother dies, the family finds a baby girl, Sophie, abandoned on their driveway. Once the members of the family break down and let Sophie into their hearts, despite the fact that her mother will be coming back for her, they are finally able to grieve for their recent loss. "MacLachlan's style remains masterly," concluded Diane Roback and Elizabeth Devereaux in *Publishers Weekly*. "It is difficult to read her sentences only once, and even more difficult to part from her novel."

When dealing with her characters and creating her stories, MacLachlan believes it is important to portray sorrow and anguish along with happiness. "I think life is a mixture of humor and sadness and poignancy and grief, all these things mixed in together," she related to Courtney in her *Language Arts* interview. "I think that books in a sense maybe don't change lives, but they have a great impact on children's lives. There's a good deal in this world that is not happy and yet there are moments here or there that I try to illuminate, the kind of thoughtful, pensive moments. We spend a lot of time inside our heads. I don't know if it's censorship or not but it's just a reflection of how I think and I must be optimistic."

Such optimism led to the writing of a successful sequel to *Sarah, Plain and Tall*. Published in 1994, *Skylark* finds Sarah and her new family facing a seemingly unending drought. Not as familiar with the prairie, Sarah starts to feel the pressure, and after the barn burns she takes Anna and Caleb to stay with her aunts in Maine. Though the children are fascinated by the sea, they miss their father terribly and all are excited when he arrives in Maine with the news that rain has fallen. Sarah, too, has news—she is expecting a baby—and when the family returns to the prairie Sarah writes her name in the dirt of her true home. MacLachlan's writing "neatly presents a very real setting and enormously powerful characters," described a *Publishers Weekly* contributor, concluding: "There are worlds in MacLachlan's words."

The worlds that MacLachlan creates, though, undergo an intense scrutiny from the author long before they ever make it into a published book. "I try to anticipate the experience of the reader," revealed MacLachlan in *Horn Book*. "I myself, of course, am the first reader, and I try to envision a small, objective, heartless Patty MacLachlan looking over my shoulder saying, 'Aw, come on!' when I am clumsy or self-indulgent." A small amount of self-indulgence is necessary for MacLachlan to write, however, for her inspiration almost always comes from events and people in her own life. "Robert Penn Warren said you write a poem or a book to solve a problem that you have or to answer a question in your life," MacLachlan stated in *Horn Book*. "If you don't have the problem or the question, there's no need to write the book. That is, quite simply, the way I write, the way I have to write. Nobody can ever assign me a topic. I'm not even sure that I assign a topic—but who I am, what happens in the lives of those I care about, does."

It is this life as a wife and mother, despite her critical and commercial success as a writer, that MacLachlan always puts first. Acknowledging her husband's valuable contributions to her successful career, she told Feitlowitz in *SATA:* "My decision to become a writer meant that we became a single-salary family with some lean years. More than once I said to my husband, 'Look, I think I should go out and get a real job,' but he never agreed. I'm not at all sure I would be at this point in my career if I hadn't had the time and space in which to develop." MacLachlan's husband is equally supportive of his wife and admires and respects her accomplishments; so much so, that he encounters difficulty when asked to find words to describe her. "Patty really describes herself," he wrote in *Horn Book*, "briefly but with exquisite accuracy, in the words Sarah writes to Jacob when she agrees to come for a month's visit. Sarah adds a postscript to that letter, for the children. '*Tell them I sing* was all it said.'"

■ Works Cited

Review of *Arthur, for the Very First Time, Publishers Weekly*, December 26, 1980, p. 59.

Babbitt, Natalie, review of *Through Grandpa's Eyes, New York Times Book Review,* September 28, 1980, p. 36.

Bauer, Ruth W., review of *Through Grandpa's Eyes, Children's Book Review Service,* April, 1980, p. 84.

Cardozo, Nancy Bray, review of *Journey, New York Times Book Review,* March 22, 1992, p. 25.

Dellett, Wendy, review of *Cassie Binegar, School Library Journal,* September, 1982, p. 124.

Review of *The Facts and Fictions of Minna Pratt, Horn Book,* July/August, 1988, pp. 495-96.

Fisher, Margery, review of *Sarah, Plain and Tall, Growing Point,* March, 1987, p. 4750.

Flowers, Ann A., review of *Cassie Binegar, Horn Book,* February, 1983, pp. 45-46.

Frederick, Heather Vogel, review of *The Facts and Fictions of Minna Pratt, New York Times Book Review,* January 8, 1989, p. 36.

Heins, Ethel L., essay on Patricia MacLachlan in *Twentieth-Century Children's Writers,* 3rd edition, St. James Press, 1989, pp. 622-23.

Jones, Trev, review of *Sarah, Plain and Tall, School Library Journal,* May, 1985, pp. 92-93.

MacLachlan, Patricia, remarks in *Junior Library Guild,* September, 1980.

MacLachlan, Patricia, interview with Ann Courtney in *Language Arts,* November, 1985, pp. 783-87.

MacLachlan, Patricia, "Facts and Fiction," *Horn Book,* January/February, 1986.

MacLachlan, Patricia, "Newbery Medal Acceptance," *Horn Book,* July/August, 1986, pp. 407-13.

MacLachlan, Patricia, and Charlotte Zolotow, "Dialogue between Charlotte Zolotow and Patricia MacLachlan," *Horn Book,* November/December, 1989, pp. 736-45.

MacLachlan, Patricia, interview with Marguerite Feitlowitz for *Something about the Author,* Volume 62, Gale, 1990, pp. 117-22.

MacLachlan, Robert, "A Hypothetical Dilemma," *Horn Book,* July/August, 1986, pp. 416-19.

Roback, Diane, and Elizabeth Devereaux, review of *Baby, Publishers Weekly,* August 16, 1993, p. 104.

Saxton, Martha, review of *Sarah, Plain and Tall, New York Times Book Review,* May 19, 1985, p. 20.

Review of *Skylark, Publishers Weekly,* November 29, 1993, p. 65.

Sutherland, Zena, review of *Arthur, for the Very First Time, Bulletin of the Center for Children's Books*, September, 1980, pp. 15-16.

Sutherland, Zena, review of *Mama One, Mama Two, Bulletin of the Center for Children's Books*, April, 1982, pp. 153-54.

Review of *Through Grandpa's Eyes, Publishers Weekly*, May 9, 1980, p. 57.

Wilms, Denise M., review of *Mama One, Mama Two, Booklist*, April 1, 1982, pp. 1019-20.

■ **For More Information See**

BOOKS

Children's Literature Review, Volume 14, Gale, 1988, pp. 177-86.

PERIODICALS

Booklist, October 15, 1980, pp. 328-29; June 15, 1988, p. 1739; September 1, 1993, p. 51; January 1, 1994, p. 827.

Horn Book, July/August, 1986, pp. 414-19; September/October, 1991, pp. 592-93.

Los Angeles Times Book Review, December 8, 1985, p. 4.

New York, February 8, 1993, p. 64.

New York Times Book Review, March 20, 1983, p. 31.

Publishers Weekly, June 4, 1979, p. 61; December 24, 1982, p. 65; January 13, 1984, p. 69; February 15, 1985, p. 100; May 20, 1988, p. 92; July 25, 1991, p. 53.

School Library Journal, September, 1979, p. 116; October, 1980, p. 149; April, 1982, p. 59; April, 1984, p. 117; July, 1991, pp. 60-61; November, 1993, p. 109.

Times Literary Supplement, November 28, 1986, p. 1344.*

—Sketch by Susan Reicha

Jay McInerney

reader, 1980-81; Syracuse University, Syracuse, NY, instructor in English, 1983. *Member:* Authors Guild, PEN, Writers Guild.

■ Personal

Born January 13, 1955, in Hartford, CT; son of John Barrett (a corporate executive) and Marilyn Jean (Murphy) McInerney; married Merry Reymond (a student), June 2, 1984 (deceased); married Helen Bransford, December 27, 1991. *Education:* Williams College, B.A., 1976; postgraduate study at Syracuse University.

■ Addresses

Home—New York, NY. *Agent*—Amanda Urban, International Creative Management, 40 West 57th St., New York, NY 10019; or Deborah Rogers, Rogers Coleridge and White Ltd., 20 Powis Mews, London W11 1JN, England.

■ Career

Writer; *Hunterdon County Democrat*, Flemington, NJ, reporter, 1977; Time-Life, Inc., Osaka, Japan, textbook editor, 1978-79; *New Yorker*, New York City, fact checker, 1980; Random House, New York City,

■ Awards, Honors

Princeton in Asia fellow, 1977.

■ Writings

NOVELS

Bright Lights, Big City, Vintage Contemporaries, 1984.
Ransom, Vintage Contemporaries, 1985.
Story of My Life, Atlantic Monthly Press, 1988.
Brightness Falls, Knopf, 1992.
The Last of the Slaves, Knopf, 1996.

OTHER

(Coauthor) *Bright Lights, Big City* (screenplay; adapted from his novel), Metro-Goldwyn-Mayer/United Artists, 1988.
(Editor) *Cowboys, Indians and Commuters: The Penguin Book of New American Voices*, Viking, 1994.

Also coauthor of the screenplay for *Big Lights, Big City*, Columbia Pictures, and the unproduced screenplay *Paint It Black*. Contributor of short stories to books, including "It's Six a.m. Do You

Know Where You Are?," *Look Who's Talking*, edited by Bruce Weber, Washington Square Press, 1986. Also contributor of short stories to periodicals, including "The Real Tad Allagash," *Ms.*, 1985; "Reunion," *Esquire*, 1987; "Smoke," *Atlantic*, 1987; "She Dreams of Johnny," *Gentlemen's Quarterly*, 1988; and "Lost and Found," *Esquire*, 1988. Contributor of articles and literary criticism to periodicals, including *Paris Review, Vogue, Village Voice, London Review of Books, Esquire, Vanity Fair, New York Times Book Review, Atlantic Monthly, Ms.*, and *New Republic*.

■ Sidelights

"You are not the kind of guy who would be at a place like this at this time of the morning. But here you are, and you cannot say that the terrain is entirely unfamiliar, although the details are fuzzy. . . . All might come clear if you could just slip into the bathroom and do a little more Bolivian Marching Powder. Then again, it might not. . . . Somewhere back there you could have cut your losses, but you rode past that moment on a comet trail of white powder and now you are trying to hang on to the rush."

Thus begins the downward spiral of the unnamed narrator in Jay McInerney's first novel, *Bright Lights, Big City*. Utilizing a second-person narrative, McInerney emphasizes just how disillusioned and removed from himself the narrator is as he struggles to deal with the loss of his model wife, his cocaine addiction, a dead-end job, and the recent death of his mother. Set against the backdrop of New York City, *Bright Lights, Big City* won both popular and critical acclaim for its satirical portrait of the early 1980s. At the same time, this first novel set down themes that return in McInerney's later novels, including *Ransom, Story of My Life*, and *Brightness Falls*.

Born in the mid-1950s, McInerney grew up in several North American and European cities as his father, an international executive, was transferred once a year or more. After having attended eighteen elementary schools, McInerney spent his high school years in Pittsfield, Massachusetts, before enrolling at nearby Williams College to major in philosophy and minor in English. Following graduation, McInerney and fellow student Gary Fisketjon (who later became the young author's editor at Random House) purchased a used car

and took off on a trip across the United States before settling down to pursue their careers.

Having determined that a writing career was his goal, McInerney worked first as a reporter in 1977 for a weekly newspaper in New Jersey, the *Hunterdon County Democrat*. Later that same year, he was able to travel to Japan on a Princeton in Asia fellowship. While overseas, McInerney served as both a teacher and a student, teaching English at Kyoto University and taking Japanese courses at the Institute for International Studies. It was also during this time that McInerney developed his strong interest in Samurai self-discipline, an art that he submerged himself in and later included in his second novel, *Ransom*.

Big Apple Breakaway

After returning in 1979 from Japan, where he had also worked as a text book editor for Time-Life, Inc., McInerney continued his publishing career as a fact checker for *New Yorker* magazine and then as a manuscript reader at Random House. By this time, McInerney's college friend Fisketjon was an editor at Random House, and it was through him that he met the short story writer and poet Raymond Carver. This established author advised McInerney to leave behind the demands of New York City for a time to pursue fiction writing. And so he did. In 1981, he went to Syracuse University on a literary fellowship to take part in the graduate writing program, which included both Carver and Tobias Wolff as teachers.

In an interview with Jean W. Ross for *Contemporary Authors*, McInerney explains how difficult and important this move from New York City was at the time. "Making the big break and leaving Manhattan, leaving a lot of friends and a job of sorts behind, I had to make a pretty big psychological commitment. I had to tell myself that there came a time when you decided to throw all of your energies behind the big ambition or else you knew ultimately the possibility of realizing that ambition—in my case, to be a novelist—would slip away."

This ambition did not slip away from McInerney, but it did not bring immediate results either. First, the author wrote a number of short stories, one of which eventually led to the writing of *Bright Lights, Big City*. McInerney had submitted a story

Told in the second person, this is the cynically humorous 1984 story of a New Yorker who, upon losing his wife, job, and mother, reacts through nightclubbing and cocaine use.

to *Paris Review* that the editors were wary of publishing. They asked if the author had anything else to submit for publication. "I had this one page in my drawer which was the only thing I wasn't really disgusted with by then," McInerney recalls in his interview with Ross. "It was pretty much the first page of the book. I'd written it down one morning and then forgotten about it. When I looked at it again, the voice seemed very exciting to me. It was written in the second person. I wasn't sure why, but there was something about that voice that had an energy I wanted to pursue and that carried me along."

Using this page as a base, McInerney sent a new short story to *Paris Review*, "It's Six a.m. Do You Know Where You Are?," and this story eventually became the first chapter in *Bright Lights, Big*

City. A few months later, McInerney revisited this second-person voice with another short story, "Amanda," which also ended up as a chapter in his first novel. "And it occurred to me that these two things were naturally connected, not only in terms of a story that might be told but also by this strange second-person voice that I was experimenting with and having a lot of fun with," relates McInerney in his *Contemporary Authors* interview. "I felt there was a very strange arc between the two things even though I didn't necessarily know what the story was going to be about in all of its detail. Shortly after I wrote that second one, I'd just finished a graduate program at Syracuse University and immediately sat down and wrote *Bright Lights, Big City*."

Bright Debut

Published in 1984 as the first original in the new Random House Vintage Contemporaries series, *Bright Lights, Big City* captures New York City in the early 1980s through the experiences of its unnamed narrator. This young man, who tells his tale in the second person, is disillusioned and lost as he faces several crises in his life at once. His method of dealing with these problems is a weeklong binge of clubbing in search of women and cocaine. During this binge he reveals different facets of his life, including his failed marriage to a model, his failed job as a fact checker at a magazine very similar to the *New Yorker*, and his failed family connections, including the recent death of his mother. By the end of this search for identity, the narrator comes to the conclusion that he will have to learn everything over again.

Bright Lights, Big City "is a very funny, oddly touching book, and something of a tour de force as well," observes Terence Moran in *New Republic*. "McInerney employs an unusual and challenging narrative device; he tells his tale through the second person in the historical present tense and fashions a coherent and engaging voice with it, one that is totally believable at almost every moment in the novel." McInerney himself was hesitant at first to maintain this unique voice throughout the entire novel. "My feeling initially was that I would probably have to stop somewhere along the line and go back and change the whole thing, but since it started that way, I was reluctant to let go," he explains to Ross. "As it turned out, I found that rather than becoming more difficult for me, it became eventually very ingrained—to the point that when I finally finished writing *Bright Lights*, it was hard not to keep writing letters and everything else in the second person."

Seeing *Bright Lights, Big City* as a familiar story, Susan Bolotin writes in *Vogue* that "McInerney takes big risks with his old story—most noticeably in his spectacularly effective use of the second-person singular voice. In lesser hands, the novel could have read like a writing-class assignment; instead, it's a fresh, if sometimes overly trendy, take on what it means to grow up." In addition to the unique second-person voice in *Bright Lights, Big City*, the satirical portrayal of New York City nightlife and the magazine where the narrator works are singled out as noteworthy

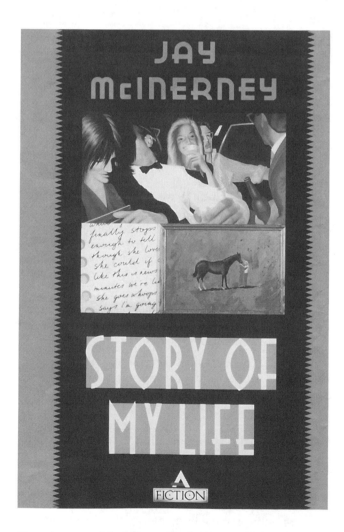

Twenty-year-old Alison Poole, an aspiring actress, and her friends indulge in the pleasures of sex and substance abuse until life spins out of control.

by several critics. "The best part of this promising debut is McInerney's humor—it is cynical, deadpan and right on target, delivered with impeccable comic timing," asserts a *Publishers Weekly* contributor. William Kotzwinkle similarly states in the *New York Times Book Review* that "McInerney's strong suit is humor, and there is lots of it in *Bright Lights, Big City*. . . . This is the echo of New York, all right, and if you have a love affair with it, you'll recognize the truth in Mr. McInerney's landscapes." And Moran concludes that in *Bright Lights, Big City* "McInerney not only jests at our slightly tawdry life, but also celebrates its abiding possibilities."

Japan Revisited

Along with its critical success, *Bright Lights, Big City* also achieved popular success, selling more than 150,000 copies within a year as it attracted an almost cult readership of young urbanites who recognized the world in which the narrator lives. With such a huge success in his first novel, McInerney was immediately thrown into the spotlight and critical expectations were high for his next work. He had originally begun his second novel, *Ransom*, before the writing of *Bright Lights, Big City* took place. McInerney had been trying to write a novel set in Japan for several years, but was unsatisfied with his progress. "I would start again and again; I really did not have the capabilities to write then the kind of book that I wanted to write, and I had hundreds of pages of manuscript that were unsatisfying to me in one way or another," reveals McInerney in his interview with Ross. "But it had become an obsession. I felt that if I abandoned this thing, it would be an admission of failure."

The stories that lured McInerney into putting *Ransom* aside brought everything but failure for the young author. While he was waiting for the publication of his first novel he returned to his tale of American expatriates in Japan. This time, however, he started over from the beginning, using a mixture of his old writings and thoughts and his new outlook on the subject matter. "I'd say the impulse for *Ransom* and some of its concerns predate *Bright Lights, Big City*, but basically the execution came afterwards," McInerney tells Ross. "I think it's my second book, but it was something I'd been working on for quite a while before the first book was done."

Ransom contains similar themes to those found in *Bright Lights, Big City*—Chris Ransom, like the unnamed narrator in the first book, is a young man searching for his identity and a semblance of meaning and direction in his life. Having taken refuge in Japan, Chris submerges himself in the study of karate in an attempt to forget recent events and a manipulative father back in the United States. Among the things Chris is trying to escape are the deaths of two friends in Pakistan during a drug deal, deaths for which he feels

---

If you enjoy the works of Jay McInerney, you may also want to check out the following books:

Caroline B. Cooney, *The Party's Over*, 1991.
Hadley Irwin, *Can't Hear You Listening*, 1990.
Robin Klein, *Came Back to Show You I Could Fly*, 1990.
Shelley Stoehr, *Crosses*, 1991.

---

responsible. At the same time, he feels guilty for the privileged life he had growing up and is resentful of his father, a playwright who "sold out" for the money involved in writing television sitcoms. In the end, the spiritual peace Chris is searching for remains out of reach.

"Jay McInerney is a serious, gifted artist," asserts Ron Loewinsohn in the *New York Times Book Review*. "His first novel, *Bright Lights, Big City*, is a brilliant and moving work—unique, refreshing, imaginatively powerful and authentically conceived. *Ransom*, on the other hand, . . . rarely rises above the level of mere competence. It feels thoroughly conventional, thoroughly uninspired." Also comparing *Ransom* to *Bright Lights, Big City*, Andrew Weinberger writes in the *Los Angeles Times Book Review* that McInerney's second effort is "wittier and more complex." And Bill Ott concludes in *Booklist*: "Writing with the same hard-edged, unadorned precision that characterized *Bright Lights, Big City*, McInerney reveals what can happen when Western individualism is mixed with Eastern moral discipline. A samurai Don Quixote is a walking time bomb."

The publication of *Ransom* in 1985 brought many comparisons to *Bright Lights, Big City*, and the majority were not favorable. McInerney believes that this second novel was not fairly reviewed, mostly because of the success of his first effort. "One thing I noticed right away in the States was that so many of the reviews of *Ransom* were just reviews of *Bright Lights* all over again," McInerney relates to Ross. "I don't think *Ransom* was so much poorly reviewed as it was *barely* reviewed. Everybody who didn't have a chance to say something about *Bright Lights* got their chance with *Ransom*, and the only thing to do after you've discovered something is to say, 'Well, it's not as good as everybody said it was.'"

City of Lights

The comparisons to *Bright Lights, Big City* continued with the publication of McInerney's third novel, *Story of My Life*. Returning the setting to New York City, McInerney introduces twenty-year-old Alison Poole, a former rich girl who is now an aspiring actress experiencing a downturn in her life as she becomes addicted to alcohol and cocaine. Alison and her girlfriends, who all speak in an unending stream of hip slang, are into excesses, especially when it comes to partying and sex. As she partakes of these pleasures more and more frequently, Alison begins to miss her acting classes and her life spins out of control, crashing under the weight of her addictions.

In a *Booklist* review of *Story of My Life*, John Brosnahan points out that "Alison, whose command of her group's lingo, values, and status symbols is awesome, tells the whole story in the first person, producing an effect akin to listening to a Valley Girl who has just discovered the stream-of-consciousness technique." Carolyn Gaiser, writing in the *New York Times Book Review*, offers similar praise, but views the overall effect of *Story of My Life* as "episodic." "McInerney has created in Alison Poole a thoroughly convincing female voice, but not a very winning character," writes Gaiser, adding: "The unrelieved use of slang, coupled with a general lack of structure, causes the novel to read, at times, like the random jottings of a diary kept by a zonked-out teenager." Deanne Stillman, on the other hand, maintains in the *Los Angeles Times Book Review* that "McInerney's authentic rendering of girl talk, his sympathetic portrayal of female characters who suffer from benign neglect, and his continuing scrutiny of the young ponies of the equestrian class . . . make *Story of My Life* highly readable. If this isn't a 'women's novel,' I don't know what is."

Another circle of Manhattan friends are introduced in McInerney's 1992 novel *Brightness Falls*. Considered to be the author's most mature work by some critics, this tale centers around Corinne and Russell Calloway, a young aspiring couple living in New York City in the months before the stock market crash of 1987. Their friends include a writer/addict, a cynical book editor, a literary intellectual, and several other Upper East Side and Wall Street types, all as corrupted by the pursuit of wealth as Russell soon becomes. Russell's corruption begins when one of his big projects at his publishing company is rejected; seeing this as a blow against his career, Russell attempts a hostile take-over of the company. As the deal progresses his marriage to Corinne is threatened as well as his moral character. At the conclusion of the novel, it becomes evident that the prosperity of the late 1980s was just a dream; the brightness of Russell and Corinne Calloway, and of all their friends, falls.

Brightness Falls "is a solid and durably plotted book," observes *Chicago Tribune* contributor Sven Birkerts. "Indeed, fueled by its images of excess and rendered biographically interesting by its undercurrents of felt remorse, it makes for a quick and compelling reading experience." Noting the similarities in McInerney's fourth novel to his earlier writings, Donna Seaman states in *Booklist*: "He's still monitoring the excesses and absurdities of New York City with caffeinic clarity, but his voice has acquired a huskiness, a deepening imbued with the wisdom of sorrow." And John Skow notes in *Time* that *Brightness Falls* is "an entirely grownup novel about the end of the '80s. It's a funny, self-mocking, sometimes brilliant portrait of Manhattan's young literary and Wall Street crowd, our latest Lost Generation." Skow goes on to conclude: "*Brightness Falls*, from an impressive height."

In the same way, McInerney's career has progressed from the "impressive height" of his first novel, despite the effects of this early spotlight. And at the center of this career is Manhattan and its many trappings, a city that both draws and repels McInerney at the same time. "Being very transient and peripatetic all my life, I (ironically, I think) feel more at home here than almost anywhere because I think it's a sort of hometown for transient ambitious Americans," McInerney describes in his interview with Ross, adding: "But I don't feel that it's terribly conducive to the sort of creative trance that I find I have to live within

in order to write a novel. So I have something of an attraction-repulsion complex with regard to New York. I think I said somewhere before that Manhattan is like malaria for me. It's in my blood and it comes around every few years and I have to live through it."

■ Works Cited

Birkerts, Sven, "McInerney's Redemption," *Chicago Tribune*, June 7, 1992, section 14, p. 3.

Bolotin, Susan, review of *Bright Lights, Big City*, *Vogue*, September, 1984, p. 578.

Review of *Bright Lights, Big City*, *Publishers Weekly*, August 10, 1984, p. 76.

Brosnahan, John, review of *Story of My Life*, *Booklist*, August, 1988, p. 1866.

Gaiser, Carolyn, "Zonked Again," *New York Times Book Review*, September 25, 1988, p. 12.

Kotzwinkle, William, "You're Fired, So You Buy a Ferret," *New York Times Book Review*, November 25, 1984, p. 9.

Loewinsohn, Ron, "Land of the Also Rising Sun," *New York Times Book Review*, September 29, 1985, p. 42.

McInerney, Jay, *Bright Lights, Big City*, Vintage Contemporaries, 1984.

McInerney, Jay, in an interview with Jean W. Ross, *Contemporary Authors*, Volume 123, Gale, 1988.

Moran, Terence, review of *Bright Lights, Big City*, *New Republic*, December 3, 1984, pp. 41-42.

Ott, Bill, review of *Ransom*, *Booklist*, August, 1985, p. 1597.

Seaman, Donna, review of *Brightness Falls*, *Booklist*, April 1, 1992, p. 1412.

Skow, John, "Onward and Yupward," *Time*, June 1, 1992, pp. 82, 86.

Stillman, Deanne, "Bright Lights, Tight Skirt," *Los Angeles Times Book Review*, August 28, 1988, p. 3.

Weinberger, Andrew, review of *Ransom*, *Los Angeles Times Book Review*, October 6, 1985, p. 8.

■ For More Information See

BOOKS

Contemporary Literary Criticism: Yearbook 1984, Volume 34, Gale, 1985.

PERIODICALS

Kirkus Reviews, July 15, 1988, pp. 1004-05.
Library Journal, September 15, 1985, pp. 93-94.

Los Angeles Times Book Review, June 7, 1992, p. 3.

New York Times Book Review, May 31, 1992, p. 7; May 26, 1996, p. 11.

Publishers Weekly, July 29, 1988, p. 219; March 23, 1992, p. 58.

Time, October 14, 1985, p. 104; September 19, 1988, p. 95.

Times Literary Supplement, August 26, 1988, p. 927.*

—*Sketch by Susan Reicha*

Pamela Sargent

1969—. *Member:* Amnesty International, Authors Guild, Authors League of America, National Wildlife Federation, Science Fiction and Fantasy Writers of America.

■ Awards, Honors

Best Books for Young Adults citation, American Library Association, 1983, for *Earthseed;* Nebula Award for best novelette, Science Fiction and Fantasy Writers of America, 1992, LOCUS Award for best novelette, 1993, and Hugo Award nomination, all for "Danny Goes to Mars."

■ Writings

YOUNG ADULT SCIENCE FICTION

Earthseed, Harper, 1983.
Alien Child, Harper, 1988.

"EARTHMINDS" TRILOGY; FOR YOUNG ADULTS

Watchstar, Pocket Books, 1980.
Eye of the Comet, Harper, 1984.
Homesmind, Harper, 1984.

SCIENCE FICTION FOR ADULTS

Cloned Lives, Fawcett, 1976.
Starshadows (short stories; includes "Shadows," "Gather Blue Roses," "Oasis," "Clone Sister," and "IMT"), Ace, 1977.

■ Personal

Born March 20, 1948, in Ithaca, NY; daughter of Edward H., Jr. (a professional singer) and Shirley (Richards) Sargent; companion to George Zebrowski (a science fiction author). *Education:* State University of New York at Binghamton, B.A. (philosophy), 1968, M.A. (philosophy), 1970.

■ Addresses

Home—Box 486, Johnson City, NY 13790. *Agent*—Joseph Elder Agency, 150 West 87th St., Suite 6-D, New York, NY 10024.

■ Career

Honigsbaum's, Albany, NY, model and sales clerk, 1965-66; Endicott Coil Company, Albany, assembly line solderer, 1966; Towne Distributors, Albany, sales clerk, 1966; Harpur College Library, State University of New York, Binghamton, typist in cataloging department, 1966-67; Webster Paper Company, Albany, office worker and receptionist, 1969; State University of New York, Binghamton, teaching assistant in philosophy, 1969-71; writer,

The Sudden Star, Fawcett, 1979, published in England as *The White Death*, Fontana, 1980.

The Golden Space, Simon & Schuster, 1982.

The Alien Upstairs, Doubleday, 1983.

The Mountain Cage, illustrated by Judy King-Rieniets, Cheap Street, 1983.

Venus of Dreams (first book in the "Venus" trilogy), Bantam, 1986.

The Shore of Women, Crown, 1986.

The Best of Pamela Sargent (short stories), edited by Martin H. Greenberg, Academy, 1987.

Venus of Shadows (second book in the "Venus" trilogy), Doubleday, 1988.

HISTORICAL FICTION

Ruler of the Sky: A Novel of Genghis Khan, Crown, 1993.

EDITOR AND CONTRIBUTOR

Women of Wonder: Science Fiction Stories by Women about Women, Random House, 1975.

Bio-Futures: Science Fiction Stories about Biological Metamorphosis, Random House, 1976.

More Women of Wonder: Science Fiction Novelettes by Women about Women, Random House, 1976.

The New Women of Wonder: Recent Science Fiction Stories by Women about Women, Random House, 1978.

Women of Wonder, the Contemporary Years: Science Fiction by Women from the 1970s to the 1990s, Harcourt, 1995.

Women of Wonder, the Classic Years: Science Fiction by Women from the 1940s to the 1970s, Harcourt, 1995.

OTHER

(Editor with Ian Watson) *Afterlives: Stories about Life after Death*, Random House, 1986.

(Editor) *Nebula Awards, No. 29*, Harcourt, 1995.

(Editor) *Nebula Awards, No. 30*, Harvest, 1996.

Contributor to numerous anthologies and science fiction and fantasy anthologies, including *Wandering Stars*, edited by Jack Dann, Harper, 1972; *Two Views of Wonder*, edited by Thomas N. Scortia and Chelsea Quinn Yarbro, Ballantine, 1973; and *Ten Tomorrows*, edited by Roger Elwood, Fawcett, 1973. Contributor to science fiction and fantasy magazines, including *Amazing Stories, Futures, Fantasy and Science Fiction, Isaac Asimov's Science Fiction Magazine, Science-Fiction Studies*, and *Twilight Zone*;

contributor to *Washington Post Book World.* Author of afterword to *The Fifth Head of Cerberus* by Gene Wolfe, Ace Books, 1976; *Fantasy Annual V*, edited by Terry Carr, Timescape, 1982; and *The Road to Science Fiction: From Here to Forever*, Volume 4, edited by James Gunn, Signet, 1982. *Bulletin of the Science Fiction Writers of America,* managing editor, 1970-73, assistant editor, 1973-75, market report editor, 1973-76, coeditor, 1983-92.

Sargent's works have been translated into several foreign languages, including Dutch, French, German, Japanese, and Spanish. Her manuscripts are kept at the David Paskow Science Fiction Collection at Temple University, Philadelphia, PA.

■ Adaptations

The short story "The Shrine" was adapted for an episode of *Tales from the Dark Side*, 1986.

■ Work in Progress

Child of Venus, the third book in the "Venus" trilogy.

■ Sidelights

When science fiction author Pamela Sargent was a young girl growing up in Ithaca, New York, she met two people who would have a great impact upon her chosen career. One was her baby-sitter Audrey, and the other was Bobby Swayze, a boy who lived next door. Audrey was a student at Cornell University and later became the first woman to graduate from that institution's school of architecture, despite the wishes of her parents and her professors' negative attitude about women architects. "My parents couldn't have picked a better role model for me if they had tried," Sargent declared in her *Contemporary Authors Autobiography Series (CAAS)* entry. Bobby Swayze, the author later wrote, "was the first person to reveal the science fictional world to me." A fan of the early television series "Captain Video," Bobby got the young Sargent interested in the genre, as well as such other unique pastimes as playing with chemistry sets and trying to hypnotize Sargent's younger brother Scott to make him their "slave."

Although enslaving her sibling didn't work out for Sargent, her interest in science fiction did. This, combined with a firm belief—inspired by her baby-sitter—that women were capable of contributing much more to society than they were currently doing, eventually led Sargent down a path that would make her a respected author for both adults and teenagers of science fiction novels and short stories featuring strong female protagonists. But in addition to writing works such as *Cloned Lives, Earthseed, Venus of Dreams,* and the "Earthminds" trilogy, Sargent has also done much to help her fellow women writers gain recognition for their contributions by editing several anthologies filled with their stories, including *Women of Wonder* and *The New Women of Wonder.*

Of course, it usually takes more than an inspiring baby-sitter and a next-door neighbor to change a person's life. Sargent had several other influences before she decided to become a writer. One

Set on a post-apocalyptic Earth, this novel confronts the question of whether to give the entire human race—with all its flaws—a second chance or let it die.

of these was not a person at all, but rather her own nearsightedness, which she endured for some years before her parents realized their daughter needed glasses. As Sargent explained in *The Sixth Book of Junior Authors and Illustrators,* "Perhaps if I had seen the world clearly from the start, I wouldn't have had so many questions about it later, the kinds of questions a writer can explore in stories." Her bad eyesight had another advantage: because television was just a blur to her, she turned to books, which she could read if she held the pages closely enough. By the time Sargent went to school, she was therefore already a good reader.

School Days

School was a series of ups and downs for Sargent. Even though she was bright, she often received bad grades in her classes. Her parents and the school authorities saw that she was intelligent and allowed her to skip kindergarten and go straight to the first grade. "Years lay ahead in which I was destined to be a big disappointment to a lot of my teachers," Sargent confessed in *CAAS.* She first went to the Henry St. John School, where her first-grade teacher, Miss Mancuso, pulled her aside one day and asked why she was doing so poorly at reading. Sargent explained that the readers were too boring, and, after her teacher asked her to read from a newspaper, Sargent proved that she was at a reading level far above the rest of the class. "I won a promotion to the advanced reading group and thrived after that," she said.

When she was in the third grade, Sargent's parent moved the family to Albany, New York, where she once again had difficulty in class. She struggled through fourth and fifth grades until she found an inspiring sixth-grade teacher, Mrs. Tabor. "Mrs. Tabor actually seemed to enjoy the classroom. My grades improved." Mrs. Tabor inspired the young Sargent to try "to convince my teacher . . . that I wasn't completely hopeless." To do this, she began writing and directing "full scale dramatic productions . . . , basing them on our history lessons." Casting her classmates in her plays' roles, Sargent and the other students made their own props and rehearsed for weeks before presenting Sargent's dramas before the school.

For the most part, however, school in Albany was a disaster for Sargent. While still in fifth grade, she learned to induce herself to vomit so that she could convince her parents she was too sick to go to class. In later years, she skipped school to go to the library and to book stores, which she found a much more fulfilling experience than the disciplined lessons and social cliques at school. By junior high, her attendance became so poor that her grades took a nosedive. "The only things saving me from complete academic failure were a good memory, an ability to cram at the last minute, and a lust for reading," she wrote in her *CAAS* entry. "A few accomplished teachers managed to salvage good work from me."

By the time she was fourteen, school had become so difficult for Sargent that she suffered a nervous breakdown. "There were plenty of early warning signs—I had run away from home twice and regularly sneaked out of the house at night to see a guy I wasn't supposed to be seeing. I ended up in a place with a lot of other troubled kids and eventually got sane enough to think of putting my life back together." Sargent pleaded with her parents to allow her to go to another school, to which they agreed. She applied to the Albany Academy for Girls, a private school with a rigorous curriculum. Normally, a student with Sargent's grades would not have been admitted, but she did so well on the entrance exam that the school granted her a full scholarship. Now in an atmosphere of small classes and demanding academic standards, Sargent once again thrived. "For the first time since my years in Ithaca, I didn't dread going to school," she recalled.

Sargent Turns to Writing

It was at the Albany Academy that Sargent's interest in writing began to flower. Working on the school's literary magazine, first on the art board and then the literary board, she began contributing stories. Sargent said in *CAAS*, "Writing had been partly an escape for me in childhood and partly a way to make some sense of a world that seemed bewildering at best. Until I had overcome a persistent stammer, writing was also my way of communicating and often the only means I had of convincing my teachers that I had learned anything at all. Now, for the first time, I began to feel that it might be a possible profession, an ambition my English teachers, Mrs. Thorstensen and Mrs. Collins, encouraged."

Sargent did so well at the Academy that she received a National Merit Letter of Commendation and a New York State Regents Scholarship, which paid her tuition to attend any college or university in the state. Her parents, however, could not afford the extra costs of university such as room and board, so Sargent selected one close to home—Harpur College in Binghamton. It was during her first semester that Sargent met the next important influence in her life: George Zebrowski. Unlike Sargent, Zebrowski had a definite ambition in life—he wanted to be a science fiction writer—which he eventually realized. It was Zebrowski who elevated Sargent's understanding of science fiction from her "Captain Video" days to the writings of luminaries like Isaac Asimov and Arthur C. Clarke.

> *"What Sargent does is to depict a world in which human potential can be realized by anyone. However, woman, in her empathic state, cuts through to truth, to new realities, new possibilities."*
> —Philip M. Rubens

After taking two years of courses at Harpur, Sargent left temporarily, partly to get her bearings and partly to earn more money for school. For a while, she worked as a solderer on an assembly line. As a pleasant diversion, she often visited Zebrowski at his apartment, where they would read and talk about science fiction. "Perhaps without that boring job and the subsequent need for diversion," Sargent pondered in *CAAS*, "I would never have read enough science fiction to acquire the background necessary to write it."

Sargent worked a couple of other minor jobs before returning to Harpur—which had just become part of the State University of New York—a year after she had left. She had decided by this time that she would major in philosophy and take classes in history as well, the only two subjects that really interested her. Since it was the 1960s, there were plenty of diversions for Sargent to get involved in—she went to some Vietnam protests, made friends with members of the Students for a Democratic Society, and experimented with drugs—but her course load, especially her classes in Greek, was demanding enough that she never became too deeply entrenched in the climate of the times. "It may be that the rigidity of [my Greek] professors and their demands were the only barriers standing between me and a totally drug-sodden, crazed sixties existence," Sargent confessed.

First Story Was Once Garbage

During her senior year, Sargent sold her first science fiction story, "Landed Minority," to the *Magazine of Fantasy and Science Fiction*. Interestingly, this first success almost ended up in the wastepaper basket. Sargent had thrown it away after writing the first few pages, but Zebrowski fished it out and encouraged her to finish and submit it. His instincts proved absolutely right. Sargent soon had a second story, "Oasis," published in an anthology called *Protostars*. By the time she had completed her master's degree, Sargent had changed her mind about getting a doctorate in philosophy and instead decided to pursue the dream of being a writer.

Sargent and Zebrowski were by this time living together in an apartment near downtown Binghamton (they have been together ever since, but have never married). They both worked diligently on their writing, while Sargent earned extra income at a paper company and Zebrowski worked as a pool filtration plant operator. Sargent completed a novel but decided it was not good enough to submit to an agent. Her first big sale turned out to be the anthology she edited, *Women of Wonder: Science Fiction Stories by Women about Women*. The first collection of its kind, *Women of Wonder* includes only science fiction featuring female protagonists and written by women authors. *Women of Wonder* sold well and received enough positive criticism to merit several similar anthologies based on the same criteria.

The year after her anthology appeared in 1975, Sargent published her first science fiction novel, *Cloned Lives*, which was based on two short stories she had written earlier, "Clone Sister" and "A Sense of Difference." As the title indicates, the story is about cloning and the issues that surround

that scientific possibility. Set sometime in the future, the story concerns astrophysicist Paul Swenson, who has several clones made of himself after a ban on the process has been lifted by the government. The novel explores the effects of cloning both from Paul Swenson's point of view and the viewpoint of his clones, in the end demonstrating that the clones are just as human as their "father," and also showing the possible benefits of the science when Paul is later brought back to life with the help of transplanted cloned organs. "The general fear of science and technology is a central problem in the novel," explains *Dictionary of Literary Biography* contributor Philip M. Rubens, "and Sargent's argument, while granting the dangers of the irresponsible pursuit of knowledge, is focused on demonstrating the greater destructiveness of fear and willful ignorance."

Books for Teens

Sargent followed *Cloned Lives* with a short story collection, *Starshadows*, and the novel *The Sudden Star*, which is about a world that has been devastated by environmental disasters. In 1980 she published her first novel for young adults, *Watchstar*, which became the first book in her science fiction "Earthminds" trilogy, including *Eye of the Comet* and *Homesmind*. The stories are set on a future Earth where people live in a primitive society but have developed the ability to link minds in a telepathic Net. One day a young girl named Daiya sees a spaceship descending to the surface and meets an alien named Reiho, who is from a comet world where people use technology to link their thoughts to Homesmind. Reiho invites Daiya to visit his world, but she becomes homesick and returns to Earth, only to find herself rejected by her people. Problems then develop when Homesmind tries to link with the Earthlings. The primitive Earthlings are afraid of the aliens' advanced technology, and their suspicions escalate into violence when Daiya's fellow villagers attack Reiho and another alien. By the novel's end, Daiya has become an outcast because of her links to the aliens, but she manages to save her baby sister—who is nontelepathic—from being killed by the villagers when the aliens accept her request to take the baby back to their world.

In *Eye of the Comet* Lydee, the baby Daiya rescued, has grown into a young women on Homesmind's world and has been asked to return to Earth, where she is supposed to serve as a sort of telepathic ambassador between the two worlds. Neither a true citizen of the comet world of Homesmind, nor comfortable among her own people who are like strangers to her, Lydee must search for her own identity, acceptance, and love. "Unlike the action that marked Daiya's quest," remarked Janice Antczak in *Twentieth-Century Young Adult Writers*, "Lydee's conflict is more philosophical and psychological. Sargent allows her character to become a sounding board for discussion of questions of death and afterlife, the existence of the soul, and powers of the mind."

The third book in the trilogy, *Homesmind*, features another new heroine, Anra. Like Lydee, Anra has been born without the telepathic capabilities of her fellow Earthlings and must use the technology of the comet world to link with the Net. A crisis comes, however, when a mysterious evil force invades the Net and it is up to Anra and others like her to save humankind. Critical reception to *Homesmind* and the other "Earthminds" trilogy books was lukewarm. Some reviewers complained that too many plot complications were added to the stories, that the author indulged in too much explication, and that characterization was sometimes flat. *Voice of Youth Advocates* contributor Rebecca Sue Taylor, for example, commented that characters in *Homesmind* "are underdeveloped and faceless" and that Sargent's *Earthseed* is a better book. And while Lyle Blake Smythers noted in *School Library Journal* that *Homesmind* does a good job "portraying how the advantages and disadvantages of mind reading can bring out crucial differences in people," he also felt that, like the previous books, the story suffers from "shallow characters" and "a thin plot."

Besides the "Earthminds" trilogy, Sargent has written two other novels for teens, *Earthseed* and *Alien Child*. *Earthseed*, which has received a Best Books for Young Adults citation from the American Library Association, is about a cybernetic spaceship that is sent to a distant Earth-like planet with a cargo of genetic material to produce settlers to colonize the new world. A few years before the ship reaches its destination, the crew is born and raised to young adulthood. The story focuses on Zoheret, a fifteen-year-old girl (like all of Sargent's young adult novel protagonists) who, along with her shipmates, must leave the ship and learn how

to survive on the uninhabited planet. According to Antczak, the novel offers a "complex examination of the motives for colonization . . . , and Sargent again focuses on the developing strengths of a young female character who finds herself in a rite of passage."

Alien Child, like *Earthseed*, is another story of human survival, only this time two young people find themselves on an Earth without humans. Long after the human race has wiped itself out through war, two aliens land on Earth and discover a repository of fertilized human eggs. By accident, the aliens activate a computer command that cause two children, Nita and Sven, to be born. Raised separately from one another, the children don't learn of each others existence until years later. After they meet they go out in search of other survivors without success, and Nita is left with the question of whether or not to take the other eggs out of their deep freeze and restore a race that very well might repeat the mistakes of the past. Although many books before *Alien Child* have been set in post-apocalyptic worlds, critics found Sargent's approach to be fresh and intriguing. A *Publishers Weekly* contributor, for example, called it a "finely crafted work" and an "honest and compelling examination" of humanity's potential for destruction. Marijo Grimes attested in *Voice of Youth Advocates* that what could have been a trite story "becomes an engaging narrative through Sargent's capable hands." Instead of creating just another survival story, Sargent offers an "invigorating . . . story probing the human flaws which could cause such a disaster."

Career Struggles

In 1982 Sargent's career reached a crisis point. "Except for Harper and Row and my editor there, Antonia Markiet, who bought my young adult novels," Sargent recounted in *CAAS*, "I had no science-fiction publisher, and the remaining editors in the field seemed uninterested in my work. I would have to start all over again." In addition, Sargent had to face the tragedy of her father's serious illness, which led to his death in 1983. Before he passed away, however, Sargent received the news that Bantam Books had agreed to buy *Venus of Dreams*, as well as two sequels. The "Venus" books concern a group of women colonists who set out to terraform Venus and must struggle to resist Earth's tyrannical patriarchal system.

The same year that *Venus of Dreams* was published, *The Shore of Women* was also released. "Without question," according to Thomas J. Morrissey in *Twentieth-Century Science Fiction Writers*, "Sargent's masterpiece . . . is *The Shore of Women*." Set in another post-apocalyptic world, the

---

If you enjoy the works of Pamela Sargent, you may also want to check out the following books:

Octavia Butler, *Dawn: Xenogenesis*, 1987; *Adulthood Rites*, 1988; *Imago*, 1989 ("Xenogenesis" series).
Ursula K. Le Guin, *The Left Hand of Darkness*, 1969.
Robert C. O'Brien, *Z for Zachariah*, 1975.
David R. Palmer, *Emergence*, 1984.
Alexei Panshin, *Rite of Passage*, 1968.

---

novel describes a society in which women and men are separated into two distinct civilizations and women become pregnant only through artificial insemination. With this premise in place, Sargent then explores the nature of sexual relationships. "Both same and opposite sex liaisons are celebrated, as individuals, couples, and friends struggle to establish loving relationships in a world in which woman-made institutions are as corrupt as the man-made institutions of our own," wrote Morrissey. "The novel's multiple narrative perspectives, lyrical eroticism, and intellectual depth should make it a classic of intelligent SF."

By 1992, however, Sargent's career was in trouble again. Her editor at Bantam decided not to publish her third volume in the "Venus" trilogy, and she was having little luck with other publishers. "It didn't seem to matter that my books had all done pretty well and that I had been encouraged to believe that I had a future at Bantam," Sargent wrote in *CAAS*. "Downsizing had come to publishing, and if that meant breaking contracts, dumping writers unceremoniously, and destroying what is left of the traditional author/editor relationship, so be it. We live in a more brutal world these days." Ironically, Sargent won a Nebula Award, LOCUS Award, and received a Hugo Award nomination for her novelette "Danny Goes to Mars" just after getting the boot from her publisher.

Just like her days in school, Sargent's writing career has seen a series of ups and downs, and, as Morrissey noted, her books have "a hard time staying in print." Nevertheless, her work has made a significant contribution to the science fiction genre, especially with regard to its promotion of women in the genre, both as writers and as strong fictional characters. As Rubens asserted, "What Sargent does is to depict a world in which human potential can be realized by anyone. However, woman, in her empathic state, cuts through to truth, to new realities, new possibilities." As for her novels for teens, Sargent, according to Morrissey, displays "a refreshing faith in the energy, flexibility, and hopefulness of youth."

■ Works Cited

Review of *Alien Child, Publishers Weekly*, January 15, 1988, p. 98.
Antczak, Janice, "Pamela Sargent," *Twentieth-Century Young Adult Writers*, St. James Press, 1994, pp. 576-77.
Grimes, Marijo, review of *Alien Child, Voice of Youth Advocates*, August, 1988, pp. 140-41.
Morrissey, Thomas J., "Pamela Sargent," *Twentieth-Century Science Fiction Writers*, 3rd edition, St. James Press, 1991, pp. 689-91.
Rubens, Philip M., "Pamela Sargent," *Dictionary of Literary Biography*, Volume 8: *Twentieth-Century American Science Fiction Writers*, Gale, 1981, pp. 96-99.
Sargent, Pamela, in *The Sixth Book of Junior Authors and Illustrators*, H. W. Wilson, 1989, pp. 262-64.
Sargent, Pamela, in *Contemporary Authors Autobiography Series*, Volume 18, Gale, 1994, pp. 327-47.
Smythers, Lyle Blake, review of *Homesmind, School Library Journal*, January, 1985, p. 88.
Taylor, Rebecca Sue, review of *Homesmind, Voice of Youth Advocates*, February, 1985, p. 339.

■ For More Information See

BOOKS

Chevalier, Tracy, editor, *Twentieth-Century Children's Writers*, 3rd edition, St. James Press, 1989.
Elliot, Jeffrey M., *The Work of Pamela Sargent: An Annotated Bibliography and Guide*, Borgo Press, 1990.

Gallo, Donald R., editor, *Speaking for Ourselves Too,* National Council of Teachers of English, 1993.

PERIODICALS

Library Journal, December, 1992, p. 188.
New York Times Book Review, January 18, 1987, p. 33; February 26, 1989, p. 32.
Publishers Weekly, November 4, 1988, p. 75; October 12, 1992, p. 64; June 19, 1995, p. 55.
School Library Journal, April, 1988, p. 113.*

—*Sketch by Janet L. Hile*

Anne Tyler

to the librarian, 1964-65. *Member:* PEN, American Academy and Institute of Arts and Letters, Authors Guild, Phi Beta Kappa.

■ Personal

Born October 25, 1941, in Minneapolis, MN; daughter of Lloyd Parry (a chemist) and Phyllis (a social worker; maiden name, Mahon) Tyler; married Taghi Mohammed Modarressi (a psychiatrist and writer), May 3, 1963; children: Tezh, Mitra (daughters). *Education:* Duke University, B.A., 1961; graduate study at Columbia University, 1961-62. *Religion:* Quaker.

■ Addresses

Home—222 Tunbridge Rd., Baltimore, MD 21212. *Agent*—Russell & Volkening, 50 West 29th St., New York, NY 10001.

■ Career

Writer. Duke University Library, Durham, NC, Russian bibliographer, 1962-63; McGill University Law Library, Montreal, Quebec, Canada, assistant

■ Awards

Mademoiselle award for writing, 1966; Award for Literature, American Academy and Institute of Arts and Letters, 1977; National Book Critics Circle Award nomination in fiction, 1980, Janet Heidinger Kafka prize, 1981, and American Book Award nomination in paperback fiction, 1982, all for *Morgan's Passing*; National Book Critics Circle Award nomination in fiction, 1982, and American Book Award nomination in fiction, PEN/Faulkner Award for fiction, and Pulitzer Prize nomination in fiction, all 1983, all for *Dinner at the Homesick Restaurant*; National Book Critics Circle Award for fiction and Pulitzer Prize nomination for fiction, both 1985, both for *The Accidental Tourist*; Pulitzer Prize for fiction, and National Book Award nomination for fiction, both 1989, both for *Breathing Lessons*.

■ Writings

If Morning Ever Comes, Knopf, 1964.
The Tin Can Tree, Knopf, 1965.
A Slipping-Down Life, Knopf, 1970.
The Clock Winder, Knopf, 1972.

Celestial Navigation, Knopf, 1974.
Searching for Caleb, Knopf, 1976.
Earthly Possessions, Knopf, 1977.
Morgan's Passing, Knopf, 1980.
Dinner at the Homesick Restaurant, Knopf, 1982.
(Editor with Shannon Ravenel, and author of introduction) *Best American Short Stories 1983*, Houghton, 1983.
The Accidental Tourist, Knopf, 1985.
Breathing Lessons, Knopf, 1988.
Saint Maybe, Knopf, 1991.
Tumble Tower (for children), illustrated by daughter, Mitra Modarressi, Orchard Books, 1993.
Ladder of Years, Knopf, 1995.
(Editor and author of introduction) *Best of the South* (anthology), Algonquin Books, 1996.

Contributor of short stories to periodicals, including *Saturday Evening Post, New Yorker, Seventeen, Critic, Antioch Review,* and *Southern Review.*

■ Adaptations

The Accidental Tourist was released as a film by Warner Brothers in 1988, starring William Hurt and Geena Davis; *Breathing Lessons* was released as a television film by CBS-TV in 1994, starring James Garner and Joanne Woodward; *The Clock Winder, Morgan's Passing, Breathing Lessons,* and *Saint Maybe* are available on audio tape.

■ Sidelights

"I think of my work as a whole. And really what it seems to me I'm doing is populating a town," Anne Tyler told Marguerite Michaels in an interview for the *New York Times Book Review.* "Pretty soon it's going to be just full of lots of people I've made up. None of the people I write about are people I know. That would be no fun. And it would be very boring to write about me. Even if I led an exciting life, why live it again on paper?"

The people who comprise this ever-growing town of Tyler's imagination are the sort of people that one might meet in everyday life. The characters in her novels and short stories grapple with recognizable issues of contemporary life such as childhood, marriage, parenthood, career, and religion. Critic Caren J. Town noted in *Dictionary of Literary Biography* that "Tyler's popularity rests in part on the apparent ordinariness of her subjects: the power of family, the struggle for personal growth, the accumulation of possessions, and the influence of religion. Yet this ordinariness is not simplicity: she treats each common situation with wry humor and fills each plot with eccentric characters and unconventional developments."

Tyler's body of work has garnered increased respect and recognition from critics over the years. *Dinner at the Homesick Restaurant, Breathing Lessons,* and *The Accidental Tourist* have all received a number of literary awards, and the latter book was made into a critically-acclaimed film. As *New York Times Book Review* contributor Edward Hoagland observed, Tyler is "blessedly prolific and graced with an effortless-seeming talent at describing whole rafts of intricately individualized people." Despite her increased popularity, though, Tyler has managed to retain a measure of privacy in her life. She has repeatedly turned down offers to teach courses, give lectures, or appear on television, and she consents to interviews only occasionally, content to devote her time instead to her writing and her family. As she indicated in one of her infrequent interviews, with Sarah English in *Dictionary of Literary Biography Yearbook,* "my main reason for doing little in public is that it's not what I'm good at—but yes, it also protects my working time. As I get older, I've learned to say 'no' more and more—and I get happier and happier."

Settling in the South

Tyler was born on October 25, 1941, in Minneapolis, Minnesota. Her father, a chemist, and her mother, a social worker, relocated the family on several occasions during Tyler's childhood. Tyler's parents were Quakers, members of a religious faith known for their pacifism. The family, which also included three younger boys, lived in various Quaker communes throughout the Midwest and South before settling in North Carolina for most of her teenage years. "There was nothing very unusual about my family life," Tyler recalled in her interview with English, "but I did spend much of my older childhood and adolescence as a semi-outsider—a Northerner, commune-reared, looking wistfully at large Southern families around

THE *NEW YORK TIMES* BESTSELLER

ANNE

Dinner at the Homesick Restaurant

TYLER

Author of SAINT MAYBE

"BEAUTIFUL...
Funny, heart-hammering, wise...
It is, from start to finish,
superb entertainment."
—THE NEW YORK TIMES

Winner of numerous honors including a 1983 nomination for a Pulitzer Prize in fiction, this tale of family relationships evolves around Pearl Tull's deathbed as her three grown children return to visit her.

me." She grew accustomed to life in the South, however, and the region serves as the setting for nearly all of her fiction.

At the age of sixteen Tyler began attending classes at Duke University in North Carolina. While at Duke she was encouraged to develop her writing ability by Reynolds Price, a novelist who had attended the same high school as Tyler. After receiving a B.A. from Duke in 1961 (and twice winning the school's Anne Flexner creative writing award), Tyler attended Columbia University, where she devoted her time to Russian studies. In 1962 she returned to Duke, where she served as the school's Russian bibliographer. A year later she married Taghi Mohammed Modarressi, an Iranian-born child psychiatrist and novelist.

Tyler's writing career began modestly. She turned out a wave of short stories, but few of them were published. Her first novel-length effort likewise met with rejection at every publishing house she sent it to. She persevered, however, and her first novel, *If Morning Ever Comes*, was published in 1964. As time has passed she has come to disown the work, noting that it was written during the first six months of her marriage, a period during which she was unemployed. Still, this tale of a young man's struggle to determine his obligations to his family after the death of his father received complimentary reviews from a number of critics. *New York Times Book Review* contributor Rollene W. Saal called the novel a "subtle and surprisingly mature story about the lack of communication between human beings, of a man's essential isolation from the world—and especially and more poignantly from his own family." Even reviewers who were critical of the novel's character development and plot movement qualified their judgments by noting that it was a promising effort from the twenty-two-year-old author.

Similar criticisms were leveled at Tyler's second novel, *The Tin Can Tree*, another work that she dismissed later in her career. By the time her third novel, *A Slipping-Down Life*, was published in 1970, Tyler's family had grown to include two infant girls. The book tells the story of a lonely, overweight girl named Evie and her efforts to establish an identity for herself. The action in the novel is triggered by the girl's decision to carve the name of a rock singer onto her forehead with scissors. In a 1980 *Dictionary of Literary Biography* essay, biographer Mary Ellen Brooks commented that *A Slipping-Down Life* "is an accurate depiction of loneliness, failure to communicate, and regrets over decisions that are irreversible—problems with which any age group can identify. Tyler, who describes *A Slipping-Down Life* as one of her most bizarre works, believes that the novel 'is flawed, but represents, for me, a certain brave stepping forth.'"

The addition of the two babies to the Tyler household in Baltimore, though, had an impact on Tyler's writing efforts, which were gaining increased attention with each new novel. Speaking of her daughters, Tyler admitted in her interview with English that "their infancy did interrupt my work for a few years—or made me shift my working time to evening, which is the same as interrupting it since I can't think past 3 p.m. Generally, I cope with interruptions like school vacations, mono, etc., by giving in gracefully—I make no attempt to work under such conditions."

Reviews of Tyler's fourth novel, *The Clock Winder* (1972), were generally favorable, and she followed with *Celestial Navigation* two years later. *Celestial Navigation* studies the life of Jeremy, an artist with an overwhelming fear of open spaces. This fear has relegated him to his studio, and the death of his mother in the novel's opening pages serves to further widen the gulf between Jeremy and the

This funny, touching story of a lonely travel writer who falls surprisingly in love with an animal trainer was awarded the National Book Critics Circle Award for fiction in 1985.

outside world. As the story unfolds he manages to establish a relationship with a boarder named Mary who, unlike him, is cheerful and outgoing. They eventually marry, but Mary's skill at shielding Jeremy from his fears only makes him withdraw further into his shell. "In the end," Brooks remarked, "each returns to his separate life, each still dominated by his innate driving characteristic. Jeremy returns to his life as a reclusive artist in a crumbling dark house while Mary prepares for winter in a run-down shack, knowing that another man will eventually provide for her and her children when her resources run out." Critics cited the complex novel as Tyler's finest to date, pointing to the book's superior plot and character development and skillful use of multiple viewpoints. In her *New York Times Book Review* assessment, contributor Gail Godwin commented that Tyler's characters are "'oddballs,' visionaries, lonely souls, but she has a way of transcribing their peculiarities with such loving wholeness that when we examine them we keep finding more and more pieces of ourselves."

By this time, a critical consensus had emerged that Tyler's style was unique in many ways. *New York Times Book Review* contributor Katha Pollitt explained that it is often difficult to classify Anne Tyler's novels: "They are Southern in their sure sense of family and place but lack the taste for violence and the Gothic that often characterizes self-consciously Southern literature. . . . The current school of feminist-influenced novels seems to have passed her by completely: her women are strong, often stronger than the men in their lives, but solidly grounded in traditional roles." Reviewers such as Pollitt also noted that while Tyler's novels are usually placed in contemporary settings, she rarely comments on contemporary issues or their impact on her characters. As a result, the time frame is often of no consequence to the primary action in the story.

Searching for Caleb was Tyler's next novel. Published in 1976, the book marked a departure for Tyler in that it was a saga that spanned four generations of a single family, the Pecks. Writing in the *New Yorker*, novelist John Updike called *Searching for Caleb* "a lovely novel, funny and lyric and true-seeming, exquisite in its details and ambitious in its design." Updike continued: "Miss Tyler's details pull from our minds recognition of our lives. These Pecks, polite and snide and tame and maddening and resonant, are *our* aunts and uncles." Time and again, Tyler's talent to portray characters that are readily recognizable in the lives of her readers has been touted as a primary reason for her critical success and popularity. In her novels, as in real life, "characters are both burdened with and supported by their families; for Tyler, families are something one simultaneously wants to escape and to create," wrote Town.

Tyler's seventh novel, *Earthly Possessions*, was published in 1977. In this book Tyler tells the story of a woman who is kidnapped during a bungled bank robbery and forced to accompany the robber on his flight from Maryland to Florida. During the journey the woman looks back on her life and takes stock. *Morgan's Passing* was published three years later. The novel, about a family man who assumes a variety of different identities ranging from street priest to French immigrant, was greeted with a mixed although generally favorable response from reviewers. The book was, however, honored with both a National Book Critics Circle fiction award nomination and an American Book Award paperback fiction nomination.

Dinner at the Homesick Restaurant (1982) also was nominated for several awards, including the Pulitzer Prize for fiction, and it received the 1983 PEN/Faulkner Award for fiction. *Dinner at the Homesick Restaurant* is one of Tyler's grimmer accounts of family relationships. Three now-grown children visit their mother, who became embittered and selfish after their father left her, as she rests on her deathbed. As the novel unfolds, the memories and feelings of all four regarding their family are laid bare, but Town remarked that "a novel that in other hands could have become a horrific chronicle of the violent legacy neglectful and cruel parents hand down to their children becomes instead a meditation on the ways people can produce sustaining families instead of reproducing destructive ones." Benjamin DeMott, writing in the *New York Times Book Review,* said that the novel goes "deeper than many living novelists of serious reputation have penetrated, deeper than Miss Tyler herself has gone before. It is a border crossing."

Acclaim for *The Accidental Tourist*

After the success of *Dinner at the Homesick Restaurant,* Tyler published another novel that received a similarly enthusiastic reception. *The Ac-*

THE *NEW YORK TIMES* BESTSELLER
WINNER OF THE PULITZER PRIZE
ANNE TYLER
Author of *LADDER OF YEARS*

BREATHING LESSONS

"More powerful and moving than anything she has done."
—*Los Angeles Times*

Tyler's eleventh novel, awarded the Pulitzer Prize for fiction in 1989, features the Morans, an ordinary middle–aged couple who, despite widely differing personalities, exemplify what makes some marriages last.

cidental Tourist (1985) examines the life of Macon Leary, a travel writer who puts together guidebooks for reluctant travelers who must do so for business or personal reasons. Macon is a cautious, methodical sort of man who separated from his wife after their twelve-year-old son was murdered. He retreats to live with his sister and two brothers, who also view interaction with the outside world with reluctance. Only after becoming involved with Muriel, an animated, vivacious animal trainer, does Macon begin to emerge from his "accidental tourist cocoon," as Tracy Chevalier wrote in *Contemporary Novelists*, "and finally he has to choose between old ways and new." Rejuvenated by the passion and exuberance that

Muriel injects into his life, Macon charts a new course for himself.

Chevalier remarked that "*The Accidental Tourist* should silence critics who have said Tyler's characters tend to end up where they started from without developing," while *Los Angeles Times Book Review* critic Richard Eder praised Tyler's development of sympathetic characters, commenting that Macon is a very odd man, "yet we grow so close to him that there is not the slightest warp in the lucid, touching and very funny story of an inhibited man moving out into life." *Chicago Tribune Book World* contributor John Blades cast a dissenting opinion, speculating whether "Tyler, with her sedative resolutions to life's most grievous and perplexing problems, can be taken seriously as a writer." Most reviewers, though, registered enthusiastic approval for the book, and it was awarded the National Book Critics Circle Award for fiction in 1985. In 1988 a film version of the novel was released. Starring William Hurt, Geena Davis, and Kathleen Turner, the movie received a number of Oscar nominations, and Davis brought home a Best Supporting Actress Award for her performance as Muriel.

Breathing Lessons, Tyler's eleventh novel, was awarded the Pulitzer Prize for fiction in 1989. Its main characters are Ira and Maggie Moran, a middle-aged couple who continue to love each other despite their very different personalities. The novel begins as the Morans embark on a trip to the funeral of a high school friend, then "moves effortlessly between the present trip to the funeral, the past of Maggie's courtship and marriage to Ira, the recent past of the breakup of her son's marriage, and the future of his former wife and Maggie's grandchild as Maggie tries to combine them all into some meaningful whole," said Town.

Novelist Wallace Stegner, writing in the *Washington Post Book World*, remarked that "Maggie Moran, who dominates the new novel, is a purely Anne Tyler creation. . . . Even while we wonder how her husband Ira has put up with Maggie for twenty-eight years, we understand why the marriage has lasted, and will. Maggie's deviousness, underlain by emotional purposes as inexorable as heat-seeking missiles, is a form of innocence." Several reviewers remarked on Tyler's skill in making her ordinary characters both familiar and interesting, with humor but not condescension. *Chicago Tribune Books* contributor Hilma Wolitzer

commented that *Breathing Lessons* "is Anne Tyler's gentlest and most charming novel and a paean to what is fast becoming a phenomenon—lasting marriage. . . . This is an honest and lovely book."

If you enjoy the works of Anne Tyler, you may also want to check out the following books and films:

Jane Austen (one of Tyler's favorites), *Sense and Sensibility*, 1811 (adapted for film, 1995), and *Pride and Prejudice*, 1813.

Alice Hoffmann, *Illumination Night*, 1987.

Flannery O'Connor, *A Good Man Is Hard to Find* (short stories), 1955.

John Updike, *Rabbit Is Rich*, 1981, and *Rabbit at Rest*, 1991.

Eudora Welty (another Tyler favorite), *The Optimist's Daughter*, 1972.

Avalon, Tri-Star, 1990.

The Member of the Wedding (based on Carson McCullers's 1946 novel), Columbia, 1952.

In 1992 Tyler published *Saint Maybe*, her twelfth novel, a work concerned with the subject of religion: "All I knew at the start was that I wondered what it must feel like to be a born-again Christian, since that is a kind of life very different from mine," she told Patricia Rowe Willrich in an *Virginia Quarterly* interview. The story centers on the Bedlows, a middle-class American family leading a prosperous existence. Ian Bedlow's life is turned upside-down, however, after his older brother Danny arrives at the house with his fiancee Lucy and her kids from an earlier marriage. As time passes, Ian comes to suspect that their newborn child, Daphne, may not be his brother's. His decision to reveal his suspicions ultimately triggers the deaths of Danny and Lucy. Ian thus becomes responsible for caring for the orphaned children, leading him to seek forgiveness in the "Church of the Second Chance." Ian is similar to many of Tyler's other characters, according to Town, for they "hope, early or later in life, to escape from the burdens and responsibilities of their families, but they find they are not trapped, and they learn that they do not really want to escape."

Ladder of Years was greeted with critical accolades upon its publication in 1995. Tyler's Delia

Grinstead, the novel's central character, is a woman on the cusp of middle age who views herself as a "sad, tired, anxious forty-year-old woman who hadn't had a champagne brunch in decades." She impulsively leaves her self-absorbed family and sets out to create a new life for herself in a strange community. Delia enjoys some triumphs but, as *Times Literary Supplement* contributor Joyce Carol Oates observed, "though the reader is solidly on Delia's side, hoping that so sweet-natured, decent and un-appreciated a woman can establish a new, it soon becomes clear that Delia isn't up to it. She lacks the inner resources, professional training and spirit to make the transition." While Oates called *Ladder of Years* a "poignant work," she added that it paints "a bleak vision somewhat at odds with the affable tone of Anne Tyler's prose and the insistent curve of her narrative towards marital accord." *Booklist* critic Donna Seaman, however, called the work a "charming, often hilarious, and astute novel. Tyler is in top form here. Her seemingly effortless prose is, like silk, rich in subtle hues and sheeny with dancing light."

Yet another milestone in a long and celebrated career, *Ladder of Years* offers further proof that the author remains a writer with "a sympathetic, forgiving eye for the textures of ordinary life," according to Oates. As Brooks observed, Anne Tyler's "work has evolved from the simple storytelling of the early novels into the carefully crafted, eloquent novels of her later career." Town agreed, concluding that "after thirty years of writing novels Tyler continues to concentrate on the family—with insight, humor, and hope."

■ Works Cited

Blades, John, review of *The Accidental Tourist, Chicago Tribune Book World*, July 20, 1986.

Brooks, Mary Ellen, "Anne Tyler," *Dictionary of Literary Biography*, Volume 6: *American Novelists Since World War II, Second Series*, Gale, 1980, pp. 336-45.

Chevalier, Tracy, "Anne Tyler," *Contemporary Novelists*, 5th edition, St. James Press, 1991, pp. 891-93.

DeMott, Benjamin, "Funny, Wise, and True," *New York Times Book Review*, March 14, 1982, pp. 1, 14.

Eder, Richard, review of *The Accidental Tourist, Los Angeles Times Book Review*, September 15, 1985, p. 3.

English, Sarah, "Anne Tyler," *Dictionary of Literary Biography Yearbook: 1982*, Gale, 1982, pp. 187-94.

Godwin, Gail, review of *Celestial Navigation, New York Times Book Review*, April 28, 1974, pp. 34-35.

Hoagland, Edward, "About Maggie, Who Tried Too Hard," *New York Times Book Review*, September 11, 1988, pp. 1, 43-44.

Michaels, Marguerite, "Anne Tyler, Writer 8:05 to 3:30," *New York Times Book Review*, May 8, 1977, pp. 42-43.

Oates, Joyce Carol, "Time to Say Goodbye," *Times Literary Supplement*, May 5, 1995, p. 22.

Pollitt, Katha, review of *Searching for Caleb, New York Times Book Review*, January 18, 1976, p. 22.

Saal, Rollene W., "Loveless Household," *New York Times Book Review*, November 22, 1964, p. 52.

Seaman, Donna, review of *Ladder of Years, Booklist*, March 15, 1995, p. 1284.

Stegner, Wallace, review of *Breathing Lessons, Washington Post Book World*, September 4, 1988. p. 1.

Town, Caren J., "Anne Tyler," *Dictionary of Literary Biography*, Volume 143: *American Novelists Since World War II, Third Series*, Gale, 1994, pp. 232-49.

Updike, John, review of *Searching for Caleb, New Yorker*, March 29, 1976, pp. 110-12.

Willrich, Patricia Rowe, "Watching through Windows: A Perspective on Anne Tyler," *Virginia Quarterly*, summer, 1992, pp. 497-516.

Wolitzer, Hilma, "'Breathing Lessons': Anne Tyler's Tender Ode to Married Life," *Tribune Books* (Chicago), August 28, 1988, pp. 1, 9.

■ For More Information See

BOOKS

Croft, Robert William, *Anne Tyler: A Bio-bibliography*, Greenwood Press, 1995.

Evans, Elizabeth, *Anne Tyler*, Twayne, 1993.

Petry, Alice Hall, *Understanding Anne Tyler*, University of South Carolina Press, 1990.

Petry, Alice Hall, editor, *Critical Essays on Anne Tyler*, G. K. Hall, 1992.

Salwak, Dale, editor, *Anne Tyler as Novelist*, University of Iowa Press, 1994.

Stephens, C. Ralph, editor, *The Fiction of Anne Tyler*, University Press of Mississippi, 1990.

Voelker, Joseph C., *Art and the Accidental in Anne Tyler*, University of Missouri Press, 1989.

PERIODICALS

Atlantic Monthly, March, 1976.

Chicago Tribune Book World, March 21, 1982.

Los Angeles Times Book Review, September 11, 1988, p. 3; September 8, 1991, p. 3; May 7, 1995, pp. 3, 16.

National Observer, July 22, 1972, p. 23.

New Leader, November 28, 1988, pp. 19-21.

New York Review of Books, November 10, 1988, pp. 40-41.

New York Times, December 23, 1965, p. L25; August 28, 1985, p. 21; September 3, 1988, p. 14; August 30, 1991, p. C21.

New York Times Book Review, December 5, 1982; September 8, 1985, p. 1; August 25, 1991, p. 1; May 7, 1995, p. 12.

Time, April 5, 1982, pp. 77-78; May 15, 1995, p. 80.

Times Literary Supplement, October 4, 1985, p. 1096; January 20, 1989, p. 57; September 27, 1991, p. 24.

Village Voice, March 30, 1982, pp. 40-41.

Washington Post Book World, August 25, 1985, p. 3; August 18, 1991, p. 1.

—Sketch by Kevin Hillstrom

H.G. Wells

■ Personal

Full name Herbert George Wells; also wrote as Reginald Bliss, Walter Glockenhammer, Sosthenes Smith, and D. P.; born September 21, 1866, in Bromley, England; died August 13, 1946, in London, England; cremated and ashes scattered over English Channel; son of Joseph (a gardener, cricketer, and shopkeeper) and Sarah (a housekeeper; maiden name, Neal) Wells; married Isabel Mary Wells, October 31, 1891 (divorced, January, 1895); married Amy Catherine Robbins (a writer), October 27, 1895 (died, 1927); children: (second marriage) George Philip, Frank Richard; (with Amber Reeves) Anna-Jane White; (with Rebecca West) Anthony West. *Education:* Attended Normal School of Science (now Imperial College of Science and Technology), 1884-87; University of London, B.S. (with honours), c. 1889, D.Sc., 1943. *Politics:* Liberal democrat.

■ Career

Rodgers & Deyner, Windsor, England, apprentice draper, 1880; pupil-teacher at school in Wookey, England, 1880; apprentice pharmacist in Midhurst, England, 1880-81; Hyde's Southsea Drapery Emporium, Hampshire, England, apprentice draper, 1881-83; student-assistant at grammar school in Midhurst, 1883-84; teacher at schools in Wrexham, Wales, 1887-88, and London, England, 1889; University Correspondence College, London, tutor, 1890-93; writer, 1893-1946. *Wartime service:* Member of Research Committee for the League of Nations, 1917; affiliated with British Ministry of Information, 1918; director of Policy Committee for Propaganda in Enemy Countries, 1918. *Member:* International PEN (international president, 1934-46), British Association for the Advancement of Science (president of educational science section, 1937), British Diabetic Association (founding president), Abortion Law Reform Society (vice-president, 1936), Film Society (co-founder), Savile Club.

■ Awards, Honors

D.Litt. from University of London, 1936; honorary fellow of Imperial College of Science and Technology.

■ Writings

NOVELS

The Time Machine: An Invention (science fiction; first published in *Science Schools Journal* as "The Chronic Argonauts," 1888), Holt, 1895.

The Wonderful Visit (science fiction), Macmillan, 1895.

The Wheels of Chance: A Bicycling Idyll (first published serially in *Today*, 1896), illustrations by J. Ayton Symington, Macmillan, 1896, published as *The Wheels of Chance: A Holiday Adventure*, Dent, 1896.

The Island of Doctor Moreau: A Possibility (science fiction), Stone & Kimball, 1896.

The Invisible Man: A Grotesque Romance (science fiction; first published serially in *Pearson's Weekly*, June-July, 1897), Arnold, 1897, published as *The Invisible Man: A Fantastic Sensation*, Robert Bentley, 1981.

The War of the Worlds (science fiction; first published serially in *Pearson's Magazine*, April-December, 1897), Harper & Brothers, 1898.

When the Sleeper Wakes (science fiction; first published serially in *The Graphic*, 1898-99), Harper & Brothers, 1899, revised as *The Sleeper Awakes*, Thomas Nelson, 1910.

Love and Mr. Lewisham: The Story of a Very Young Couple, George H. Doran, 1899.

The First Men in the Moon (science fiction; first published serially in *Strand Magazine*, December, 1900-August, 1901), Bowen-Merrill, 1901.

The Sea Lady (first published serially in *Pearson's Magazine*, July-December, 1901), D. Appleton, 1902 (published in England as *The Sea Lady: A Tissue of Moonshine*, Methuen, 1902).

The Food of the Gods, and How It Came to Earth (science fiction; first published serially in *Pearson's Magazine*, December, 1903-June, 1904), Scribner, 1904.

A Modern Utopia (first published serially in *Fortnightly Review*, October, 1904-April, 1905), illustrations by E. J. Sullivan, Scribner, 1905.

Kipps: A Monograph (first published serially in *Pall Mall*, 1905), Scribner, 1905, published as *Kipps: The Story of a Simple Soul*, 1905.

In the Days of the Comet (science fiction; first published serially in *Daily Chronicle*, 1905-06), Century, 1906.

The War in the Air, and Particularly How Mr. Bert Smallways Fared While It Lasted (first published serially in *Pall Mall*), Macmillan, 1908.

Tono-Bungay, Duffield, 1908.

Ann Veronica: A Modern Love Story, Harper & Brothers, 1909.

The History of Mr. Polly, Duffield, 1909.

The New Machiavelli (first published serially in *English Review*, May-October, 1910), Duffield, 1910.

Marriage, Duffield, 1912.

The Passionate Friends: A Novel (first published serially in *Grand Magazine*, March-November, 1913), Harper & Brothers, 1913.

The Wife of Sir Isaac Harman, Macmillan, 1914.

The World Set Free: A Story of Mankind (science fiction; first published serially in *English Review*, December, 1913-May, 1914), E. P. Dutton, 1914.

Bealby: A Holiday (first published serially in *Grand Magazine*, August, 1914-March, 1915), Macmillan, 1915.

(Under name Reginald Bliss) *Boon, The Mind of the Race, The Wild Asses of the Devil, and The Last Trump: Being a First Selection From the Literary Remains of George Boon, Appropriate to the Times, Prepared for Publication by Reginald Bliss With an Ambiguous Introduction by H. G. Wells*, George H. Doran, 1915, published under name H. G. Wells, Unwin, 1920.

The Research Magnificent, Macmillan, 1915.

Mr. Britling Sees It Through (first published serially in *Nation*, May-October, 1916), Macmillan, 1916.

The Soul of a Bishop (first published serially in *Collier's Weekly*, 1917), Macmillan, 1917 (published in England as *The Soul of a Bishop: A Novel—With Just a Little Love in It—About Conscience and Religion and the Real Troubles of Life*, Cassell, 1917).

Joan and Peter: The Story of an Education, Macmillan, 1918.

The Undying Fire: A Contemporary Novel (first published serially in *International Review*, March-June, 1919), Macmillan, 1919.

The Secret Places of the Heart (first published serially in *Nash's* and *Pall Mall*, December, 1921-July, 1922), Macmillan, 1922.

Men Like Gods: A Novel (science fiction; first published serially in *Westminster Gazette*, December, 1922-February, 1923), Macmillan, 1923.

The Dream: A Novel (first published serially in *Nash's* and *Pall Mall*, October, 1923-May, 1924), Macmillan, 1924.

Christina Alberta's Father, Macmillan, 1925.

The World of William Clissold: A Novel at a New Angle, George H. Doran, 1926.

Meanwhile: The Picture of a Lady, George H. Doran, 1927.

Mr. Blettsworthy on Rampole Island, Doubleday, Doran, 1928.

The King Who Was a King: An Unconventional Novel, Doubleday, Doran, 1929 (published in England as *The King Who Was a King: The Book of a Film*, E. Benn, 1929).

The Autocracy of Mr. Parham: His Remarkable Adventures in This Changing World, Doubleday, Doran, 1930.

The Bulpington of Blup: Adventures, Poses, Stresses, Conflicts, and Disaster in a Contemporary Brain, Hutchinson, 1932, Macmillan, 1933.

The Shape of Things to Come: The Ultimate Revolution, Macmillan, 1933.

The Croquet Player, Chatto & Windus, 1936, Viking, 1937.

Star-Begotten: A Biological Fantasia (science fiction), Viking, 1937.

Brynhild; or, The Show of Things, Scribner, 1937 (published in England as *Brynhild*, Methuen, 1937).

The Camford Visitation, Methuen, 1937.

Apropos of Dolores, Scribner, 1938.

The Brothers: A Story, Viking, 1938.

The Holy Terror, Simon & Schuster, 1939.

Babes in the Darkling Wood, Alliance Book, 1940.

All Aboard for Ararat (science fiction), Secker & Warburg, 1940, Alliance Book, 1941.

You Can't Be Too Careful: A Sample of Life, 1901-1951, Secker & Warburg, 1941, G. P. Putnam's Sons, 1942.

The Wealth of Mr. Waddy: A Novel (early draft of *Kipps*), edited with introduction by Harris Wilson, preface by Harry T. Moore, Southern Illinois University Press, 1969.

A Story of the Days to Come (science fiction), Corgi, 1976.

SHORT STORIES

Select Conversations With an Uncle, Now Extinct, and Two Other Reminiscences, Merriam, 1895.

The Stolen Bacillus and Other Incidents (science fiction), Methuen, 1895.

The Red Room, Stone & Kimball, 1896.

A Perfect Gentleman on Wheels (first published as "A Perfect Gentleman on Wheels; or, The Humours of Cycling" in *Woman at Home*, April, 1897), published in *The Humours of Cycling*, James Bowden, 1897.

Thirty Strange Stories (science fiction), Arnold, 1897.

The Plattner Story, and Others (science fiction), Methuen, 1897.

A Cure for Love, E. Scott, 1899.

Tales of Space and Time (science fiction), Doubleday & McClure, 1899.

The Vacant Country, A. E. Kent, 1899.

Twelve Stories and a Dream (science fiction), Macmillan, 1903.

The Door in the Wall, and Other Stories (science fiction), M. Kennerley, 1911.

The Country of the Blind, and Other Stories (science fiction), Thomas Nelson, 1911.

The Star (in simplified spelling), Sir Isaac Pitman & Sons, 1913.

The Country of the Blind (science fiction), privately printed, 1915, Golden Cockerel Press, 1939.

The Short Stories of H. G. Wells (science fiction), E. Benn, 1927, Doubleday, Doran, 1929, published as *The Complete Short Stories of H. G. Wells*, E. Benn, 1966, St. Martin's, 1970.

The Adventures of Tommy (for children), self-illustrated, Frederick A. Stokes, 1929.

The Valley of Spiders, London Book, 1930.

The Stolen Body, and Other Tales of the Unexpected, London Book, 1931.

The Favorite Short Stories of H. G. Wells, Doubleday, Doran, 1937, published as *The Famous Short Stories of H. G. Wells*, Garden City Publishing, 1938.

Short Stories by H. G. Wells, notes and questions by A. J. J. Ratcliff, T. Nelson, 1940.

The Land Ironclads, Todd Publishing, 1943.

The New Accelerator (science fiction), Todd Publishing, 1943.

The Empire of the Ants, Todd Publishing, 1943.

The Inexperienced Ghost, Todd Publishing, 1943.

The Truth About Pyecraft, and Other Short Stories, Todd Publishing, 1943.

The Inexperienced Ghost and The New Accelerator, Vallancey Press, 1944.

Twenty-eight Science Fiction Stories, Dover, 1952.

Seven Stories, Oxford University Press, 1953.

Tales of Life and Adventure, introduction by Frank Wells, Collins, 1953.

Tales of the Unexpected, introduction by Frank Wells, Collins, 1954.

Tales of Wonder, introduction by Frank Wells, Collins, 1954.

The Desert Daisy (for children), introduction by Gordon N. Ray, Beta Phi Mu, 1957.

Selected Short Stories, Penguin Books, 1958.

The Inexperienced Ghost, and Nine Other Stories, Bantam, 1965.

Best Science Fiction Stories of H. G. Wells, Dover, 1966.

The Man With a Nose: And the Other Uncollected Short Stories of H. G. Wells, edited with an introduction by J. R. Hammond, Athlone Press, 1984.

NONFICTION

Text-Book of Biology, two volumes, introduction by G. B. Howes, W. B. Clive, Volume I, 1892, Volume II, 1893, revision by A. M. Davies published as *Text-Book of Zoology*, 1898, 7th edition, revised and rewritten by J. T. Cunningham and W. H. Leigh-Sharpe, 1929.

(With R. A. Gregory) *Honours Physiography*, Joseph Hughes, 1893.

Certain Personal Matters: A Collection of Material, Mainly Autobiographical, Lawrence & Bullen, 1898.

Anticipations of the Reaction of Mechanical and Scientific Progress Upon Human Life and Thought (first published serially as "Anticipations: An Experiment in Prophecy" in *Fortnightly Review*, April-December, 1901), Harper & Brothers, 1902, with new introduction, Chapman & Hall, 1914.

Mankind in the Making (first published serially in *Fortnightly Review*, September, 1902-September, 1903), Chapman & Hall, 1903, Scribner, 1904, with new introduction, Chapman & Hall, 1914.

The Future in America: A Search After Realities (first published serially in *Harper's Weekly*, July 14-October 6, 1906), Harper & Brothers, 1906.

First and Last Things: A Confession of Faith and a Rule of Life, G. P. Putnam's Sons, 1908, definitive edition, Watts, 1929.

New Worlds for Old, Macmillan, 1908, revised edition, Constable, 1914.

Floor Games (for children; first published in *Strand Magazine*, December, 1911), self-illustrated, Frank Palmer, 1911, Small, Maynard, 1912.

(Editor with G. R. S. Taylor and Frances Evelyn Warwick, and contributor) *The Great State: Essays in Construction* (first published as "Socialism and the Great State" in *Harper's*, 1911), Harper & Brothers, 1912, published as *Socialism and the Great State: Essays in Construction*, 1914.

Little Wars: A Game for Boys From Twelve Years of Age to One Hundred and Fifty and for That More Intelligent Sort of Girls Who Like Boys' Games and Books, with an Appendix on Kriegspiel (first published serially in *Windsor Magazine*, December, 1912, and January, 1913), Small, Maynard, 1913.

Social Forces in England and America (essays), Harper & Brothers, 1914 (published in England as *An Englishman Looks at the World: Being a Series of Unrestrained Remarks Upon Contemporary Matters*, Cassell, 1914).

The War That Will End War (essays), Duffield, 1914.

The War and Socialism, Clarion Press, 1915.

What Is Coming? A European Forecast, Macmillan, 1916 (published in England as *What Is Coming? A Forecast of Things After the War*, Cassell, 1916).

Introduction to Nocturne, G. H. Doran, 1917.

God, the Invisible King, Macmillan, 1917.

Italy, France, and Britain at War, Macmillan, 1917 (published in England as *War and the Future: Italy, France, and Britain at War*, Cassell, 1917).

In the Fourth Year: Anticipations of a World Peace, Macmillan, 1918 (abridged edition published in England as *Anticipations of a World Peace*, Chatto & Windus, 1918).

(With Viscount Grey, Lionel Curtis, William Archer, H. Wickham Steed, A. E. Zimmern, J. A. Spender, Viscount Bryce, and Gilbert Murray) *The Idea of a League of Nations: Prolegomena to the Study of World-Organisation*, Atlantic Monthly Press, 1919.

(With Viscount Grey, Gilbert Murray, J. A. Spender, A. E. Zimmern, H. Wickham Steed, Lionel Curtis, William Archer, Ernest Barker, G. Lowes Dickinson, John Hilton, and L. S. Woolf) *The Way to the League of Nations: A Brief Sketch of the Practical Steps Needed for the Formation of a League*, Oxford University Press, 1919.

(With Arnold Bennett and Grant Overton) *Frank Swinnerton: Personal Sketches; Together With Notes and Comments on the Novels of Frank Swinnerton*, G. H. Doran, 1920.

(With advice and editorial help of Ernest Barker, H. H. Johnston, E. Ray Lankester, and Gilbert Murray) *The Outline of History: Being a Plain History of Life and Mankind*, illustrations by J. F. Horrabin, Macmillan, 1920, published as *The New and Revised Outline of History: Being a Plain History of Life and Mankind*, Garden City Publishing, 1931, published as *The Enlarged and Revised Outline of History: Being a Plain History of Life and Mankind*, Triangle Books, 1940, under original title revised and brought up to the end of World War II by Raymond Postdate, Garden City Publishing, 1949, published as *The Outline of History: Being a Plain History of Life and Mankind From Primordial Life to Nineteen-sixty*, Cassell, 1961, under original title revised and brought up to date by Postdate and G. P. Wells, Doubleday, 1971.

Russia in the Shadows (first published serially in *Sunday Express*, October 31-November 28, 1920), Holder & Stoughton, 1920, George H. Dolan, 1921.

The Salvaging of Civilization: The Probable Future of Mankind, Macmillian, 1921.

A Short History of the World, Macmillian, 1922.

Washington and the Riddle of Peace (first published in *New York World*, November-December, 1921), Macmillian, 1922 (published in England as *Washington and the Hope of Peace*, Collins, 1922).

The Story of a Great Schoolmaster: Being a Plain Account of the Life and Ideas of Anderson of Into. (biography; first published serially in *New Leader*, September 14-October 26, 1923), Macmillian, 1924.

A Year of Prophesying (articles), Unpin, 1924, Macmillian, 1925.

A Short History of Mankind, adapted from *A Short History of the World* by E. H. Carter, Macmillian, 1925.

Mr. Bello Objects to "The Outline of History," George H. Dolan, 1926.

Wells' Social Anticipations, edited with introduction by Harry W. Ladler, Vanguard Press, 1927.

(Editor and author of introduction) *The Book of Catherine Wells,* Chatty & Winds, 1928.

The Way the World Is Going: Guesses and Forecasts of the Years Ahead; Twenty-six Articles and a Lecture, E. Been, 1928, Double day, Dolan, 1929.

The Open Conspiracy: Blue Prints for a World Revolution, Double day, Dolan, 1928, published as *The Open Conspiracy: Blue Prints for a World Revolution; a Second Version of This Faith of a Modern Man Made More Explicit and Plain,* Hogarth Press, 1930, revised edition published as *What Are We to Do With Our Lives?,* Double day, Dolan, 1931, published as *The Open Conspiracy,* Gordon Press, 1979.

(With Bertrand Russell, Fannie Hurst, Theodore Dreiser, Warwick Deeping, Rebecca West, Andre Maurois, and Lionel Feuchtwanger) *Divorce as I See It,* Douglas, 1930.

(With G. Lowes Dickinson, Dean Inge, J. B. S. Haldane, Sir Oliver Lodge, and Sir Walford Davis) *Points of View: A Series of Broadcast Addresses,* Allen & Unpin, 1930.

(With H. R. Knickerbocker, Sir John Russell, Sir Bernard Pares, Margaret S. Miller, B. Mouat-Jones, Stafford Talbot, and Frank Owen) *The New Russia: Eight Talks Broadcast,* Faber & Faber, 1931.

(With Julian S. Huxley and G. P. Wells) *The Science of Life: A Summary of Contemporary Knowledge About Life and Its Possibilities,* Amalgamated Press, 1930, Double day, Dolan, 1931 (portions published severally as "The Science of Life" series, Double day, Dolan, 1932; various volumes published in England by Cassell, 1937).

Selections From the Early Prose Works of H. G. Wells, University of London Press, 1931.

The Work, Wealth, and Happiness of Mankind, Double day, Dolan, 1931, published as *The Outline of Man's Work and Wealth,* Garden City Publishing, 1936.

After Democracy: Addresses and Papers on the Present World Situation, Watts, 1932.

Experiment in Autobiography: Discoveries and Conclusions of a Very Ordinary Brain (Since 1866), self-illustrated, Macmillian, 1934.

The New America: The New World, Macmillian, 1935.

The Anatomy of Frustration: A Modern Synthesis, Macmillian, 1936.

World Brain (essays and addresses), Double day, Dolan, 1938.

The Fate of Man: An Unemotional Statement of the Things That Are Happening to Him Now, and of the Immediate Possibilities Confronting Him, Longmans, Green, 1939 (published in England as *The Fate of Homo Sapiens: An Unemotional Statement of the Things That Are Happening to Him Now, and of the Immediate Possibilities Confronting Him,* Secker & Warburg, 1939).

Travels of a Republican Radical in Search of Hot Water, Penguin Books, 1939.

The Common Sense of War and Peace: World Revolution or War Unending, Penguin Books, 1940.

H. G. Wells, S. de Madariaga, J. Middleton Murry, C. E. M. Joad on the New World Order, National Peace Council, 1940.

The New World Order: Whether It Is Attainable, How It Can Be Attained, and What Sort of World a World at Peace Will Have to Be, Secker & Warburg, 1939, Knopf, 1940.

The Rights of Man; or, What Are We Fighting For?, Penguin Books, 1940.

Guide to the New World: A Handbook of Constructive World Revolution, Gollancz, 1941.

The Pocket History of the World, Pocket Books, 1941.

Modern Russian and English Revolutionaries: A Frank Exchange of Ideas Between Commander Lev Uspensky, Soviet Writer, and H. G. Wells, privately printed, 1942.

The Conquest of Time (written to replace his *First and Last Things*), Watts, 1942.

The Outlook for Homo Sapiens: An Unemotional Statement of the Things That Are Happening to Him Now, and of the Immediate Possibilities Confronting Him (an amalgamation and modernization of *The Fate of Homo Sapiens and The New World Order*), Secker & Warburg, 1942.

Phoenix: A Summary of the Inescapable Conditions of World Reorganisation, Secker & Warburg, 1942.

Crux Ansata: An Indictment of the Roman Catholic Church, Penguin Books, 1943.

'42 to '44: A Contemporary Memoir Upon Human Behaviour During the Crisis of the World Revolution, Secker & Warburg, 1944.

(With J. S. Huxley and J. B. S. Haldane) *Reshaping Man's Heritage: Biology in the Service of Man*, Allen & Unpin, 1944.

The Happy Turning: A Dream of Life, Heinemann, 1945.

(With Joseph Stalin) *Marxism vs. Liberalism: An Interview*, New Century, 1945, published as *H. G. Wells' Interview With J. V. Stalin (Marxism v. Liberalism)*, Current Book Distributors (Sydney), 1950.

Mind at the End of Its Tether (first published in *Sunday Express*), Heinemann, 1945.

Henry James and H. G. Wells: A Record of Their Friendship, Their Debate on the Art of Fiction, and Their Quarrel (correspondence), edited with introduction by Leon Edel and Gordon N. Ray, University of Illinois Press, 1958.

Arnold Bennett and H. G. Wells: A Record of a Personal and a Literary Friendship (correspondence), edited with introduction by Harris Wilson, University of Illinois Press, 1960.

George Gissing and H. G. Wells: Their Friendship and Correspondence, edited with introduction by Royal A. Gettmann, University of Illinois Press, 1961.

Journalism and Prophecy, 1893-1946: An Anthology (addresses, essays, and lectures), compiled and edited by W. Warren Wagar, Houghton, 1964.

H. G. Wells's Literary Criticism, edited by Patrick Parrinder and Robert M. Philmus, Harvester Press, 1980.

H. G. Wells in Love: Postscript to an Experiment in Autobiography, edited by G. P. Wells, Little, Brown, 1984.

Treasury of H. G. Wells, Octopus Books, 1985.

OTHER

Socialism and the Family (pamphlet; contains "Socialism and the Middle Classes" and "Modern Socialism and the Family"), A. C. Fifield, 1906.

This Misery of Boots (pamphlet; first published in *Independent Review*, December, 1905), Fabian Society, 1907, Ball Publishing, 1908.

The H. G. Wells Calendar: A Quotation From the Works of H. G. Wells for Every Day in the Year, selected by Rosamund Marriott Watson, Frank Palmer, 1911.

Great Thoughts From H. G. Wells, selected by Rosamund Marriott Watson, Dodge, 1912.

Thoughts From H. G. Wells, selected by Elsie E. Morton, Harrap, 1913.

The Works of H. G. Wells: Atlantic Edition, 28 volumes, Scribner, 1924-27.

The Essex Thin-Paper Edition of the Works of H. G. Wells, 24 volumes, E. Been, 1926-27.

Democracy Under Revision: A Lecture Delivered at the Sorbonne, March 15th, 1927 (pamphlet), George H. Dolan, 1927.

Things to Come: A Film Story Based on the Material Contained in His History of the Future "The Shape of Things to Come" (science fiction), Macmillian, 1935.

Man Who Could Work Miracles: A Film by H. G. Wells, Based on the Short Story Entitled "The Man Who Could Work Miracles," Macmillian, 1936 (published in England as *Man Who Could Work Miracles: A Film Story Based on the Material Contained in His Short Story "Man Who Could Work Miracles,"* Cresset Press, 1936).

The H. G. Wells Papers at the University of Illinois, edited by Gordon N. Ray, University of Illinois Press, 1958.

Hoopdriver's Holiday (dramatization of his novel *The Wheels of Chance*), edited with notes and introduction by Michael Timko, English Department, Purdue University, 1964.

H. G. Wells: Early Writings in Science and Science Fiction, edited with critical commentary and notes by Robert M. Philmus and David Y. Hughes, University of California Press, 1975.

H. G. Wells Science Fiction Treasury, Crown, 1987.

Also author of *Two Hemispheres or One World?*, 1940, and many pamphlets. Author of film scripts, including *Bluebottles*, *Daydreams*, and *The Tonic*. Contributor of introductions and prefaces to numerous books.

Work represented in anthologies, including *Thirty-one Stories by Thirty and One Authors*, edited by Ernest Rhys and C. A. Dawson Scott, Butterworth, 1923, and *Masterpieces of Science Fiction*, edited by Sam Moskowitz, World Publishing, 1967.

Contributor of reviews, letters, essays, and stories to periodicals, including *Clarion*, *English Review*, *Fortnightly Review*, *Independent Review*, *Labour Leader*, *London Daily Mail*, *London Times*, *Nation*, *New Age*, *Times Literary Supplement*, and *Saturday Review*.

■ Adaptations

Numerous works by Wells have been adapted as comic books, films, plays, sound recordings, and radio and television productions, including *The*

Shape of Things to Come, adapted as the film "Things to Come," 1936, and *The War of the Worlds,* adapted by Orson Welles and broadcast by Columbia Broadcasting System (CBS-Radio) on October 30, 1938; the broadcast sparked a widespread panic by listeners who thought a real alien invasion had taken place.

■ Sidelights

"The thing the Time Traveller held in his hand was a glittering metallic framework, scarcely larger than a small clock, and very delicately made, There was ivory in it, and some transparent crystalline substance. . . . Then . . . he said, 'Now I want you clearly to understand that this lever, being pressed over, sends the machine gliding into the future, and this other reverses the motion. This saddle represents the seat of a time traveller. Presently I am going to press the lever, and off the machine will go. It will vanish, pass into future Time, and disappear. Have a good look at the thing. Look at the table too, and satisfy yourselves there is no trickery. I don't want to waste this model, and then be told I'm a quack.'. . .

"We all saw the lever turn. I am absolutely certain that there was no trickery. There was a breath of wind, and the lamp flame jumped. One of the candles on the mantel was blown out, and the little machine suddenly swung round, became indistinct, was seen as a ghost for a second perhaps, as an eddy of faintly glimmering brass and ivory; and it was gone—vanished! Save for the lamp the table was bare."

With these chilling words, the British science fiction writer H. G. Wells introduced the Victorian reading public to the potential of the twentieth century in his influential 1895 novel *The Time Machine.* Wells broke new ground in early science fiction with his broad imagination and his social conscience. His works foretold the development of atomic weaponry, and the advent of chemical warfare and global conflicts. They also offer comments on the society of late-Victorian England and the development of twentieth-century socialism. "Wells," stated *Concise Dictionary of British Literary Biography* contributor Michael Draper, "is an author whose achievement is as impossible to ignore as it is difficult to fit into readily assessed categories." "Quite simply," wrote W. Warren Wagar in *Twentieth-Century Science-Fiction Writers,*

"he is to science fiction what Albert Einstein is to modern physics, or Pablo Picasso to modern art."

Although Wells is best remembered today for his early science fiction novels—especially *The Time Machine, The War of the Worlds, The Invisible Man,* and *The Island of Doctor Moreau*—he was also a prolific author of social criticism, journalism, literary criticism, film scripts, and political manifestos. "Over a career that spanned five decades," declared Brian Murray in the *Dictionary of Literary Biography,* "H. G. Wells produced nearly a hundred full-length books, a large portion of them novels and collections of short fiction." His literary output ranged from essays to autobiography, from history to biology—an output that, according to Draper, earned him a reputation as "the most serious of the popular writers and the most popular of the serious writers of his time."

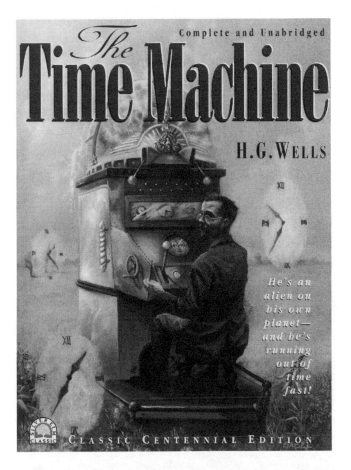

Wells's first and most influential novel, this work of science fiction, initially published in 1895, introduced Victorian readers to the possibilities of the twentieth century.

Herbert George Wells was born in Bromley, Kent, in 1866, the youngest son of lower-middle-class parents. "His father, Joseph Wells, was a celebrated cricket player turned failed shopkeeper," Murray explained. At one time he had also been a gardener—a "service" occupation—in an upper-class household. "All his days," Wells wrote in his *Experiment in Autobiography,* "my father was a happy and appreciative man with a singular distaste for contention or holding his own in the world. He liked to do clever things with his brain and hands and body, but he was bored beyond endurance by the idea of a continual struggle for existence."

Wells's "rather domineering mother, Sarah Neal Wells," Murray continued, "was a housekeeper

This classic account of a scientist who attempted to change animals into humans through surgery roused the ire of critics who called it blasphemous in 1896.

and lady's maid whose fondest dream was that young 'Bertie' and his two older brothers should become respectable tradesmen in service to the upper classes." According to Wells's statements in his *Experiment in Autobiography,* she urged her youngest son to become a draper's apprentice at the age of fourteen, where he was "given so bad a time as to stiffen my naturally indolent, rather slovenly, and far too genial nature into a grim rebellion against the world." An attempt to apprentice the young Wells to a chemist also failed. Finally, "when he was nearly seventeen," Murray declared, "Wells finally convinced his mother that apprentice positions . . . had left him desperately unhappy. She allowed him to enroll as a pupil-tutor at the Midhurst Grammar School, and—two years later—to accept a scholarship at the Normal School of Science in South Kensington."

"I am probably the only completely unsatisfactory student turned out by the Normal School, who did not go the pace there and who yet came up again and made a comparative success in life," Wells declared in *Experiment in Autobiography.* Wells's program of study included biology, geology, astronomy, and physics. The only subject in which he succeeded, however, was biology, taught by the Darwinist Thomas Huxley. "Wells neglected the study of science after a successful first year," stated Draper, "and turned in preference to the role of 'philosophical desperado.'" "My very obstinate self-conceit was also an important factor in my survival," Wells explained. "I shall die, as I have lived, the responsible centre of my world. . . . [I refused to believe] that I was a failure as a student and manifestly without either the character or the capacity for a proper scientific career. I had convinced myself that I was a remarkable wit and potential writer. There must be compensation somewhere."

The Construction of a Writer

Wells's attitude toward organized religion and his belief in the powers of science were inherited in part from his teacher Thomas Huxley. Huxley, a founder of the Normal School, was best known to his Victorian contemporaries as "Darwin's bulldog." In 1860, Huxley had faced down Bishop Wilberforce in the "Oxford Debate," defending the radical theory of evolution by means of natural selection against the dogma of the Christian church. Huxley's students, including Wells, came

The Invisible Man
by H.G. Wells

With an Introduction by
Anthony West

BANTAM BOOKS
A BANTAM CLASSIC · A BANTAM CLASSIC · A BANTAM CLASSIC · A BANTAM CLASSIC · A BANTAM CLAS

In this suspenseful novel, the scientist Griffin has discovered the secret of invisibility, but his manipulation of science to self–serving ends leads to his own destruction.

to think of science in general and biology in particular as radical and revolutionary, and it encouraged them to question previously-held views, no matter how well established they were. Huxley's definition of biology also took in social and cultural studies, now classified as sociology and anthropology, providing the basis for Wells's later political views.

The Normal School was also important for Wells because it gave him a way to escape from his lower-middle-class origins. The scholarships it offered gave Wells the only chance he had to obtain a higher education. Schools like Oxford and Cambridge were far beyond the means of fami-

lies like the Wells, and scholarships were usually limited to the sons of gentlemen. Such schools also tended to concentrate on classics and humanities—Latin, Greek, theology, and literature—rather than on the sciences, which were regarded as lower-class studies. Even after Wells became famous, with a world-wide reputation, some of his contemporaries regarded him as a "counter-jumper," a former draper's assistant unworthy to be ranked among the great men of the British nation.

"After leaving college in 1887," Draper continued, Wells "taught for a time at private schools in Wales and London." After an accident in a football match in Wales, his health broke down altogether. His lungs hemorrhaged and one of his kidneys received severe damage. His local doctor suspected tuberculosis, which would plague Wells for the rest of his life. "I was put upon my back," Wells explained in *Experiment in Autobiography*, "ice-bags were clapped on my chest and the flow [of blood] was stopped. I was satisfying all the conventional expectations of a consumptive very completely. I lay still for a day or so and then began to live again in a gentle fashion in a pleasant chintz-furnished, fire-warmed, sunlit room."

The attending physician, however, had a different idea. He "was a brilliant young heretic in the medical world of those days . . . and he rather dashed my pose as a consumptive and encouraged my secret hope of life by refusing to recognize me as a tuberculous case." "Summer passed into spring and I grew stronger every day," Wells continued. "One bright afternoon I went out by myself to a little patch of surviving woodland amidst the industrialized country, called 'Trury Woods.' There had been a great outbreak of wild hyacinths that year and I lay down among them to think. It was one of those sun drenched afternoons that are turgid with vitality. Those hyacinths and their upright multitude were braver than an army with banners and more inspiring than trumpets. 'I have been dying for nearly two-thirds of a year,' I said, 'and I have died enough.'"

The damage to Wells's health prevented his returning to teaching full-time. Once he received his degree from the University of London in 1889, he began working as a tutor in a biology correspondence course. "With this secure income," Draper explained, "he married his cousin Isabel Mary Wells in 1891, settled in Wandsworth, southwest London, and expanded his career in educational journalism." He published a couple of biological textbooks in 1893, one of which was co-written with R. A. Gregory. "I went on writing, indeed, as a toy-dog goes on barking," Wells concluded in *Experiment in Autobiography*. "I yapped manuscript, threateningly, at an inattentive world."

Wells suffered another severe hemorrhage in 1893. "No more teaching for me for ever," he wrote in a letter cited in *H. G. Wells: A Sketch for a Portrait*. As he slowly recovered, he struck up a close friendship with one of his biology students, Amy Catherine Robbins, "the embodiment of all the understanding and quality I desired in life," he recalled in *H. G. Wells: A Sketch for a Portrait*. "We talked—over our frogs and rabbits. . . . Our friendship grew swiftly beyond the bounds of friendship and I was amazed to find that she could care for me as much as I did for her." Wells obtained a divorce from his first wife in 1895 and married Robbins the same year.

Robbins was the first of many mistresses in Wells's active private life. Perhaps the best-known of these was the writer and reviewer Rebecca West, who celebrated sexual liberation as much as Wells himself did. The son born of their union, Anthony West—himself a writer of no little renown—told the story of his parents' affair in his memoir *H. G. Wells: Aspects of a Life*. Although West made no secret of his parents' complicated relationship, he also emphasized his father's public career and requested that his name be remembered for his literary achievements.

Commencing a Writing Career

At the same time, Wells began publishing the works for which he is best remembered—the scientific romances *The Time Machine, The War of the Worlds, The Invisible Man,* and *The Island of Doctor Moreau*. Wells apparently had little intention of making his living by writing. However, his bouts of tuberculosis, which ended his teaching career, left him with few other options. His first professional work was for newspapers and magazines, and were collected in *Selected Conversations with an Uncle, Now Extinct, and Two Other Reminiscences,* published in 1895, and *Certain Personal Matters: A Collection of Material, Mainly Autobiographical,* published in 1898. On the basis of his articles, Wells was able to obtain a position as fiction reviewer of the English *Saturday Review*. He worked at this job for three years, but gave it up to work on his own publications.

As early as 1888, while Wells was teaching in Wales and in London, he had worked on a promising story idea. He published an early draft of the story in his college paper under the title "The Chronic Argonauts." In 1895, Wells produced a revised version of the earlier story and published it as *The Time Machine*. It was the first of his scientific romances, which have since proved to be his most popular and enduring works. "Just as science was exploding the nineteenth-century frames of reference which had once bound Wells," explained Draper, "so in these stories fantastic events erupt into the commonplace Victorian world and demonstrate the unrecognized precariousness of that world." Wells expressed in his stories a pessimism about the future of science and technology that differed greatly from the optimism that had dominated the nineteenth century. "Inventions threaten to radically disrupt human existence in 'The New Accelerator' and 'The Land Ironclads,'" Draper stated; "hostile creatures emerge from the sea or jungle in 'The Sea Raiders' and 'The Empire of the Ants'; people's perceptions suddenly come adrift from their bodies in 'Under the Knife' and 'The Remarkable Case of Davidson's Eyes;' man-made objects are mistaken for gods and even receive human sacrifice in 'Jimmy Goggles, the God' and 'The Lord of the Dynamos.'"

The Time Machine tells the story of an inventor, known only as the Time Traveller, who creates a machine that can navigate into the past or into the future. When the machine is completed the Time Traveller undertakes a journey into the distant future, to the year 802,701 AD. He discovers there what appears to be a pastoral world, inhabited by pretty, childlike beings called the Eloi, who live lives of pure leisure. He also discovers an underworld in which dwell the Morlocks, a nocturnal race that lives underground. The Morlocks manage the technology that keeps the Eloi in comfort and in turn use the Eloi as a food source. The Time Traveller makes friends with an Eloi named Weena, loses the time machine to the Morlocks, and visits the end of the earth before returning to share his story with his friends. After telling them his story, he starts on another voyage in time. "The Time Traveller vanished three years ago," the narrator of the story concludes. "And, as everybody knows now, he has never returned."

Wells's first published novel presents some of the major themes that recurred throughout his works, fictional and non-fictional. "*The Time Machine*," said Frank McConnell and Samuel Hynes in their essay "The Time Machine and The War of the Worlds: Parable and Possibility in H. G. Wells," "is a parable of [a] late-Victorian state of mind— a parable in which science is used as the vehicle for meanings that are profoundly anti-scientific." By the end of the nineteenth century, the reviewers argued, social critics had realized that the unbounded optimism that had characterized the century's early years was unfounded. Industrialization and scientific advances had created as many, if not more, problems than they had solved. Slums alongside factories, weapons of destruction, massive differences in levels of wealth and quality of living were all visible signs of the imbalance brought by scientific "progress." The ultimate expression of Wells's despair of human progress can be found in the climactic scene of the distant future, after the Time Traveller has fled the Morlocks who have taken Weena. "Escaping on the recovered time machine into the infinite future," explained fellow science fiction writer and critic Jack Williamson in *H. G. Wells: Critic of Progress*, "he finds mankind extinct and the solar system itself near death, the earth spiraling inward toward the dying sun." Yet, in the midst of desolation, "life persists," Williamson concluded: "bright green moss grows on the sunward faces of the rocks, and enormous crab-like things crawl along the shores of an oily, tideless sea."

The Time Machine also justifies Wells's own adherence to socialism. The period the Time Traveller spends among the Eloi and the Morlocks, according to McConnell and Hynes, "is a parable of the social consequences of science." Although mankind has been able to establish a fully leisured class, it has done so at the cost of splitting itself into two distinct species. It has also suffered the loss of its competitive spirit. "The Eloi and the Morlocks offer a parable of the class structure in a capitalist society," the critics stated—"the workers thrust underground and deprived of light and the natural world, the rich living idly and softly on the surface, on the profits of the workers' labor." By making the Morlocks cannibals, they concluded, "Wells is saying . . . that those to whom evil is done do evil in return, that exploitation makes monsters, that cruelty is an inevitable product of a cruel system, and inhuman conduct is an inevitable product of inhumanity."

The Island of Doctor Moreau examines the topic of inhumanity by revisiting the same themes that Mary Shelley had looked at in her novel *Frankenstein*. It tells of a scientist who tries to turn animals into human beings through surgery. "Moreau is both a misguided exponent of progress and a personification of natural evolution," declared Draper. "His doctrines challenge the traditional view of man as a distinct creation; his actions burlesque Christian mythology. The Beast People he has created worship him in a vain attempt to appease his wrath and preserve their unstable human qualities." After Moreau's death, the Beast People lose their humanity and return to their animal condition.

If you enjoy the works of H. G. Wells, you may also want to check out the following books and films:

Jack Finney, *Time and Again*, 1970.
Jules Verne, *A Journey to the Center of the Earth*, 1864.
Back to the Future, Universal, 1985.
Frankenstein, Universal, 1931.
Invasion of the Body Snatchers, Republic Pictures, 1956.

Critics have termed the novel a satire reminiscent of Jonathan Swift's *Gulliver's Travels*. Although the narrator, Prendick, returns safely to London, stated John Huntington in his *The Logic of Fantasy: H. G. Wells and Science Fiction*, he is haunted by the experiences of Moreau's island: "Prendick, like Gulliver, sees beasts when he looks at humans: 'I go in fear. I see faces keen and bright, other dull or dangerous, others unsteady, insincere; none that have the calm authority of a reasonable soul. I feel as though the animal was surging up through them; that presently the degradation of the Islanders will be played over again on a larger scale.'"

In *The Invisible Man*, Wells presents a parable of the potential for self-destruction that is inherent in science. "The principal character, Griffin," revealed *Twentieth-Century Young Adult Writers* contributor Fred McEwan, "is a scientist . . . who has discovered this secret and has made himself invisible to all. The story is grim, owing something to the tradition of the Gothic novel, but it is replete with adventure as Griffin turns against everyone and finally meets his destruction by being beaten to death with shovels in the hands of irate citizens." The character of Griffin, like that of Moreau, resembles that of Shelley's Victor Frankenstein, stated Darko Suvin in his *Metamorphoses of Science Fiction: On the Poetics and History of a Literary Genre*. "The delineation of Griffin hesitates between a man in advance of his time within an indifferent society and the symbol of a humanity that does not know how to use science," the critic stated. "This makes of him almost an old-fashioned 'mad scientist,' and yet he is too important and too sinned against to be comic relief." Griffin is both a tragic and an ironic figure, a rational thinker—a scientist—who cannot escape the consequences of his own irrationality.

"The most celebrated of all Wells's ventures into science fiction," wrote Draper, "is *The War of the Worlds*." Over a ten day period in the late nineteenth century, astronomers observe a series of large explosions on the surface of the planet Mars. Within a few days, huge cylinders begin dropping on sites in southern England near London. From the cylinders emerge the Martians: giant octopus-like creatures possessed of greatly superior technology. "Men, curious and friendly at first," wrote Williamson, "are stung into armed resistance by the unprovoked Martian attacks, and finally driven out of London in dazed and helpless panic. Although two or three Martians are killed, their superior weapons easily crush the best human defenses. Their victory seems secure—when suddenly they die, rotted by the micro-organisms of decay." "Documentary in style," Williamson concluded, "the narrative is so appallingly convincing that Orson Welles was able to create an actual panic in New Jersey on an October evening of 1938, with a radio version of it."

Many critics have interpreted *The War of the Worlds* as an assault on Victorian imperialism and complacency. "Wells repeatedly compares the Martians' brutal treatment of their victims to civilized man's treatment of animals and supposedly inferior races," declared Draper. "The overdeveloped brains, lack of emotions, and artificial bodies of the Martians parody the characteristics of modern man and suggest his evolutionary destiny." "The germs that kill the Martians appear at first glimpse to be coincidental, simply a convenient *deus ex machina* invented by the author to bring about a pleasing conclusion," Williamson said. "A second glance, however, shows this solution arising logically from the theme that progress is con-

trolled by biological laws—which bind Martians, no less than men. Meeting a competing species of life against which they have no biological defenses, the Martians are eliminated. Ironically, their lack of defenses is probably the result of their own past progress." Progress, if successful, leads to an inevitable decline.

The psychological effect of the invasion on the world is as much Wells's theme as is the fate of the Martians themselves. The narrator of the story meets two men that represent different approaches to the breaking of their worlds. One is a clergyman, a curate, and the other is a soldier, an artilleryman. The curate believes that the Martians are an instrument of the wrath of God, and he is too paralyzed by fear to resist. In fact, his fatalistic fear eventually leads to his death in a Martian camp. The artilleryman intends to live among the Martians like a rat among humans, struggling for existence, in constant danger of death but with the possibility of revenge close at hand. Although the artilleryman dreams of overthrowing the Martians, he lives in a drunken stupor most of the time by looting abandoned houses. "Those two central forces behind the early Wells parables, his Bible-centered religious heritage and his education as a Darwinian evolutionist and technologue, are in fact projected and redefined in these equally failed characters," wrote McConnell and Hynes; "and between their extremes lies, at the end of the book . . . the measured optimism and heroic rationality of the narrator himself. It is this voice, tested and refined by the alternatives of passive superstition and feckless revolutionism, that utters the epitaph for the last, dying Martian war machine."

"A Purely Imaginative Writer"

To the end of his life, Wells considered his scientific romances as inconsequential. Most contemporary critics agreed with him, including his distinguished colleague, the French science fiction writer Jules Verne. "Some of my friends," Verne told interviewer Gordon Jones in *Temple Bar*, "have suggested to me that his work is on somewhat similar lines to my own, but here, I think, they err. I consider him, as a purely imaginative writer, to be deserving of very high praise, but our methods are entirely different. I have always made a point in my romances of basing my so-called inventions upon a groundwork of actual fact, and of using in their construction methods and materials which are not entirely without the pale of contemporary engineering skill and knowledge." "The creations of Mr. Wells, on the other hand," he continued, "belong unreservedly to an age and degree of scientific knowledge far removed from the present, though I will not say entirely beyond the limits of the possible." "I am casting no disparagement on Mr. Wells' methods," he concluded; "on the contrary, I have the highest respect for his imaginative genius."

The writer Kingsley Amis, in his book-length study of science fiction *New Maps of Hell*, agreed with Verne's assessment of Wells's work. "The long scientific lectures interpolated in his stories . . . however, tedious, are highly germane to what Verne was doing," Amis stated. "Wells, on the other hand, is nearly always concerned only to fire off a few phrases of pseudo-scientific patter and bundle his characters away to the moon or the 803rd century with despatch." "It is often said that Wells's main interest was not in scientific advance as such," declared Amis. "Although this is true of some of his works . . . it is patently not true of the ones which had the most immediate effect on the growth of science fiction." "The real importance of these stories is that they liberated the medium from dependence on extrapolation," the critic continued, "and in doing so initiated some of its basic categories. The time machine itself, the Martians and their strange irresistible weapons in *The War of the Worlds*, the monsters in the first half of *The Food of the Gods*, the other world coterminous with ours in 'The Plattner Story,' the carnivorous plant in 'The Flowering of the Strange Orchid,' all these have had an innumerable progeny. What is noticeable about them is that they are used to arouse wonder terror, and excitement, rather than for any allegorical or satirical end." Even in *The First Men in the Moon*, which contains "some satirical discussions of war and human irrationality, . . . Wells's main drive here," Amis concluded, "is simple delight in invention, in working out an alien ecology, typical of what I might call primitive science fiction."

Martian attack ships fly over Earth's landscape in this 1953 film adaptation of *The War of the Worlds*.

It was not until Bernard Bergonzi published his 1961 study *The Early H. G. Wells: A Study of the Scientific Romances* that critics began to take his early works seriously. His contemporaries felt the works for which his reputation would be established were his social comedies, including *Kipps* and *The History of Mr. Polly*, and his social criticism, such as *Tono-Bungay*. These were the works that won Wells a reputation as the preeminent British novelist of the early twentieth century, surpassing even his friend Arnold Bennett. However, as social conditions in England changed, Wells's novels became less relevant. He turned instead to a long, drawn-out campaign to promote worldwide socialism—but the works he wrote in support of socialism were neglected even in their own time. Bergonzi's assessment, that Wells's early science fiction were his only works of lasting merit, is now accepted by most critics.

A Peculiar Socialist

Critics generally agree that Wells wrote his best science fiction before 1901. By that time, he had earned enough from sales of his writing to build his own home, Spade House, near the English coast in the county of Kent. By that time, he was firmly established as a professional writer. "Some of his works had already been translated into French and Italian," reported Draper. "He decided to offer his growing public a nonfictional expression of his ideas in a volume of speculations on man's future." He called the resulting volume *Anticipations*, and it was published in 1901. "Much of the book now seems naive," the *Concise Dictionary of British Literary Biography* contributor concluded, "and there are places where its sweeping proposals become uncomfortably fascistic. It does, however, put forward an idea which was to inform nearly all of Wells's later work: that the growth of communication and transport facilities, which lies behind modern social tensions and conflicts, might in the longer term, under the direction of a technocratic elite, make possible a just, efficient world order."

Kipps, one of Wells's best-known and best-loved non-science-fiction novels, reflects the author's own upbringing as well as his socialist convictions. "Wells presents the simple, likable Arthur Kipps and shows how he escapes from a repressive lower-class environment," Murray explained. "After experiencing life among men and women obsessed with money and eager for social respect-

ability, he winds up running a small bookshop and finally securing peace of mind." Wells uses Arthur Kipps to satirize contemporary social values. "Wells takes the opportunity to make general social comments," declared Draper, "but minimizes their disruptive effect by using two minor characters as mouthpieces. . . . Wells succeeds in persuading readers to identify with an unprecedentedly lower-class character." In 1967, Paramount Pictures filmed the story as a musical under the title *Half a Sixpence*.

Tono-Bungay tells the story of George Ponderevo, "a housekeeper's son," according to Murray, "whose up-and-down life, like Wells's, included a stint as a druggist's apprentice and the study of science at a new university in South Kensington." It is the story of how Ponderevo loses his idealism to crass commercialism. He leaves college and goes into business with his uncle Edward, selling a worthless medicine called Tono-Bungay. "Eventually," wrote Draper, "the Ponderevos' fraudulent business empire collapses; Edward dies in squalor; and George, deserted by his aristocratic lover Beatrice Normandy, is left to reflect on the significance of his life." The book, which was hotly debated by critics, Draper concluded, "is such a resourceful performance that it must nonetheless be reckoned a modern classic."

The third of Wells's great social novels was the one Draper termed "his comic masterpiece, *The History of Mr. Polly*." The book tells the story of Alfred Polly, a storekeeper whose business and marriage have both failed. In despair, Polly decides to kill himself and simultaneously set his store on fire so his wife can collect his insurance. The plan misfires, and Polly becomes a local hero for rescuing a lady from the fire he set himself. Instead of completing his suicidal plans, Polly decides to run away. He finds shelter and a new home at the Potwell Inn. "With his cheerful mispronunciation of words and innocent yearning for a richer life," Draper declared, "Mr. Polly is Wells's most memorable and vital character. The book's appeal comes from Wells's success in transforming a realistic world into a gratifying one of romance without denying the inevitability of conflict, suffering and individual limitation."

A Dim View of Human Progress

Despite his fame and the popularity of his writing, Wells continued to resent the criticism he suffered at the pen of the prominent socialist and playwright George Bernard Shaw. Wells had attempted to take control over the objectives of the Socialist Fabian Society, and Shaw resisted his efforts. The two became bitter rivals, challenging each other in print for the next two decades. Wells left the Fabian Society in 1909 and pursued his socialist goals on his own. His experience with his fellow socialists and his sparring with Shaw left him embittered. The furor that followed the publication of his novel *Ann Veronica*, on the subject of female emancipation, did nothing to lighten his mood. "Life is filthy with sentimental lying," Wells stated in *H. G. Wells: A Sketch for a Portrait*. "Every man who would tell of reality does it at his personal cost amidst a chorus of abuse."

Wells's *Outline of History*, written with the assistance of prominent advisors, was the first attempt to present the story of mankind using biological, anthropological, and sociological models. It proposed world socialism as a means of promoting world peace. In many ways, Wells intended it as the first volume of a series—including *The Science of Life* and *The Work, Wealth and Happiness of Mankind*—that would revolutionize education. If *The Outline of History* was taught in schools, Wells believed, mankind would drop such empty values as nationalism and patriotism in favor of a world society—based, of course, on socialism. The work was an enormous popular success. "In Britain and the United States together," wrote Draper, "the completed work sold more than two million volumes."

However, history for Wells was not only a story about the past. *The Shape of Things to Come* revealed his ideas and hopes for the future. The motion picture based on his work was filmed by Alexander Korda in 1936. It was the first big-budget science fiction film, an ancestor of *2001: A Space Odyssey* and *Star Wars*. However, Wells's efforts to use the film as a propaganda device for the spread of world socialism interfered with audiences's enjoyment of the film. *Things to Come* failed at the box offices. Its message about the "war to end all wars" was regarded as unconvincing and meaningless.

Wells was greatly disappointed. The fact that World War II—the war he predicted—broke out three years later was of little comfort. He contributed to the war effort a book entitled *The Rights of Man*, which later formed the basis for the United Nations' Declaration of Human Rights. Wells made lasting contributions to the problem of human rights abuse, but he had no illusions about the future of the human race. "Against the dark background of the interwar years," wrote Draper, "he championed [human progress] as a necessary goal, but his assessment of its actual likelihood swung between extremes of optimism and pessimism. . . . In the year of his death he painted a mural of evolution on a wall behind his house, placing beneath man the caption 'Time to go.'" His body was cremated in accordance with his wishes, and his ashes were scattered over the English Channel.

Wells might have been referring to himself in his description of the Time Traveller with which he ends *The Time Machine*: "He, I know . . . *thought but cheerlessly of the Advancement of Mankind, and saw in the growing pile of civilization only a foolish heaping that must inevitably fall back upon and destroy its makers in the end. If that is so, it remains for us to live as though it were not so. . . . And I have by me, for my comfort, two strange white flowers—shrivelled now, and brown and flat and brittle—to witness that even when mind and strength had gone, gratitude and a mutual tenderness still lived on in the heart of man.*"

■ Works Cited

Amis, Kingsley, "Starting Points," *New Maps of Hell*, Ballantine, 1960, pp. 11-35.

Draper, Michael, "H. G. Wells," *Concise Dictionary of British Literary Biography*, Volume 6: *Modern Writers, 1914-1945*, Gale, 1991, pp. 398-421.

Huntington, John, *The Logic of Fantasy: H. G. Wells and Science Fiction*, Columbia University Press, 1982.

McConnell, Frank, and Samuel L. Hynes, "The Time Machine and The War of the Worlds: Parable and Possibility in H. G. Wells," *The Time Machine/The War of the Worlds: A Critical Edition*, edited by Frank McConnell, Oxford University Press, 1977, pp. 345-66.

McEwen, Fred, "H. G. Wells," *Twentieth-Century Young Adult Writers*, St. James, 1994, pp. 682-88.

Murray, Brian, "H. G. Wells," *Dictionary of Literary Biography*, Volume 70: *British Mystery Writers, 1860-1919*, Gale, 1988, pp. 303-16.

Suvin, Darko, "Wells as the Turning Point of the SF Tradition," *Metamorphoses of Science Fiction: On the Poetics and History of a Literary Genre*, Yale University Press, 1979, pp. 208-21.

Verne, Jules, "Jules Verne at Home" (interview with Gordon Jones), *Temple Bar*, June, 1904, pp. 664-71.

Wagar, W. Warren, "H. G. Wells," *Twentieth-Century Science Fiction Writers*, 3rd edition, St. James, 1991, pp. 852-56.

Wells, H. G., *Experiment in Autobiography: Discoveries and Conclusions of a Very Ordinary Brain (Since 1866)*, Macmillian, 1934.

Wells, H. G., *The Time Machine/The War of the Worlds: A Critical Edition*, edited by Frank McConnell, Oxford University Press, 1977.

West, Geoffrey H. (formerly Geoffrey H. Wells), *H. G. Wells: A Sketch for a Portrait*, Howe, 1930, reprinted, Folcroft Library Editions, 1972.

Williamson, Jack, "Wells and the Limits of Progress," *H. G. Wells: Critic of Progress*, Mirage Press, 1973, pp. 47-62.

■ For More Information See

BOOKS

Batchelor, John, *H. G. Wells*, Cambridge University Press, 1985.

Bello, Hilaire, *A Companion to Mr. Wells's "Outline of History,"* Sheed & Ward, 1926.

Bello, Hilaire, *Mr. Bello Still Objects*, Sheed & Ward, 1926.

Beresford, John Davys, *H. G. Wells*, Nisbet, 1915, reprinted, Haskell House, 1972.

Bergonzi, Bernard, *The Early H. G. Wells: A Study of the Scientific Romances*, Manchester University Press, 1961.

Bergonzi, Bernard, editor, *H. G. Wells: A Collection of Critical Essays*, Prentice-Hall, 1976.

Bloom, Robert, *Anatomies of Egotism: A Reading of the Last Novels of H. G. Wells*, University of Nebraska Press, 1977.

Brooks, Van Wyck, *The World of H. G. Wells*, Unpin, 1914, M. Kennerley, 1915, reprinted, Gordon Press, 1973.

Costa, Richard Hauer, *H. G. Wells*, Twayne, 1966, revised edition, 1985.

Dictionary of Literary Biography, Volume 34: *British Novelists, 1890-1929: Traditionalists*, Gale, 1985.

Dilloway, James, *Human Rights and World Order*, H. G. Wells Society, 1983.

Edel, Leon, and Gordon N. Ray, editors, *Henry James and H. G. Wells: A Record of Their Friendship, Their Debate on the Art of Fiction, and Their Quarrel*, University of Illinois Press, 1958, reprinted, Greenwood Press, 1979.

Foot, Michael, *H. G.: The History of Mr. Wells*, Counterpoint/Bessie, 1996.

Gill, Stephen, *The Scientific Romances of H. G. Wells*, Vesta, 1975.

H. G. Wells: A Comprehensive Bibliography, H. G. Wells Society, 1972.

Haining, Peter, *The H. G. Wells Scrapbook*, New English Library, 1978.

Hammond, J. R., *Herbert George Wells: An Annotated Bibliography of His Works*, Garland Publishing, 1977.

Hammond, J. R., *An H. G. Wells Companion: A Guide to the Novels, Romances, and Short Stories*, Macmillian, 1979.

Hammond, J. R., editor, *H. G. Wells: Interviews and Recollections*, Macmillian, 1980.

Hawley, Elizabeth, and Columbia Rossi, *Bertie: The Life After Death of H. G. Wells*, New English Library, 1973.

MacKenzie, Norman, and Jeanne MacKenzie, *H. G. Wells: A Biography*, Simon & Schuster, 1973.

MacKenzie, Norman, and Jeanne MacKenzie, *The Time Traveller: The Life of H. G. Wells*, Simon & Schuster, 1973.

McConnell, Frank, *The Science Fiction of H. G. Wells*, Oxford University Press, 1981.

Meyer, Mathilde Marie, *H. G. Wells and His Family, As I Have Known Them*, International Publishing, 1956.

Niles, P. H., *The Science Fiction of H. G. Wells: A Concise Guide*, Auriga, 1980.

Parrinder, Patrick, *H. G. Wells*, Oliver & Boyd, 1970, Putnam's, 1977.

Parrinder, Patrick, editor, *H. G. Wells: The Critical Heritage*, Routledge & Kegan Paul, 1972.

Raknem, Ingvald, *H. G. Wells and His Critics*, Allen & Unpin, 1962.

Ray, Gordon N., *H. G. Wells and Rebecca West*, Macmillian, 1974.

Short Story Criticism, Volume 6, Gale, 1990.

Suvin, Darko, and Robert M. Philmus, editors, *H. G. Wells and Modern Science Fiction*, Bucknell University Press, 1977.

Twentieth-Century Literary Criticism, Gale, Volume 6, 1982, Volume 12, 1984, Volume 19, 1986.

Wells, Frank, *H. G. Wells: A Pictorial Biography*, Jupiter, 1977.

Wells, Geoffrey H., *The Works of H. G. Wells, 1887-1925: A Bibliography, Dictionary, and Subject-Index*, George Routledge & Sons, 1926.

West, Anthony, *H. G. Wells: Aspects of a Life*, Random House, 1984.

Wood, James Playsted, *I Told You So! A Life of H. G. Wells*, Pantheon, 1969.

Wykes, Alan, *H. G. Wells in the Cinema*, Jupiter, 1977.

PERIODICALS

Los Angeles Times Book Review, December 9, 1984.
Newsweek, May 28, 1984.
New York Times Book Review, March 3, 1985; September 21, 1986.
Times (London), October 4, 1984.
Times Literary Supplement, January 25, 1985; February 7, 1986; September 18-24, 1987, p. 1020.
Washington Post Book World, January 6, 1985.

■ **Obituaries**

PERIODICALS

Christian Century, August 28, 1946.
New York Times, August 14, 1946.
Publishers Weekly, August 24, 1946.
Wilson Library Bulletin, October, 1946.*

—Sketch by Kenneth R. Shepherd

Acknowledgments

Acknowledgements

Grateful acknowledgement is made to the following publishers, authors, and artists for their kind permission to reproduce copyrighted material.

ISABEL ALLENDE. Bauer, Jerry. Portrait of Isabel Allende. Reproduced by permission./ From the cover of *Of Love and Shadows.* By Isabel Allende. Bantam Books, Inc., 1988. Cover art copyright © 1988 by Leo and Diane Dillon. Reproduced by permission of Bantam Books, Inc., a division of Bantam Doubleday Dell Publishing Group, Inc./ From the cover of *The House of the Spirits.* By Isabel Allende. Bantam Books, Inc., 1993. Cover art © 1993 Neue Constantin Film. All rights reserved. Reproduced by permission of Bantam Books, Inc., a division of Bantam Doubleday Dell Publishing Group, Inc./ From the cover of *The Stories of Eva Luna.* By Isabel Allende. Bantam Books, Inc., 1992. Cover art © 1991 by Leo and Diane Dillon. Reproduced by permission of Bantam Books, Inc., a division of Bantam Doubleday Dell Publishing Group, Inc.

WILLIAM ARMSTRONG. Armstrong, William H., portrait of. Reproduced by permission./ Barkley, James. From the jacket of *Sounder.* By William H. Armstrong. HarperCollins, 1969. Illustrations copyright © 1969 by James Barkley. Reproduced by permission of HarperCollins Publishers, Inc./ Pinkney, Jerry, From the cover of *Sour Land.* By William H. Armstrong. HarperTrophy, 1992. Cover art © 1992 by Jerry Pinkney. Cover © 1992 by HarperCollins Publishers. Reproduced by permission of the publisher.

W. H. AUDEN. Auden, W. H., photograph of. Wide World Photos, Inc. Reproduced by permission./ Gerson, Mark. Photograph of John Betjeman. Reproduced by permission. / Photograph of a page from *O Love, the interest itself in thoughtless Heaven* in Auden's 1932 poetry book. Houghton Library, Harvard University. Reproduced by permission of the Houghton Library, Harvard University./ Auden, W. H., photograph of. The Bettmann Archive. Reproduced by permission.

TERRY BROOKS. Brooks, Judith. Photograph of Terry Brooks. Reproduced by permission of Ballantine Books, a division of Random House, Inc./ From the cover of *The Elf Queen of Shannara.* By Terry Brooks. Ballantine Books, 1992. Copyright © 1992 by Terry Brooks. All rights reserved. Reprinted by permission of Ballantine Books, a division of Random House, Inc./ Parkinson, Keith. From the cover of *The Druid of Shannara.* By Terry Brooks. Ballantine Books, 1991. Copyright © 1991 by Terry Brooks. All rights reserved. Reproduced by permission of Ballantine Books, a division of Random House, Inc./ Parkinson, Keith. From the cover of *The Scions of Shannara.* By Terry Brooks. Ballantine Books, 1990. Copyright © 1990 by Terry Brooks. All rights reserved. Reproduced by permission of Ballantine Books, a division of Random House, Inc./ Sweet, Darrell K. From the cover of *The Black Unicorn.* By Terry Brooks. Ballantine Books, 1987. Copyright © 1987 by Terry Brooks. All rights reserved. Reproduced by permission of Ballantine Books, a division of Random House, Inc.

OCTAVIA E. BUTLER. Butler, Octavia E., portrait. O.M. Butler. Reproduced by permission. Barlowe, Wayne./ From the cover of *Wild Seed* by Octavia E. Butler. Popular Library, 1980. Copyright © 1980 by Octavia Butler. Reproduced by permission of Warner Books, Inc./ Butler, Octavia E. From the cover of *Adulthood Rites.* Popular Library, 1988. Copyright © 1988 by Octavia Butler. Reproduced by permission of Warner Books, Inc./ Palencar, John Jude. From the cover of *Parable of the Sower.* By Octavia E. Butler. Warner Books, 1993. Copyright © 1993 by Octavia E. Butler. Reproduced by permission of Warner Books, Inc.

PATRICIA CALVERT. Calvert, Patricia, portrait of. Reproduced by permission./ Calvert, Patricia. From the cover of *The Stone Pony.* Signet, 1983. Copyright © 1982 by Patricia Calvert. Reproduced by permission of Signet, an imprint of New American Library, a division of Penguin USA.

PAM CONRAD. Conrad, Pam, portrait of. Reproduced by permission./ Deas, Michael. From the cover of *Taking the Ferry Home.* By Pam Conrad. Harper Keypoint, 1990. Cover art © 1988 by Michael Deas. Cover © 1990 by HarperCollins Publishers, Inc. Reproduced by permission of the publisher./ Zudeck, Darryl S. From the jacket of *Prairie Songs.* By Pam Conrad. Harper & Row, Publishers, 1985. Jacket art © 1985 by Darryl S. Zudeck. Reproduced by permission of HarperCollins Publishers, Inc.

BERLIE DOHERTY. Doherty, Berlie, portrait of. Reproduced by permission./ Dooling, Michael. From the cover of *Granny Was a Buffer Girl.* By Berlie Doherty. Beech Tree Paperback Books, 1993. Reprinted by permission of Beech Tree, a division of William Morrow & Company, Inc./ Lisi, Victoria. From the cover of *Dear Nobody.* By Berlie Doherty. Beech Tree Paperback Books, 1994. Illustration copyright © Victoria Lisi. Reprinted by permission of Beech Tree, a division of William Morrow & Company, Inc.

CLINT EASTWOOD. Eastwood, Clint, photograph of. Wide World Photos, Inc. Reproduced by permission./ Movie still from *Dirty Harry.* © 1971 Warner Brothers. Inc. and The Malpaso Company. Reproduced by permission./ Movie still from *In The Line of Fire*. Reproduced by permission of Archive Photos, Inc./ Movie still from *Unforgiven*. Reproduced by permission of Archive Photos, Inc.

ALLAN W. ECKERT. Eckert, Alan W., portrait of. Reproduced by permission of John Hawkins & Associates, Inc./ From the cover of *The Frontiersmen*. Bantam Books, 1970. Cover art copyright © by Lou Glanzman. Reproduced by permission of Bantam Books, Inc., a division of Bantam Doubleday Dell Publishing Group, Inc./ Schoenherr, John. From the cover of *Incident at Hawk's Hill*. Bantam Books, 1987. Cover art copyright © 1987 by Bantam Books. Reproduced by permission of Bantam Books, Inc., a division of Bantam Doubleday Dell Publishing Group, Inc.

LOUISE FITZHUGH. Fitzhugh, Louise, portrait of. Reproduced by permission./ From an illustration in *Harriet the Spy*. Harper & Row, 1964. Copyright © 1964 by Louise Fitzhugh; renewed 1992 by Lois Morehead. Reproduced by permission of Lois Morehead./ Velasquez, Eric. From the cover of *Nobody's Family is Going to Change*. By Louise Fitzhugh. Farrar, Straus, and Giroux, Inc., 1993. Cover art © 1986 by Eric Velasquez. Reproduced by permission of Farrar, Strauss, and Giroux, Inc.

ERNEST J. GAINES. Crampton, Nancy. Portrait of Ernest J. Gaines. © Nancy Crampton. Reproduced by permission./ *Autobiography of Miss Jane Pittman*. Courtesy of Viacom. Reproduced by permission./ From the cover of *The Autobiography of Miss Jane Pittmann*, by Ernest J. Gaines. Bantam Books, 1971. Copyright © 1971 by Ernest J. Gaines. Reproduced by permission of Doubleday, a division of Bantam Doubleday Dell Publishing Group, Inc.

NANCY GARDEN. Morse, Tim. Portrait of Nancy Garden. Reproduced by permission./ Norman, Elaine. From the cover of *Annie on My Mind*. By Nancy Garden. Aerial Fiction, 1982. Cover art © 1992 by Elaine Norman. Reproduced by permission of Farrar, Strauss, and Giroux, Inc.

ALAN GARNER. Garner, Alan, portrait of. Reproduced by permission of William Collins & Sons Co., Ltd.\ Halverson, Janet. From the jacket of *The Owl Service*. By Alan Garner. Henry Z. Walck, 1968. © Alan Garner 1967. Reproduced by permission of Henry Z. Walck, Incorporated./ Schleinkofer, David. From the cover of *The Weirdstone of Brisingamen*. By Alan Garner. Ace Books, 1960. Copyright © 1960 by Alan Garner. Reproduced by permission of The Berkley Publishing Group.

MICHAEL HAGUE. Hague, Michael, portrait of. Reproduced by permission./ From an illustration in *Dream Weaver*. By Jane Yolen. Collins, 1979. Illustrations copyright © 1979 by Michael Hague. Reproduced by permission of the publisher./ Hague, Michael. From an illustration in *The Hobbit; or, There and Back Again*. By J. R. R. Tolkien. Houghton Mifflin, 1966. Illustrations copyright © 1984 by Oak, Ash & Thorn Ltd. Reprinted by permission of the publisher.

NATHANIEL HAWTHORNE. From the cover of *The Scarlet Letter*. By Nathaniel Hawthorne. Signet, 1980. Reproduced by permission of Signet Classic, an imprint of Dutton Signet, a division of Penguin USA./ Palmer, Frances. From the cover of *The House of Seven Gables*. By Nathaniel Hawthorne. J. M. Dent, 1995. Reproduced by permission of the publisher.

LEE BENNETT HOPKINS. Nunno, Rocco. Portrait of Lee Bennett Hopkins. Reproduced by permission of Lee Bennett Hopkins./ From an illustration in *Moments: Selected by Lee Bennett Hopkins*. Illustrations copyright © 1980 by Michael Hague. Reproduced by permission of Harcourt Brace & Company./ Mikolaycak, Charles. From the cover of *Voyages: Poems by Walt Whitman. Selected by Lee Bennett Hopkins*. Harcourt Brace & Company, 1988. Illustrations copyright © 1988 by Charles Mikolaycak. Reproduced by permission of Harcourt Brace & Company.

JAMES A. HOUSTON. Houston, James A., portrait of. Reproduced by permission./ From the jacket of *River Runners: A Tale of Hardship and Bravery*. Atheneum, 1979. Copyright © 1979 by James Houston. All rights reserved. Reproduced with the permission of Atheneum, an imprint of Simon & Schuster, Inc.

IRENE HUNT. Hunt, Irene, portrait of. American Library Association. Reproduced by permission./ Illustration by Jim Sharp from a cover of *No Promises in the Wind*. By Irene Hunt. Berkley, 1993. Copyright © 1970 by Irene Hunt. Reproduced by permission of The Berkley Publishing Group./ Illustration from a cover of *The Lottery Rose*. By Irene Hunt. Berkley Books, 1986. Copyright © 1976 by Irene Hunt. Reproduced by permission of The Berkley Publishing Group./ Illustration from a cover of *Up a Road Slowly*. By Irene Hunt. Tempo Books, 1966. Copyright © 1966, by Irene Hunt. Reproduced by permission of The Putnam & Grosset Group./ Illustration by Louis Glanzman from the cover of *Across Five Aprils*. By Irene Hunt. Berkley Books, 1986. Copyright © 1964 by Irene Hunt. Reproduced by permission of The Berkley Publishing Group.

PATRICIA MACLACHLAN. Nulty, Judith, portrait of Patricia MacLachlan. Reproduced by permission./ Sewall, Marcia. From the cover of *Sarah, Plain and Tall*. By Patricia MacLachlan. HarperTrophy, 1985. Cover art © 1985 by Marcia Sewall. Cover © 1985 by Harper & Row, Publishers, Inc. Reproduced by permission of HarperCollins Publishers./ Sewall, Marcia. From the jacket of *Skylark*. By Patricia MacLachlan. HarperCollins, 1994. Jacket art copyright © 1994 by Marcia Sewall. Jacket © 1994 by HarperCollins Publishers. Reproduced by permission of the publisher.

JAY MCINERNEY. Bauer, Jerry, portrait of Jay McInerney. Reproduced by permission./ Jeff Carpenter, Jeff. From the jacket of *Story of My Life: A Novel*. By Jay McInerney. The Atlantic Monthly Press, 1988. Copyright © 1988 by Jay

McInerney. Reproduced by permission of the publisher./ Tauss, Marc. From the cover of *Bright Lights, Big City.* By Jay McInerney. Vintage Books, 1984. Copyright © 1984 by Jay McInerney. Reproduced by permission of Random House, Inc.

PAMELA SARGENT. Bauer, Jerry. Portrait of Pamela Sargent. Reproduced by permission. Nasta, Vincent./ From the jacket of *Alien Child.* By Pamela Sargent. Harper & Row, 1988. Jacket art © 1988 by Vincent Nasta. Jacket © 1988 by HarperCollins Publishers, Inc. Reproduced by permission of HarperCollins Publishers, Inc.

ANNE TYLER. Walker, D. Portrait of Anne Tyler. Gamma-Liaison. Reproduced by permission./ Cover design of *Breathing Lessons.* By Anne Tyler. Berkley Books, 1989. Copyright © 1988 by ATM, Inc. Reproduced by permission of The Berkley Publishing Group./ Illustration from a cover of *Dinner at the Homesick Restaurant.* By Anne Tyler. Ballantine Books, 1992. Copyright © 1982 by Anne Tyler Modarressi. Reproduced by permission of Ballantine Books, a division of Random House, Inc./ Cover design of *The Accidental Tourist.* By Anne Tyler. Berkley Books, 1986. Copyright © 1985 by Anne Tyler Modarressi. Reproduced by permission of The Berkley Publishing Group.

H. G. WELLS. Wells, H. G., photograph of. The Granger Collection, New York. Reproduced by permission./ Gabel, Matt. From the cover of *The Time Machine.* By H. G. Wells. Worthington Press, 1995. Illustrations © 1995 by Worthington Press. Reproduced by permission of the publisher./ Kastel, Roger. From the cover of *The Invisible Man.* By H. G. Wells. Bantam Books, 1987. Reproduced by permission of Bantam Books, a division of Bantam Doubleday Dell Publishing Group, Inc./ Le Douanier, Rousseau. From the cover of *The Island of Dr. Moreau.* Bantam Books, 1994. Reproduced by permission of Bantam Books, a division of Bantam Doubleday Dell Publishing Group, Inc./ Movie still from *War of the Worlds.* Reproduced by permission of Archive Photos, Inc.

Cumulative Index

Author/Artist Index

The following index gives the number of the volume in which an author/artist's biographical sketch appears.